THE GUITAR BOOK

Reprinted in 2019, 2023

This edition published in 2017

First published in 2010

Material previously published as Play Guitar and Learn to Play Guitar Like the Greats

Published by
Amber Books Ltd
United House
North Road
London N7 9DP
United Kingdom
www.amberbooks.co.uk
Instagram: amberbooksltd
Facebook: www.facebook.com/amberbooks
Twitter: @amberbooks

ISBN: 978-1-78274-472-6

Project editors: James Bennett and Sarah Uttridge
Design: Keren Harragan, Nicola Hibbert and Zoe Mellors
Picture Research: Terry Forshaw and Natasha Jones

Manufactured in China

THE GUITAR BOOK

The Ultimate Guide to Playing Like the Greats

General Editors:
Charlotte Greig and Nick Powlesland

amber
BOOKS

CONTENTS

GENERAL INTRODUCTION

If you're not playing like one of the world's great guitarists by the end of *The Guitar Book*, it's because you've developed your own individual style! From basic techniques to the most advanced chords, from blues to gypsy jazz to rock and pop, and from acoustic to electric, *The Guitar Book* takes you through each step to playing excellent guitar.

Arranged in three parts, the first part features 39 practice sessions ranging from first notes to advanced solos. Each session has sample song arrangements from well-known songs. the second part features major guitarists such as Eric Clapton, Robert Johnson and Kurt Cobain, showing you how to play their best-known songs in their signature styles. In addition there are biographies on each featured guitarist's life and music. The final part is a reference section covering all the chords introduced in the practice sessions. this provides an at-a-glance reminder of valuable chord constructions.

Spanning all the major genres of popular guitar music, *The Guitar Book* is your essential companion to becoming the guitarist you've always dreamed of being.

FIRST NOTES & CHORDS

The key to mastering your guitar is to combine good technique with a secure knowledge of individual notes and chords. Follow these easy instructions and soon you'll be wowing the audience!

The first session guides you through everything you need to know to play an arrangement of Paul Weller's *Wild Wood*. Specifically, this involves three chord shapes and a simple solo passage. Let's get started.

Playing open strings

This exercise focuses upon your plectrum technique, as you also get to know the sound and location of the six guitar strings. Play each string once, starting from the lowest sound of the 6th string. Aim to keep the plectrum strokes small and even, using a short downward flick of the wrist each time.

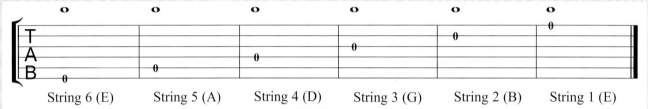

String 6 (E) String 5 (A) String 4 (D) String 3 (G) String 2 (B) String 1 (E)

Finger tip

Hold the plectrum lightly, towards the tip, between thumb and first finger.

Play the note E on the open 6th string.

Play the note G on the open 3rd string.

Keep the wrist fairly low over the strings.

Open strings in two count notes

Play each string twice in the same order as above. You'll find that each note lasts for two counts. This is shown below by a different note symbol above the TAB numbers. Remember that the lines on the TAB each represent a string on your guitar, and the '0' on a line indicates an 'open' string.

Open strings in one count notes, with backing

To develop flexibility and control of your plectrum work, play each string four times. The symbol for one count notes can be seen above each TAB number. You should aim to keep each stroke as relaxed and even as possible.

As for the plectrum itself, various shapes and weights are available. Try and find the one that suits you.

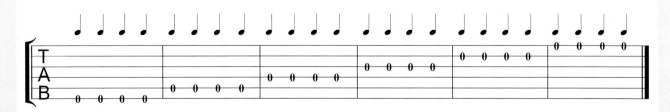

Open string four with varied rhythm

Music is made up of a variety of notes and different note lengths. In this next piece, you'll remain on note D, the open 4th string, from start to finish.

However, you'll need to count carefully, as the note lengths you've practised so far are combined irregularly, to create a much more interesting effect.

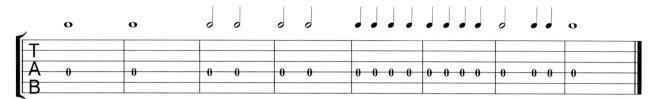

Left: You play the note D by striking string 4. The left-hand fingers are not used at all, so this note is described as 'open'.

Keep the fingers of your left hand close to the fretboard, even when they're not being used, so they'll be ready to play the notes that follow.

Introducing the left hand

A guitar's fretboard is divided into sections by metal strips called 'frets'. The fret closest to the headstock is known as fret 1.

Place the middle finger of your left hand behind fret 2 on the 4th string in order to play another type

of E note. Each note is four counts long. While playing the notes, try to keep your thumb low and upright, directly behind your middle finger. The two-dot sign at the end of the line of TAB is there to tell you to repeat the whole piece a second time.

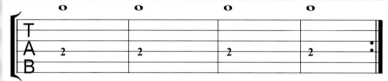

Left: Place your middle finger behind the 2nd fret on the 4th string to play another type of note E. Try to curve your left-hand fingers to improve both pressure and accuracy.

Finger tip

BUZZING OR MUFFLED NOTES
If a note buzzes, or sounds odd when you strike it, try squeezing the string more tightly, and make sure that your finger is positioned just behind – but not on top of – the fret.

String four – E – with varied rhythm

The left-hand finger remains behind fret 2 throughout, but be wary of the changing note

lengths. Try and follow the notation above the TAB, which was introduced earlier.

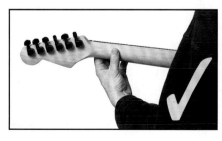

Left: The thumb is positioned correctly, low behind finger 2.

Left: Poor thumb positioning hinders hand and finger mobility.

Tied notes

This piece continues to use the 4th string, fretted note E. The curved lines linking some of the note symbols show that they are 'tied'. This means that you should strike only the first note, then allow the string to keep ringing for the length of the second note too. The brackets around some of the TAB numbers are a further indication that the note should not be struck again.

Repeat and play along

This exercise is identical to the previous one except the repeat sign.

The repeat sign (two dots) at the end indicates that the whole piece should be played twice.

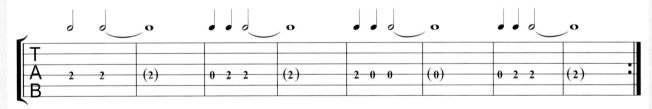

Alternating E and D notes

Now to put the finishing touch to your *Wild Wood* solo. Follow the music below, replacing fret 2 notes with open strings wherever marked. You'll find that the rhythm is exactly the same as in the previous two exercises, although the tempo is a little faster. The repeat sign tells you to play the piece twice.

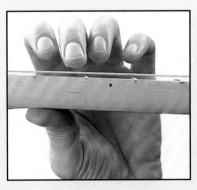

Left: When you play the open D string, keep finger 2 of your left hand close to the 2nd fret, as shown in this shot, taken from above. It'll make it easier to replace the finger.

Finger tip

DISJOINTED PLAYING

If your playing sounds disjointed, you may be releasing the pressure on fretted notes too early, or placing your left-hand finger on the fret too soon. Either way, the answer is to slow down, watch and listen to what you are doing. Release or place the left-hand finger as precisely as you can with the new right-hand stroke. Build your speed up again gradually.

The E minor chord

Instead of playing strings individually, you're now going to play all six together as a 'chord'. This is shown as a column of numbers in the TAB. Place your left-hand fingers to create the E minor (Em) chord shape (right), then, with your right hand, 'strum' evenly down all the strings to produce the chord.

Left: E minor can also be shown using a chord box, like this.

Keep your thumb low behind the neck, so your 2nd and 3rd fingers can reach round to the 2nd fret on the 4th and 5th strings.

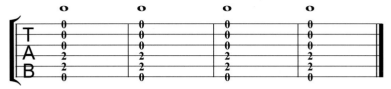

The A minor chord

The chord of A minor (Am) uses three left-hand fingers. Fingers 2 and 3 remain behind the 2nd fret, but this time on the 4th and 3rd strings. Place your index finger on the 2nd string behind the 1st fret. Strum downwards from the 5th string, counting four beats for each strum.

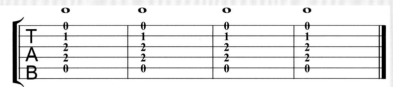

Left: The A minor chord shape.

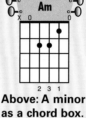

Above: A minor as a chord box.

Alternating A minor and E minor chords

This exercise lets you practise changing between the two chords learned so far. The shift to E minor (Em) means releasing finger 1 and moving the other two fingers to strings 4 and 5.

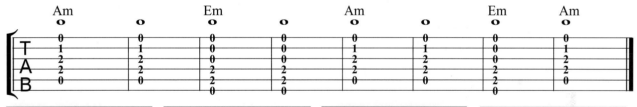

Place your fingers in the A minor chord shape.

Strum chord A minor from string 5 to string 1.

Move fingers 2 and 3 and release finger 1.

Strum chord E minor from string 6 to string 1.

The D minor chord

D minor (Dm) is the last new chord for this issue. Place finger 1 on the 1st string behind the 1st fret, and finger 2 on the 3rd string behind fret 2. Try putting your 3rd finger on the 2nd string behind fret 3, but if this is too much of a stretch, use finger 4. Note the similarity to the A minor shape.

Left: the D minor chord using finger 3 on the 2nd string at fret 3.

Above: D minor using finger 4 on the 2nd string at fret 3.

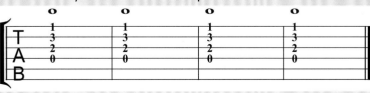

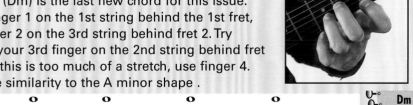

Left: The D minor chord box.

Alternating E minor and D minor chords

The next three pieces concentrate on smooth, relaxed shifting from one chord to another. It's a good idea to watch the left-hand changes closely, until you can memorize the chord shapes.

```
       Em          Dm          Em          Dm     Em
       o      o      o      o      o      o      o      o
   ┌─────0──────0──────1──────1──────0──────0──────1──────0────┐
 T │     0      0      3      3      0      0      3      0     │
 A │     0      0      2      2      0      0      2      0     │
 B │     2      2      0      0      2      2      0      2     │
   │     2      2             2      2                   2     │
   └─────0──────0──────────────────0──────0──────────────0────┘
```

1 Form the left-hand finger shape for E minor.

2 Strum all six strings to produce E minor.

3 Change the left-hand fingers to the D minor shape.

4 Strum from string 4 to produce D minor.

Alternating D minor and A minor chords

Always look for similarities between chord shapes as a starting point for your finger shifts. In this example, chords D minor and A minor share the same finger 1 and 2 shapes. You should aim to change fingers 1 and 2 as a unit, while bringing the other left-hand finger into place.

```
       Dm     Am     Dm     Am     Dm     Am     Dm     Am
       o      o      o      o      o      o      o      o
   ┌─────1──────0──────1──────0──────1──────0──────1──────0────┐
 T │     3      1      3      1      3      1      3      1     │
 A │     2      2      2      2      2      2      2      2     │
 B │     0      2      0      2      0      2      0      2     │
   │            0             0             0             0     │
   └───────────────────────────────────────────────────────────┘
```

Left: The D minor chord with fingers 1 and 2 highlighted.

Left: The A minor chord with fingers 1 and 2 highlighted.

Putting the three chords together

Here, for the first time, are the A minor, E minor and D minor chords within the same piece. Play the chords and you'll hear how the melody develops.

Prepare each chord in plenty of time to keep your four count strums on the first beat of the bar. Note the repeat sign.

```
       Am                 Em                 Dm          Am
       o      o      o      o      o      o      o      o
   ┌─────0──────0──────0──────0──────1──────1──────0──────0────┐
 T │     1      1      0      0      3      3      1      1     │
 A │     2      2      0      0      2      2      2      2     │
 B │     2      2      2      2      0      0      2      2    :│
   │     0      0      2      2                    0      0     │
   └───────────────────0──────0───────────────────────────────┘
```

Wild Wood sequence in two beat strums

To play this chord sequence, strum every two counts, as shown in the notation below. This means you'll be playing each chord twice in a bar instead of just once. The brackets above the last two bars (1. and 2.) show that you have to play bar 9 instead of bar 8 the second time you play through this exercise.

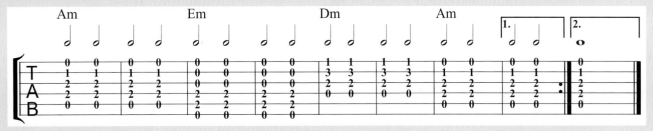

Strumming off the beat

Strumming on count two and four of each bar is referred to as strumming 'off the beat'. This exercise holds a static A minor chord shape – notice the one count rest symbol in bars 1 and 3.

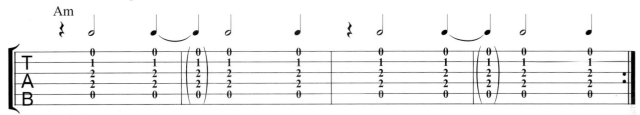

Right: The A minor chord shape.

Below: The A minor chord box.

Finger tip

BLOCKING OPEN STRINGS
Check that your chord shapes are ringing clearly by playing each string individually. Moving your wrist slightly forward can improve the curvature of the fingers and overcome the common problem of blocking open strings.

The full *Wild Wood* chord sequence and rhythm

By adding 'off-beat' strumming to the chord changes, you can play a full verse of this Paul Weller song. The brackets (1. and 2.) mean exactly the same as they did in the two-beat strums exercise.

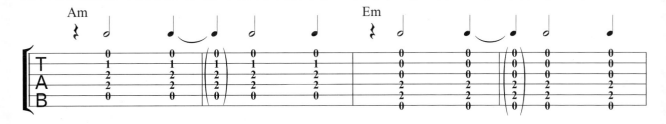

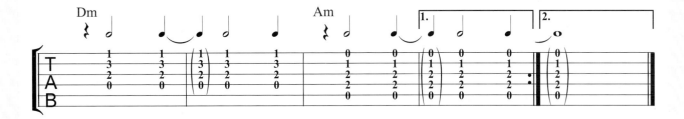

NOTES, RHYTHMS & CHORDS

The basic techniques from the first session are developed and combined with new ones in this section, enabling you to play an arrangement of a classic Beatles' track.

Here, you focus in detail upon a number of new notes, rhythms, chords and techniques. Combining all these moves will enable you to give an assured performance of a true classic: *I Saw Her Standing There*, taken from The Beatles' first album, *Please, Please Me* (Parlophone, 1963).

Try and play all of these pieces regularly as practice makes perfect.

The six open strings using one and two count notes

Begin by reminding yourself of the six strings, both in terms of their appearance on the page and their sound as you strike them with your plectrum. Bar one requires you to play the open 6th string three times. This is the lowest sounding string, which is why it is often referred to as the 'bass' string. The names of the open strings as played here are: E-A-D-G-B-E. The length of each note is shown in Standard Notation above every bar: two one count notes followed by a two count note.

Remember to hold the plectrum between your thumb and index finger. Only the tip of the plectrum protrudes to strike the open 6th string, E.

Finger tip

ACHIEVING OPTIMUM RIGHT HAND CONTROL
For a smooth, relaxed right hand action, always use small plectrum strokes when playing single strings. Large strokes move your hand too far away from the strings and your control of the plectrum tip is greatly reduced.

Use your elbow as a pivot point on the edge of your guitar and move your forearm up or down to the required string. With the plectrum just above the string, a slight downward twist of the wrist provides the momentum to create the stroke.

The open 5th string, A.

The open 4th string, D.

The open 3rd string, G.

The open 2nd string, B.

The open 1st string, E.

String crossing using open strings

Use the same rhythm as in the first piece throughout this eight bar exercise. Aim to produce notes that are fully sustained by carefully timing each plectrum stroke. Always strike the strings with equal strength and relocate the plectrum in readiness for the change of string that follows each two count note.

Revising your A minor, D minor and E minor chords

Spend a little time going back over these three chords. Remember that the key to good chord changes lies in small left-finger movements and a systematic approach. When you shift from A minor to D minor in the first bar, move fingers 1 and 2 of your left hand as a unit, because both chords share this same finger shape. Check that you are strumming the correct number of strings.

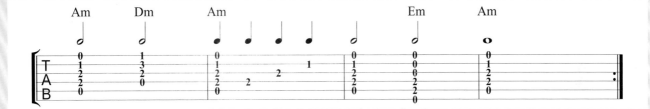

A minor as a chord box

The A minor (Am) chord shape. Keep the thumb low and upright behind the middle finger.

 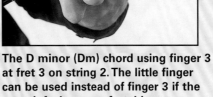

D minor as a chord box

The D minor (Dm) chord using finger 3 at fret 3 on string 2. The little finger can be used instead of finger 3 if the stretch feels uncomfortable.

 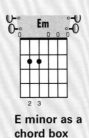

E minor as a chord box

The E minor (Em) chord raises fingers 2 and 3 onto the 5th and 4th strings at fret 2.

SOUNDBITE

'I play a Gibson Les Paul guitar live because it's reliable, powerful, strong enough and heavy enough to work really well and survive.' Graham Coxon, Blur

'My guitar playing developed because I had that great unit [Led Zeppelin] to work with. I don't think I have a technique, as such, when you think of people with technique'. Jimmy Page

The note A, using the left hand

Each bar of this piece contains a four count note, illustrated by the oval symbol above each TAB number. Keep your left thumb low and vertical behind the neck of your guitar, as this position will allow a good curve of the left middle finger (finger 2) onto the 2nd fret.

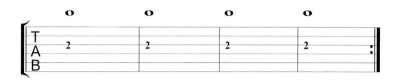

Right: This photo, taken from above, shows the ideal placement of the left-hand fingers and thumb when playing the note A.

Alternating between notes B and A

The note B is played on the open 2nd string. This is marked by a '0' on the second of the six parallel lines that make up the TAB stave. Always have the left finger ready and close to fret 2 for a smooth and accurate change of note.

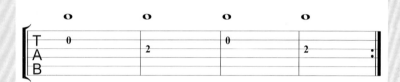

Finger tip

MUTING A STRING

If you are curving the left finger well when playing note A, you'll hear this sound clash with the previously played open B string. This can be prevented by an intentional slight drop of the middle finger as you play the A note, so that its underside touches string 2 and mutes the sound.

The note C

Hold fret 1 on the 2nd string throughout, using finger 1 of your left hand. The rhythmical interest is provided by a combination of two and four count notes. The 5th and 6th notes are linked by a curved line called a 'tie', which means that the two beat note is struck and then left to sound for a further four beats to make a six count note in all.

The note C is played by striking string 2 while placing finger 1 of the left hand at fret 1.

Combining notes C, B and A

The three notes you have just played are now used in the same piece. The right hand must be alert to the switches between string 2 and string 3. Also, keep left fingers 1 and 2 close over these frets to help prevent problems with timing and coordination. One, two and four count notes are used, so count carefully.

Right: Fingers 1 and 2 remain close to the frets when not being used.

The note F sharp and the three count rhythm

The word 'sharp' refers to the raising of a note on the guitar by one fret. This takes an F from fret 1 on the 1st string over into fret 2 and provides you with the necessary note for The Beatles' song we're preparing to play. Also, notice that the dot after a two count symbol gives it a three count note value. Be aware of the one beat then three beat combination in every other bar of this piece.

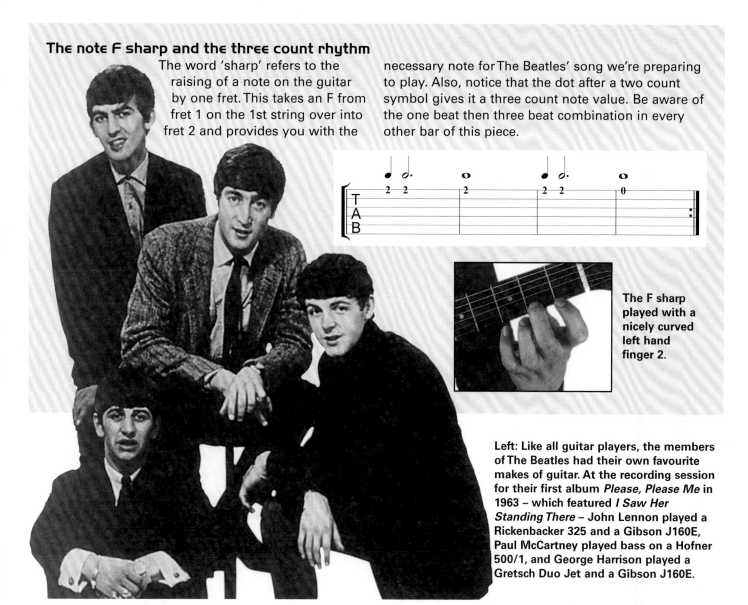

The F sharp played with a nicely curved left hand finger 2.

Left: Like all guitar players, the members of The Beatles had their own favourite makes of guitar. At the recording session for their first album *Please, Please Me* in 1963 – which featured *I Saw Her Standing There* – John Lennon played a Rickenbacker 325 and a Gibson J160E, Paul McCartney played bass on a Hofner 500/1, and George Harrison played a Gretsch Duo Jet and a Gibson J160E.

Solo: *I Saw Her Standing There*

The notes and rhythms now combine to take the form of a complete melody from *I Saw Her Standing There*. Note the two one count 'rest' symbols above bar one. These symbols indicate that you start to play on the third beat of the bar.

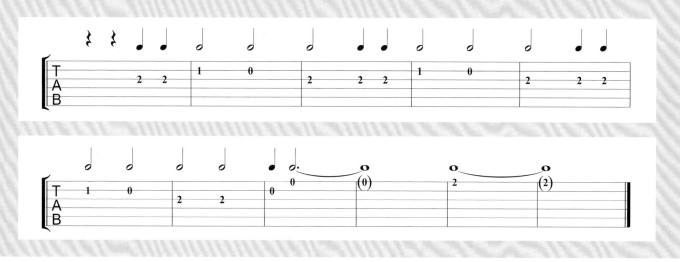

The A power chord

Power chords are used constantly by rock guitarists. Formed of only two or three strings, these chords offer the 'powerful' bottom range of the full chord shape and give you the agility to shift rapidly from one power chord to another. In this feature, we're going to study a trio of two note power chords.

Looking at the TAB below, you can see that the open 5th string and fret 2 on the 4th string combine to form an A power chord. Practise striking both strings together with equal strength, while avoiding any contact between the plectrum and string 3. You should find that a tiny adjustment is all that's required to achieve this.

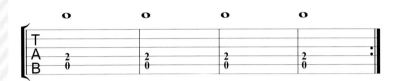

The A power chord uses finger 2 of the left hand only.

The D power chord

The method is the same as for the A power chord but, as the TAB clearly shows, you will now be playing strings 4 and 3. Taking a close look at the music before trying to play will help you to understand all of these exercises better. Learn to 'hear' the rhythm simply by looking at the music.

The D power chord shape is created by moving finger 2 of the left hand across to string 3.

Combining A and D power chords

Use the same rhythm pattern as in the exercise above. Aim to shift between the A and D power chords smoothly, leaving each small finger 2 change to the last possible moment to achieve this.

The E power chord

Providing you have mastered the previous power chords, this ought to be a straightforward exercise. Just like the others, the E power chord consists of an open string with a fret 2 on the neighbouring string. Even before you hear this, the TAB prepares your ear for a lower sounding chord, utilizing the bottom two strings of your guitar.

Left: The plectrum strikes strings 6 and 5 together to help form an E power chord.

Right: The E power chord needs left finger 2 at the 2nd fret on string 5.

I Saw Her Standing There, using two and four count chords

By bringing the three power chords together, you can hear the main body of this song taking shape. When you are practising this, always try to look ahead in the printed music to avoid having to make sudden, or late, shifts – particularly as the chord changes are quite irregular in this piece.

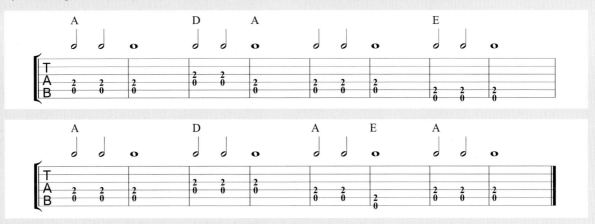

I Saw Her Standing There, using one and four count chords

The structure here is precisely that of the previous tracks, so your chord changes happen in exactly the same places as before. Four one count strums replace the two beat chords. This livens up the finger shift between bars 3 and 4 and also between bars 13 and 14.

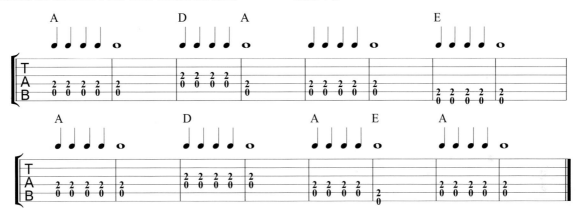

I Saw Her Standing There, using mainly one count chords

A suitably driving rhythm is created for this song by removing the four count chords and replacing them with four one count chords. So, apart from the final chord, each strum should last for one beat. Avoid potential tension in the right hand by keeping the strokes light and from the wrist.

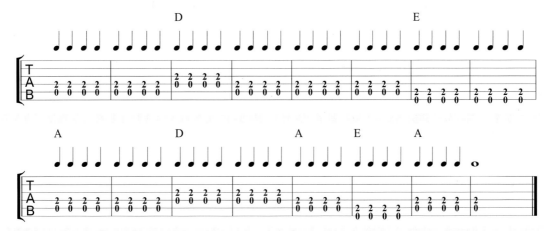

ALTERNATE PICKING & POWER CHORDS

The techniques in this session will help you play a rendition of The Riverboat Song **by Ocean Colour Scene.**

There are plenty of new notes and rhythms to learn in this session, as we work towards playing the full version of *The Riverboat Song*. We'll also be taking a first look at the techniques of alternate picking and two finger power chords.

Look closely at the music for each exercise and read the instructions carefully. The photographs are there to help you achieve good hand positions. Listen to the original song to familiarize yourself with the rhythm and beat before you try playing it yourself.

The open strings using alternate picking

In the music below, you'll see a row of arrows above the notes. These refer to the technique known as 'alternate picking'. Follow every downstroke with an upstroke of the plectrum. Continue

to swap the stroke direction throughout all six bars. The abbreviation *sim.* (for 'similar') indicates that the note lengths and stroke directions remain the same for the all bars that follow.

Playing string 6 with an upstroke.

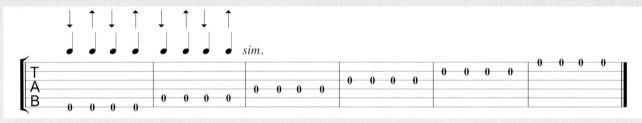

Crossing open strings using alternate picking

Alternate picking is taken a step further, as you now have to change string after each note you play. If your plectrum strokes are small and your arm remains fairly still, this should feel as natural as using all downstrokes. By way of a TAB

reminder, the first note is a one count open 2nd string. This is followed by a one count open 1st string, picked in an upwards direction. The last downstroke is four counts long and is played on the open 6th string.

String 1 is played open with an upstroke.

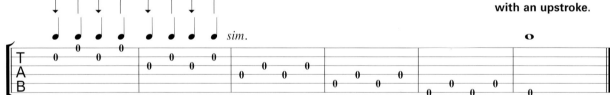

Clapping the rhythm

Every exercise, riff and song we've studied so far in *Play Guitar* has had a rhythm based upon four beats in a bar. By varying the combination of notes, note values, chords and speeds of the pieces, we have created different styles and moods. Ocean Colour Scene's *The Riverboat Song* is unusual in rock music

because it has six beats in a bar. The intricacies of the written rhythm will be covered in later sessions. For now, read the box on new notes (see opposite page). For this exercise, count the 12 half beats evenly, as shown, and clap your hands on the underlined numbers.

COUNT: <u>1</u> 2 3 <u>4</u> 5 6 <u>7</u> 8 <u>9</u> 10 <u>11</u> 12 | <u>1</u> 2 3 <u>4</u> 5 6 <u>7</u> 8 <u>9</u> 10 <u>11</u> 12 | <u>1</u> 2 3 <u>4</u> 5 6 <u>7</u> 8 <u>9</u> 10 <u>11</u> 12 | <u>1</u> 2 3 4 5 <u>6</u> <u>7</u> 8 <u>9</u> 10 <u>11</u> 12

The Riverboat Song rhythm, using open string 5

The repeated one bar rhythm pattern from the previous piece is crucial to many of the exercises in this session. Here, you can focus upon the rhythm pattern by using your right hand only to play the note A on open string 5. The third note in every bar should be played with an upstroke, as this method will ensure a relaxed and fluent performance. Try and practise this exercise a few times before continuing.

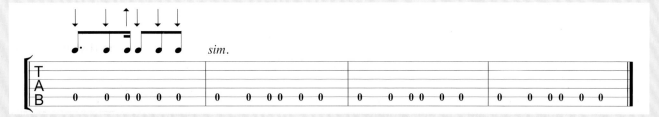

First, play the open string 5 (note A) with a downstroke.

Now that the plectrum is below the 5th string, it can be played with an upstroke.

NEW NOTE SYMBOLS

The note symbol ♪ represents a quarter count note, so four of these equal a one count note (♩). When joined together, quarter count notes are written as ♫♫, while ♫ represents a half count note followed by a quarter count note. The dot after the first note symbol in each bar adds half of the note's value again, making a three-quarter count note in total.

The Riverboat Song rhythm, crossing open strings

Start on string 5, but cross to the 4th string for the next two notes. Do the same thing to form the second half of the bar. Keep the picking and rhythm the same as before, and remember the upstroke on the third note of each bar. Switch to the D and G strings in bar three and note the repeat sign at the end of the line which tells you to play the exercise twice through.

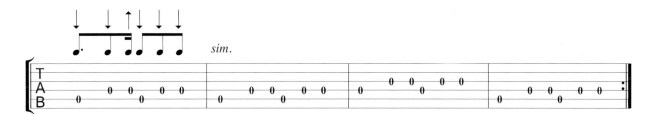

Playing a downstroke on string 5 leaves your hand in the correct position ...

... to play a downstroke on string 4.

When your plectrum is beneath string 4, play it again with an upstroke.

The Riverboat Song riff – Shape 1

Now it's time to introduce the left fingers to this one bar pattern. Because of the quick change between the third and fourth notes it's better to play these with different left fingers. So, use finger 1 for the 2nd fret note played on the 5th string, and finger 2 for the 4th string note played at fret 2. The combination of right-hand picking and this left-hand fingering will provide you with the firepower to deal with this riff.

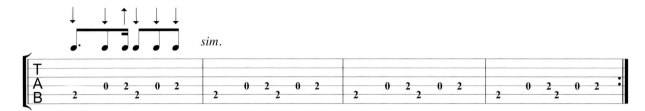

1st finger at the 2nd fret on string 5, with the 2nd finger poised over the 4th string.

This view from above clearly shows the 2nd finger poised to play string 4.

The fingers swap: the 2nd finger now frets string 4 at fret 2, and the 1st finger is raised.

The 1st finger is lifted off the 5th string, with finger 2 on string 4 at fret 2.

Finger tip

DEVELOPING A MORE FLUENT TECHNIQUE
The repetitive nature and target speed of this riff mean that the development of a relaxed and fluent technique is supremely important.

Even the slickest shift of the same finger across these fret 2 notes results in tension and a drop in performance quality. By using two fingers, you spread the left hand workload and reduce strain.

The Riverboat Song riff – Shape 2 moving to Shape 1

Shape 1 described the one bar riff pattern that was repeated throughout the previous exercise. Shape 2 uses the same rhythm, the same right-hand stroke pattern and even the same left-hand finger combination. The one essential difference is the move across to strings 4 and 3.

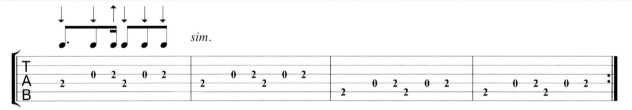

Finger 1 plays the 4th string at fret 2, with the 2nd finger ready over string 3.

The view from above, showing finger 2 poised over string 3.

Finger 2 frets string 3 at fret 2, and the 1st finger is lifted off string 4.

Finger 1 is lifted off the 4th string, while finger 2 is on the 3rd string at fret 2.

The Riverboat Song riff – Shape 3 moving to Shape 1

Shape 3 is created by shifting the entire Shape 1 riff onto the 6th and 5th strings. This pattern forms the first two bars, with a return to Shape 1 played on strings 5 and 4 to complete the line of music. Observe the repeat sign and play these four bars through twice.

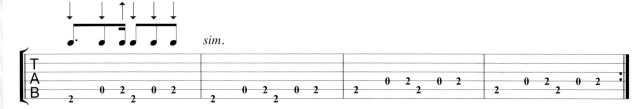

Finger 1 at fret 2 on the 6th string, with finger 2 poised over string 5.

The view from above, showing finger 2 ready in position over string 5.

Finger 2 placed on the 5th string at fret 2, with finger 1 lifted off string 6.

Finger 2 on the 5th string at the 2nd fret, with finger 1 clearly lifted off string 6.

OCEAN COLOUR SCENE
Before finally hitting the big time, the back-to-basics guitar skills of Ocean Colour Scene's Steve Cradock (far left) and Damon Minchella (left) so impressed their hero Paul Weller that he hired them for his backing band.

Often derided in the music press for their unashamed 'Sixties retro. approach, the band have a fan base that includes Noel Gallagher and Pete Townshend and sell millions of albums.

Retrospective they may be, but their largely unadorned playing style requires scrupulous technique that doesn't rely solely on spectacular effects and electrical trickery.

Linking together the three shapes of The Riverboat Song riff

Shape 1 is used predominantly in this twelve bar piece, forming bars one to four, seven to eight and eleven to twelve. Link these figures together with Shape 2 in bars five to six and Shape 3 in bars nine to ten. With lots of practice, you'll find that your fingers automatically begin to move to these locations. You will also appear to have more time and be able to think more clearly.

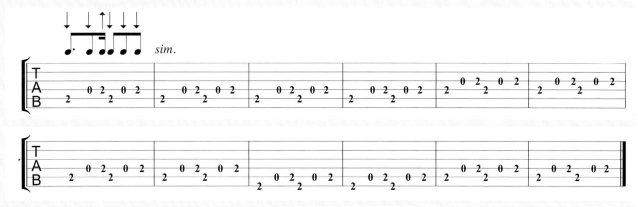

Two-finger power chords

One of the mainstays of the rock guitarist is the power chord. This exercise takes the open string power chord we studied in session 2 a stage further, as both notes are now going to require fretting. Start by placing finger 1 on fret 2 of the 5th string to make the note B. At the same time, add finger 3 to the 4th string at fret 4 to form the note F sharp (F#). In bar one, play the two notes separately, then strike both strings together in the second bar. Leave the left-hand fingers on these notes throughout the exercise.

Place your 1st finger on string 5 at fret 2.

Now add your 3rd finger on string 4 at fret 4.

LABELLING POWER CHORDS

Power chords are labelled by the letter name of the lowest note, followed by the number 5.

This means that the B power chord (right) is labelled B5.

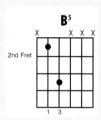

Shifting power chords

Before you begin this exercise, position your fingers in the B power chord (B5) shape practised in the previous piece. Remember to position your left thumb low behind your middle finger, so that there's some curve in the fingers and the stretch feels comfortable. In bar two, move the left hand as an entire block up one fret, so that your fingers still end up two frets apart – at frets 3 and 5 – thus creating the C power chord (C5). Notice that every other chord played is B5, with bigger shifts each time in the even numbered bars, right the way up to the 7th fret with finger 1. (# = *sharp*)

Move finger 1 up to fret 3 on the 5th string, with finger 3 at fret 5 on string 4. This makes the C power chord (C5).

The same shape moved up, so that finger 1 is at fret 7 on string 5, and finger 3 is at fret 9 on string 4, makes the E power chord (E5).

Finger tip

MUTING STRING 3
When you are playing power chords, there's a likelihood that your plectrum will accidentally hit the 3rd string some of the time. This unwanted string noise can easily be prevented.

With the 3rd finger of your left hand on its fretted note, touch the underside of this finger lightly against the 3rd string. The plectrum contact with string 3 will not then be heard through the sound of your power chord.

The power chord shape with finger 3 leaning against string 3 to prevent it ringing, i.e. 'dampening' the string.

The Riverboat Song chorus, using one power chord per bar

Once again, begin with a B power chord (B5) before shifting through D5, E5 and A5 in the next three bars.

The fret locations are given, as always, by the numbers shown in the TAB. Bars one to four are repeated four times here (indicated by *x4*) and also in the following exercise. For the first time in this session, we see the use of a tie, joining two six count chords at the end of the piece.

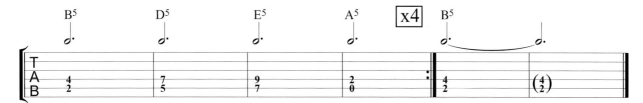

The B power chord (B5).

The D power chord (D5).

The E power chord (E5).

The A power chord (A5).

NOTE: Finger 3 is used on string 4 at fret 2 for an easy change back to the B5 chord.

The Riverboat Song chorus, using two power chords per bar

The power chords are played in the same sequence as the last exercise. You need to repeat each chord twice per bar, counting three beats for each chord.

Remember to flatten the 3rd finger a little, so that it touches lightly against string 3, preventing the unwanted ringing of this string.

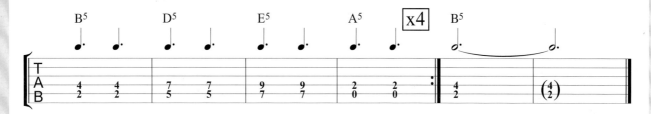

The link between the verse and chorus of *The Riverboat Song*

The Shape 1 pattern studied earlier pauses on the fourth note in bar two. This lets you prepare the power chord fingering needed in bar three. These are played in a new location, on strings 6 and 5, but the principle is the same as before. The power chord shape moves finger 1 up from fret 2 to fret 3, and finally to fret 5. There is a one count rest or pause at the start of bar five before the final flourish of bass notes.

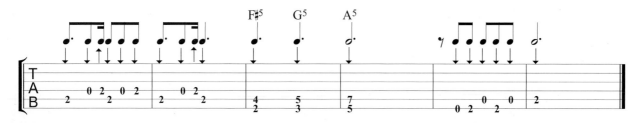

Finger 1 on string 6 at fret 2, with finger 3 on string 5 at fret 4 produces F#5.

Bar 5 needs finger 1 on string 6 at fret 2, with finger 2 poised over string 5.

The final note has finger 2 on string 5 at the 2nd fret, with finger 1 lifted off string 6.

CHORD SHIFTING & THE UPSTRUM

Master the five new chord shapes introduced in these practice pieces and you'll be ready to play the whole of Wonderwall, this session's selection from Oasis.

Most of these exercises involve strumming one or more of five new chord shapes and linking them fluently to play this session's arrangement. Check the matching chord chart on page 221 for a quick guide to left hand finger positions. Pay special attention to the newly-introduced technique of upstrumming.

The six open strings and the rhythm pattern
You should recognise the manner in which this exercise moves through the six open strings, one bar at a time, starting from the bass string – we've used it in previous issues. However, the rhythm pattern is new and best understood if you listen to the Oasis song and try playing along with it.

The right hand, ready to play a downstroke on string 6.

Adding upstrokes to the rhythm pattern
This faster version of the piece above uses upstrokes for the third and fourth notes of each bar. These are marked by the line of arrows over the TAB numbers. After a little practice, the right hand should feel more relaxed using this combination of up- and downstrokes.

The right hand about to play an upstroke on string 3.

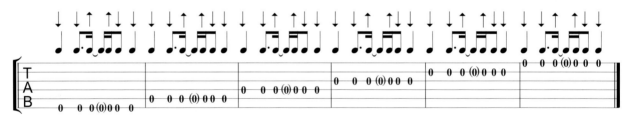

The upstrum and revision of the E minor chord
Use fingers 1 and 2 of the left hand to place the fret 2 notes of this chord shape. The vertical column of six numbers at the start of the line of TAB shows that all six strings are strummed and indicates the frets for your left hand fingers. The downward arrow indicates a downward strum, starting with the bass string. Leaving the left fingers in place, strum upwards through strings 1, 2 and 3 only, to complete the first bar. Notice the repeat sign.

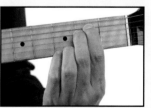
E minor, played with the 1st and 2nd fingers.

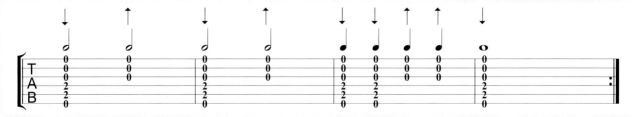

The E minor chord and the rhythm pattern

Now it's time to put together the repeated one bar rhythm, already studied in the first and second piece, with the E minor chord shape. The third and fourth strums are both upwards and should strike the first three strings only. Keep the right-hand work relaxed by strumming lightly down or up from the wrist. The fourth bar is a single four count downstrum, so let it carry on ringing throughout the bar.

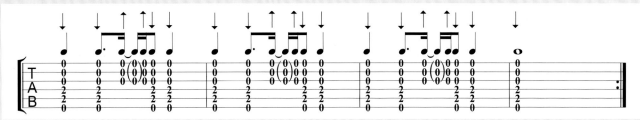

Preparing fingers 3 and 4 of the left hand

All five chords that you'll play in *Wonderwall* use fingers 3 and 4 at the 3rd fret of strings 2 and 1 respectively. These constant notes add poignancy to the song. With fingers 3 and 4 firmly in place, your 1st and 2nd fingers are now ready to fret the lower strings. Use downstrokes throughout.

Right: With your 3rd and 4th fingers in position, curve fingers 1 and 2 towards, but not onto, the lower strings.

The Eminor7 chord

Place your 3rd and 4th fingers in the same position as in Track 11. Add an E minor shape using fingers 1 and 2 to form Eminor7 (Em7).

Ensure your hand has sufficient space to make this chord; your thumb should be upright, halfway down the back of the neck, behind the 2nd fret. Curve your wrist, giving your 1st and 2nd fingers the stretch they need to reach strings 4 and 5.

Now play an even downward strum of all six strings on the first beat of every four count bar.

Em7

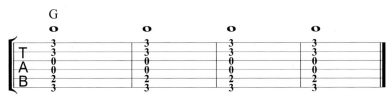

Above: The Em7 chord position. Keep your fingers in the Track 11 position, adding finger 1 at fret 2 on string 5 and finger 2 at fret 2 on string 4.

The G chord

The 3rd and 4th fingers remain on the 1st and 2nd strings at fret 3, just like the Eminor7 chord. Finger 1 also stays put on the 5th string. By shifting finger 2 over to fret 3 on the 6th string, you have the G chord.

G

With fingers 3 and 4 still in the same position as above, move finger 2 onto string 6 at fret 3 to make the G chord.

Alternating between the Eminor7 and G chord

This piece helps develop tidy changes between the two chords. When changing to the G chord, move finger 1 up close to fret 2 to allow your 2nd finger to stretch to fret 3 on the 6th string. Note the repeat sign at the end of bar four.

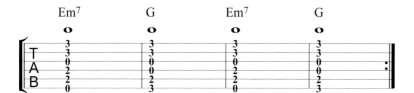

Em7 with finger 2 lifted off.

Finger 1 shifted up close to fret 2 on string 5, with finger 2 ready to play string 6 at fret 3.

Incorporating the strum pattern

Now add the strum pattern to the chord changes of the previous piece. Your downstrokes should strike all six strings, but your upstrokes should only strike strings 1 to 3. (*sim.* = similar playing style as before)

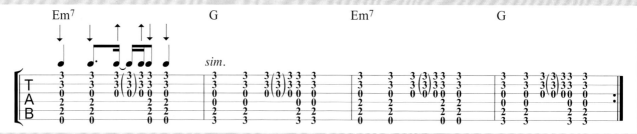

The Dsus4 chord

The TAB below has no numbers written on the bottom 2 lines – which means the third *Wonderwall* chord doesn't use strings 6 or 5 at all. Fingers 3 and 4 stay at fret 3 on the first two strings and the 4th string is played open. Use finger 1 to fret string 3 at fret 2. Hold this chord throughout the piece.

With fingers 3 and 4 kept in the same position, finger 1 now moves onto string 3 at fret 2. String 4 is left open, to form the Dsus4 chord.

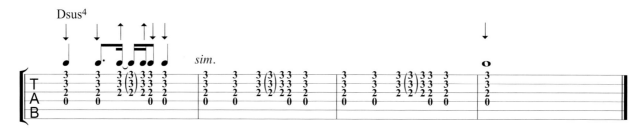

Linking the Eminor7, G and Dsus4 chords

Adding Dsus4 to the chord chain is not too hard. Fingers 3 and 4 stay on the first two strings, so only fingers 1 and 2 move. At the end of bar two, form the Dsus4 chord by removing finger 2 from the G shape and shifting finger 1 to string 3, fret 2.

We've replaced the rows of numbers in the TAB with their chord symbols. This means that you need to memorize the chord shapes, but it's much clearer and easier to read, so we've adopted it for many of the remaining exercises.

Above: Lifting finger 2 from the G shape before shifting finger 1 to fret 2 on string 3 to form Dsus4.

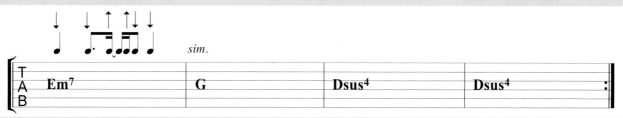

The A7sus4 chord

As with all the chords in this song, fingers 3 and 4 stay on the first two strings at fret 3. The 4th string is fretted by finger 1 at fret 2, and strings 5 and 3 are played 'open'. TAB numbering returns while you learn this chord.

With fingers 3 and 4 still in place on the 1st and 2nd strings, place finger 1 at the 2nd fret on string 4, leaving string 3 'open'.

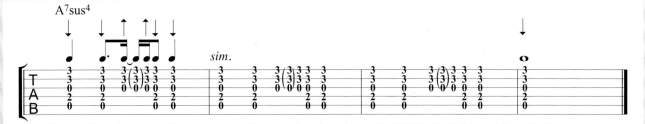

Linking the four chords

This exercise adds the new A7sus4 shape in the fourth bar. You should find the change into bar four straightforward, since you only need to shift finger 1 across to string 4.

In addition to paying close attention to your left-hand changes, try to keep your right-hand strumming fluent and accurate, only hitting the correct strings for each chord.

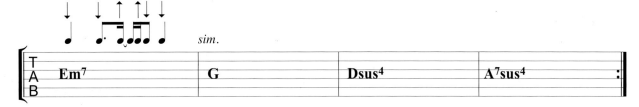

The Cadd9 chord

The fifth and final *Wonderwall* chord. Fingers 3 and 4 stay rooted to the first two strings, and finger 1 stays on the 4th string at fret 2 – like an A7sus4. The chord is transformed by placing finger 2 at fret 3 on string 5. Hold this chord throughout the piece and use the same rhythm and strum pattern from the earlier practice pieces, but avoid striking string 6.

Make an A7sus4 shape, then fret string 5 at fret 3 with finger 2 to form this chord – Cadd9.

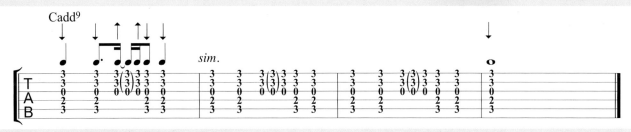

The closing chord sequence of the verse

Once again, only the chord symbols are given here, so make sure you know your left-hand shapes before you try playing along to the song. You can always refer to the matching chord chart for an at-a-glance guide. Try to use small finger movements as you change between the chords.

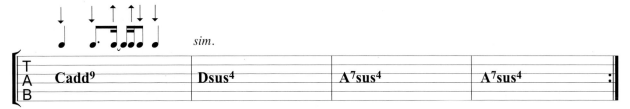

The verse chord sequence with half bar changes

This is a very important exercise in your preparation for playing fluently, so be sure to give it lots of practice. For the first time, you need to change to a different chord half way through each bar. Apart from bar eight, each bar contains only the first three strums of the one bar rhythm pattern we've used up until now. The chord change coincides with the third strum, which happens to be an upstroke.

If this is at all unclear, try listening to the original and follow the music below. You'll hear the chord changes and the held third strum, which gives you time to plan the next bar.

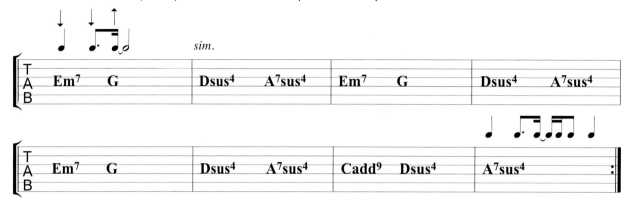

The complete verse

The chord changes are already familiar, but the complete rhythm and strum pattern has returned to complete your work on the verse of the song. Notice how bars one and two are, in fact, played three times in a row before the chord sequence is used in condensed form in bars seven and eight.

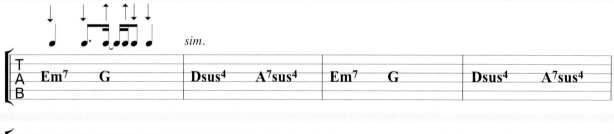

Start with the Em7 chord.

Move finger 2 onto string 6 at fret 3 to form the G chord.

Lift off finger 2 and move finger 1 over to string 3 to form the Dsus4 chord.

Move finger 1 onto string 4 at fret 2 to form the A7sus4 chord.

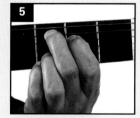
Add finger 2 to string 5 at the 3rd fret to form the Cadd9 chord.

Finger tip

PRACTISE USING ONE HAND AT A TIME
Try shifting your left hand through the chord changes without playing them with your right hand. This will help you focus on finger movements and adjustments to the angle of your wrist, and helps build a mental picture – your hand will begin to 'remember' the shapes.

It's equally important to work on your right hand technique. Try holding one chord shape and concentrate on your strumming, paying attention to the lightness, evenness and direction of your plectrum strokes.

The bridge

The 'bridge' referred to is the section of the song that comes between the verse and the chorus. In other words, it 'bridges' the gap between the two major parts of the song's structure. Bars one, three and five are the same, with two downstrummed Cadd9 chords, followed by four Dsus4 chords in the remainder of the bar. Remember to change chord on the first upstrum. Bars two and four use Eminor7 throughout and the piece finishes on a single sustained G chord.

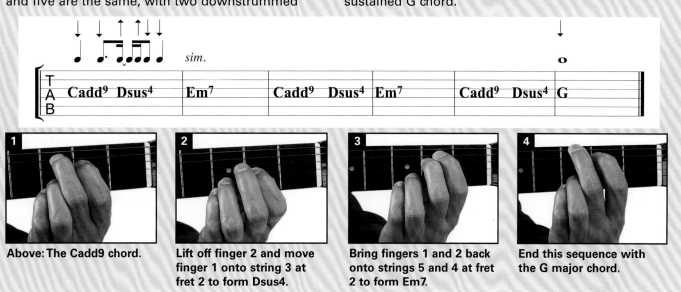

Above: The Cadd9 chord.

Lift off finger 2 and move finger 1 onto string 3 at fret 2 to form Dsus4.

Bring fingers 1 and 2 back onto strings 5 and 4 at fret 2 to form Em7.

End this sequence with the G major chord.

The end of the bridge

Bars one to five of the previous track are fused to the three bar sequence below, forming the entire bridge. A simple shift of finger 2 to the 4th string turns the G chord into Eminor7. The A7sus4 shape is easily created by removing finger 2 and replacing it with finger 1.

The chorus

The last exercise brings yet another permutation of the chords studied in this issue. In this piece, only Cadd9, Eminor7 and G are used in a regular two bar sequence. The symbol above the final two count note value indicates a 'pause'. This means that you should let the Eminor7 chord ring for longer than usual.

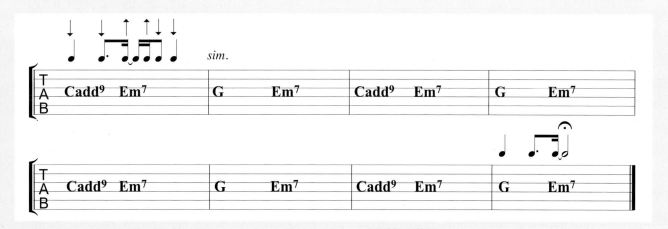

ARPEGGIOS, BENDS & SLIDES

There are plenty of new ideas to work at in these exercises. Practise carefully and your reward will be a dazzling version of Eric Clapton's timeless song, Wonderful Tonight.

Picking out the notes of a chord shape one by one creates what is known as an 'arpeggio' effect. This is an important skill to develop, and you'll get lots of opportunities to try it out over the next few pages. We are also going to look in more detail at string bending as well as getting to grips with the 'slide'.

Revising the G major chord and alternate picking

Throughout this piece, keep your four left-hand fingers in the G major chord shape. Notice the four half counts followed by a two count note symbol above bar 1. Follow the arrows to alternate between the downstrokes and upstrokes. End the piece with a full four count strum of the G chord.

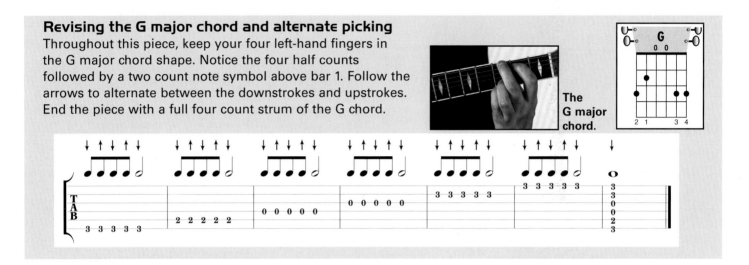

The G major chord.

The arpeggio and the G chord

This piece demonstrates the arpeggio technique using the G chord. Note that string 5 is left out of this arpeggio pattern and that downstrokes are used throughout. The first three bars adopt the rhythm pattern of the previous exercises, with a full four count strum of the G chord to finish.

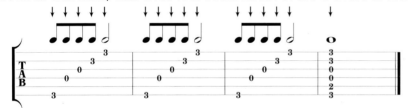

THE ARPEGGIO

To achieve an arpeggio, or 'broken chord', the strings of the chord are not strummed together. Instead, they are struck one by one and then allowed to ring over each other, creating a harp-like effect. Endless variations are possible by changing the playing order of the strings.

The D major chord

The D chord is one of the most commonly used chord shapes on the guitar. Fingers 1, 2 and 3 should form a comfortable triangular shape. A downward strum of four strings makes up most of this piece, with an arpeggio pattern in the 3rd bar. Be sure to leave your three left-hand fingers in place throughout bar 3 and observe the direction of the plectrum strokes.

The D major chord with a low thumb and curved fingers.

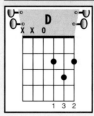

Linking the G and D chords

The secret to this shift lies in holding finger 3 in exactly the same place for both chords. If you rotate the other fingers around this pivotal 3rd finger, the shift is much easier than it at first appears. Remember the thumb's key role. It should be low, straight at the joints and pointing vertically upwards behind the 2nd fret. Avoid moving the thumb when you change chord for a quicker, more controlled shift.

The G major chord. Finger 1 is placed but not used.

Leaving finger 3 in place as you change to the D chord.

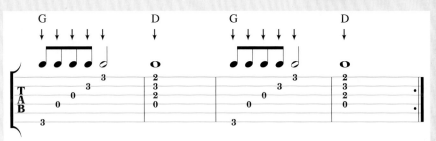

The D major chord is located with minimal finger movement.

Adding the D chord in arpeggio form

If the chord changes were working in the previous piece, this should not pose too many problems. The 3rd finger stays on string 2, leaving only small finger movements to locate the next chord. As before, mind the alternate picking in the D chord bars. Notice the repeat sign at the end of the line and leave the finger changes as late as you dare for smoother links between bars.

Finger tip

WHY COMBINE UP- & DOWNSTROKES? It's all about economy of movement. By moving the plectrum towards the next string you need to play, you reduce hand travel. This gives greater control and a better performance.

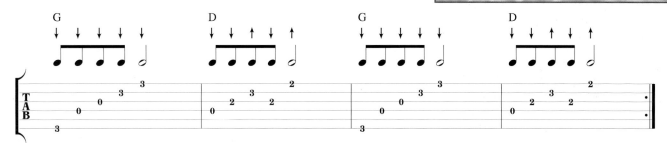

The C major chord

This is the pure form of the Cadd9 chord covered in Oasis' *Wonderwall*. Providing you keep a low thumb and nicely arched fingers, you should get the hang of this shape. Hold the C chord from start to finish, and try to stretch your fingers over to the right hand side of each fret, where the notes need less pressure to make a good sound. Use three upstrokes to end bar 3.

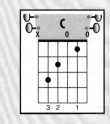

The C chord with fingers stretched.

Putting the two new chords together

There is no obvious thread linking the C and D chord shapes, making this piece tricky at first. Each of the three fingers has to move to a new location, so the closer you can skim your fingers across the strings the better. Aim to keep the thumb in the same place all the way through. If it helps, change chord position during the two count note in bar 1, or trim the long chord in bar 2 so that you are ready for bar 3.

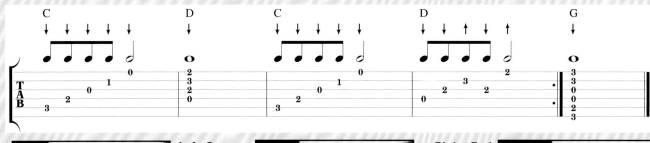

Left: Start with the C chord.

Right: Keep the thumb still as you shift to the D chord.

Right: End on a full strum of G major.

The opening chord sequence of *Wonderful Tonight*

Now we need to link together the G, D and C chord shapes. Remember to leave finger 3 in position when changing from G to D and vice versa. When you reach with finger 3 for the 5th string note that begins the C arpeggio, try to pull the 1st finger down towards string 2 to form the shape of the C chord.

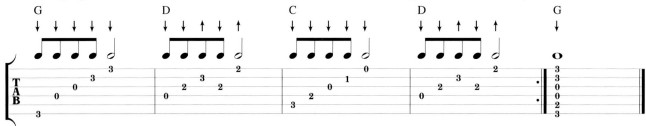

A crucial linking passage and the E minor chord

Place the 1st note with finger 3. Hold this through the open 4th and 3rd string notes that follow. Try to let the next three notes ring on by using fingers 1 and 2 for the left hand work. The final E minor chord of this piece was introduced on page 13. This time, play the fret 2 notes with fingers 1 and 2, making an easier shift out of bar 3.

Left: Finger 3 plays the 1st note on string 6.

Right: Fingers 1 and 2, together, end bar 1.

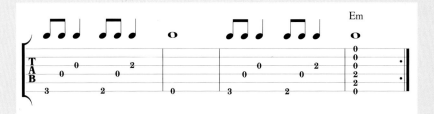

Right: Use fingers 1 and 2 to play the E minor chord.

Adding the E minor chord in arpeggio form

This is almost the same as the previous piece, but the strings of the E minor chord need to be picked separately in bars 2 and 4, and on the repeat. The rhythm is the same as for the G, D and C arpeggios played in this issue. Use small, even downstrokes to create the light, rippling effect required for this song.

Adding C and D arpeggios

This familiar section of *Wonderful Tonight* brings together the previous piece and the C and D arpeggios. Most of the chord names are self-explanatory, but bar 3 is an exception. The first three notes belong to the G chord. The next three notes create the harmony of a D chord but have an F sharp as the bass note, hence D/F#. If this makes little sense, don't panic! We'll return to the idea later.

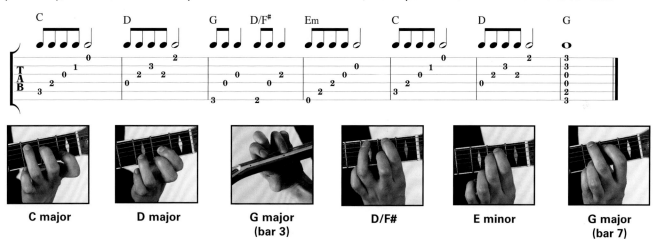

| C major | D major | G major (bar 3) | D/F# | E minor | G major (bar 7) |

The 'bridge' chord sequence

This song is unusual in that it doesn't have a specific chorus. Instead, the song is broken up by the solos and a 'bridge' section between verses 2 and 3. The melody is different, but your guitar part is almost identical to the previous exercise. Add another C major arpeggio pattern in bar 7 and a strummed D major chord on the first beat of bar 8. This chord should ideally sound for four beats, but place the final G major shape a little early if this helps you achieve the required strum on beat 1 of the last bar.

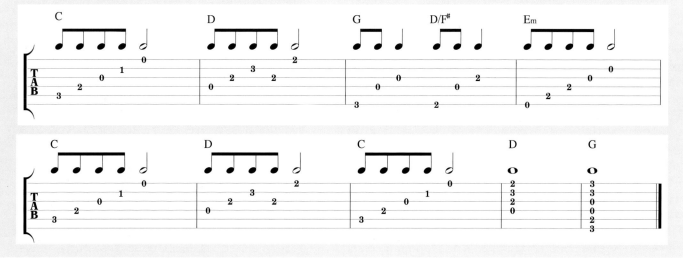

Preparing to bend string 2

Now start piecing together this famous solo. The TAB and the photos will help you locate the right notes. Placing fingers 1 and 2 behind finger 3 will give your hand more strength for the string bend coming up in the next piece. Raise the left-hand thumb in readiness for the string bending technique.

Finger 1 plays the 2nd note at fret 8.

Start with fingers 1, 2 and 3 on the 2nd string at frets 8, 9 and 10, respectively.

The fret 9 note on string 3 employs finger 2.

The full bend

Start by positioning your left hand as you did in the last exercise. Strike the fret 10 note on string 2, then use the fingers to push the string up. This will mean displacing the 3rd string and probably the 4th string as well. Then maintain the finger pressure as you gradually release the fingers back to where they started. The bend is represented on the TAB by a dotted bracket.

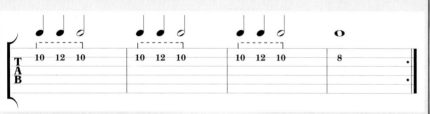

The left hand, ready to bend fret 10 on string 2.

Finger tip

BENDING NOTES

A half bend involves raising the note pitch by the equivalent of one fret. A full bend requires a two fret stretch of the string, hence the 12 in the centre of the bracket. Generally speaking, it is best to push the string upwards. This allows space for the bend as well as being easier to control.

The full bend in action, displacing strings 3 and 4.

A faster bend of the fret 10 notes

As in the last piece, the bracket shows a bend of fret 10 up to the pitch of a fret 12 note, before letting the string drop back to fret 10 again. Only the first note within the bracket is struck with the plectrum. Therefore, it is vital that a firm contact is maintained if the rise and fall effect of the bend is to be achieved. The floating rhythm value is now above the 12. This means that the upwards bend needs to be quick, so that you can hear the top of the bend on the first beat of the bar.

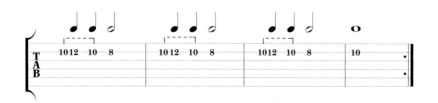

Finger tip

BENDS ON AN ACOUSTIC

Full bends are tough on the acoustic guitar. A half bend will sound perfectly acceptable for this song.

That famous Clapton solo

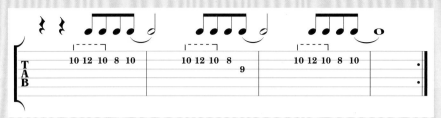

The initial bend is quick, but try to measure the fall of the string back to fret 10 before releasing fingers 2 and 3 to access the fret 8 note with finger 1. Replace fingers 2 and 3 to complete the first bar, allowing this note to carry on ringing until the next bend for a smooth line.

The slide

A slide is created by literally sliding a left-hand finger along a string from one fret position to another. It is marked on the TAB by a diagonal line between the fret numbers. The second half of this solo uses no less than three slides in a single bar! Starting bar 2 with finger 1 makes things easier. You can then slide the 1st finger along the string to fret 12, so that you can hear fret 12 without restriking it. With the same finger, slide from fret 12 to 13. Use finger 3 to slide from fret 15 to fret 17. Finish the piece by playing fret 15 with finger 1.

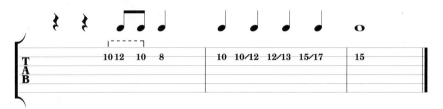

Finger 1 slides from frets 10 to 12, then to fret 13.

Finger 3 takes over at fret 15...

...then slides up from fret 15 to fret 17.

Finger tip

ATTENTION ACOUSTIC PLAYERS!
Frets 15 and 17 are hard to access, unless you have a cutaway style of guitar. Do not despair! You can achieve an identical effect by relocating the last notes at frets 10 and 12 on string 1. It is easier to use finger 3 for all but the final slide. For this and the final note, use finger 1.

The entire Clapton solo

A good performance of this solo is not easy to achieve – after all, you are playing it in exactly the way that Eric plays it himself! So go easy on yourself and work slowly but often at the aspects covered in these exercises. Acoustic guitarists should change the ending as discussed in the Finger Tip. Good luck!

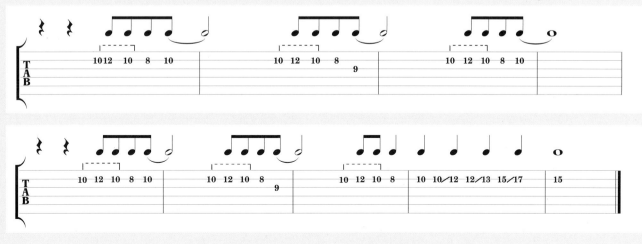

A NEW STRUM & THE HAMMER-ON

As always, there are a host of things to learn in this session. We shall study a new strum pattern, three more chord shapes and a specialist guitar technique called the 'hammer-on'.

The ideas in this session's practice pieces fuse with some further power chord work inspired by a song by

The Cranberries, *Zombie*. Try to practise each exercise at least a few times before moving on to the next.

A new rhythm pattern and the E minor chord

Place the E minor chord shape with fingers 1 and 2 of your left hand. This should be familiar, having featured previously. Leave the fingers in place throughout, allowing the sound of each string to overlap. Remember that the arrows above the rhythm values indicate the direction of the plectrum strokes, and that '*sim.*' is short for 'similar' – it means that bars 2 and 3 keep the same rhythm and stroke configuration as bar 1.

The E minor chord with fingers 1 and 2.

Striking the 3rd string, G. A reminder of good right hand shape.

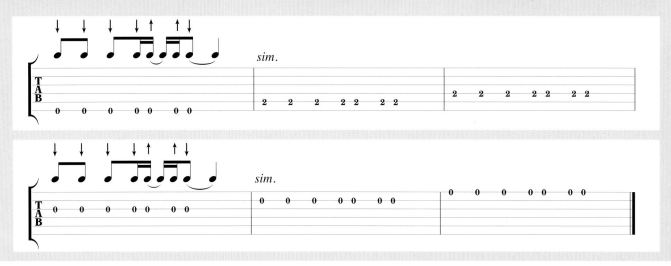

The same rhythm using strummed E minor chords

Try to strum lightly and evenly through the four downstrums that begin bar 1, before flicking the plectrum up through strings 1 to 3 for the next two chords. Bar 1 ends with another downstrum of all six strings. This rhythm figure repeats in bars 2 and 3, with a four count strum taking up all of bar 4. Finally, remember the repeat sign at the end of the TAB line.

UPSTRUMS AND DOWNSTRUMS

You may have noticed that upstrums always include less strings than downstrums. This isn't always the case, but upward strummed chords generally sound better when only the higher sounding strings are struck. This is because a lighter sound is more appropriate to chords played between the main beats of the bar.

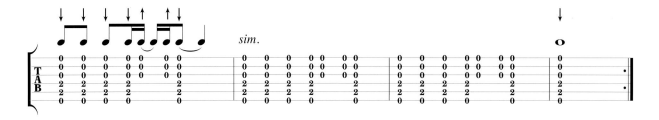

The C major 7 chord (Cmaj7)

Our first new chord is very similar to the E minor shape – finger 2 of the left hand remains in the same place, while finger 1 is replaced by the 3rd finger on string 5 at fret 3. The strum pattern is identical to the previous tracks, but avoid striking string 6 as it is not a part of the C major 7 chord. In bar 4, shift back to E minor, keeping finger movements to a minimum to make the task of chord changing easier.

The C major 7 chord.

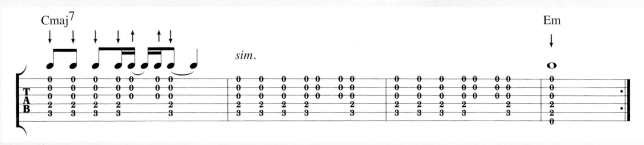

Shifting between E minor and C major 7

The one bar strum pattern, covered in previous exercises, features in every bar of this piece as you switch between these two chords, starting with E minor. Try to have your 3rd finger close to string 5 so that the change from finger 1 to 3 for the C major 7 chord is comfortable and smooth. Take care not to strike string 6 during the C major 7 bars, so spend some time watching the right hand at work.

Release finger 1 of the E minor shape.

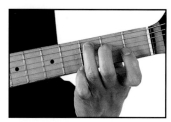

Add finger 3 to complete a smooth shift to C major 7.

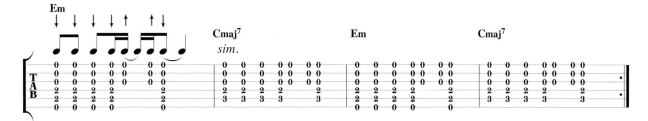

The G6 chord joins the chain

Bars 1 and 2 are identical to the previous piece. Form the new G6 chord by shifting the C major 7 shape to strings 6 and 5. Strum all six strings and hold this shape for bars 3 and 4, before returning to E minor to repeat the exercise. To perfect the strum pattern, check your right hand position (including the way you are holding the plectrum) and strive for a fluid, controlled motion of the forearm and a flexible wrist.

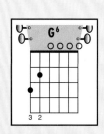

The G6 chord.

The Em11/F# chord completes the sequence

Despite the awful name, this new chord shape is very easy. Place finger 1 on string 6 at the 2nd fret, and that's all there is to it. Using finger 1 allows the easiest shift back to E minor after the repeat in bar 4. All of the other five strings are played open (do not use the left hand) producing a menacingly discordant sound.

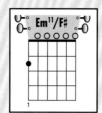

The Em11/F# chord.

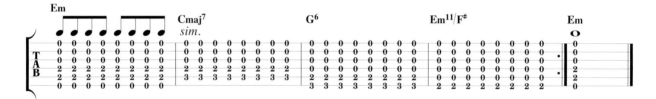

The same four chords in driving half beats

The Cranberries' song begins with the gently brooding strum pattern and chord sequence just completed, but then turns nasty as the same four chords are powered out in punishing downstrums, eight to the bar. If you are an electric player and you have any effects pedals, try clicking a heavy distortion in for this exercise, which you should practise a few times before moving on.

The E minor chord.

Shift to the C major 7 chord.

The G6 chord.

The Em11/F# chord.

A new rhythm figure

Let the E minor chord that starts this piece ring for 3 counts. Follow with a downward strum of open strings 1 to 3 on the 4th beat of the bar. Allow the strings to keep ringing and place finger 3 at fret 3 on string 5 to form the note C. The bar 2 note is 4 counts long. Repeat these two bars another three times.

The note C on the 5th string.

Introducing the 'hammer-on'

This new technique is shown on the TAB by a curved, dotted line joining pairs of fret numbers. Strike the 1st note in the usual manner. Then, keep finger 1 in place and literally hammer finger 2 onto fret 8. Fret 8 sounds without you restriking the string with the plectrum. Use the same technique in bar 3, but move your left hand to frets 2 and 3.

Finger 1 at fret 7 on string 1. Finger 2 at the ready.

Finger 2 hammers onto fret 8.

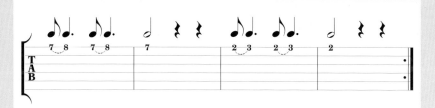

Hammer-ons using finger 3

The principle here is just the same as in the last exercise. Play fret 5 on the 1st string with the plectrum, then hammer finger 3 onto fret 7 whilst finger 1 stays in place. As long as your hammer-on makes a good, firm contact with the string, this ought to transfer the weight of the fret 5 stroke to your 3rd finger and result in a reasonably strong fret 7 sound. Do the same thing in bars 3 and 4 at the 3rd and 5th frets on string 1.

Note 1 is fret 5 on the 1st string.

Finger 3 hammers onto fret 7.

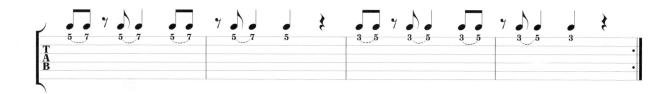

Putting the hammer-ons together

You can build most of the song's solo by combining the two hammer-on variations. Use fingers 1 and 2 for adjacent fret hammer-ons, and fingers 1 and 3 for those with a two fret gap. Notice that each hammer-on in bars 1 and 2 is followed by a shift down the neck from fret 7 to 5 to 3 to 2. Try to observe the rests (shown as ⅞ above the TAB) by muting the strings with the side of the right hand.

The 3rd hammer-on starts at fret 3 with finger 1.

Finger 3 hammers onto fret 5.

The right hand creates the rests.

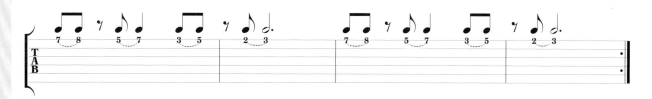

The *Zombie* solo

The four hammer-ons from the last piece are followed by two D notes. Play these at fret 3 on the 2nd string with the 3rd finger. This makes the change easier from the previous hammer-on and frees up fingers 1 and 2 to place the final E minor chord. The last melody note of the solo is string 2 open, so the strum should omit string 1. Let the chord ring for two whole bars (eight beats) before repeating.

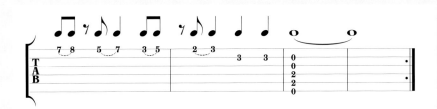

Play D on string 2 at fret 3 with the 3rd finger.

Putting the pieces together

In this piece, the pounding chords, sustained sounds and *Zombie* solo come together to create the most richly varied exercise covered so far in *Play Guitar*.

Bear in mind that the mood softens in bar 5, so remember to turn off your distortion pedal if you have been using one.

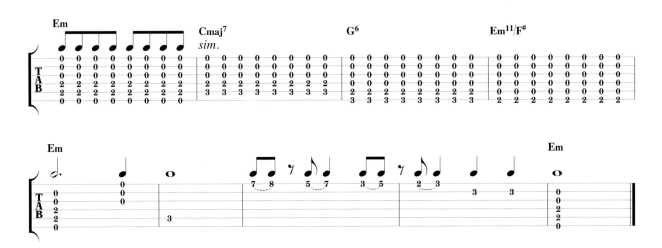

The E minor chord reducing to E power chords

Now you are going to prepare the verse of your Cranberries' song. Hold an E minor chord shape down throughout this exercise and concentrate upon the right hand work here. As you can see from the vertical column of numbers at the start of each bar, the E minor chord is played without touching string 1. Then reduce the plectrum strums to two strings only as you play seven E power chords (known as E5 chords) to complete the bars. The right hand needs to be flexible, so aim for a light, floating action.

The E minor chord is placed throughout.

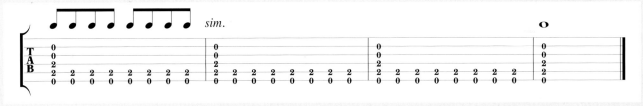

Adding C5 to the E power chords

In bar 1, use finger 1 to make the E power chord. For bar 2, shift this finger up to fret 3 on string 5, adding finger 3 at fret 5 on string 4 to form the C power chord shape. You have plenty of time to shift at first, but the gaps start to close until you have eight even power chords in each bar. Change across the strings with your plectrum as you move into each new bar.

The E power chord (E5).

Finger 1 moves up to fret 3.

Add finger 3 at fret 5 on string 4.

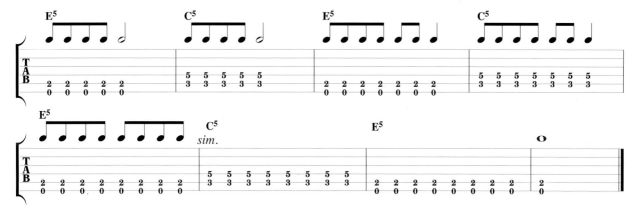

The concept of power chords being a two bass string shape should be familiar from sessions 2 and 3. A number 5 is used to differentiate these from major chords. G5 is the same shape as C5, but involves a shift across to strings 6 and 5. Though predominantly eight half beat strikes in a bar, this piece has a sustained two beat chord at the end of the line.

The G power chord (G5) on strings 6 and 5.

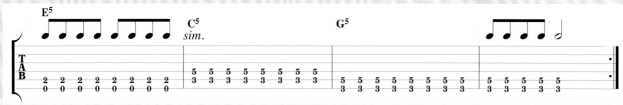

Completing the verse using the D/F# shape

This shape is a two note chord, but not a power chord – the distance between the two notes is slightly too big and so we can best refer to it as D/F#. The first three bars are identical to the first three bars of the piece above. Bar 4 involves holding firm with finger 3 from the G5 chord while reaching back to fret 2 on string 6 with finger 1.

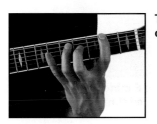

The D/F# chord.

Alternative fingering to make the stretch easier.

Finger tip

MAKING THE STRETCH

If you find the sudden stretch to the D/F# shape difficult, try playing the fret 5 note with your little finger. This leaves plenty of room for finger 1 to move down to fret 2. For an even smoother changeover, try playing all the fret 5 notes, from the C5 chord onwards, with your 4th finger.

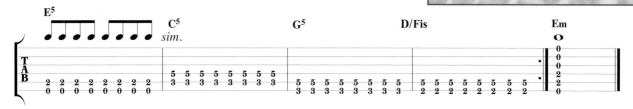

THE BASS-STRUM STYLE

*In this session, new right hand techniques, more chords and a great solo gradually come together as you build up to one of Radiohead's finest songs, **Fake Plastic Trees**.*

For most of the guitar part of *Fake Plastic Trees*, you have to strike the bass note of each chord on its own and then strum the other strings. This is a common rhythm guitar approach that is called the bass-strum style of playing.

An introduction to the bass-strum technique

Form the A major chord shape (you first used this chord for the *Pretty Vacant* riff in one of the earlier sessions) and hold this shape throughout the exercise. Play the 5th string on its own, then follow with a strum of the remaining four A-chord strings, before repeating the open 5th string. Use only downstrokes, whether you are picking single notes or strumming the chords.

The A major chord using fingers 1, 2 and 3.

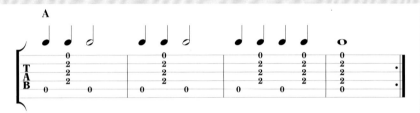

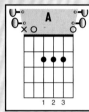

Adding upstrums

Use the A chord again for this exercise, but this time follow each downstrum with an upward strike of the first three strings. With a little work, the upstrum should make playing the next single bass note easier, as it returns your hand to the bass string area. Keep your right hand action light and relaxed, and end with a full strum of the A chord.

THE BASS-STRUM STYLE

The bass-strum method of playing makes an effective way to accompany a vocal part. Because the bass note alternates with the strummed chords, the sound is naturally lighter than a full strum and lends itself well to ballads or the softer sections of rock and pop songs.

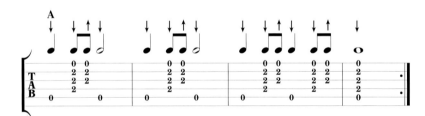

Completing the main strum pattern

For this exercise, you need to squeeze in another downstrum before each upstrum. Your plectrum movement will have to be fast, so keep the strums and strokes economical with a flexible wrist. The rhythm of bars 3 and 4 will appear in many of the exercises in this session, so try hard to get it perfect.

The plectrum ready to strike string 5.

The strum ends just below string 1 of the A chord.

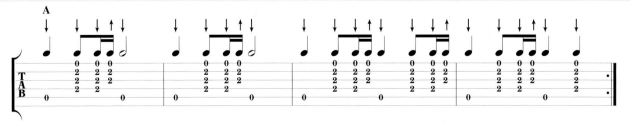

The Dmaj9/F# chord

Despite the complex name, this chord is easy to play. From the A chord shape, simply move finger 1 over to the 6th string and you have it. The chord box has a cross above string 5, so let the 1st finger lean lightly down onto this string to mute it (don't worry if it still rings a little, the chord sounds OK without muting). In this piece, play string 6 on its own, followed by two downstrums of strings 1 to 4 and a three-string upstrum to finish off the main rhythm motif.

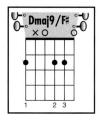

The Dmaj9/F# chord. A low thumb improves the arch of the fingers.

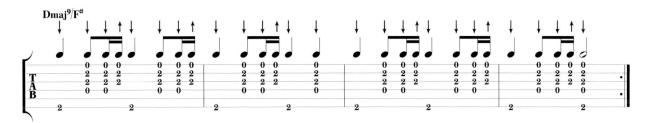

Switching between the A and Dmaj9/F# chords

For bars 1 and 2, place the A chord and then use the bass-strum style of previous exercises (i.e. a bass string 5, two downstrums of strings 1 to 4 and an upstrum, repeated three times). End bar 2 with another open 5th string followed by a whole beat downstrum. Shift finger 1 to fret 2 on string 6, forming the Dmaj9/F# chord at bar 3. Strum all six strings for the last chord, but block string 5 with finger 1 to stop it from sounding.

The A major chord.

Finger 1 is released.

Place finger 1 on string 6 for Dmaj9/F#.

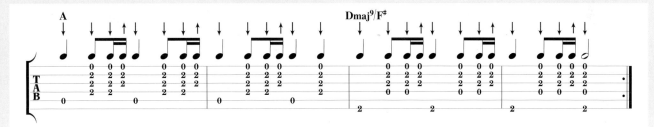

The E6 chord

For this exercise, you need to swap between Dmaj9/F# and the new E6 chord shape. Use finger 3 as the anchor and shift fingers 1 and 2 onto the 3rd and 4th strings. Give some thought to the right hand work as you shift between the chords – Dmaj9/F# involves all six strings while E6 only uses four strings.

The E6 chord. Don't play strings 5 and 6.

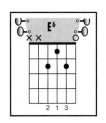

Bringing back the bass strum

Although this exercise only uses E6 and Dmaj9/F#, the combination of bass strum and faster chord shifts makes it difficult to master. The curved line between note values on the TAB is called a tie. It links the one- and two-count note values together, so take care to hold these E6 chords for three counts.

In Dmaj9/F#, mute string 5 with finger 1.

Remove fingers 1 and 2, but leave finger 3 in place.

For E6, add fingers 1 and 2 to strings 3 and 4.

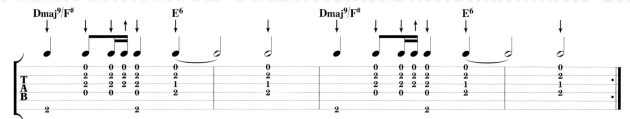

The Dsus2 chord

To form the Dsus2 chord, place finger 2 on the 3rd string at fret 2, finger 3 on string 2 at fret 3, but keep strings 1 and 4 open. Use the bass-strum approach again – start with the open 4th string, then two downstrums of strings 1 to 3, followed by a small upward flick of strings 1 and 2. An open 4th string, strum and open 4th string again complete the Dsus2 pattern. End bars 2 and 4 with two E6 chords.

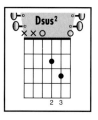

The Dsus2 chord.

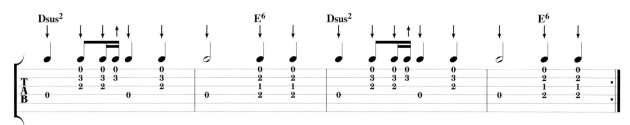

The chord changes so far

Let's recap the four chords used so far. The rhythm is easy; each two-count strum is followed by a pair of one-count strums. This allows you to concentrate on the left hand shifts and striking the correct number of strings in each chord. After the repeat of bars 1 to 4, end with a four-count A major chord.

The A major chord.

The Dmaj9/F# chord.

The E6 chord.

The Dsus2 chord.

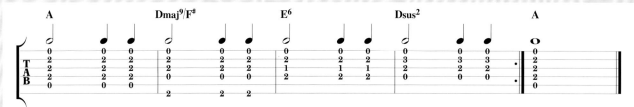

Adding the bass strum to the chord changes

Begin this piece from the Radiohead song with the A chord in bars 1 and 2, then move finger 1 to the 6th string, forming Dmaj9/F# for most of bars 3 and 4. The last chord of bar 4 is the E6 shape.

Slip finger 3 up one fret and shift finger 2 to string 3, creating Dsus2 in bar 5. One bar of A major and two bars of Dsus2 precede the final A major chord.

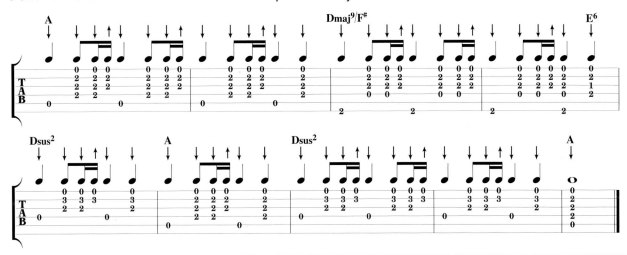

The Bm11 chord

Bm11 is best thought of as a Dsus2 shape plus finger 1 at fret 2 on the 5th string. Keep your fingers arched to stop them falling against neighbouring strings. Use the bass-strum pattern and change to A major for bars 3 and 4. Finger 2 stays at the same fret for both chords, but shifts slightly to the centre of the fret to make space for the other A chord fingers.

The Bm11 chord.

Shift fingers 1 and 3 to form A major.

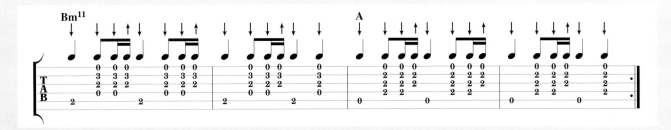

Solo work

On the original Radiohead recording, the solo is understated and very much background to the vocals. In our arrangement though we've given Jonny Greenwood's guitar work greater prominence. Begin with two A power chords (A5). The second of these rings well into bar 2, before being taken over by a melodic phrase of notes on strings 2 and 3.

The A5 chord: string 5 open, finger 1 at fret 2 on string 4.

Finger 2 plays fret 2 on the 2nd string.

Finger 3 plays fret 3 on the 2nd string.

The final fret 2 note on string 3 uses finger 1.

Revising the finger slide

This part of the solo picks up where the previous exercise left off, with finger 1 on string 3 at fret 2. Strike the 1st note and slide finger 1 up to fret 6 for the 2nd beat of the bar, without striking the fret 6 note. Use downstrokes for all remaining notes: shift the 1st finger up and then back down string 3.

COUNTING THE RHYTHMS

Improve the accuracy of your rhythm by counting an evenly spaced '1+2+3+4+' in each bar of the *Fake Plastic Trees* solo as you play it. This has the effect of subdividing the bar into eight half beats, which should help you to play each note in the right place.

In bar 1, finger 1 slides up to fret 6 on the 3rd string. Keep the thumb centred behind the fingers.

Finger 1 at fret 11 on string 3.

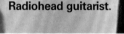

Jonny Greenwood, Radiohead guitarist.

Finger tip

READING BASS-STRUM TAB
Although the notes of a chord played in the bass-strum style are split up on the TAB, you should not place them individually. Always form the full chord shape as soon as it is marked, then pick out the individual bass strings or strums until a further chord change is labelled.

Solo work, continued

Think of the final note of the previous exercise as the 1st note of this section. Use your 1st finger all the time as you follow the TAB up the 3rd string. Start with three notes at the 2nd fret, then move up to fret 4 for the next two notes and so on up to the 9th fret. Watch out for the unequal durations of the last three notes and observe the one-bar rest before repeating the line.

Solo work, the end

For this final section of the solo, start at fret 9 with finger 1 on the 3rd string and keep your left hand at this point of the neck throughout. Use finger 2 for the 10th fret notes, finger 3 for the 11th fret notes and finger 4 for the 12th fret notes. Notice where the TAB numbers swap lines and move your fingers across to the 2nd string at the 5th note. Bars 3 and 4 are a repeat of the first two bars.

The 1st note is at fret 9 on string 3.

Change to finger 3 for the 3rd note at fret 11.

The last note is on string 2 at fret 10.

Putting the solo parts together

The previous exercises dovetail to make the solo. Hopefully, you will know the four separate parts well, so this is going to be about practising the joins now that those long final notes of earlier exercises are removed. Use the same fingering as before and count carefully.

Finger tip

There are no rests marked in this solo; you need to create one long, flowing stream of notes. Try not to release left-finger pressure for more time than is necessary when shifting between notes, and don't let the plectrum rest down onto the strings too early, as this will stop the sound of the string.

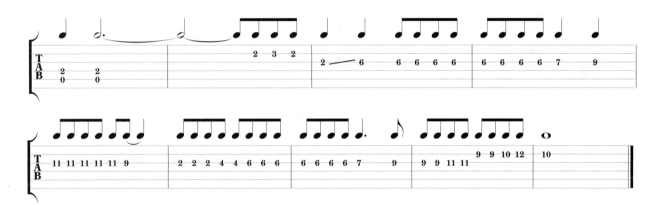

Heavier strumming to follow the solo

The song powers on after the solo as the bass-strum style changes to full, heavier downstrums. The rhythm patterns remain the same as in earlier exercises, and upstrums are still used on the 4th strum of bars 1 to 5 and the last chord of bar 2. Let the final Dsus2 chord ring for two whole bars.

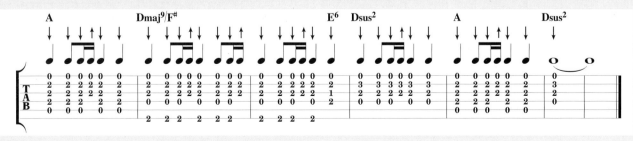

STRUMMING, POWER CHORDS & RIFFS

This session begins with the commonly used chord of E major, played to a new strum pattern. There's also further opportunity to brush up on your power chords.

These riff exercises are based on *This Is A Call* by Foo Fighters. The first riff is prominent in the chorus and will test your finger placement and alternate picking skills. The second one is an instrumental bridge – it's a meaty, repeated two-bar phrase played on the bass strings.

The E major chord

You studied the E minor chord in the first chapter of *Play Guitar*. To turn this sombre minor chord into its brighter major form, keep fingers 2 and 3 on strings 5 and 4, then add finger 1 to fret 1 on string 3. For this exercise, hold the E major shape and only use downstrums. One-, two- and four-count note values form the rhythm.

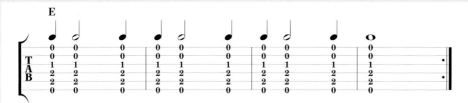

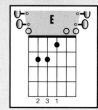

The E major chord.

Adding upstrums

Add two upstrums of strings 1, 2 and 3 to the previous exercise, between the 2nd and 3rd strums in bars 1 to 3. As before, hold the E major chord shape all the way through, and end the piece with a four-count downward strum. Try to feel the pulse of the music by evenly counting the marked '1+2+3+4+' in each bar, either aloud or in your head.

Finger tip

ACHIEVING A RELAXED STRUM
Your plectrum should glide through the strings without force. By using more wrist action and less forearm movement, you can minimize follow-through after strumming, and be better prepared for the next strum.

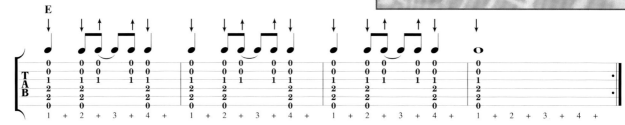

Bringing back the G major chord

G major has featured in a number of earlier exercises, so the shape used in bars 1 and 2 should be familiar. Think of the shift to E major in bar 3 as a small diagonal movement to the left of fingers 1 and 2 – the fingers open out to rest on the 3rd and 5th strings. Finally, add finger 3 underneath finger 2 on the 4th string. This piece uses the same rhythm and strum pattern as the last in bars 1 and 3, while a four-count strum fills bars 2 and 4.

A reminder of the G major chord.

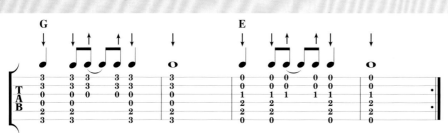

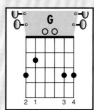

Revising the A major chord

You have used the A chord frequently, so the left hand shape should still be fresh in your mind. Having strummed this chord at the start of bar 1, release all three fingers and place finger 1 on string 3 at fret 1. Fingers 2 and 3 move to strings 4 and 5 for a smooth change to E major in bar 2. Reverse the diagonal finger movement of the previous exercise to form the G chord. Slip finger 3 back a fret and release the other fingers as you prepare for the A chord shift in bar 4.

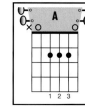

The A major chord.

The A major chord featured heavily in the last chapter.

Move finger 1 to fret 1 on string 3 to end bar 1.

Add fingers 2 and 3 for E major in bar 2.

Slip finger 3 down string 2 to fret 2 in bar 3.

Finger tip

SLICK CHORD CHANGES
For slick chord changes, look for a common thread that links the two chords together. Check for a finger that stays in the same place for both (such as finger 3 in Dmaj9/F# to E6), or a finger that can slip up or down the same string (such as finger 3 in D major to A major).

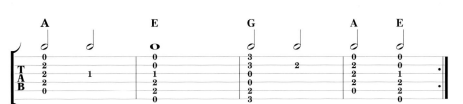

Putting together the strummed chord sequence

Bars 1 to 4 are identical to this session's second piece. For smoothness, leave the change to the G chord as late as you can, but do shift during the 4th bar if the change to the G chord is causing problems. The toughest part of this exercise occurs in bars 6 and 7, where you are called upon to shift smartly from G to A to E major. Keep the fingers close to the frets for accurate finger placement.

E major.

G major in bars 5 and 6.

A major is the second chord in bar 6.

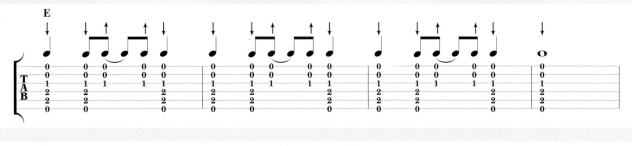

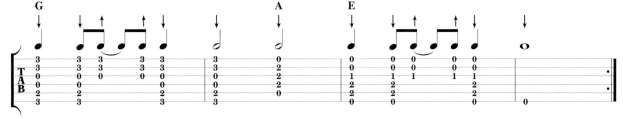

The E power chord (E5)

This two-string power chord combines an open 6th string with fret 2 on string 5. To make shifting to other power chords easier in the coming pieces, use finger 3 for the fretted note. For this piece, leave finger 3 on fret 2 from start to finish. Bar 1 contains five open 6th string notes played to this issue's main rhythm pattern. For bar 2, strike the upper string of the E5 chord throughout, before combining the two notes in the 3rd and 4th bars.

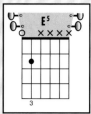

The E power chord using finger 3 on string 5 at fret 2.

Shifting between E and G power chords

To make the G power chord (G5), move the two E power chord notes up three frets each – the open string 6 becomes fret 3 with finger 1, and finger 3 moves up to the 5th fret on string 5. When you are playing the E5 chord, see if you can keep the 1st finger stretched away from the 3rd finger, as this will make the shift back to G5 much easier.

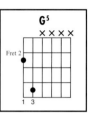

G5 uses fingers 1 and 3 at frets 3 and 5.

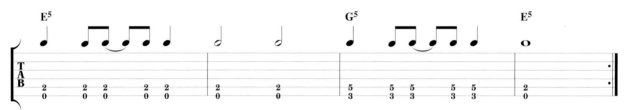

The link between the strummed and power chord sections

The rhythm and left hand movement in bar 2 are quite awkward, so be certain to shift up to the G5 chord as soon as you have released the E chord at the end of bar 1. If you listen to the original song, you will grasp the offbeat placement of the G power song. As in the previous exercise, slip finger 3 down from fret 5 to fret 2 as you move into bar 3 and the E5 chords that finish the line. Notice the 'N.C.' label at the start of bar 2. This means that there is No Chord played here (just a single open string 6 note).

Bar 1 uses the E chord.

Right hand picks the open string 6 in bar 2...

...followed by a G5 chord.

Finger 3 slips down to fret 2 to form E5.

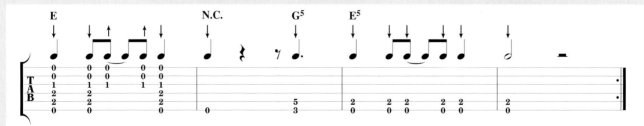

Adding A5 to the power chord chain

Use the one-bar rhythm pattern for all but the final bar. Start with the open E5 chord shape before moving your left hand up to frets 3 and 5 to form G5. The last two chords of bar 4 involve a further two-fret shift of the power chord shape up the guitar neck as A5 makes a brief appearance. Repeat bars 1 to 4, then finish with a single, sustained E5 chord.

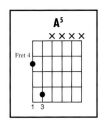

Frets 5 and 7 on the lowest two strings make A5.

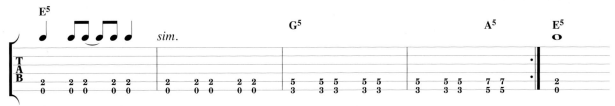

The complete power chord section

Here's a chance for you to put the last few exercises into their proper context. Begin with the spiky rhythm studied in the link between strummed and power chord sections, before settling into four bars of E power chords. Use the same rhythm pattern as you shift finger 3 quickly up to fret 5, and add finger 1 to the 6th string at fret 3 for the G5 chords. In bar 7, you need to move the G5 shape up two more frets for the pair of A power chords. Drop finger 3 down string 5 to fret 2, and combine this note with the open string 6 for a final flourish of E5.

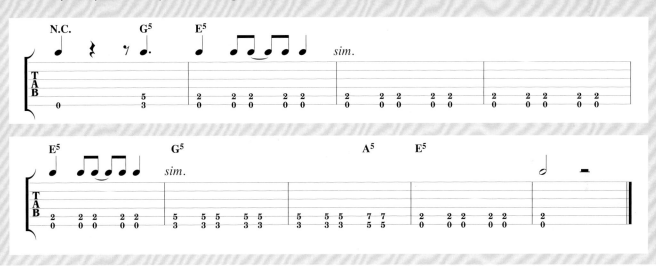

Starting the chorus riff

Keep finger 3 on string 3 at fret 3 throughout this piece. Follow the initial note with an open string 2, open string 1 and open string 2 again. End bar 1 with a further strike of the 3rd string. You will notice that you need to keep the same one-bar rhythm pattern used in many earlier exercises. Be careful not to block string 2 with the underside of finger 3, as this riff relies strongly on the over-ringing of the three strings. Also, try to use upstrokes on the 3rd and 4th notes to ensure a more comfortable passage across the strings.

Note 1 is at fret 3 on string 3 with finger 3.

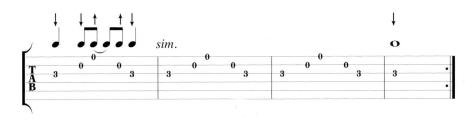

The same pattern with string 3 shifts

Keep the same string crossing, rhythm and picking as in the previous exercise, but change the fret position on string 3 at the start of each new bar. For bar 1, begin with finger 3, then change smoothly to finger 2 at fret 2 in bar 2, and finger 1 for the fret 1 notes in bar 3. Repeat bars 1 to 3 before finishing with a strum of all three strings, keeping finger 1 on the 3rd string at fret 1.

Left:
Finger 2
at fret 2
in bar 2.

Right:
Finger 1
at fret 1
in bar 3.

Beginning the bridge riff

The next four exercises piece together the instrumental riff that punctuates the Foo Fighters' song. Start by striking two open 6th strings and an open 4th string in quick succession. After a short pause, place finger 2 at fret 3 on string 6 (this will lead on well to the notes in the pieces to follow) and hold this note into bar 2. Bars 3 and 4 are a direct repeat of the first two bars.

The only fretted note is finger 2 at fret 3 on string 6.

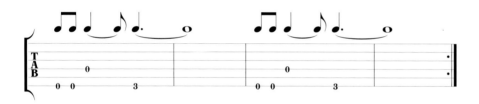

Developing the bridge riff

This exercise adds two further notes to the riff. From finger 2 at fret 3 on string 6, change to finger 3 at fret 4 on the same string (this is a quick change so have the fingers close to the frets), then play the open 5th string immediately after. This note is tied through bar 2, so let it ring. The second half of the line is the same as the first. The swift string crossing and finger changes make this piece a real challenge.

Change finger 2 on string 6...

...to finger 3 at fret 4.

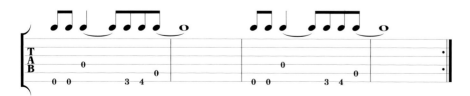

The second half of the bridge riff

Use finger 1 to place the 1st note at fret 2 on string 5, then follow with an open string 4 note. Finger 2 at fret 3 on string 6 comes next, before giving way to the open string 6 note that begins bar 2.

The piece is made up of these four notes linked at the end of the 2nd bar by a single open string 5 note.

Aim to get the rhythm right and try to practise regularly

Play note 1 with finger 1 at fret 2 on string 5.

Note 2 is an open 4th string.

Use finger 2 for the string 6, fret 3 note.

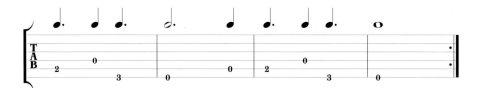

Dave Grohl, Foo Fighters frontman.

LEFT HAND POSITION

In this exercise the left hand is described for the first time as being in the 'second position'. This means that the 1st finger is positioned at fret 2. Despite the piece starting with open strings, the hand is still referred to as being in the second position because of the location of finger 1 on the neck.

The two-bar bridge riff

To complete the bridge riff, you need to put together the music from the last two exercises. Keep your left hand in the 'second position' throughout, as discussed in the blue box above (i.e. fingers 1, 2 and 3 placed on frets 2, 3 and 4, respectively). This choice

of fingering makes the note shifts easier. Repeat bars 1 to 4 before ending the riff with two fast E power chords, for which you should use finger 1 to play the 5th string notes. Damp the strings swiftly after the final power chord for a crisp ending.

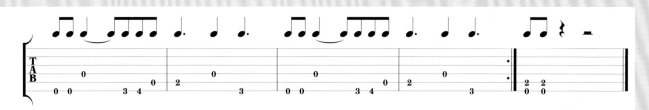

AN OUTSTANDING RIFF AND A MIGHTY SOLO

This session's exercises, based on Come As You Are by Nirvana, breaks down into four key areas of practice: the riff, two power chord sequences and a lead solo.

Nirvana's original recording of this song involved the unusual approach of tuning every guitar string down by the equivalent of two frets. We've kept the practice pieces at standard pitch to spare you potential tuning problems. However, there will be a tuning alteration later on in the solo exercise.

Beginning the riff

This early outline of one of rock's best riffs is all played on string 6. Begin after the two-and-a-half beats rest marked in bar 1. Two open strings are followed by frets 1 and 2 with the corresponding left hand fingers. The 4th note is sustained before you play another pair of fret 2 notes, then fret 1 to end the 2nd bar. An open string completes the sequence, which repeats a further two-and-a-half times.

Finger 1 at fret 1 on string 6.

Finger 2 at fret 2 on string 6.

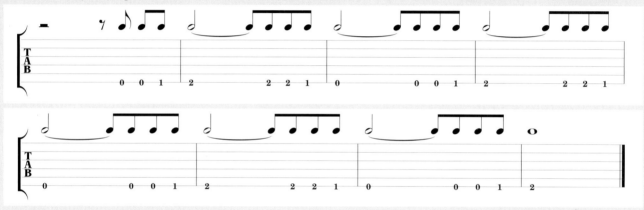

Overlapping the bass string notes

Only two different notes are used in this piece, starting with fret 2 on string 6. Play this note with your 2nd finger and leave it in position throughout as you strike the open 5th string. Arch the 2nd finger so that no contact is made with string 5. Alternate between these two notes as shown, remembering to repeat the line, as indicated by the pair of dots that precede the double bar line.

Finger 2 is curved to avoid touching string 5.

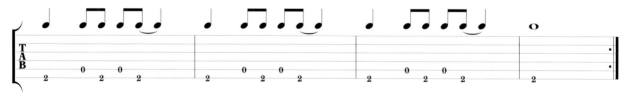

The first half of the riff

The *Come As You Are* riff starts to take shape as you combine the last two exercises. Prepare fingers 1 and 2 over the frets before you play, then use small movements when placing these fingers on the strings. Bars 2 and 3 repeat a total of three times before you play the final four-count note on string 6 with finger 2 at fret 2.

The right wrist remains low as you play all down-strokes.

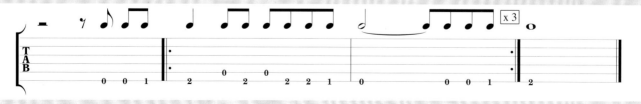

Sustaining the string 5 notes

This piece is similar to the second exercise. The fret 2 note is played with finger 2 and retained for most of the piece, only this time the notes are on string 5. Swap between open string 6 and fret 2 on string 5 as you work through the piece. As you play the last open string of the line, release finger 2 in readiness for the fretted string 6 notes that follow. Try to understand the written rhythm above the TAB.

Finger 2 remains on string 5 at fret 2 for most of the piece.

The complete riff

Replace the first two notes in bar 3 of the first half of the riff with the opening passage of the previous piece to form the whole Nirvana riff. Smooth note changes and the over-ringing of the bass strings are important, so time your left finger shifts carefully and don't mute any strings with the right hand. Repeat bars 2 and 3 three times before you play the final fret 2 note in bar 4.

Finger tip

LEFT HAND FINGER PLACEMENT
The point within each fret at which you place your left fingers greatly affects the sound quality of your notes. When you are playing individual notes, as opposed to chords, always place the left hand fingers just behind the fret wires. You might have found out the hard way that fingers placed to the left or even centrally within frets can produce an unpleasant buzzing noise, only remedied by pressing uncomfortably hard on the strings. If your notes sometimes sound muffled, it is likely that your fingers are landing on top of the fret wires instead of close behind them.

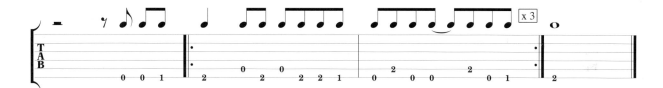

Making a start on the chorus

Now there is a shift of emphasis, as individual notes are replaced by the commonly used power chord shape covered on many previous occasions. The F#5 chord consists of finger 1 at fret 2 on string 6, plus finger 3 at fret 4 on string 5. The chord shape remains in this position for the entire piece, so concentrate on accurate rhythm and strumming of the two strings. Finger 3 can mute string 4 by leaning against it; this is a useful insurance policy against strumming more than just strings 6 and 5.

F#5 uses the familiar power chord fingering.

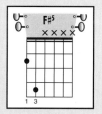

The F#5 chord.

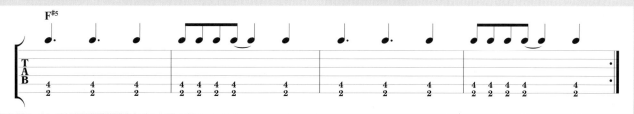

Alternating between F#5 and A5 chords

The rhythm throughout is identical to that of the last piece. Bars 1 and 3 even use the same F#5 chords. The difference lies in the power chord shift up to the 5th and 7th frets to form the A5 shape. As has been discussed before, aim to hold a firm hand shape as you move position. This enables the fingers to arrive at their new location, ready to fall straight onto their respective strings and frets.

From F#5 in bar 1...

...to A5 in bar 2. The thumb remains central behind finger 2.

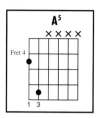

The A5 chord.

The link between the riff and the chorus

The majority of the riff studied earlier makes up the first two bars. You will finish on open string 6 at the end of the 2nd bar, at which point you should quickly move the left hand up to 2nd position in preparation for the four F# power chords that follow. Damp the strings with the side of the right hand to observe the two-beat rest that ends bar 4. During this silence, move the left hand back to 1st position so that finger 2 can place the opening note of the repeat. Try and practise this piece a few times.

1 Start on string 6 at fret 2 with finger 2.

2 The last note of bar 1 uses finger 1 at fret 1.

3 Finger 2 is needed for the fretted notes in bar 2.

4 Mute all six strings with the right hand in bar 4.

The full chorus linking to the riff

Practising the join between the short segment of riff and the power chord chorus ensures a smoother passage when putting the song together. The two-bar power chord figure from the first piece on the previous page is repeated three times. The fourth repeat is curtailed a chord early in bar 8, as you shift the left hand smoothly and swiftly down from 5th to 1st position for the opening notes of the riff.

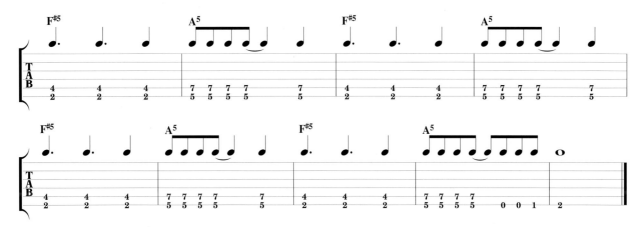

The bridge

This section is built upon the only two remaining chords used in the Nirvana song. Place the power chord shape for B5, which is situated at frets 7 and 9 on the lowest two strings. As always, fingers 1 and 3 are employed. A low, vertical thumb position allows good reach over to the 6th and 5th strings as well as enabling the fingers to curve. In bar 2, move the power chord shape three frets up the guitar neck to make D5 at frets 10 and 12. Try and listen to the original song to pick up the new rhythm patterns.

B5 at frets 7 and 9 on strings 6 and 5.

Shift up 3 frets to 10th position for D5.

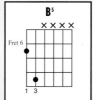
The B5 chord.

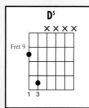
The D5 chord.

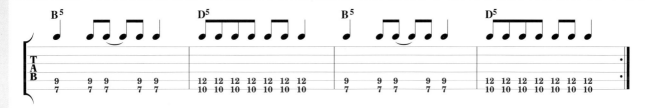

Joining the chorus and bridge

The song's four power chord shapes are brought together in this exercise. Begin with F#5 in bar 1, using fingers 1 and 3 in the usual manner. Place the fingers just behind frets 2 and 4 so that there is less risk of buzzing or muffled notes. From this starting point in 2nd position, move the shape up the neck to 5th position for the A5 chords in bar 2. After seven strums, let the power chord shape travel two further frets up the neck to 7th position for the B5 chords in bar 3. The single D5 chord in bar 4 is at 10th position.

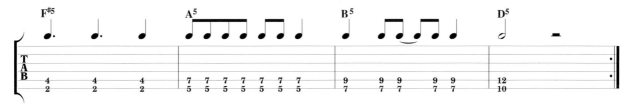

From bridge to riff and preparing for the solo

Bars 1 to 4 use the B5 and D5 chords again, with almost the same configuration as in the bridge exercose. You can see from the TAB that the riff covered in the early exercises enters towards the end of bar 4. Stay alert, as the open 6th string E follows on immediately from the stream of D5 chords. This is made tougher still by the shift from 10th position down to 1st. The last two notes of the piece prepare your hand for the lead guitar solo. Dampen the open 6th string that starts bar 8 with the side of the right hand, then use the rests to move finger 1 up to fret 6 on string 3.

Mute the strings with the right hand after the open E string in bar 8.

The last two notes shift finger 1 to fret 6 on the 3rd string.

Solo work, the start

This solo is great to play, as you sweep up and down string 3 throughout. The first note picks up where the last piece left off, with finger 1 at fret 6. After one-and-a-half beats, slide this finger up to fret 9 for the next note. Prepare for the string bend needed in the next group of tracks by leaving finger 1 at fret 9 and adding fingers 2 and 3 at frets 10 and 11. Play fret 11 twice, then let these fingers slide along the string as your hand returns to fret 6 for bar 2. The next two bars are identical, whilst a four-count fret 6 note occupies the 4th bar.

Begin the solo with finger 1 at fret 6 on string 3.

Slide finger 1 up to fret 9.

End bar 1 with a pair of fret 11 notes, using finger 3.

Bending string 3 in the solo

In this piece, you will need to bend the 3rd string note but play the 2nd string at the same time. Place fingers 1, 2 and 3 along string 3 at frets 9, 10 and 11. After three fret 11 notes, bend the note by pushing the three fingers upwards until you get the pitch of a fret 13 note (acoustic guitar strings will not bend this far, however). The bend is indicated by the dotted bracket on the TAB. Strike the open string 2 at the same time as string 3. Keep the three fingers in place as you release the bend sharply in bar 2 back to a fret 11 pitch.

Fingers 1, 2 and 3 prepare for the string bend at frets 9, 10 and 11 on string 3.

A full bend on string 3, taking care to avoid contact with string 2.

Place finger 1 at fret 9 in the 4th bar.

Finger 1 slips down to fret 6 for the final note.

The full solo

Merge the musical material of the last two exercises to form the central solo section of *Come As You Are*. Count the two-and-a-half beats rest before playing the first fret 6 note. Use the same fingerings as before to simplify the shifts of left hand position. Play bars 2 to 5 four times before you reach the last note at fret 6.

Linking the solo to the chorus

As a piece of music in its own right, this exercise will feel a little strange. However, the change from fret 6 on string 3 to an A5 chord via a right hand damping of the strings is exactly what happens in Nirvana's original song. The power chord shifts should be familiar as you studied them earlier in this session.

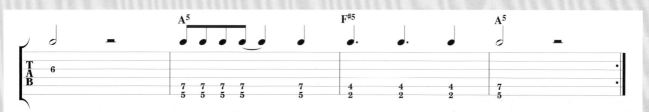

Begin with finger 1 at fret 6 on the 3rd string.

Move the hand down a fret for the A5 chords in bar 2.

A three-fret shift down the bass strings gives you F#5.

ARPEGGIOS & THE NEW F CHORD

You will learn arpeggios, a new rhythm pattern and another chord shape in these practice pieces based on The House Of The Rising Sun *by The Animals.*

You may recall that arpeggios involve placing the full left hand chord shape, then picking the strings of the chord individually.

These exercises employ a $\frac{6}{8}$ time signature, so you should count six half beats in every bar.

A minor and the arpeggio

A minor was one of the very first chord shapes you learned in *Play Guitar*. Use downstrokes to play strings 5, 3 and 2, then swap to upstrokes for strings 1 and 2. For the last note of bar 1, remove finger 3 for an upstroke of open string 3. An open string 5 fills the six half beats of bar 2, during which time you should replace finger 3 on string 3 at fret 2. Repeat bars 1 and 2 in bars 3 and 4.

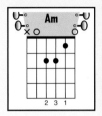

The A minor chord.

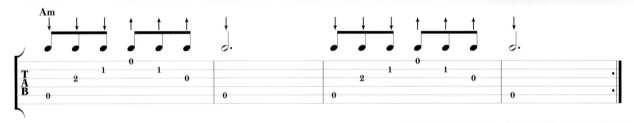

The C major arpeggio

Remove finger 3 on the last note of the A minor arpeggio in bar 1 and place it on string 5 at fret 3 to form C major for bar 2. In bar 4, use the full C major arpeggio pattern, individually striking strings 5, 3, 2, 1, 2 and 3, using a combination of three down- and three upstrokes per bar. Repeat bars 1 to 4, then end with a six-count open string 5.

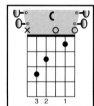

The C major chord.

Adding the D major chord

Bar 1 is the same as in the previous two pieces. Form C major in bar 2, keeping the combination of three downstrokes and three upstrokes. Release all the left hand fingers to play the three-count open 4th string that starts bar 3. During this note, place the D major chord shape to play strings 3, 2 and 1 to end bar 3. A single three-count strum of D major completes the line.

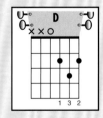

The D major chord.

Developing the sequence

As in previous exercises, remove finger 3 to shift to C major in bar 2. The change to D major in bar 3 is swift. If you can't get all three fingers in place at the same time, the arpeggio gives you the chance to position them one at a time in the necessary order, beginning with finger 1 on string 3, then finger 3 and lastly finger 2. Remove finger 1 to play the open string 3 that ends bar 3, and the open 4th string gives you time to prepare A minor for the repeat.

Release finger 1 of D major for the last note in bar 3.

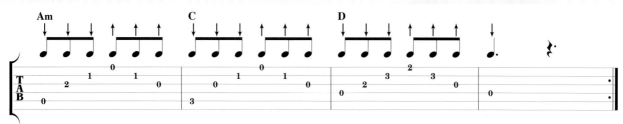

Preparing the F major chord

This practice piece involves the technique of using finger 1 to bar two strings at the same time. The same idea is adopted here, so lay the top of your 1st finger across strings 1 and 2 just behind fret 1. The string tension is at its greatest here, so plenty of pressure is necessary if both strings are to ring clearly in this piece.

Barring strings 1 and 2 at fret 1 with finger 1.

The F major chord

F major is an important step towards playing bar chords (see Finger tip). Position the fingers for this new chord in the order they need to be played – finger 3 at fret 3 on string 4, followed by finger 2 at fret 2 on string 3, then lay finger 1 across strings 1 and 2 at fret 1. Keep this shape throughout. This chord shape seldom feels comfortable straight off, so practise it often to get the muscles of your hand to adapt to its demands.

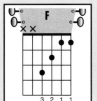

The F major chord with finger 1 barring strings 1 and 2.

Finger tip

BAR CHORDS
Barring finger 1 across two strings (as in F major) is the first step towards playing bar chords. For these you will need to fret four, five or even all six strings at the same time with finger 1, and use other combinations of fingers to complete the bar chord shapes. A chord involving the barred 1st finger and no open strings can be moved to any fret position.

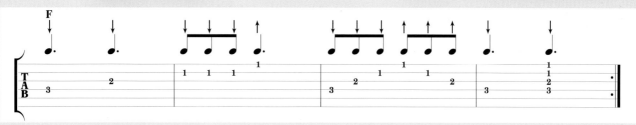

Linking the D and F arpeggios

Now you need to approach F major from the D major shape. In bar 1, pick strings 4, 3, 2, 1, 2 and 3 of D major separately, one on each half beat, with the usual mix of down- and upstrokes. The open string 3 note gives you a moment to release the D shape and prepare the F

chord for bar 2. You might find it useful to put the F chord fingers on one at a time – begin with finger 3 at fret 3 on string 4, then add finger 2 and then the 1st finger bar. Release the F chord to play the open strings 3 and 5 that complete the piece.

Begin with the D major chord placed.

Release the D chord fingers on the last note of bar 1.

Start bar 2 with finger 3 at fret 3 on string 4.

The full F chord is in position by the middle of bar 3.

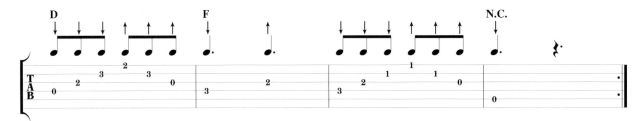

Putting together the four arpeggios

In bar 1, play the usual six-note arpeggio pattern in A minor. Use the open string 3 at the end of the bar to change to C major for bar 2. The D major arpeggio follows in bar 3. Like bar 1, bar 3 ends

with an open 3rd string, which gives you a moment to regroup your fingers for the F major arpeggio in bar 4. Once again, an open string 3 note is the key to a sleek shift back to A minor for the repeat.

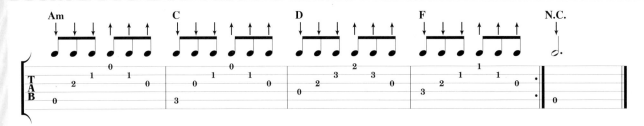

The E major chord

The Foo Fighters' song *This Is A Call* used E major a lot, so the shape should already be familiar to you. In fact, it is the same pattern as A minor, with each of the three fingers moved up one string. Place the full chord shape, even though you won't be playing all the strings within the arpeggio (you will be strumming the full chord later). The last note of each bar is, once again, an open string 3. Use this point in each bar to release the chord shape and prepare for the next shift of the fingers.

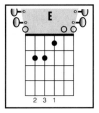

The E major chord featured previously.

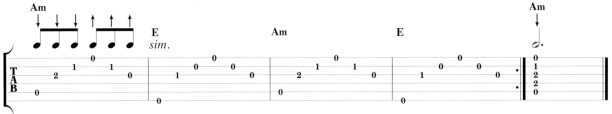

The C to E chord change

The change from C to E major is the final arpeggio pattern to learn. Begin by playing the A minor and C major arpeggios already practised. Release the C chord at the end of bar 2 and move finger 2 to fret 2 on string 5, finger 3 to fret 2 on string 4 and finger 1 to fret 1 on string 3 to build E major. Leave finger 1 on string 3 at the end of bar 3 because the E arpeggio plays for two bars in succession.

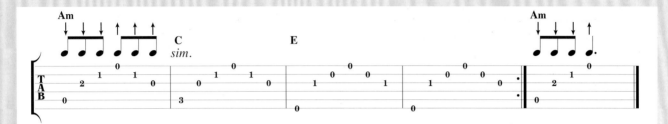

Solo work, the beginning

This is the first of four pieces that, when joined together, make up the guitar solo in the middle of *The House Of The Rising Sun*. The solo begins in 1st position, which means that finger 2 plays the first two notes at fret 2 on string 3. An open string 2 ends bar 1, followed by two fret 1 notes on string 2 with finger 1. Use finger 3 for the fret 3 note in bar 3 before returning to fret 2 on string 3.

The first two notes at fret 2 on string 3 with finger 2.

Note 3 is an open 2nd string, B.

Finger 1 at fret 1 on string 2.

The 3rd full bar starts with finger 3 at fret 3 on string 2.

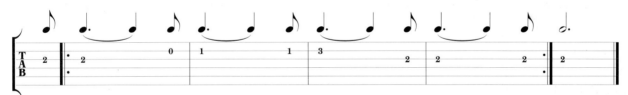

The second part of the solo

For note 1, slide finger 3 from fret 3 on string 1 up to fret 5. Strike string 1 twice more with finger 3 at fret 5, then use finger 1 to place fret 3 in the 2nd full bar. The rhythm of the solo is dominated by bars consisting of a five-count note and a one-count note.

Finger 3 is ready to slide at the start of the piece.

Slide finger 3 up to fret 5 on string 1.

Use finger 1 for the fret 3 note in the 2nd full bar.

The third phrase of the solo

Music, just like sentences, is constructed in phrases. This solo consists of four phrases, of which this section is phrase three. Start in the same way as the previous piece (the second phrase), but shift the left hand back down to 1st position as you strike the open string 1 at the end of the 2nd full bar. This will allow you to use fingers 2 and 1 for the last two notes. Observe the rest by damping your right hand onto all six strings.

In bar 3, finger 3 plays fret 3 on the 2nd string.

This note is followed by finger 2, fret 2, string 3.

End with finger 1 at fret 1 on string 2.

Finishing the solo

Each of the four phrases that make up the solo starts with a single half-count note, known as an up-beat. Having ended phrase three in 1st position, you can now stay there throughout this final section of the solo. Use finger 1 for fret 1 and finger 2 for fret 2. Downstrokes are fine for the whole solo, as the note changes do not involve much string crossing or an especially quick tempo.

The first three notes use finger 2 at fret 2 on string 3.

Next comes fret 1 on string 3 with finger 1.

The lowest note, E, is at fret 2 on string 4 with finger 2.

The complete solo

With slight adaptation, this solo links together the last four pieces of music. The repeat signs have been removed, as have the last two notes of the first, second and fourth phrases. Aim to link your notes and phrases smoothly, bearing in mind that the majority of the rests have now disappeared.

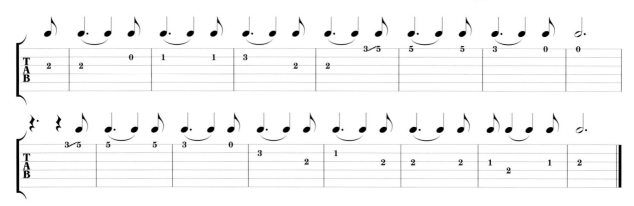

The verse using strummed chords

Strummed chords replace the arpeggio style for verse 4 of *The House Of The Rising Sun*. This creates a louder sound that is appropriate to the last verse of the song, as well as lending some useful variety. The chord shapes are the same as those played earlier in the session, and you have the 5th and 6th counts of almost every bar to shift your left fingers to the next chord. Bar 7 is the exception, in which you pound out half-count strums on every beat of the bar.

A minor is used in the 1st bar.

Shift to C major for the 2nd bar.

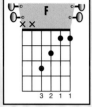
A reminder of the F major chord.

On to D major for the 3rd bar.

F major comes in the 4th bar.

E major fills bars 7 and 8.

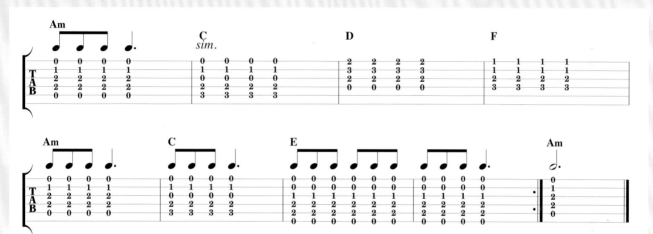

The conclusion and the D minor chord

You need a new chord in the last few bars of *The House Of The Rising Sun*. A four-note A minor arpeggio in bar 1 gives you time to place the D minor chord, studied in the first chapter of *Play Guitar*.

Leave the changes back to A minor as late as you can to avoid gaps in the sound. Bars 1 to 4 repeat before one more A minor chord completes this session.

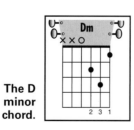
The D minor chord.

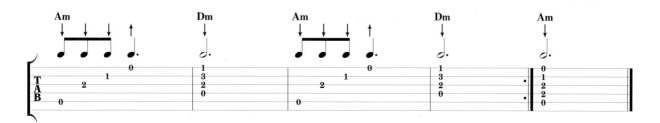

THREE-STRING POWER CHORDS

Practising for this session's** When I Come Around **by Green Day builds on your palm muting skills and serves as an introduction to three-string power chords.

The strident sound of a two-string power chord is further intensified by adding a third string to its shape. This always involves placing finger 4 at the same fret as finger 3, but on the next string across. Though not essential, palm muting gives definition to notes and style to your performance, so work hard on this technique.

Palm muting and the G5 chord

To form G5, place finger 1 at fret 3 on the bottom E (6th) string and finger 3 at fret 5 on the A (5th) string. Palm mute the chords with P.M. written above them by dropping the heel of the right hand lightly onto the bridge. Two half-beat quavers followed by a one-beat crotchet form the main rhythm pattern of the piece.

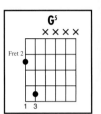

The G5 chord. Use this chord throughout.

Palm muting on the bridge for a muffled tone.

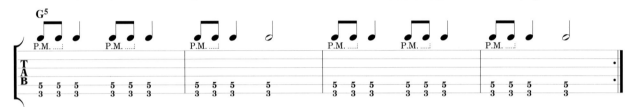

Three-string power chords

With the G5 chord still in place, add finger 4 to the D (4th) string at fret 5. Adding this upper octave note makes G5 sound even stronger. Play the three bass strings separately in bar 1, aiming for a clean sound on each note. The three strings are struck together on each of the four chords in bar 2. Bars 3 and 4 repeat the opening two bars.

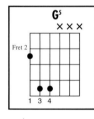

The three-string version of G5.

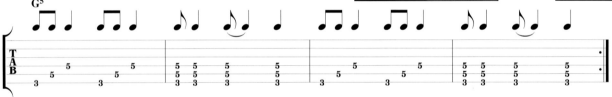

Power chord shifts

Start bar 1 with two palm muted, two-string G5 chords. The three-string version of G5 follows, so have finger 4 already in place. Lift the right hand off the bridge for chords 3 and 4 to contrast the palm muted and clean chords. Use an identical approach in bars 2 to 4, but shift the three-string power chord shape up through 5th, 7th and 8th positions.

The A5 chord (the G5 shape in 5th position).

The B5 chord (the G5 shape in 7th position).

The C5 chord (the G5 shape in 8th position).

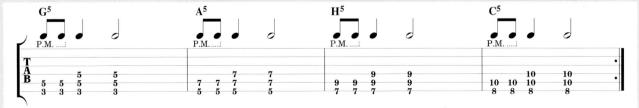

Moving the power chord to the inner strings

Release the G5 chord at the end of bar 1 but keep the hand shape as you move up two frets and diagonally across to strings 5, 4 and 3. With careful practice, the fingers will stay in the power chord shape, ready to form the D5 chord. Apply the same process in reverse as you return to G5 in bar 3, not forgetting to attempt the palm muting on the first two chords. For bar 4, play the D5 chord in arpeggio form but try to place all three fingers together at the beginning of the bar.

The G5 shape moves up to strings 5, 4 and 3 to form D5.

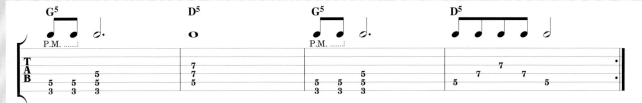

Speeding up the left hand shifts

The dotted minim (three-count) and semibreve (four-count) chords of the last piece gave you plenty of time to make the shifts between G5 and D5. In this piece, however, you have only two counts to make the shifts.

Leave the changes as late as you can, but be sure to have the new chord in place for the start of each bar. Aim to make a clear distinction between the two-string muted chords and the three-string clean-sounding chords.

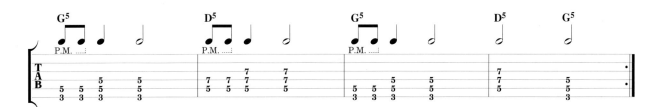

The verse riff takes shape

You still have to use the G5 and D5 shapes in this piece, but now the rhythm is mostly built upon one-count crotchets and half-count quavers. This means that your chord shifts will need to be even faster. The right hand work should be feeling more instinctive by now, so pay particular attention to your left hand. Remember that for neat shifts you want to be looking ahead to the next chord position. As you approach the end of bar 1, focus your eyes on fret 5, string 5 so that your 1st finger knows exactly where it's going for the D5 chord. The 3rd and 4th fingers should follow.

Finger tip

A DUAL ROLE FOR FINGER 1
As well as using finger 1 to place the lowest-sounding note of your three-string power chords, you can let the bottom part of this finger rest lightly across the treble strings. Should your plectrum accidentally strike these unwanted strings, which is more than likely at first, they will be muted and make no obvious sound.

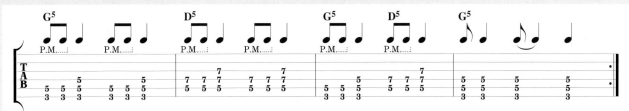

Moving between E5 and C5

This piece prepares you for the second half of the verse riff. The E5 and C5 chord shapes are modelled on the D5 chord. E5 is formed by moving D5 up two frets to 7th position. From here, C5 involves dropping the same shape four frets down the guitar neck to 3rd position. Both are played as three-string power chords throughout. You'll need neat plectrum work to avoid making contact with strings 6, 2 and 1.

E5 is played in 7th position.

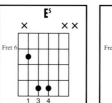

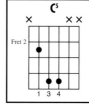

Move the E5 shape down to 3rd position for C5.

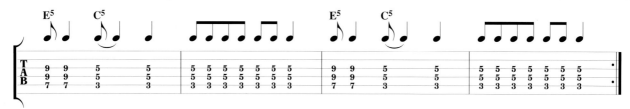

The E minor chord in 7th position

There are many different ways of playing the same chord on the guitar. Adding finger 2 at fret 8 on the B (2nd) string to the E power chord changes it to a minor chord (it adds note 3 of the E minor scale). Leave this shape in place for the entire piece, and pick the strings separately in bars 1 to 3. Observe the stroke direction arrows for a tidy right hand technique.

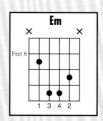

The E minor chord with finger 1 muting string 1.

The riff is nearly complete

You have played bars 1 and 3 before. Place the full, three-string G5 chord at the start but only strike the bottom two strings for the opening two palm muted chords. Lift the right hand off the bridge for the full G5 chord, then move to 5th position for the D5 chords. Shift up two frets in bar 2 and play strings 4 and 5 together, before adding finger 2 to string 2 and playing the four-string E minor chord. Use the one-beat crotchet rest at the end of bar 2 to replace the G5 shape.

Finger tip

PALM MUTING AND CLEAN CHORDS
Good right hand technique allows you to switch between palm muted and clean chords with a minimum of hand movement. Don't press down too hard on the bridge when palm muting or the result may be no sound at all. Experiment with different pressures until you can create the muffled tone but still distinctly hear the notes. The wrist should require only a fractional lift to clear the bridge and should have virtually no effect on the plectrum position.

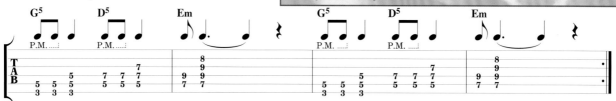

The finished verse riff

It's time to fill the spaces in bars 2 and 4 of the previous piece by moving your left hand down from 7th to 3rd position for the two C power chords. As you make this change, be sure to remove finger 2 since this is not part of the C power chord. You are then left with a straightforward shift across to the bottom three strings at the same frets for the return to G5.

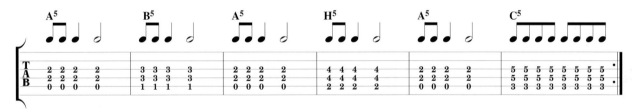

Preparing the chorus chord changes

For the four chords in bar 1, place finger 3 at fret 2 on the D (4th) string and finger 4 at fret 2 on the G (3rd) string to form A5, then add an open A (5th) string. The reason behind this fingering becomes clear as you move each note up one fret in bar 2. Shift your 3rd and 4th fingers to fret 3, leaving finger 1 available for the fret 1 note on string 5. The 3rd and 5th bars are the same as bar 1, while, respectively the B5 and C5 chords in bars 4 and 6 shift the power chord shape to 2nd and 3rd positions.

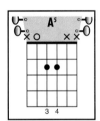

The A5 chord using the open 5th string.

B♭5 in 1st position.

Move A5 to 2nd position for B5.

The chorus accompaniment

The absence of palm muted chords in the chorus of *When I Come Around* creates an effective contrast to the verse. Unusually short at only four bars long, the chorus consists of A5 and C5 chords. These are punched out in half-beat quavers, making the shifts a bit tougher than in the last piece. There are five chords in bar 4, the last of which is the only one-beat chord. Observe the crotchet rest by damping the side of the right hand down onto the strings, then reposition the hand ready for the repeat.

The chorus begins with A5 chords.

Fingers 3 and 4 slip along the strings to fret 5 as you add finger 1 to form C5.

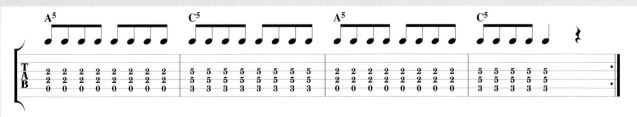

Solo work, the beginning

Use finger 1 to bar strings 1 and 2 at fret 3 throughout this piece. The 3rd note is an open G (3rd) string, so be careful not to allow finger 1 to extend too far. Add finger 3 to the top E (1st) string for the 5th note in bar 1 and keep it on until the end of the bar. Combine down- and upstrokes as shown by the arrows above the TAB to enhance and relax your performance.

Finger 1 bars the E and B strings at fret 3.

Add finger 3 at fret 5 on the E string.

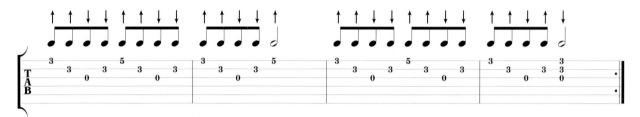

Stage two of the solo

The role of the left hand is very much the same as for the previous exercise. Finger 1 bars the top E (1st) and B (2nd) strings throughout, with the G (3rd) string remaining open. Finger 3 is added at fret 5 for one chord only in the middle of bars 1 to 3. Move the plectrum downwards through a mixture of three-string chords and individual open G notes. The exception is the last chord of bar 3, which is strummed upwards because of the quickness of the quarter-beat semiquavers.

USING MORE MUSICAL TERMINOLOGY

This session's text makes regular reference to the letter names of open strings and to musical terms, such as crotchets and quavers, when describing note values. Explanation of these terms each time they appear will be phased out, so commit these note names and terms to memory as you go along.

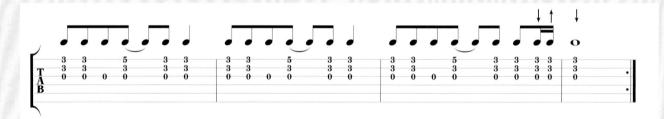

Downstrums and upstrums

A down-down-up-down strum pattern is the key to this section of the *When I Come Around* solo. This is the only way to deal with the quick rhythm figures used throughout bars 1 to 3. Your left hand retains the 3rd position bar across the top E (1st) and B (2nd) strings and adds finger 3 for chords 4 to 7 in the first three bars. A nifty shift of finger 1 across to fret 2 on the G (3rd) string is required to implement the slide from fret 2 up to fret 4 that ends the line.

Finger 1 slides from fret 2 up to fret 4.

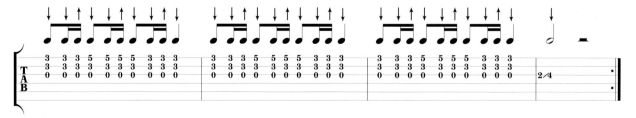

Sliding up to two-string chords

The finger slide that ended the previous piece is the starting point of this exercise. With finger 1 at fret 2, strike the G (3rd) string, then swiftly slide up to fret 4 – don't restrike the string as you arrive at fret 4. Add finger 3 at fret 5 on the B (2nd) string to play a pair of two-string chords. Bars 3 and 4 repeat bars 1 and 2, but with an extra chord. For this, leave fingers 1 and 3 in place and add finger 2 to fret 5 on the G (3rd) string.

Finger 3 joins finger 1 after the slide.

Finger 2 is added to fret 5 in bars 3 and 4.

Sliding down to A5

Use finger 1 to slide all the way down the bass E string from fret 12. This fret is often marked with a double dot because it is one octave higher than the open string. The slide is quick, but try to line up fingers 3 and 4 with the D (4th) and G (3rd) strings so that you can place these fingers swiftly for the A5 chords. In this piece, use the one-beat crotchet rest to move the 1st finger smartly back up to fret 12.

Finger 1 slides all the way down string 6 from fret 12.

An A5 chord follows the slide.

The entire solo

The solo of *When I Come Around* may be brief but it does contain a lot of variety. Leave finger 1 barring the top E (1st) and B (2nd) strings for bars 1 to 3. Use an arpeggio picking style for bar 1, followed by a mixture of down- and upstrummed three-string chords in the 2nd and 3rd bars. Bar 4 combines the upward slide and two-string chords of the piece at the top of this page with the descending slide from the previous piece. End with a semibreve (four-count) A5 chord.

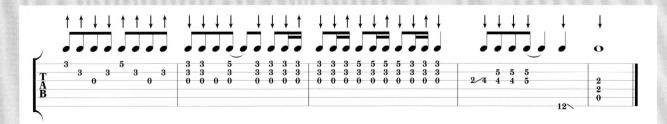

THREE-STRING BARRING

In this session, we study a riff played on the bass strings and muted power chords that lead into a trio of strummed chords.

The new concept contained within this arrangement of *And She Was* by Talking Heads involves using finger 1 to bar three strings, instead of just the two that you practised previously in *The House Of The Rising Sun* by The Animals It will take precise finger placement and focused pressure to make all three strings sound clearly.

Placing the 3rd finger

With your thumb low behind fret 3, spread your fingers apart, ensuring that finger 3 is just above fret 4 on the bottom E (6th) string. Play two open E strings, then place finger 3 onto fret 4. Repeat this process on the A (5th) string, again holding finger 3 close to fret 4 while you play the open strings. The three-count dotted minims reduce to one-count crotchets in bar 3, while the 4th bar consists of a single open E.

Finger 3 on the bottom E (6th) string at fret 4.

Finger 3 at fret 4 on the A (5th) string.

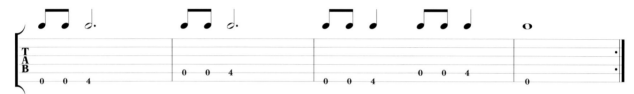

Bringing in the 1st finger

Keep your left fingers in 2nd position throughout (finger 1 at fret 2). Begin as in the previous piece, playing two open E strings followed by a fret 4 note placed with finger 3. Complete bar 1 by using finger 1 to play a fret 2 note on the A (5th) string. Bar 2 imitates bar 1 but on the A and D (4th) strings. Four half-beat quavers and a two-beat minim rest make up bars 3 and 4.

Finger 1 at fret 2 on the A (5th) string.

Finger 1 on the D (4th) string in bars 2 and 4.

The song's opening riff

Most of the riff that accompanies the song's verse is formed by joining together the notes from bars 3 and 4 of the previous piece and removing the rests. The 9th and final note of the figure is simply another open E. As all nine notes are quavers, aim to keep them smooth and even. The remainder of bar 2 is silent, so count the rests carefully. Bars 3 and 4 are a repeat of the first two bars.

Finger tip

PALM MUTING THE RIFF
To give this riff an authentic feel, mute all the notes by resting the heel of your right hand lightly on the bridge as you pick the strings with your plectrum. The result, as demonstrated in previous sessions, is a muffled tone through which the notes can still be heard.

Bb5 and C5 chords

After using three-string power chords in the last chapter, we return to the two-string shape for the song's pre-chorus power chords. Bb5 consists of finger 1 at fret 1 on the A (5th) string, together with finger 3 at fret 3 on the D (4th) string. This chord remains in place until bar 3, when a two-fret shift up the guitar neck to 3rd position makes the C5 chord.

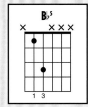

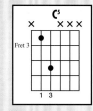

Bb5 in 1st position.

C5 is the same shape, two positions higher.

F5 on strings 4 and 3

In this piece, the F5 shape joins the Bb5 and C5 chords. For the song, you need to play F5 on the D (4th) and G (3rd) strings. Although this power chord sounds higher than the others, it is formed in exactly the same way. From Bb5 in bar 1, release and move the shape up to 3rd position, at the same time moving up one string. Aim to hold each chord for its full two-count minim value (four counts in bar 4), as this will encourage swift, accurate changes.

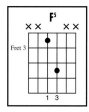

F5 in its higher octave location.

Quicker power chord shifts

To complete the first half of the pre-chorus, you need to combine the three power chords with the rhythm as shown above. The key to success here lies in always keeping the same spread between your 1st and 3rd fingers as you move between chord positions. Trim the length of all but the bar 4 chord as described in the Finger tip box, and be particularly alert to the tricky shift between Bb5 and F5 in bar 1.

Finger tip

LEFT HAND MUTING
To achieve a clipped sound for the power chords in the pre-chorus, you need to observe the rests. By releasing the finger pressure on the frets just after each chord is struck, the sound can be muted without removing the fingers from the strings. An example of this technique was used in the Elastica riff in an earlier session.

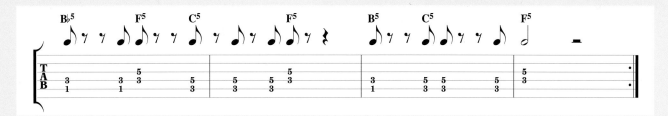

G5 and a new rhythm pattern

The second half of the pre-chorus brings G5 into the song. From the opening B♭5 chord, shift the power chord shape up two frets and down onto the bottom E (6th) and A (5th) strings to play a pair of G5 chords. Stay in 3rd position for the C5 chords on the A and D (4th) strings. Bar 2 consists of a crotchet (one count), four quavers (half counts) and another crotchet. Keep the C5 chords smooth in contrast to the muted chords in bars 1 and 3.

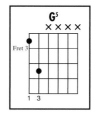

The final power chord shape used in the song is G5.

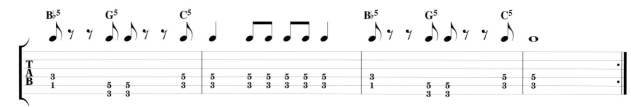

Talking Heads, playing live on stage.

The complete power chord section

The first four bars are identical to the section studied in the last piece on the previous page, and bars 5 and 6 are simply a repeat of bars 1 and 2. Bars 7 and 8 take their musical material from the previous piece as you bring in the G5 chord and the sustained sequence of seven C5 chords. To build up a sense of momentum towards the repeat, it is effective to strike each C5 chord progressively harder.

E and A major chords

Work on the song's chorus begins with revision of the six-string E major chord and the five-string A major chord. Hopefully, the chords and the changes between them won't feel too taxing. You'll need to concentrate on the rhythm, so keep your strums swift and punchy. The rests are crucial to the feel of the chorus: you achieve them by dropping the side of the right hand onto all six strings.

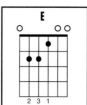
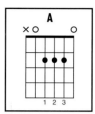

The E major chord.
Finger 1 avoids contact with the open B string.

A major with all three fingers at fret 2.

The four-string D major chord

After the three spiky A chords, shift to D by slipping finger 3 over from fret 2 into fret 3. At the same time, release fingers 1 and 2 and drop them onto the G (3rd) string and the top E (1st) string. An open D (4th) string completes the D major chord. Pay special attention to the quick change between the last two chords in bar 4. Aim to use finger 3 as the lead finger when moving back to the A chord.

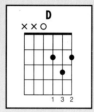

Slip finger 3 up a fret as you form D major.

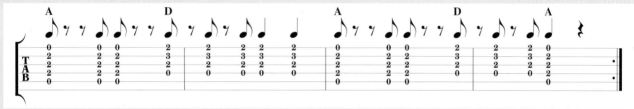

The finished chorus

The chorus accompaniment brings together the E, A and D major chords. At first glance there is a lot to take in. However, the eight bars are just bars 1 and 2 repeated four times. The only variation occurs in bar 8, where you play one A chord instead of the usual two. If muting the chords is proving difficult, let them ring until you can comfortably make the chord shifts, then try to incorporate the muting process later.

The side of the right hand creates the silence between chords.

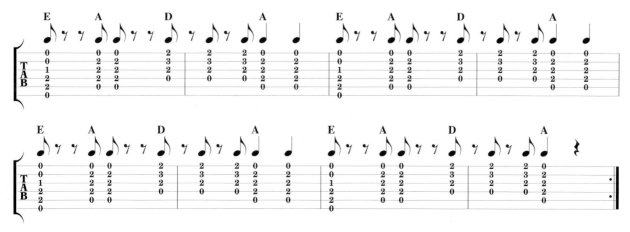

The C5 to E major chord change

This piece will come in useful when you are putting together the practice pieces because it focuses on the link between the pre-chorus and the chorus. Place C5 using fingers 1 and 3 and hold this shape throughout the six strums in bar 1. Three E chords follow in bar 2, and you should aim to get all six strings ringing clearly. Try to achieve the right hand muting to contrast the E chords with the sustained C5 chords. Bars 3 and 4 are an exact repeat of the first two bars.

Finger tip

SIMPLIFYING CHORD CHANGES
Always look for a common thread when changing between chords. This reduces the pressure on your technique and results in a more fluid performance. In the case of C5 to E major, finger 3 stays on string 4, so it makes sense to build your chord shift around this. From C5, release finger 1 and run finger 3 along the D string to fret 2. With practice, you will also be able to prepare the 1st and 2nd fingers as you shift.

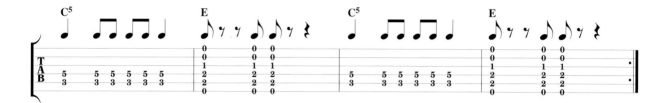

Barring the E, B and G strings

Lie finger 1 flat across the top three strings just behind fret 7. Keep the thumb low so that finger 1 can remain straight at the joint nearest the tip. This is necessary if you are to achieve a good contact across each string. The left hand can stay in this position for the whole piece, so pay close attention to the order in which the strings need to be struck. The direction of the plectrum strokes is indicated for the first time; following the directions shown should help the right hand stay relaxed.

Finger 1 bars three strings at fret 7.

Shifting the finger bar

Keep the three-string finger bar from the previous piece and add finger 2 at fret 8 on the B (2nd) string, making sure you avoid contact with string 1. Pay attention to the direction of the plectrum strokes. Remove finger 2 for the 1st chord in bar 3, which consists of the top E (1st) and B strings only. As you shift finger 1 down to fret 5 and then to fret 3, keep the finger across all three strings but strike only two of them. Use the open strings that end bar 3 to return the left hand to 7th position in time for the bar 4 chord.

With finger 1 barring fret 7, add finger 2 at fret 8 on the B string.

Slide the finger bar down to fret 5 in bar 3.

Finger 1 falls two more frets to 3rd position.

Putting the bridge together

By combining some of the bars from the previous two exercises, you can form the complete bridge section of *And She Was*. The three-string finger bar continues to play a vital role, so be sure to position your 1st finger accurately, while allowing for the addition of finger 2 in the 3rd bar.

Tidy finger placement in 9th position

This piece uses a new solo idea based upon barring the first three strings at 9th position. You will be playing chords on the B (2nd) and G (3rd) strings throughout, so make a firm contact with these strings. Though not essential, you could try to keep the finger pressure light on the top E (1st) string by slightly bending the finger outwards, so that the finger mutes out any accidental plectrum contact. Add finger 2 at fret 10 for the 2nd chord, and then finger 3 as well at fret 11 in bar 2.

Finger 1 bars the B and G strings at fret 9.

Finger 2 is added at fret 10.

In bar 2, add the 3rd finger at fret 11 on the G string.

Final exercise

In this last piece, the B (2nd) and G (3rd) string chords change in the same order as in the previous piece, but now you must use a new rhythm and be aware of the number of times each chord is played. As before, keep the finger bar at fret 9 and avoid any plectrum contact with the top E (1st) string. Bars 1 and 2 repeat three times, but you need to release finger 2 for the very last chord of bar 6. Play with your right hand wrist low, and aim to observe the marked half-beat quaver rests by damping the side of the hand down onto the strings, before lifting it fractionally again in time for the next plectrum stroke.

A FRESH APPROACH TO RHYTHM GUITAR PLAYING

There are no full chords in your latest session. Instead, power chords form the basis of a more fluid style of rock song accompaniment.

You'll need to embellish the power chord shapes in this session by occasionally adding and removing one finger, along the lines of the Blues shuffle.

Hammer-ons and string bends, so far associated with lead playing, weave in among the power chord lines to give an exciting new sound to your guitar playing.

Barring the D and G strings
To bar the D and G strings with finger 1 for the opening A5 chord, you will have to rest your finger across the top E and B strings. Strike the A, D and G strings separately in bar 1. Then, in bar 2, play two three-string strums, avoiding contact with the E and B strings. With the finger bar still in place, add finger 3 to fret 4 on the D string as you pick out the notes of bar 3. Remove this extra finger to leave the original A5 chord ready for you to play in bar 4.

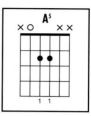

The A5 chord using finger 1.

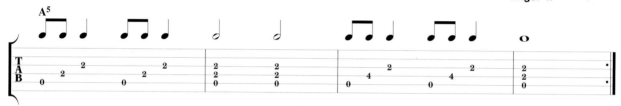

Developing the three-string chords
For this exercise, keep the finger shapes of the first piece but strum three-string power chords. Use finger 3 for the fret 4 notes on the D string and hold this finger close over the fret when it is not being used. The rests after the 2nd chord in each bar are vital to the overall effect, so even at this early stage, see if you can use the right hand muting technique to create these silences.

Mute the strings with the right hand.

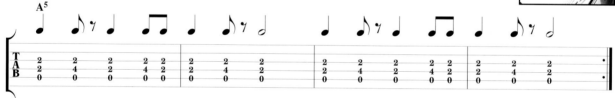

Breaking down the G major chord
The form of G major used here is different from the shape you have studied before. However, it still uses finger 2 for the fret 3 note on the bottom E string and contains an open D and an open G string. An open B string completes the chord shape for this piece. Do not play the chord as one full strum. Instead, strike the notes very carefully, aiming to make contact only with the notes required. Use right hand muting for the rests and replace finger 2 with a 1st finger bar across fret 2 for the final A5 chord.

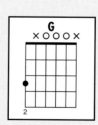

G major using finger 2 to mute the A string.

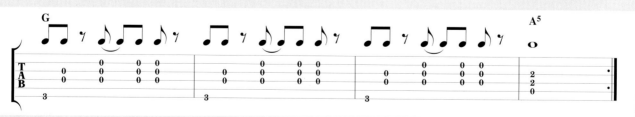

Incorporating a new D5 shape

This D5 shape is played in a different position than the one you learnt before. Bar 1 is the same as in the second piece, which leaves finger 2 free to play the fret 3 note on the bottom E string at the start of bar 2. Leave finger 2 in place as you play the open D and G strings together, then use fingers 1 and 3 on the G and B strings, along with an open D, for the first of three D5 chords to finish bar 2. Bars 3 and 4 repeat the process, followed by a repeat of bars 1 to 4 and a final strum of A5.

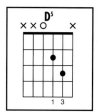

Place the D5 chord with fingers 1 and 3.

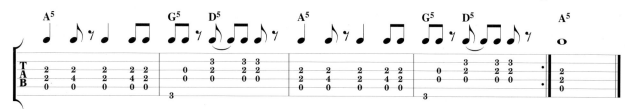

A challenging rhythm figure

The rhythm of the entire song is challenging, but the next two pieces are particularly tricky. The '1+2+3+4+' below the TAB represents the division of the four beats in each bar into half-beat quavers. Say this as you play to help place your notes on the right counts. Although there is no open A at the bottom of the 1st chord shape, A5 is strongly implied, which is why the chord name is there. The same theory applies to the G5 chord in bars 2 and 4. Play the D and G strings together for each of the chords, with finger 1 barring fret 2 for the A5 shapes, and with open strings forming G5. Use the right side of your palm for the rests.

Finger tip

LEFT HAND MUTING

It might feel easier to mute with the left hand where no open strings are used. To do this, release the finger pressure while maintaining contact on the fretted notes. This approach could be adopted to mute the A5 chords in this exercise.

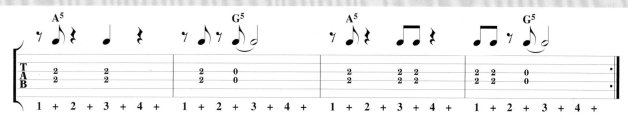

Bending the A string

This piece breaks up the power chord guitar work. It keeps the rhythm of the piece above, but slots a 1st finger string bend into bars 2 and 4. Use the 1st finger to bar the D and G strings for the three A5 chords, then release this finger for the open string shape referred to as G5. As you release finger 1 and play the open strings, move the same finger over to the A string for the bend at fret 2. As soon as you place finger 1, pull downwards towards string 4 to effect the half bend. Aim to achieve a note change equivalent to putting a finger one fret higher onto fret 3. Maintain finger pressure as you release the bend and end the figure with an open A.

Finger 1 is ready to bend the A string at fret 2.

Pull the string downwards to create the bend.

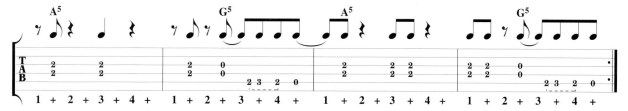

From hammer-on to power chord

Hammer-ons always act as a prelude to a power chord. Keep the opening A5 chord in place, then add finger 2 to fret 3 on the A string for the initial note of the hammer-on. Without removing either finger 1 or finger 2, hammer-on at fret 4 on the A string with finger 3. Remove the hammer-on fingers and you are left with finger 1 for the next A5 chord.

Begin with the three-string A5 chord.

Add finger 2 for the 3rd fret note.

Finger 3 executes the hammer-on.

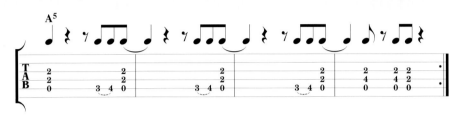

Taking shape

Begin as you did in the exercise above before punching out the two-string A5 and G5 shapes studied earlier. The D5 chord comes next with the three-string A5 shape rounding things off up to the repeat. Don't forget to rock the 3rd finger on and off fret 4 in the 4th and 5th bars. Bar 4 is called the '1st time bar' because it is played first time through only. Following a repeat of bars 1 to 3, you skip over bar 4 and go to bar 5, known as the '2nd time bar'. This is what the brackets above the TAB refer to.

1ST AND 2ND TIME BARS

These are useful abbreviating tools, eliminating the need to write out a piece for a second time when only a slight adaptation of the ending is required. The 1st time bar bracket sometimes spans more than one bar.

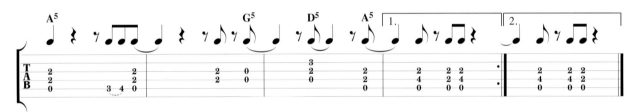

Damping the A string with finger 2

For the opening E5 chord, place finger 1 at fret 2 on the A string. The shuffle idea returns as you add finger 3 to play the fret 4 notes in bars 1 and 3. For G5, use finger 2 for the fret 3 note on the bottom E string and damp the A string with the underside of finger 2. This allows you to play strings 6 and 4 together without hearing string 5. Add finger 1 at fret 2 on the D string for the minim chord in bar 2, while continuing to damp out the A string.

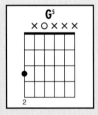

The first chord is E5.

Add finger 3 at fret 4 on string 5 in bars 1 and 3.

The 1st and 2nd fingers together in bars 2 and 4.

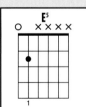

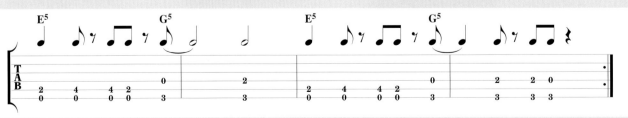

An effective rhythmical device

This two-bar riff consists of a hammer-on followed by a two-string A5 chord, played four times in all. Each pairing of a hammer-on and A5 chord starts at a different point within the two bars, which intentionally blurs the effect of four beats in a bar. You have to play a single quaver before the 1st full bar, so count carefully. Use fingers 2 and 3 for the hammer-on and then finger 1 for the 2nd fret note in the A5 chords. Because of the quaver upbeat at the start, there are only three-and-a-half beats in bar 4 – this is necessary to keep four beats to a bar in the repeat.

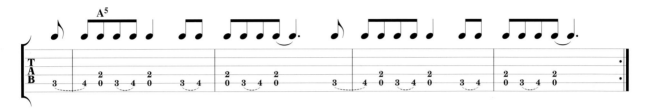

The same riff on the D and G strings

Start with the two-string E5 shape and its fret 4 extension using finger 3, then change to finger 2 for G5. The shuffle effect runs through bar 2, as you add and then release finger 1 on the D string. The riff from the piece above follows, before an almost identical repeat of bars 1 and 2 starts on the last chord of line 1. Move the hammer-on and power chord riff across to the D and G strings, and then repeat the entire piece over again.

The 1st note of the D string hammer-on.

Finger 3 hammers-on at fret 4.

Use finger 1 between the hammer-ons.

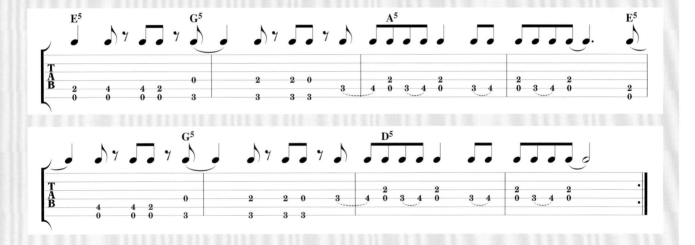

The song's chorus

Bar 1 is based on the A5 chord, with the fret 4 notes adding the shuffle that is a rock'n'roll guitarist's trademark. Remember to keep finger 1 in place when using finger 3. The remainder of the chorus is virtually identical to the end of the piece above; just watch out for the slight alteration to the rhythm on the first G5 chord and the crotchet rest at the end of bar 4. Stick to rests between chords using the right hand muting technique.

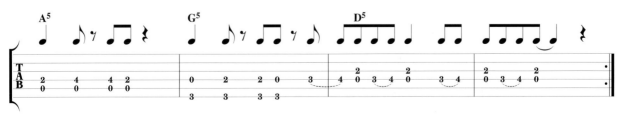

Further intricate rhythms

The rhythm throughout the song is complex, so you'd benefit from tapping it out before playing. In this exercise, A5 occurs both with and without the open A string, G5 appears as a three-string chord, with the A string damped out by the underside of finger 2 as before. Bar finger 1 across fret 2 for the A5 chords, use finger 2 to place the bottom note of G5, and use fingers 1 and 3 to place D5.

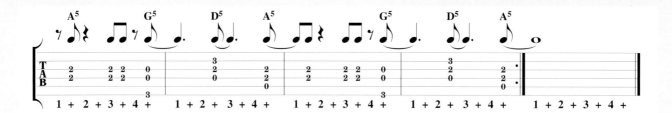

The first half of the solo

Start in 5th position, with finger 3 at fret 7 on the D string. Finger 1 plays the fret 5 notes on both the G and D strings through to the string bend in bar 2. For this, leave finger 1 at fret 5 and add fingers 2 and 3 along string 3 at frets 6 and 7. Play the fret 7 note, then push the fingers upwards for a full, two-fret bend. Return the fingers to their starting positions to make fret 7 sound again without re-striking the string.

The solo starts at fret 7.

Finger 1 also plays fret 5 on the D string.

All three fingers bend the G string in bars 2 and 4.

The remainder of the solo

Stay in 8th position for this piece. With finger 1 at fret 8 and finger 3 at fret 10, strike the top E string. Finger 3 pulls the string downwards – hold finger 1 firm and you should hear the fret 8 note sound. Jump finger 3 over to string 2 at fret 10 while retaining finger 1, then use fingers 1 and 3 for the last two notes of bar 1. Bars 2 and 3 are the same, followed by a fret 10 string bend.

Fingers 3 and 1 ready for the pull-off.

Finger 3 moves onto the B string.

Finger 3 pulls off fret 10.

A full bend on string 1.

THE D MAJOR 7 CHORD

The warm, mellow sound of the D major 7 chord lies at the heart of this session's arrangement of Babies by Pulp.

This session contains a new and commonly used form of G major to learn, plus the opportunity to bar four strings at the same time with finger 1 for the A6 chord. E minor returns to complete the set of strummed chords, which combine with four imaginatively crafted lead guitar lines to create practice pieces full of variety.

Shifting from 6th to 4th position

This piece will loosen up your fingers and focus your plectrum work, as well as prepare the opening notes of *Babies*. Place finger 2 at fret 7 on the D string and finger 1 at fret 6 on the G string. Starting with the D string, alternately strike these two strings, using down- and upstrokes as indicated. Shift the whole hand down two frets to 4th position for bars 3 and 4. After the repeat, play a semibreve D5 chord by dropping the left hand two further frets, using finger 1 at fret 2 with an open D.

Fingers 1 and 2 in 6th position.

Shift this shape to 4th position.

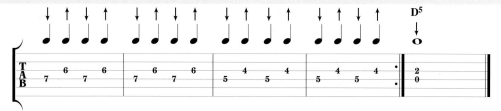

Quicker use of alternate strokes

This piece uses the same notes and left hand fingerings as the previous exercise, but the plectrum work is faster and virtually continuous, so you'll need to follow the marked combination of down- and upstrokes carefully. Keep the right wrist low and the plectrum strokes small to help you deal with the pace, bearing in mind that it will be quicker still should you wish to play along to the original recording.

Use finger 1 for the final D5 chord.

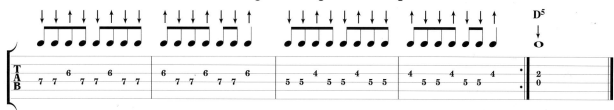

D major 7 (Dmaj7) and a new G major shape

The jazz-tinged flavour of the major 7 first appeared when you played the C major 7 chord. The finger pattern for D major 7 is very similar to that of A major, except that the fingers are on the top three strings at fret 2 instead of on strings 2, 3 and 4. An open D string completes the chord. The G major chord in bars 3 and 4 is subtly different from previous versions – it requires an open B string, which allows finger 3 to place the 1st string note while finger 4 is not used.

The new Dmaj7 chord.

G major with an open B string.

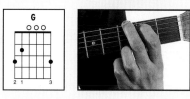

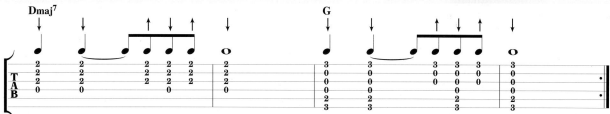

Developing the strum pattern

To create the song's main strum pattern, you need to replace the semibreves in bars 2 and 4 of the previous piece with five quicker strums. Use downstrokes to play the chords containing all the strings and upstrokes to strike the top three strings only. Try to achieve a light, fluid strumming action with lots of flexibility at the wrist. When changing from D major 7 to G, lead with finger 3 by slipping it up one fret on the same string.

A relaxed right hand position for strumming.

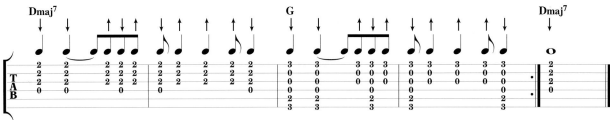

THE CHORD CHART: AN ALTERNATIVE LAYOUT

You will sometimes see the chord names written within the music stave instead of TAB numbers (you might recall this from *Wonderwall* by Oasis). This method relies upon a sound knowledge of the chord shapes involved, but avoids the 'tower blocks' of numbers that can be more of a hindrance than a help when learning a new song. It will be used in two later exercises. The practice piece below is written out in this format. Give it a go and try playing from it – you'll get used to the format quite quickly.

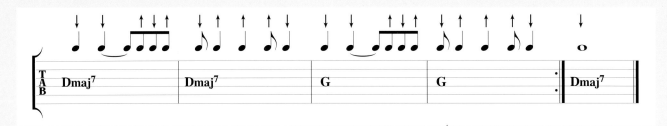

A simple but effective lead line

Each melodic phrase consists of only three notes. Keep your left hand in 3rd position throughout, using fingers 1, 2 and 3 to play the 3rd, 4th and 5th fret notes on the top E string. Begin with finger 1 at fret 3, then add finger 2 for the next note and finger 3 for the 3rd note. This method allows you to peel the fingers off one at a time when the three notes are played in reverse order, making the finger work easier and smoother. To play the next note at the right time, count the lengths of the tied notes carefully.

Start with finger 1 at fret 3.

Add finger 2 at fret 4.

Finger 3 joins the string at fret 5.

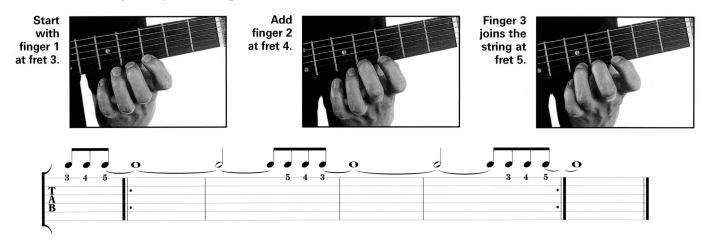

A left hand muting exercise

The emphasis now switches to the bottom strings as you learn another riff. The small dot under each of the crotchets tells you to clip the length of each note for that spiky effect aimed for in previous sessions. Play the 1st note with finger 3 at fret 5 on the bottom E string, then almost immediately release the left finger pressure to deaden the sound. Be sure to keep your finger in contact with the string, however. Do the same thing for the finger 2 notes at fret 4 and the finger 1 notes at fret 3.

Finger 3 at fret 5 on the bottom E string.

Finger 2 is used for the fret 4 notes.

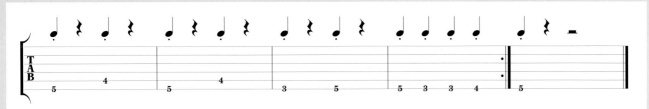

The rhythm of an important riff

The notes are intentionally simple in this piece so that you can concentrate on the repeated two-bar rhythm pattern. Bar 1 has two crotchets, followed by two quavers and finally a crotchet rest. Bar 2, however, is syncopated, which makes the rhythm more of a challenge – you might find that it helps to think in half-beats to subdivide the bar. Use finger 3 at fret 5, and finger 1 for the fret 3 notes, all of which are played on the bottom E string. Not all the notes are muted here, so try to release the left hand finger pressure only on the notes with a dot beneath them.

Finger 1 stays at fret 3 for bars 3 and 4.

Completing an essential riff

By combining the notes and rhythms of the two previous pieces, you can complete the riff that accompanies the second half of the song's verses. Play each note with a downstroke and keep the strokes small to improve control as you switch between the bottom E and A strings. The brackets above the TAB represent the 1st time bars and the 2nd time bars – you need to play bars 3 and 4 the first time around and bars 5 and 6 instead on the repeat.

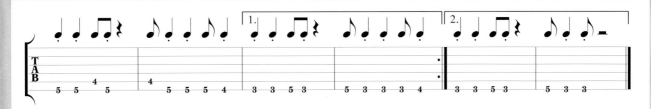

Adding the E minor chord

This piece is written out using the chord chart system discussed on page 88. Most of the information you need to play this chorus section – the chord names, the rhythm pattern and strum directions – is still present. When playing upstrokes, strum only the top three strings. Place E minor with fingers 1 and 2 as on many previous occasions. You can then leave finger 1 in the same place for E minor and the subsequent G chord shape.

E minor has already been used many times.

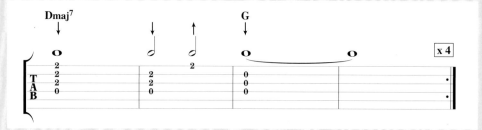

Preparing a new accompaniment figure

Another part of *Babies* is formed by splitting up the notes of D major 7 and linking them to the open strings at the heart of this issue's G chord shape. Strum all four strings of D major 7 together, letting them ring for the whole of bar 1. Omit string 1 as you strum the chord again, this time for a minim count. Play the 1st string note from D major 7 separately on the 2nd minim of bar 2 using an upstroke. Release D major 7 to play the open D, G and B string chord that rings throughout bars 3 and 4.

A reminder of the Dmaj7 chord.

Precise plectrum work

The principles of the previous piece go a stage further to finish this light accompanying figure. The opening D major 7 chord is made one beat longer by the tie into bar 2. The same chord is then broken down into a strum of strings 4, 3 and 2 together, followed by single upstrokes of strings 1, 2 and then 3. The G chord in bar 3 is the same as in the previous piece and rings for eight beats. Notice that the line repeats four times because of the x4 sign above the standard repeat mark.

Alternative Dmaj7 fingering: finger 1 bars strings 1 to 3.

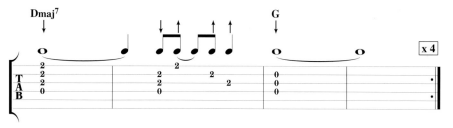

Finger tip

ALTERNATIVE FINGERING FOR D MAJOR 7
For D major 7, you might prefer to use finger 1 to bar strings 1, 2 and 3 at fret 2 (see left). Try both fingerings to see which you prefer. The three-finger version works better for the change to the G major chord, but this needs to be weighed against the benefit of using only one finger to form the entire shape.

Finger 2 in a static role

This looping, two-bar riff contains only four notes. Begin with finger 3 at fret 3 on the top E string. Use finger 1 for the next note at fret 2 on the same string. This leaves finger 2 ready for the 3rd note, which is on the B string at fret 3. Leave finger 2 at this location for the rest of the piece. Ensure that it is arched to avoid contact with the open top E string, which alternates with the B string note to complete bars 1 and 2.

Use finger 3 for the 1st note.

Change to finger 1 for the fret 2 note that follows.

Add and then keep finger 2 at fret 3 on the B string.

A repeating phrase over changing chords

This piece is very similar to the previous one and builds a nice lead guitar line. At the end of bar 1, replace the open E that ends the 1st bar of the previous exercise with another fret 3 note. The remaining space produced by a shorter tied note is filled by extra notes at fret 2 on the E string and fret 3 on the B string.

As before, keep finger 2 in place for a flowing rendition. Remember to replace bars 3 and 4 with bars 5 and 6 on the repeat.

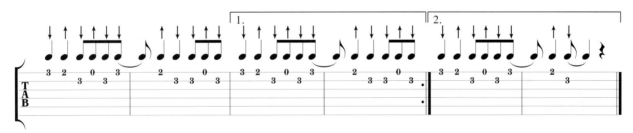

Finger barring the A6 chord

Although it is just about feasible to use four different fingers in the placement of the A6 chord, the finger bar across strings 1 to 4 at fret 2 is likely to be the most straightforward option. An open A string completes the A6 chord shape. As you can see, the chord chart method has been adopted again, and the strum pattern is identical to that used earlier in the session. Your priority should be the preparation of fingers 2 and 3 over the strings in readiness for the G major chord change.

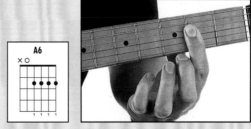

A6 with finger 1 barring four strings at fret 2.

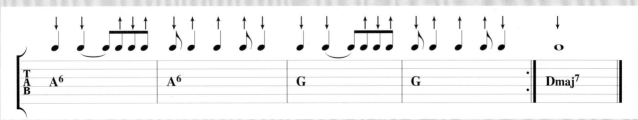

HARMONICS AND DYNAMICS

Featuring dynamics – how loud or soft to play – and the bell-like tones of harmonics.

This session's practice pieces concentrate on power chords, as used in *Swallowed* by Bush. However, you will often have to pick out the notes of the power chord shapes individually. This results in a sound more like the broken chord approach of earlier sessions and contrasts with the original song's bludgeoning power.

The A♭ major chord

The opening chord is, in fact, A♭5 with finger 2 added to string 3 at fret 5. For the D♭5 shape that follows, lift the A♭ chord across one string and remove finger 2. In bar 3 you need to pick out the D♭5 notes one at a time. Allow each string to sustain as indicated by the 'let ring' marking under the relevant notes and use finger 1 for the fret 6 note in bar 4.

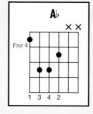

The A♭ major chord in 4th position.

Remove finger 2 and shift up one string for D♭5.

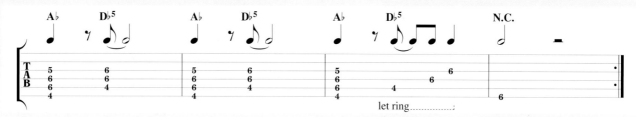

Measured finger slides and F5

Place the opening note with finger 1, strike the bottom E string, then slide the finger up to fret 8 to sound on the 1st beat of the bar. The three-string F5 chord is also in 8th position, so move finger 1 onto the A string and add fingers 3 and 4 at fret 10 on the D and G strings. Play the F5 notes separately as shown in bar 3, followed by an open A as you shift the power chord shape down to A♭5 on the bottom three strings in 4th position.

F5 in 8th position.

A♭5 is similar to A♭ major, but without finger 2.

Adding the broken C5 chord

The piece begins with A♭5 in 4th position. Next, place the full D♭5 chord, then play strings 5 and 4 together, followed by single string 3 and string 4 notes from the chord. To end bar 1, quickly slide up from fret 6 on the bottom E string to fret 8. With finger 1 in place, add fingers 3 and 4 to form the broken C5 chord that runs into bar 2. Drop the C5 shape onto the A, D and G strings for F5 to complete the repeating two-bar phrase. Pick the F5 notes out separately in the 2nd time bar to end the piece.

The notes of C5 are added one at a time.

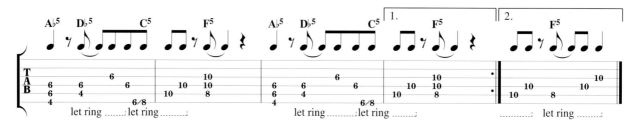

The opening takes shape

Fragments of the three previous pieces come together to make this verse accompaniment. Start with A♭ major, adding finger 2 to the three-string A♭5 chord shape. Place the full D♭5 chord shape but play the three notes separately. A measured slide of finger 1 from fret 6 up to fret 8 takes you to 8th position. Move finger 1 over to the A string, at the same time adding fingers 3 and 4 of F5. Use the open A string at the end of bar 2 to get back to 4th position. The remaining notes use identical material from the previous piece, with an open A and a final fret 4 note rounding things off.

The last note of bar 1 is at fret 6 on the bottom E string.

Slide finger 1 up to fret 8.

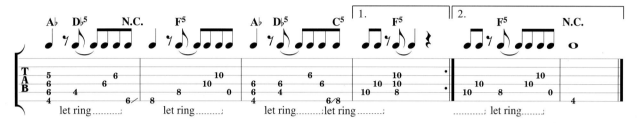

Adding some subtle variations

The musical outline is the same as in the exercise above, but a sprinkling of small differences provides new interest. You begin with a single A♭ note instead of a major chord (hence the N.C. sign, meaning No Chord). Bar 2 ends with an open D string instead of an open A, before bar 3 starts with an A♭5 chord, but breaks it up into a two-string chord followed by the 4th string note. The penultimate note of the same bar is the 3rd string note again from D♭5 and not the 4th string. Finally, a two-string F5 chord replaces the three-string form used above.

Finger tip

PLACING THE BROKEN POWER CHORDS

If you can place the entire power chord shape when the notes are written separately, your left hand work will benefit from a feeling of space and ease. However, there is nothing technically wrong with placing the fingers on their notes one at a time, and this is necessary when approaching the power chord shape from a quick finger slide.

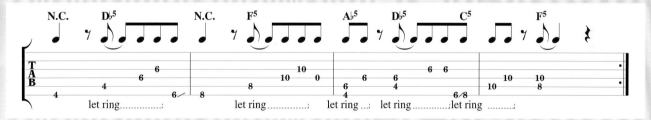

The chorus power chords

After a complicated start to the session, you'll be glad to lay into some straightforward full power chords with no variation of rhythm or shape. The A♭5, C5, D♭5 and B♭5 chords in this piece are all played on the bottom three strings with the customary 1st, 3rd and 4th fingers. The rhythm is built on driving quavers, apart from the final semibreve chord. The only real problem that you might experience is with quick transfer of the power chord through 4th, 8th, 9th and 6th positions. Remember to look ahead to the point on the strings where the next chord should land.

D♭5 in 9th position.

B♭5 in 6th position.

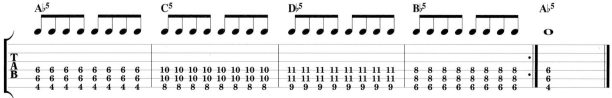

Percussive muted notes

This is a new technique that will give your playing more style. The crosses on the TAB tell you to release the finger pressure of the previously played chord or note, but leave the finger(s) in light contact with the string(s). Then strike any strings with crosses on them to produce a percussive click. Begin with two A♭5 chords before playing a muted chord. The remaining bars feature single notes and percussive mutes, all placed with finger 1.

Use finger 1 at fret 8 in bar 3.

Release the finger pressure for the percussive sound.

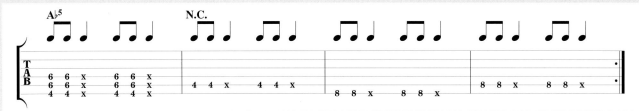

A first look at dynamics

In this piece, you have to alter the strength of the plectrum strokes (and therefore the volume) at marked intervals, as discussed in the box on the right. The notes are similar to those played previously, starting with three A♭5 chords (the last one muted). Move finger 1 onto the A string at fret 4 for three clean sounds followed by one muffled note, made by lifting the finger 1 pressure. Watch your left hand as finger 1 executes a rapid slide from fret 6 to fret 8. Continue to mix pure notes and percussive mutes in even quavers.

DYNAMICS

If you stroke a string gently, it will produce a soft note, indicated in music by the letter '*p*'. A firm strike results in a loud note, which is marked by the letter '*f*'. These symbols are referred to collectively as 'dynamics'. Other dynamic terms are defined opposite.

ff	=	very loud (from the Italian *fortissimo*)
f	=	loud (from *forte*)
mf	=	moderately loud (from *mezzo forte*)
mp	=	moderately soft (from *mezzo piano*)
p	=	soft (from *piano*)
pp	=	very soft (from *pianissimo*)
>	=	gradually softer
<	=	gradually louder

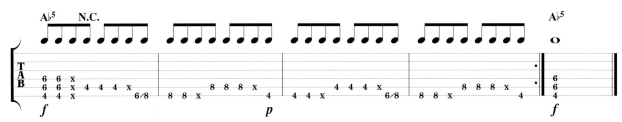

More subtle dynamic contrast

The dynamic changes in this piece are less obvious. Start off moderately loud, then, as you move through the short passage of notes at the end of bar 3, play gradually quieter to finish up at a moderately soft volume. There are frequent open strings between chords, which add another level of interest to the sound. The notes are chiefly full A♭5 and two-string D♭5 chords, with a quick ascent to C5 and F5 in 8th position at the end of the line.

The two-string version of D♭5.

The two-string version of C5.

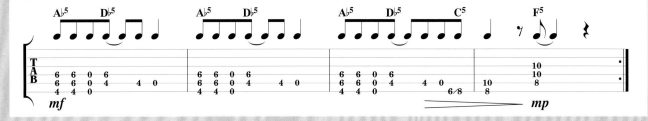

Using the left hand only

This piece is a bit of fun, as you make every sound by hammering-on and pulling-off the left hand fingers. Place a full F5 chord in 8th position, then pull the fingers off the strings and slightly downwards to hear the open strings ring softly. In bar 2, hammer-on the power chord shape in 4th position, before pulling the fingers off again to produce another gentle open string chord. Move the power chord shape up one string and hammer-on to end the pattern. Repeat the process in bars 3 and 4.

F5 is placed but not played with the plectrum.

Pull the fingers off to make the open string chord.

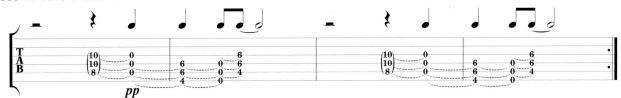

Harmonics

You might recall harmonics from a previous session. Place finger 1 very lightly on the D string, right over the 7th fret wire. Strike the string with the plectrum and lift your finger away. If you time your lift well, you will hear the harmonic. Repeat the process on the G and B strings at the same fret, then lie finger 1 over all three of these strings. The harmonic chord in bar 2 is made by lifting the finger bar off the strings as you strike them with the right hand.

The finger only just touches the A string in bar 3.

Finger tip

HARMONICS
Harmonics are pure, bell-like sounds. They can be created at any point on the strings, but are at their strongest at fret 12, the exact half-way point along the strings. The purity of sound makes them a very accurate tuning aid.

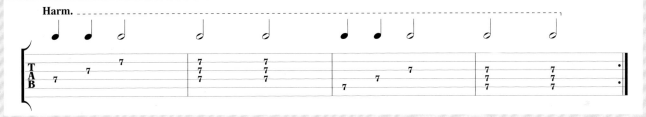

A host of effects

Crash into this exercise with pairs of power chords, divided by a quaver rest, made by damping the side of the right hand onto the strings. Five beats of silence follow, giving impact to the further power chords in bar

3. Bars 3 and 4 were rehearsed earlier, after which you go into your left hand only routine. A very softly struck finger slide precedes the loudest pair of harmonic chords that you can manage.

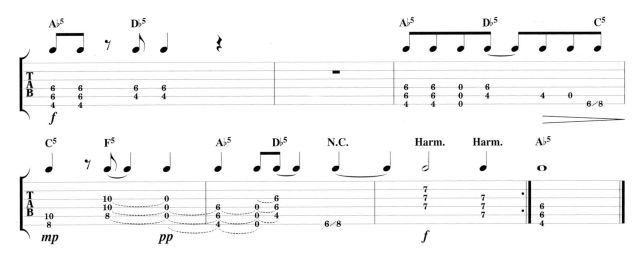

A gradual half bend

The solo is preceded by a sudden rush of semiquavers played with finger 2. Use alternate down- and upstrokes to achieve an even stream of notes. Begin to push finger 2 upwards fractionally from the 5th note of bar 2 all the way through to the final crotchet beat of the bar. This is shown by the solid curving line above the note values. Each note should sound slightly sharper the more you bend the string, until you reach the equivalent of a fret 10 pitch. Play these two bars four times, then drop finger 1 down to fret 6 on the D string.

Finger 2 is at fret 9 virtually throughout. **The half bend that ends bar 2.**

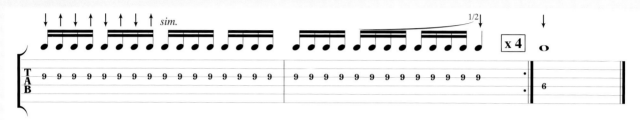

Solo, part one

Use finger 1 to play the opening four fret 6 notes on the D string, then play the fret 8 note that follows with finger 3 and rapidly slide up to fret 10. Fingers 1 and 2 place the G string notes that end bar 1. The 2nd bar alternates finger 2 with finger 3 at fret 10 on the D string. At the end of bar 2, slide finger 3 along string 4, but switch to finger 1 for the near identical repeat that occurs in bars 3 and 4.

The 1st note of the solo. **The top of the finger slide is at fret 10.** **Fret 8 on the G string uses finger 1...** **...swapping to fret 9 with finger 2.**

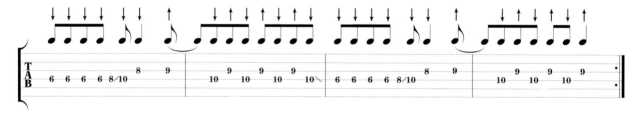

Solo, part two

Fingers 2 then 1 take care of the quavers in bar 1. After the quaver rest at the start of bar 2, use finger 1 for the fret 8 notes on the top E string, and finger 3 for the slide from fret 10 up to fret 12.

Use finger 1 throughout bar 3 and for the fret 13 notes that follow. Repeat bars 1 to 3 before jumping to the 2nd time bars. The fret 15 note is quite a stretch, so have finger 3 as close to the A string as possible when you play the fret 13 notes. Slide finger 3 down the A string and damp the string on beat 3 of the final bar.

The 2nd finger starts things off. **The fret 13 notes are easiest with finger 1.** **The final note with finger 3 at fret 15.**

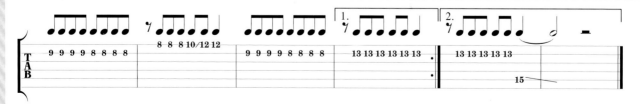

LEFT THUMB FRETTING

Some guitarists use the left thumb to fret notes on the bottom E string – a technique essential for certain chord shapes, as featured in this session.

You have played several of the chords used in these exercises before, such as D major, A major and E minor. However, these three chords are combined in sequence for the first time. Upstrums get a heavier treatment than usual, and open string strums appear in a chord-linking role.

D major and the principal strum pattern
Retain the triangular D major chord shape throughout. The underside of finger 3 often blocks the top E string note, so check each note of the chord separately. Here, the upstrums as well as the downstrums include all four strings. The result is a fuller sound perfectly suited to our practice pieces based on *Freak Scene* by Dinosaur Jr.

The D major chord.

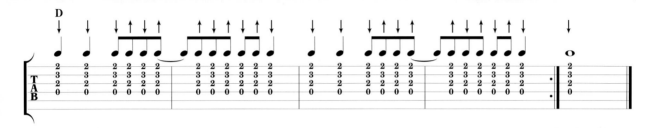

The open strings as a linking device
E minor joins D major in this piece. The nature of the strum pattern means that you have to make the chord changes in just half a beat. For this reason, the brief spaces needed for the shift of hand position are filled with open string strums. The open strum before E minor in bar 1 consists of four strings (as with the D chord), whereas the open string chord that ends bar 2 uses only three strings. This lighter upstrum prevents the open bottom E and A strings from blurring the D chords that follow.

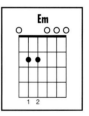

A reminder of E minor.

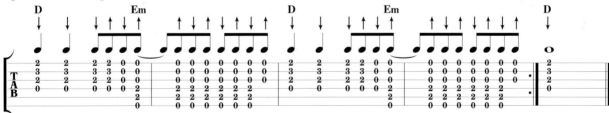

Revisiting the chord chart system
Compare the identical first half of the previous piece with this exercise, and you can see the benefit of the chord chart system. Shift to A major for bars 3 and 4 by moving fingers 1 and 2 up one string at the same fret, while adding finger 3 to complete the shape. Hold A major to the end of bar 4, then slip finger 3 up one fret as a smooth method of returning to the D chord.

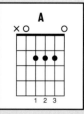

The A major chord.

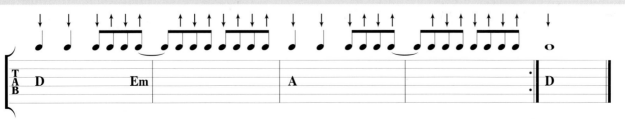

Rapid alternate strumming

The first two bars retain most of the strum pattern used so far in this session. This consists of two downstrummed crotchets followed by a stream of alternately strummed quavers, with a single tied chord adding rhythmical spice across the bar line. At the end of bar 2, make a quick change to D major, then strum the three chords almost as fast as you can. Count the sustained chord precisely, then repeat the three-strum flourish.

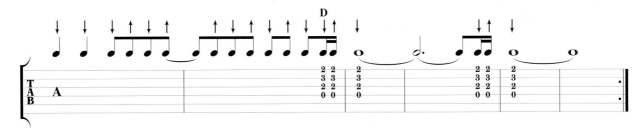

Finger tip

RELAXING THE RIGHT ARM
When called upon to strum or play notes quickly, the tendency is to tighten the muscles, resulting in a build-up of tension. Always try to keep the right arm and wrist relaxed so that the plectrum can flow smoothly through the strings.

Shifting between E5 and A5

This exercise highlights the five-fret leap from the E5 chord up to A5. It makes sense to use fingers 3 and 4 (along with the open bottom E string) in the first two bars. This allows you to run the fingers along the strings to fret 7 for a smoother A5 shift. The chief technical difficulty is executing the fast alternate strums that end bars 1 and 3. Be sure to keep the right arm and wrist completely relaxed so that the plectrum flows through the strings.

E5 using fingers 3 and 4 to ease the shift to A5.

Add finger 1 in 5th position for A5.

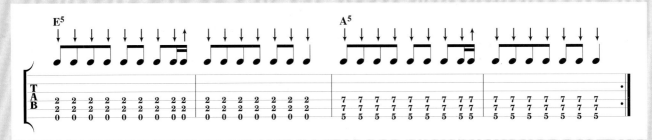

The Aadd9 chord

The new Aadd9 chord introduced in bar 3 of this piece uses the same left hand shape as Ab major, but moved up one fret to 5th position. Alternatively, you could view this chord as A5 from the exercise above, plus finger 2 on string 3 providing the vital ingredient for that major sound. The new chord is completed by the addition of the open B and top E strings. Concentrate on the contrast between tight power chords and full six-string chords.

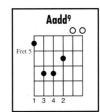

Aadd9 with open 1st and 2nd strings.

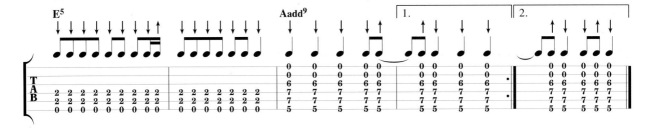

E major and a new strum figure

E major is a chord that you should recognize and be feeling comfortable with by now. Although the TAB looks tricky in bars 2 and 4, you shouldn't have too many problems, providing you hold the E chord shape throughout the piece. It's worth memorizing the exercise so that you can watch the plectrum strike the required groups of strings.

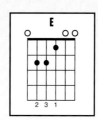

The familiar E major shape.

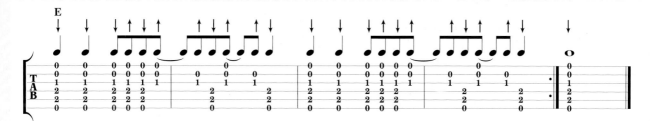

Fretting with the left thumb

Here's a new technique that you'll come across from time to time. Instead of using the left thumb just for support, you can wrap it around the top of the guitar neck and fret notes on the bottom E string. Keep the thumb very high as you play bar 1 in 1st position, then slip the hand into 2nd position with finger 1 still on the G string in bar 2. Bend the top joint of the thumb so that it rests on the bottom E string at fret 2 with just enough pressure to make the note. You might find that finger 1 blocks out the open string notes, but persevere and experiment with the arm, wrist and finger angles until the notes ring clear.

The thumb ready to fret the bottom E string.

The thumb wraps round onto fret 2.

F# minor 11 (F#m11) using the left thumb

This chord is virtually unplayable without the left-thumb fretting approach. If it were not for the open top E and B strings, you could bar finger 1 across all the frets, an approach you will study soon. The first two bars of this exercise are identical to the first piece on this page, with a shift of the hand up to 2nd position for bars 3 and 4. To do this, slip finger 1 along the G string to fret 2, drop the thumb onto the bottom E string and add fingers 3 and 4. Retain this F#m11 shape for the picking detail in bar 4.

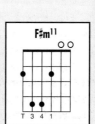

Using the thumb allows an open B and top E string in F#m11.

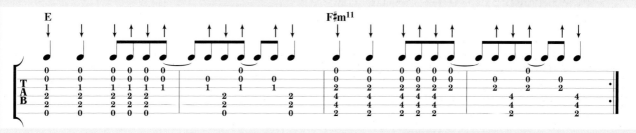

A sequence of fret 9 bends

The next five pieces break down the song's substantial, 16-bar guitar solo. The first two bars of this exercise consist entirely of full bends of string 3 at fret 9. As always, you can achieve further leverage and control by placing fingers 1 and 2 on the same string. Strike the opening two note bends separately with the plectrum, and aim to release a part, if not all, of each bend quickly in between each strike. The longer dotted bracket in bar 1 indicates a plectrum stroke only on the initial bend, with the left fingers releasing, bending, then releasing the bend again.

A full bend at fret 9 on the G string.

Use finger 1 in bar 3.

More 7th position soloing

This passage of the solo begins with a series of half bends at fret 7. These should be manageable with just finger 1 exerting the upwards pressure on the B string. If not, feel free to use finger 2 with finger 1 behind at fret 6 for some extra power. Measure the bends and their release in even quavers, restriking the string on the 3rd quaver beat. For the hammer-ons, marked with curved dotted lines, use fingers 1 and 3 in 7th position.

A firm upwards push of finger 1 creates the opening bends.

Leave finger 1 in place for the 2nd hammer-on in bar 2.

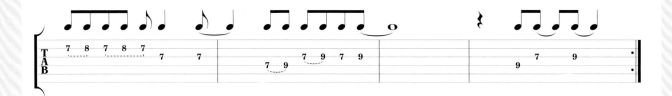

Full bends at the 15th fret

The most exhilarating passage of the song's solo consists of four consecutive full bends up at the 15th fret on the B string. This practice piece separates the individually struck bends with clean fret 15 notes. There are no surprises regarding the best fingering – place finger 3 at fret 15, with fingers 1 and 2 lending extra weight at frets 13 and 14 on the same string. For the best effect, electric guitarists should crank up the distortion for this one.

AN ACOUSTIC ALTERNATIVE TO FULL BENDS

It's harder to bend notes on an acoustic guitar due to the greater tension of the strings. Some difference of pitch is attainable but a full bend is often impossible. A finger slide between the two TAB numbers representing the bend can prove to be an effective alternative.

Staccato notes

Use finger 1 to place all the notes here, apart from the 2nd note of each hammer-on, which uses finger 3. As this makes playing the notes relatively easy, aim to shape the piece musically. Try to keep the rhythm tight – take particular care to watch out for the quaver rest that starts bar 2. Also, clip the two notes with a small dot beneath them (the staccato symbol) by releasing the left finger pressure to mute the string.

Finger 1 at fret 11 in bar 2.

Finger 1 slips down to fret 7.

The end of the solo

You can play all these notes in 7th position, which takes some pressure off the left hand. The full bend in bar 1 works best with finger 3 at fret 9, and with fingers 1 and 2 placed on the frets behind to help push the string upwards. This is one of the easier places to make a noticeable string bend on an acoustic, so even if you choose to avoid the others, have a go at this one. There's a finger 2 to finger 1 pull-off in the 3rd bar, so have finger 1 ready at fret 7 while you play the fret 8 notes that start the bar.

SIMPLIFYING THE SOLO

Instead of struggling with string bends or finger slides between the 15th and 17th frets in the solo, acoustic guitarists could try sliding from fret 10 up to fret 12 on the top E string. The notes are identical, but the hand position is much more comfortable.

The Songbook outro

We've adapted this phrase from the original version of *Freak Scene* and given it greater prominence as an effective but not too involved way of rounding the song off. The notes are, once again, all played in 7th position and mostly located on the B string. The exception is the hammer-on from finger 1 to finger 4 in bar 4 and the single strike of fret 7 that follows. Improve the smoothness of your note changes by holding the fingers close to the frets when not in use.

Begin with finger 4.

Hold finger 1 in place as you hammer-on finger 4 in bar 4.

FINGERPICKING AND THE BARRE CHORD

Fingerpicking features heavily in these exercises based on an Alanis Morissette song. The first full barre chord is another landmark in your development as a player.

Fingerpicking sections interchange with strummed chords that require a plectrum, ensuring that your right hand remains central to your thinking in this session.

Before you play anything, attach your capo at the 4th fret and leave it in place for all of the practice pieces.

Fingerpicking four-string chords

Use your thumb, index, middle and ring fingers (t, i, m and r) simultaneously to play the 1st chord in each bar. Push your wrist out from the strings so that the fingers are curved and relaxed. Leave the full C major 7 chord in place for bars 1 and 2, then shift the same shape up two frets for the second half of the piece. Don't forget to capo fret 4.

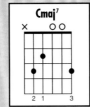

The C major 7 chord.

An ideal right hand position.

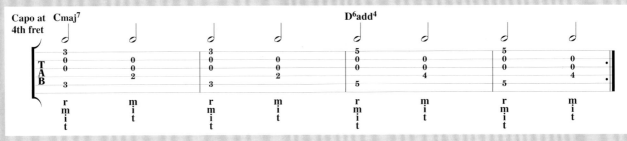

An important rhythm pattern

Both the intro and bridge of *Ironic* feature the complex, one-bar repeated rhythm pattern of this piece. Place the D6add4 chord and use the ring, middle and index fingers to play strings 1, 2 and 3, respectively, while the thumb switches between the A and D strings.

The D6add4 chord.

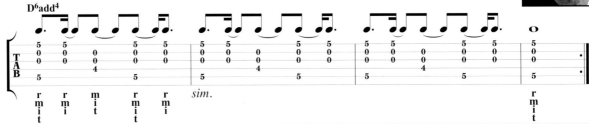

The complete intro

In bars 1 to 3, keep the rhythm and right hand finger pattern of the previous piece while swapping the left hand between C major 7 and D6add4. Bar 4 has a similar rhythmical approach but the chords are thinned down to two strings. Leave C major 7 in place for the 1st chord of bar 4, then release fingers 1 and 3 and move finger 1 over to the top E string at fret 2.

The 2nd chord of bar 4.

Change the top note for chord 3.

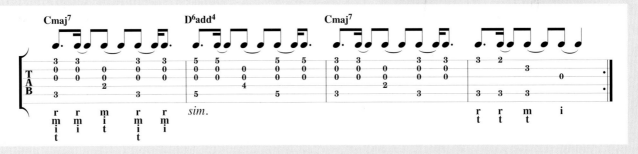

Three new verse chords

For Gadd9, keep finger 2 in place and add finger 3 to the bottom E string at fret 3, together with finger 4 on the B string at fret 3 – an open D string completes the chord. For D/F# in bar 2, remove finger 3 and place finger 1 at fret 2 on the bottom E string. E minor 7 consists of the open G, D and bottom E strings only.

Start with a two-string D/F# chord.

The 2nd chord in bar 1 is Gadd9.

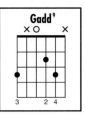

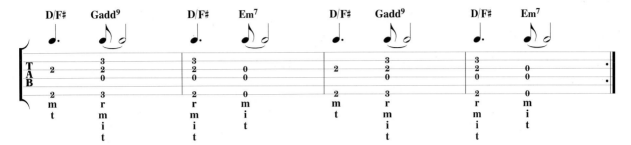

Varying the verse sequence

The first two bars are the same as in the piece above. These represent the basic verse chord pattern, which is then varied slightly in bars 3 and 4 to enhance the accompaniment. At the start of bar 3, use the full D/F# chord instead of the two-string version. Begin bar 4 by changing the bottom E string to fret 2 with finger 1, followed by the B string note only from the same chord. The inclusion of this 4th finger note on its own gives the last bar an interesting rhythmical twist.

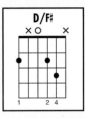

Use the fuller form of D/F# in bar 3.

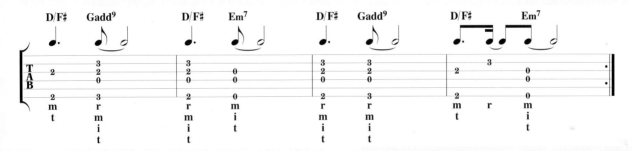

Adding further subtle variations

Each pair of bars uses the same chord sequence and yet no consecutive pairs are quite the same. In bars 5 and 7, an open A string replaces the open D in the Gadd9 chords. When playing these chords, move your index finger off the D string to pluck string 5. Otherwise, the thumb plays string 6, the index finger plays string 4, the middle finger plays string 3 and the ring finger plays the 2nd string notes.

Finger tip

RIGHT HAND FINGERING
Wherever possible, allocate a set finger to each string for the fingerpicked sections. This prevents the right hand from having to move any more than is necessary. This rule does not apply to the thumb, which can be used to play any of the bottom three strings.

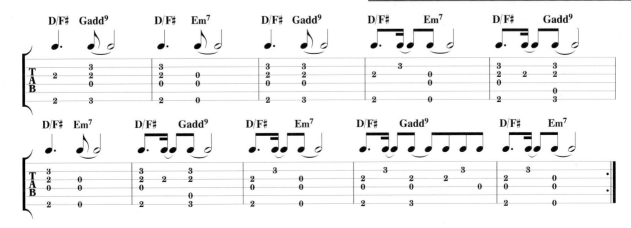

Two familiar chords

Use your plectrum for the first time in this session to strum the chords of D major and G major. You should know these two shapes from previous sessions, but check the chord boxes and photographs if you are in doubt. Leave finger 3 in place as you switch between the two shapes. The chord chart system gives you no clues as to how many strings to play in your strums of the indicated rhythm. Since these chords accompany the heavy chorus of the song, full down- and upstrums work extremely well.

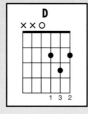

A standard D major chord.

The four-fingered G major shape is an easier change from D major.

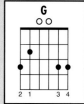

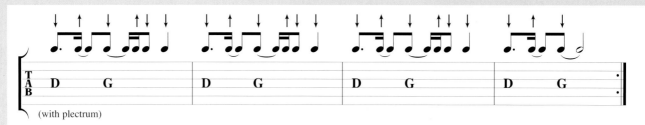

(with plectrum)

Another outing for E minor

In this exercise, the much-used E minor chord is integrated with the D and G chords of the previous piece. Fingers 1 and 2 are the best choice for E minor, bearing in mind its position between D major chords. Pay close attention to the strum pattern to ensure a fluid right arm action.

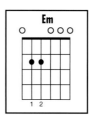

E minor with fingers 1 and 2.

The F major barre chord

The full F major chord, as opposed to the four-string version in an earlier session, is formed by moving the E major chord shape up one fret and barring all six strings at fret 1 with your 1st finger. This means you have to use fingers 2, 3 and 4 for the E major part of the chord shape. Place this new chord for the whole piece, as you work your way across the strings towards a final six-string strum in bar 4. The word 'barre' will be used from now on to distinguish between a bar of music and a barre chord.

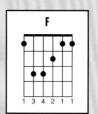

The F major barre chord.

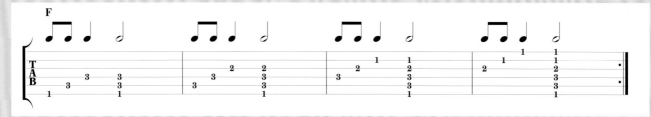

F major and C major

Bar 3 features the new F major barre chord. From E minor in the previous bar, place the 3rd and 4th fingers to begin with, followed by finger 2 on the G string at fret 2. Finally, place finger 1 across all six strings at fret 1 above the capo, keeping the finger as straight and flat as you can. The C major chord appears for the first time in the session and is best formed by leaving finger 3 in place as you change from F major. The less your thumb moves as you shift between the five chords, the better your performance will be.

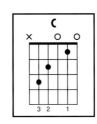

C major is the last of the chorus chords to feature.

E minor 7 as a six-string chord

Use your plectrum to strum the chords in this piece, which is based on the fingerpicked verse played earlier. The D/F# shape is the same as before, but using finger 3 on the B string makes the change to the G major chord that follows much smoother. Also, because you are now strumming, try to mute both the A and top E strings by dropping your 1st finger lightly into contact with these strings. Play the full G chord used in the chorus, and use fingers 1, 2 and 3 to place the full version of E minor 7 in bars 2 and 4.

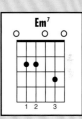

Keep finger 3 on the B string for E minor 7 in bars 2 and 4.

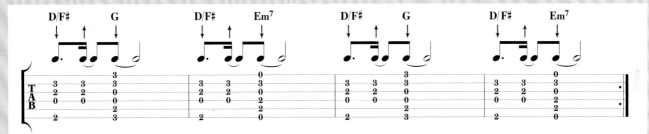

Filling in the strum pattern

The chord sequence and fingering are identical to the previous piece, but you need to add a more intricate strum pattern to the 2nd half of bars 1 to 4. This consists of a full upstrum, then a single downstroke of the bottom E string. Next, you need to strum down through all six strings, before ending with a light upstrum of just the top three strings. Practise the complete one-bar strum pattern slowly, without the CD. The `·//·` symbol means repeat the previous two bars identically.

Finger tip

A STATIC 3RD FINGER

The D/F#, G major and E minor 7 chords used in the previous and in this exercise can all be played by leaving finger 3 at fret 3 above the capo on the B string. This simplifies the left hand work and results in smoother chord changes.

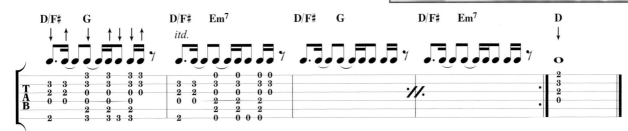

Colouring the D6add4 chord

This piece uses C major 7 and D6add4 chords and a familiar rhythm pattern. However, here the chords are strummed instead of fingerpicked. The 4th chord in the D6add4 bars adds finger 4 at fret 7 above the capo on the top E string, creating melodic colour. Leave finger 3 in place at fret 5 for a smooth release of the fret 7 note as you strum the final chord of bars 2 and 4. Use fingers 3, 1 and then 3 again for the fretted notes in bar 5.

D6add4 with finger 4 added at fret 7.

The 2nd note in the final bar is F#.

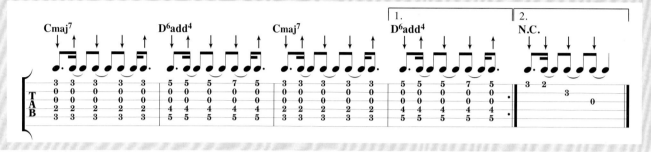

A tricky combination

Although all the techniques and chord shapes have already been analysed, there are some potential pitfalls as you fuse these subtly varied passages together. There is only a single downstrum of E minor 7 in bar 2, which is tied through the two-beat bar that follows.

During this sustained chord, put your plectrum on your lap (or between your lips if you prefer), then fingerpick the next four bars along the lines of verse 1. Pick up your plectrum again straight after the E minor 7 chord in bar 7 for the final D and G chord strums.

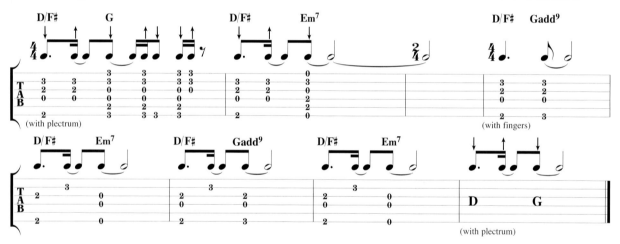

Slowing down the ending

It's common for a song, particularly a ballad, to slow down, resulting in a more expressive ending. After three bars of C major 7 and D6add4 strums identical to those played in the piece at the top, the 4th bar continues with C major 7 chords. There are only four strums in this bar as the rhythm broadens out.

The symbol 'rit.' means slow down gradually, and applies through to the end.

Feel free to shape these final two bars in your own way, since the placement of notes and chords in a free rhythm ending such as this is very much a matter of personal taste.

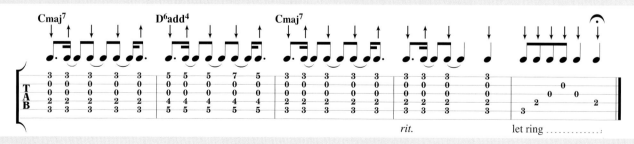

After numerous forays into rock and pop, it's time to investigate the distinctive swinging beat and punchy rhythm guitar sound of reggae.

Clipped chords played on the 2nd and 4th beats of each bar lie at the heart of reggae guitar. Crisp strums (or chops) of the top strings are another characteristic, counteracting the heavy bass lines that are an essential ingredient of the style. You'll find plenty of examples as you prepare for this session's exercises.

The A major barre chord

This new barre chord uses the same finger shape as the F major chord studied earlier. The only difference is that the left hand is placed in 5th position, meaning that finger 1 forms a barre across all six strings at fret 5. To achieve the most comfortable and efficient hand shape, start by placing fingers 3 and 4, then add finger 2 to the G string. Keep these fingers arched and relaxed as you add a straight finger barre to fret 5.

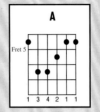

The A major barre chord.

Alternate strumming of the barre chord

This forms the intro to a Bob Marley classic, *Buffalo Soldier,* and is the only part of the song to use anything other than a three-string chord. Try to feel the natural swing of the reggae rhythm, a feature of the remaining practice pieces. Holding the A major barre chord throughout, alternately strum the bottom four strings for all but the second half of bar 2.

The thumb is low and vertical behind fret 6.

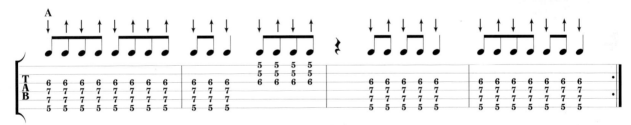

Introducing the reggae style

An emphasis on beats 2 and 4 is a key element of reggae, as demonstrated here in bars 1 to 3. Place the finger barre across only the top three strings in this lighter version of the A major chord. Strum firmly without resorting to force to achieve the accents marked by the small arrows under the note values, and mute each chord crisply through a release of the left finger pressure.

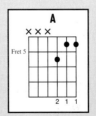

A major played on the top three strings only.

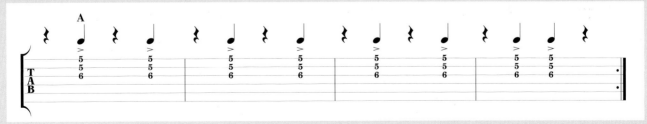

Adding muted upstrums

The columns of crosses on the TAB stave represent percussive mutes. Play the new chord shape of F# minor throughout, using the fingering shown in the photograph and the chord box. Release the finger pressure immediately after each downstrum to produce a crisp 1st chord. With the left fingers still in light contact with the frets, strum lightly upwards to achieve a three-string muffled click.

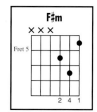

F# minor in 5th position.

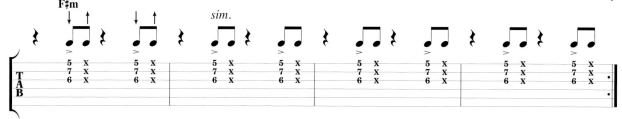

Combining the A major and F# minor chords

This exercise completes the accompaniment to the opening verses of *Buffalo Soldier* by bringing together the three-string chords from the previous two pieces. Once again, you need to observe the crotchet rests on beats 1 and 3, so be careful to wait an extra beat before playing the opening A major chord. As in the previous piece, follow each left hand muted downstrum with a percussive muted upstrum.

Finger tip

A SWING APPROACH TO QUAVERS
The swing rhythm of reggae means you have to play pairs of quavers in a slightly different way from rock and pop music. Instead of allowing half a beat each, the 1st quaver takes two-thirds of a beat, leaving one-third for the 2nd quaver.

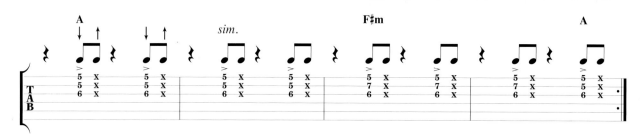

Two new chord shapes

Play both D major and C# minor as three-string chords, with finger 1 barring the top three strings. The addition of fingers 3 and 4 completes the D major shape played in 5th position. Fingers 2 and 3 on the B and G strings make up the remainder of C# minor, which is attained by shifting the finger barre down to 4th position. The rhythm and technique are identical to those used in the piece above.

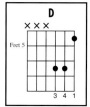

D major as a three-string chord.

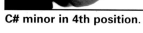

C# minor in 4th position.

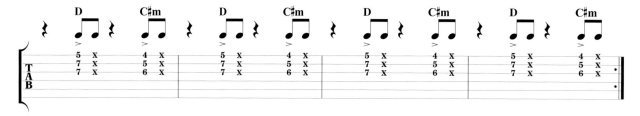

The three-string E major chord

In keeping with the reggae style, E major is played as a three-string chord in this session. Use finger 1 to form a barre across the top three strings at fret 7, and place fingers 3 and 4 at fret 9 on the G and B strings. The chord shares the same shape as D major, but because E is two semitones higher than D, it needs to be placed two frets higher, in 7th position instead of 5th. The piece uses the same rhythm figure again, so you have a good opportunity to master the combination of downstrums, mutes and muffled upstrums.

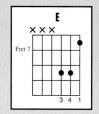

E major in 7th position.

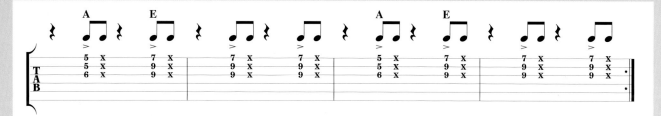

The five chorus chords

You should by now be feeling more comfortable with the reggae rhythm and the weight of your down- and upstrums. The principal challenge of this piece lies in the lively shifts between five three-string chord shapes. You have already practised the shifts between D major and C# minor in bars 1 and 2 and the changes between A and E in bar 3, so concentrate on moving from C# minor to A major, as well as from E major to F# minor to improve these new shifts.

Finger tip

THE HALF-BARRE AS A CONSTANT
The three-string chords in this session are all played with finger 1 barring the top half of your six strings, hence the term 'half-barre'. Each chord could be fingered differently to avoid this half-barre, but it provides the most fluent method of shifting between chords.

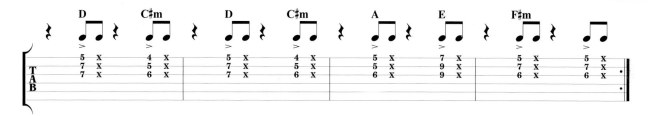

Another form of F# minor

The component notes of an F# minor chord are F#, A and C#. Both the new F# minor chord shape played in 9th position and the 5th position version studied previously include these three notes. The new shape, used in the 1st time bar, has the note C# at the top of the chord instead of at the bottom, resulting in its placement higher up your guitar neck. Compare the sounds of these two F# minor shapes as you work your way through the piece and pay attention to the accompanying rhythm change in the 1st and 2nd time bars.

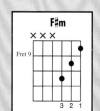

The 9th position version of F# minor.

A new phase

In this practice piece, your playing switches to the lower strings. Place the root note and 3rd degree of the A chord in 3rd position (finger 3 at fret 5 on the bottom E string and finger 2 at fret 4 on the A string). Keep this hand position for bars 1 and 2 as you play downstrums of the two-string chords. Release the left hand finger pressure to mute chords 3 and 5 in each bar, or you might prefer to mute these with the side of the right hand. In bar 3, shift up to 5th position for two bars which are identical to the end of the previous exercise.

The two-string A chord used in verses 3 and 4.

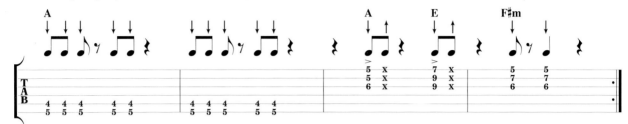

An important riff

This four-bar passage of music plays a key role in this session, repeating four times as an accompaniment. Start bar 3 with finger 3 at fret 4 on the D string. This puts your left hand into 2nd position, where it can remain through to the end of the line, despite the finger slide in bar 4. For this, reach back with finger 3 to fret 3 but avoid moving your thumb. The finger slide returns your hand to 2nd position. You should observe the rests and mute the open strings with your right hand. For this reason, you might find it less confusing to use right hand mutes throughout.

Finger 3 at fret 4 on the D string.

Finger 3 reaches back to fret 3 for the slide.

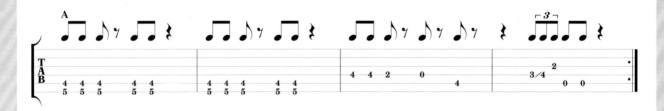

A subtle variation of the riff

Most of the material of bars 1 to 3 is identical to that in the previous exercise. Follow the open A string on the 4th beat of bar 3 with a 4th bar consisting of open and fret 2 notes on the D string, and a further open A to finish. In contrast to the rhythmic chops on beats 2 and 4 of so many of the earlier pieces, these final four session passages of music are much more firmly on the beat. If you listen to the original song, you will find that the clipped chords of the rhythm guitar are still strongly in evidence in the backing.

Finger 1 on the 2nd fret notes.

An ideal right hand muting position.

Palm muting in the bridge section

Palm muting has featured several times before in *Play Guitar*. As a reminder, the aim of palm muting is to muffle the tone and yet allow the notes to be distinguishable from one another. This is what sets the technique apart from percussive muting, where the strings are struck but the pitch of the notes is not heard. You should recall that palm-muted notes are achieved by striking the strings while resting the heel of your right hand lightly against the strings just in front of the bridge.

Use finger 1 for each 2nd fret note.

Palm muting the bottom E string.

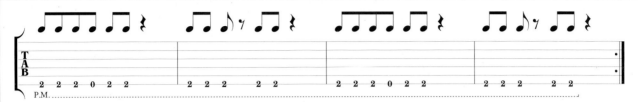

The complete bridge section

This final session piece breaks up palm-muted passages with a new riff, played in 2nd position. Palm mute the notes in bars 1 and 2, remembering to lift finger 1 off the bottom E string for the open note on the 4th quaver. To maintain the muting position of the right hand, aim to observe the crotchet and quaver rests by releasing the 1st finger pressure from the 2nd fret. Lift the right hand off the strings for a clean execution of bars 3 and 4. Stretch finger 4 up to fret 5 on the A string as you begin the new riff in bar 3. Bars 5 to 8 are a slight variation of bars 1 to 4. End the piece with fingers 2 and 3 on the two-string A major chord rehearsed earlier.

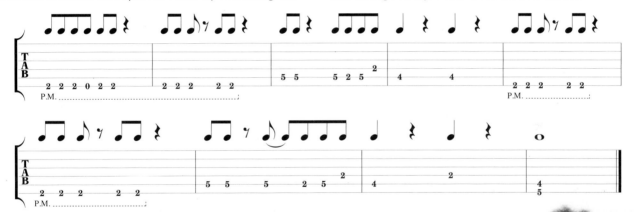

Start bar 3 with your 4th finger at fret 5...

...then change to finger 1 at fret 2.

109

THE A SHAPE BARRE CHORD

This session follows on from your study of the E shape barre chords of F major and A major by taking a first look at the five-string barre chord of B major.

This session focuses on an arrangement of *One To Another* by The Charlatans, which features a monumental riff that will test your left hand skills as well as your right hand control. You'll learn how to play Dsus2 and add another strum pattern to your repertoire. Make sure you place your capo at fret 1 for the exercises.

Revising the pull-off

The curved, dotted lines indicate pull-offs between fret 2 and open G string notes. You could use finger 1 or finger 2 for all the fret 2 notes in this riff, but we've chosen finger 1 for consistency throughout the session. Once you've played the opening fret 2 note, pull finger 1 downwards to create the open G without a further plectrum stroke. As you pull finger 1 down off fret 2, move the finger out slightly to prevent it from touching the B string. A tight, swift circular motion takes the finger back up to the D string for the next note.

Use finger 1 for note 1.

Developing the main riff

Approach the pull-off at the start of each bar in exactly the same way as you did in the exercise above. Continue to use finger 1 at fret 2, lifting the finger out slightly from the string for the open D notes. The riff in the original song is very fast. If you want to play at the same speed, it's best to follow the suggested directions of the plectrum strokes.

Use finger 1 on the D string.

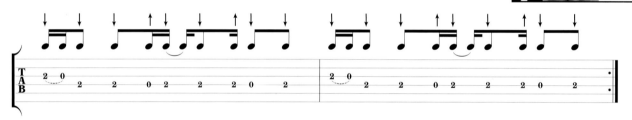

Connecting a hammer-on

Now try adding a hammer-on right before the previously rehearsed pull-off to take the riff one step nearer to completion. Strike the 1st open G, with finger 1 close and ready to hammer down onto fret 2 to produce the next sound. Although it may feel strange when taken out of the context of the whole riff, use an upstroke for each hammer-on and pull-off combination.

Finger tip

HAMMER-ON OR PULL-OFF?
You've seen the curved, dotted line used on many previous occasions to represent both hammer-ons and pull-offs. If the linked TAB numbers go up, you need to hammer-on. Conversely, if the numbers joined by the dotted line fall, a pull-off is required.

The complete riff

The moment of truth has arrived as you bring together the concepts studied so far to play this repeating one-bar riff. The piece begins on the 1st beat of the bar with a pull-off, followed by the series of D string notes studied in the second exercise. A semiquaver upstroke of the open G string at the end of bar 1 precedes the hammer-on and pull-off combination, which runs straight into a repeat of the riff. Persevere with the stroke directions and play a bit faster each time you practise.

Finger 1 ready to hammer-on.

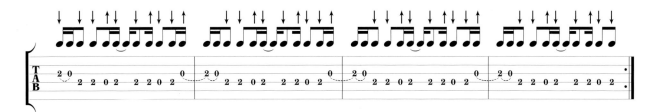

The key chord

The pivotal chord around which all the others revolve is known as the 'key chord', which, in the case of *One To Another*, is E major. Bars 1 and 3 are identical to the bar studied in the second practice piece, with the E major chord used in the even-numbered bars. The chord shape ought to be at your fingertips by now, but check the photo and chord box to be sure. Switch to finger 3 for the last note of bars 1 and 3 for a smooth change to E major.

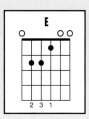

A reminder of the E major chord.

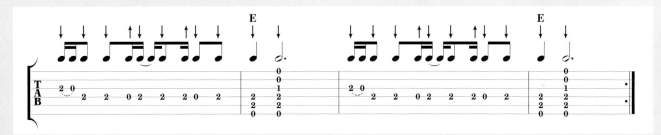

A new idea for the verse

The song's verses combine long, sustained E major chords with one-bar bursts of lead playing. In this exercise, place the full E shape but play only the bottom three strings of the chord together at the start of bar 1. Strum the full chord on the 2nd beat and leave it to ring right through to the end of bar 2. Next, release the E major shape but shift finger 3 up the D string to fret 4. Add fingers 1 and 2 on the top E and B strings, letting all three notes merge. Remove the fingers for the open string notes, and hammer-on finger 1 as you move into bar 4. While keeping finger 1 in place, quickly add the 2nd and 3rd fingers for the full strum of E major that follows.

The 1st note of bar 3.

Add finger 1 on the top E string.

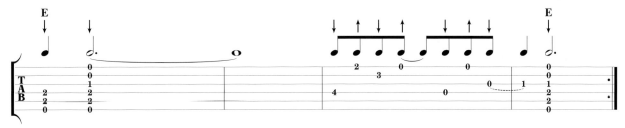

111

Another lead guitar lick

2nd position is the best starting point, so use fingers 3 and then 1 for the opening notes. Release each finger as you change note to ensure a smooth melodic line with no over-ringing strings. Slide finger 3 from fret 4 to fret 6, using a single plectrum stroke for both notes. After the slide, finger 2 is perfectly situated for the pair of fret 5 notes on the B string. For a definition of the word 'lick', see the blue box lower down this page.

Slide finger 3 up to fret 6 above the capo.

Use finger 2 for fret 5 on the B string.

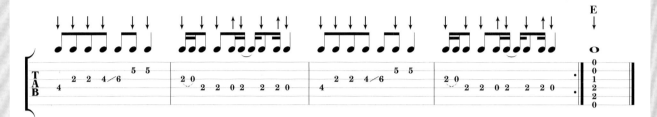

A slight variation of earlier material

Rather than directly repeating the 1st verse, verse 2 uses this pattern. As you can see, bar 1 is similar to the 3rd bar of the last piece on the previous page. As you now need to place fret 2 for a final crotchet beat of the bar, it is best to use your 2nd finger. This has the advantage of moving your left hand into 1st position, where it will need to be for the following 1st finger note at fret 1 on the G string. Keep this finger in place and add the remainder of the E major chord for the full strum on the 2nd beat.

LICKS

Short lead guitar phrases, such as the one that appears in the 1st and 3rd bars of the piece above, are sometimes referred to as licks. They're not the dominant musical material in the same way that a riff is, instead their purpose is to provide melodic interest to complement the vocal line.

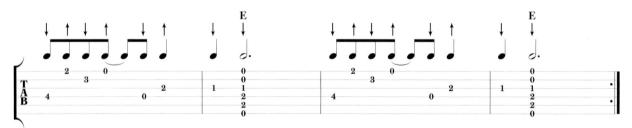

The Dsus2 chord

The next five pieces break down the song's chorus. Your first task is to learn Dsus2, a chord identical to D major, except that it has an open top E string. Even though this means that finger 2 is available, using finger 3 on the B string results in a more comfortable hand position. The shift between the two different chords is made easier by keeping finger 1 in contact with the G string and slipping it up one fret as you change from E to Dsus2.

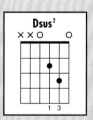

The Dsus2 chord.

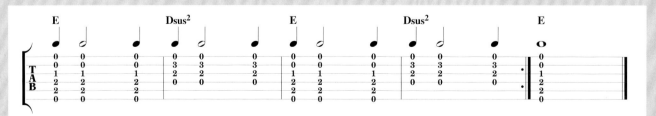

The B major barre chord

So far, the barre chords you have played have been six-string chords based on the E major shape. By using fingers 2, 3 and 4 to form A major and then adding a five-string barre two frets behind the other fingers, this shape can be shifted to any fret position on the neck to make many more major chords. As with the other exercises, consider the capo at fret 1 as the nut of your guitar, then place the A major shape at the 4th fret using fingers 2, 3 and 4. An open A string completes your quota of notes for the first two bars. For bars 3 and 4, add a five-string finger barre at fret 2 as you continue to use downstrokes for each note.

The A major shape at fret 4.

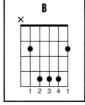

The B major barre chord.

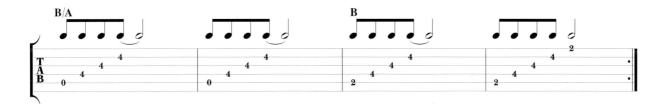

A tricky chord change

Placing the B major chord is hard enough at first, even if you have plenty of time in which to do it, so achieving a quick shift from an unrelated shape will really push your ability. However, you can make life easier by approaching the change in the correct manner. As before, use fingers 1 and 3 for Dsus2 and don't forget to strum just four strings. Leave the release of the fingers as late as you can, then try to form the A major chord shape with fingers 2, 3 and 4 as you move them to their 4th fret location on the D, G and B strings. As you place these, reach back to add a firm, straight finger barre at the 2nd fret.

Keep the thumb low and still throughout.

Shifting between B and A major

Here's another opportunity to practise your new barre chord shape, this time in conjunction with an easier change from the similarly shaped A major. In bar 1, use the same B major fingering as before, then slip fingers 2, 3 and 4 down to fret 2 above the capo for the A major chords in bar 2. So that the return to B major is as relaxed as possible, try to keep the finger barre extended out towards the capo. Remember to repeat bars 1 to 4 before ending with a semibreve strum of the B chord in bar 5.

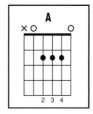

A major using fingers 2, 3 and 4.

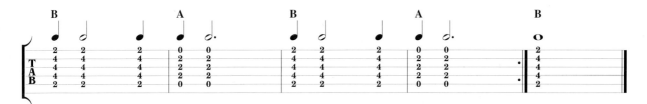

The chorus chord sequence

E major, Dsus2, B major and A major all come together to form an accompaniment to the song's chorus. The only change you have not practised already is from A back to E for the repeat. Using fingers 2, 3 and 4 for A major helps this change, since fingers 2 and 3 only need to move across the same 2nd fret while finger 1 can prepare for its placement at fret 1 on the G string. Notice that you've got a three-count Dsus2 chord, which gives you a little more time to prepare for the B barre chord. The last bar is here to get you used to returning to the riff after the chorus.

Finger tip

BARRING THE BOTTOM E STRING

If you prefer, you can place the finger barre across all six strings for any A shape barre chords, provided you don't make plectrum contact with the bottom E string. You might find this more comfortable and convenient, particularly when switching between six-string and five-string barre chord shapes.

Two more familiar chords

This instrumental passage brings in the G major and D major chords. The G shape used is the three-finger version with an open B string, so it's probably more comfortable to use finger 3 on the top E string instead of finger 4. The G and D chords take it in turns to combine with E major. Use finger 1 as your lead finger when changing between D and E, since it only needs to shift by one fret on the same G string.

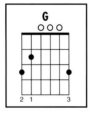

The three-fingered G major shape.

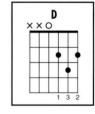

The familiar D major chord.

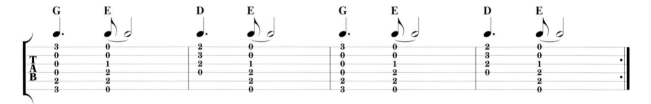

A useful strum pattern

This one-bar strum pattern links to the final four plays of the riff. There's little to choose between the two possible left hand fingerings for A major, though using fingers 2, 3 and 4 keeps things consistent. You're sure to come across other songs that sound great strummed to this pattern, so memorize the combination of down- and upstrums. You could try strumming like this instead of using the more sustained and straightforward pattern suggested in the practice piece at the top of the page.

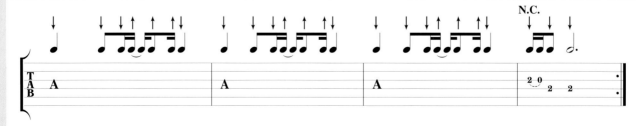

NEW RHYTHM GUITAR TECHNIQUES

This session investigates the subtle art of good rhythm guitar playing.

Although these pieces based on *Alright* feature familiar chords, some new shapes are used , notably Dsus4 and Asus4. There's also an elaborate piece of lead guitar at the start and a great sounding solo.

A major revisited

To form A major, place fingers 1, 2 and 3 in a straight line across fret 2. If the fingers are arched, you should be able to strum through all five strings and hear each ringing clearly. On beat 4 of bars 1 and 3, strike the A and D strings together, but let the plectrum continue downwards until it lies just beyond the top E string – it's then ready for the upstroke of the top E string that follows. Keep your right wrist relaxed for the quick, triple strum at the centre of the piece.

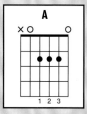

A reminder of A major.

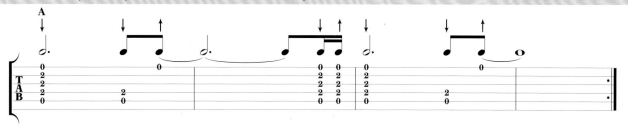

A different approach to the hammer-on

This repeating phrase sounds best if you let the fretted notes overlap. When playing the hammer-ons, release finger 1 from fret 2 on the D string at the same time as you hammer-on finger 3 two frets higher. With finger 3 still in place, add finger 2 and then finger 1 to complete the broken chord effect in the 1st and 3rd full bars. Take all three fingers off together as you play the open G at the end of these bars.

Release finger 1 as you hammer-on finger 3.

The 2nd and then 1st finger join finger 3.

A new form of A major

In the 2nd full bar, use finger 1 for the pull-off from fret 2 to the open G string. Fingers 2, 3 and then 1 form the broken D major chord shape that follows. Let the fretted notes ring over one another before releasing the fingers for the open G and then the open A that fills bar 3. Use this sustained note to prepare the two different versions of A major in the 1st and 2nd time bars.

Form D major in the 2nd full bar.

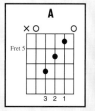

A

Fret 5

3 2 1

Finish with the new A chord in 5th position.

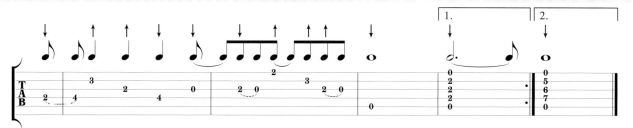

The Gmaj9/A chord

Place the full 5th position A major chord at the start of this exercise, as this ensures that your hand is ready for the three strums of this chord that follow. To form the elaborately titled Gmaj9/A chord that ends bar 1, drop the 5th position A major shape to 3rd position and add finger 4 at fret 5 on the top E string. Keep this shape in place as you move into bar 2 and play the top E string note on its own. Just release the 4th finger for the remaining two notes in bar 2. Bars 3 and 4 are identical to the opening two bars.

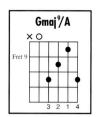

The Gmaj9/A chord in 3rd position.

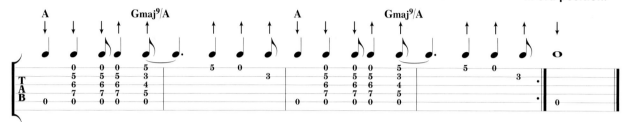

The triplet

There are two sets of triplets in bars 1 and 3 of this piece, indicated on your music by brackets with a number 3 in the middle. You have to play these three equal notes in the time of two, which is why there are six crotchets in these bars instead of four. Play the 1st note of each triplet on the beat, and the remaining two notes evenly either side of the following beat. Triplets are complex rhythm figures. Apart from the final A major chord, leave finger 1 at fret 2 on the top E string, and finger 2 at fret 3 on the B string throughout. Add finger 4 where necessary to reach the 5th fret notes.

Keep fingers 1 and 2 in place for bars 1 to 4.

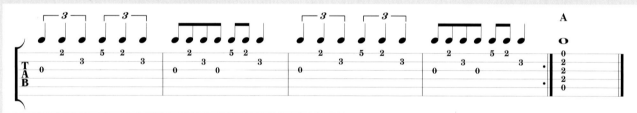

The complete intro

The first full bar is preceded by a pair of A major strums. Your 1st finger is perfectly situated to instigate the hammer-on in bar 3, after which the remainder of the 1st line runs identically to the phrase practised in the session's third exercise. Two open string notes are all the preparation time you have for the shift to 5th position for the A major chords, and you'll need to move back to 2nd position for the previously rehearsed fingerings in bars 3 and 4 of the 2nd line.

Finger tip
SIMPLIFYING THE CHORD SHIFT TO A
You can ease the placing of the final A major chord in the following piece by switching to finger 3 for the fret 3 note that ends the penultimate bar. From here, slide finger 3 back along the B string for a smooth change to A major.

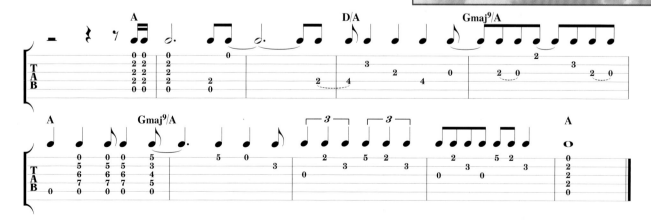

116

Strumming muted strings

Good rhythm guitar playing is all about injecting the right feel into your strumming. The blocks of crosses indicate percussive muting, so you'll need to release the A chord finger pressure slightly for these. As you do this, pull the wrist back to cause the slight collapse of the fingers needed to mute the top E string. Straight after the muted downstrum, replace the fingers for a clear upstrum of the top three strings.

The fingers mute the A chord.

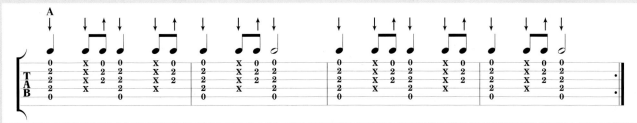

Combining A and G chords

A natural occurrence in rhythm guitar involves a slightly early shift towards the next chord. The purpose is to buy a little time in which to prepare the next chord change. For the last upstrum of bars 1 and 3, release the muted A chord fingers and replace them with the top part of the G major chord, using fingers 3 and 4. Add the lower part of the chord for the full G major strum, then mute all six strings through a slight release of pressure and the collapse of the fingers across the open strings.

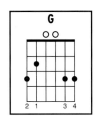

G major in bars 2 and 4.

Slightly release and collapse the fingers for the percussive mute.

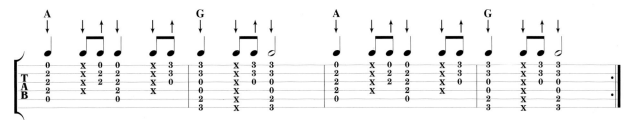

Bringing D major into the equation

This piece serves two main purposes. Firstly, it introduces the familiar shape of D major in sequence with the A and G chords. Secondly, it brings a new rhythm figure into play in bars 3 and 4. The last upstrum of bar 2 contains just three strings and is designed to prepare the D chord through the release of all but finger 3 of G major. For the 1st chord of bar 3, add the remainder of the triangular D shape and leave this in place through to the end of the line.

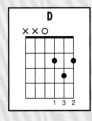

Leave finger 3 in place at the end of bar 2.

Add fingers 1 and 2 for D major in bars 3 and 4.

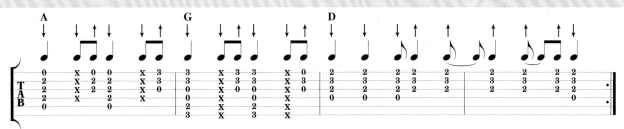

The Dsus4 chord

Dsus4 translates as a D chord with a suspended 4th. In other words, the 4th note of the D scale is 'suspended' (or tagged) onto the D major chord. When this occurs, the usually present major 3rd degree is omitted, leaving notes 1, 4 and 5 of the scale. It's common for a sus4 chord to alternate with the pure major form of the same chord, as is the case in this piece. The rhythm stays the same as in the previous exercise, although the presence of only D chords at the end of the repeat necessitates the use of a 1st and 2nd time bar.

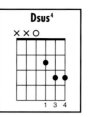

Add finger 4 to D major to form Dsus4.

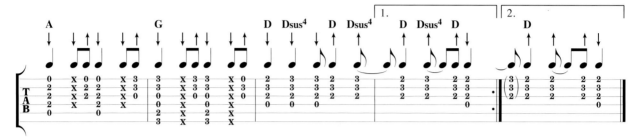

Shifting between G major and Dsus4

The chord chart system is adopted for the remaining strummed pieces in this session. The four chords in the piece have all been played in earlier exercises, so the shapes should be fresh in your mind. You can leave fingers 3 and 4 in place as you change from G major to Dsus4. Replace finger 4 with finger 2 at fret 2 to form D major.

The strum pattern for the first half of the repeated two-bar pattern is new, so give it special attention and try to practice it regularly.

Another sus4 chord

The same theory applies for the new Asus4 chord in this piece as for Dsus4 in the exercise at the top of the page. The result is a subtle harmonic shift as you add finger 4 at fret 3 on the B string to the usual A major chord. Alternating between A and Asus4 is simply a matter of adding and releasing finger 4, provided you retain the full A chord fingering when finger 4 is in place. Use this piece to get accustomed to the omission of strum directions. The strum directions from bar 1 of the previous piece are ideal, and remember to strum only the top three strings on the upstrums.

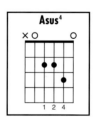

Adding finger 4 for Asus4.

Solo work, the first half

The guitar solo frequently proves to be the most demanding part of a song to learn. However, after the intricacies of the intro, you'll be pleased to discover that there's not much to this solo. Begin in 4th position, so that finger 2 is at fret 5 on the D string. Finger 1 is the obvious choice for the 4th fret notes, and an open D completes bar 1. This and the following open string give you time to shift up one position for the next stage, using fingers 1 and 3 at frets 5 and 7 respectively. Slide finger 3 swiftly up to fret 9 in the 3rd bar, from which position all the remaining notes can be reached comfortably.

Start with finger 2 at fret 5.

Slide up to fret 9 in bar 3.

The remainder of the solo

This is the more straightforward section of the solo, particularly since bar 1 is exactly the same as in the previous piece. During the tied open D note, shift the left hand up to 7th position. From here, use finger 1 for the 7th fret notes, with finger 2 naturally taking care of the single fret 8 in bar 2. A measured finger slide drops your 1st finger to fret 5 in the 3rd bar, and then it's repetitions of the same B string note all the way through to the eight-beat tied note at the end of the line.

A final new chord

The concept and sound of major 7 chords should be familiar from earlier sessions. The new G major 7 chord needed for this piece retains the 2nd and 3rd finger locations of the full G major chord, but mutes out the A string with the underside of finger 2 and has finger 1 at fret 2 on the top E string. When changing from D major, try keeping finger 3 in place, as this provides stability for fingers 1 and 2 to stretch out to opposite strings. The quaver rests are best created using the side of the right hand, after which repeated downstrums of the A chord offer the necessary driving power for this passage.

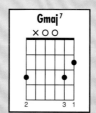

G major 7 with the A string muted.

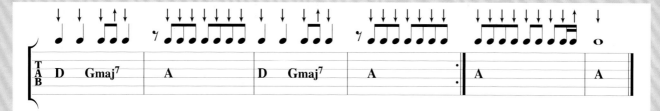

THE CLASSIC ROCK'N'ROLL STYLE

Where better to start looking at vintage rock'n'roll than through the artistry of Elvis Presley's 'guitar man', Scotty Moore?

Jailhouse Rock, a classic which contains punchy rhythm work, an inspired lead solo and one of the most famous rock'n'roll riffs ever played, is an essential song to have in your repertoire.

Setting up the A barre chord shape

To start this session, here's a straightforward piece alternating between two three-string power chords. D#5 is played in 6th position with finger 1 on the A string and fingers 3 and 4 on the D and G strings at fret 8. After four counts, shift the D#5 shape up one fret to 7th position to form E5. You'll find the shifts between chords smoother if you keep your thumb behind fret 7 throughout. Hold each chord for a full four counts.

The D#5 chord.

E5 uses the D#5 shape in 7th position.

Muting the top E string

To form D# major, place an A major chord shape at fret 8 using fingers 2, 3 and 4, then add finger 1 at fret 6 on the A string. This is virtually the A barre chord shape you played in one of the earlier sessions. The difference lies in the omission of a top E string note, which means you don't have to place the finger barre across the strings. Instead, make a strong contact on the A string and let the very tip of finger 1 touch the bottom E string. The other end of the finger lightly covers the top E string to mute any sound.

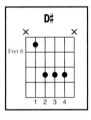

The D# major chord in 6th position.

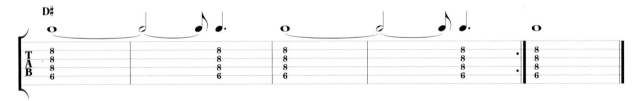

Alternating between D# and E major

The notes D# and E are a semitone apart, so by shifting each note of the D# major chord up one fret to 7th position, you can create an E major chord. Use the same fingering and string muting approach as you did for the D# chord in the previous piece. Apart from in the final bar, hold the E chords for a full six-and-a-half beats, before shifting back one fret for D# major.

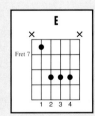

E major with finger 1 muting the top E string.

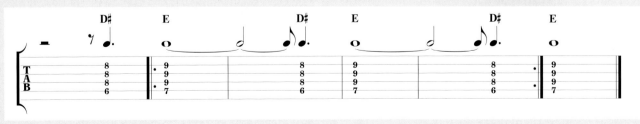

A classic rock'n'roll riff

This famous one-bar pattern is based on the major chord triad, which consists of notes 1, 3 and 5 of the A major scale. Note 6 of the scale (fret 4 on the D string) is added for the 7th quaver in bars 1 to 3. Keep your left hand in 2nd position throughout, using fingers 3 and 1 for the 4th and 2nd fret notes, respectively.

Fret 4 on the A string with finger 3.

Fret 2 on the D string.

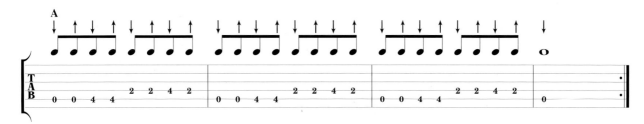

The same riff for the E chord

In bars 3 and 4, transfer the notes rehearsed in the previous exercise across to the bottom E and A strings to play an E major version of the same riff. Eight quaver beats fill all but the final bar, which makes the rhythm straightforward. The problem with a repetitive rhythm figure such as this is that it tends to emphasize any unevenness in your alternate plectrum strokes, so you'll need to concentrate hard on this area. Palm mute every note and keep your left fingers spread in 2nd position and close to the relevant strings at all times when not in use.

Finger tip

RETAINING THE 1ST FINGER

Leave finger 1 at the 2nd fret for the 2nd half of the eight-note riff. This allows you to focus on the neat placement and accurate removal of finger 3.

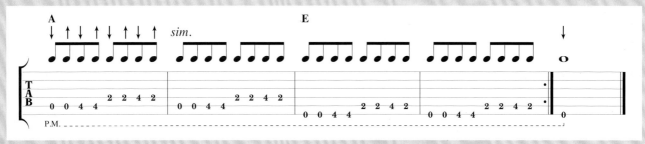

Extending the 4th finger

It's now time to play the riff of the two previous pieces using notes from the B major chord. The fingering is more complicated this time, beginning with a stretch from finger 1 at fret 2 on the A string up to finger 4 at fret 6 on the same string. For the 2nd half of the eight-note riff, try to use fingers 2 and 4, although fingers 1 and 3 are an acceptable alternative. Whichever fingering you choose, leave the 4th fret finger on the D string as you play and then remove the fret 6 note. Finger 3 works well for the 2nd minim in bar 2, as it relocates your hand for the return of finger 1 to the 2nd fret at the start of bar 3.

The 1st note of the riff based on the B chord.

Extend finger 4 up to fret 6.

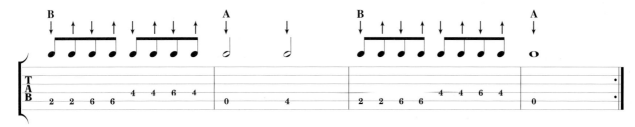

Linking the B and A chord riffs

Although each riff picks out the notes of a chord individually, it's easiest to refer to them by the name of the chord they relate to. This piece takes the previous one a stage further by filling in most of the notes of the A chord riff. Bars 7 and 8 contain a tied open bottom E string, which should be left to ring fully. In readiness for the song's chorus, palm mute the strings with the heel of the right hand.

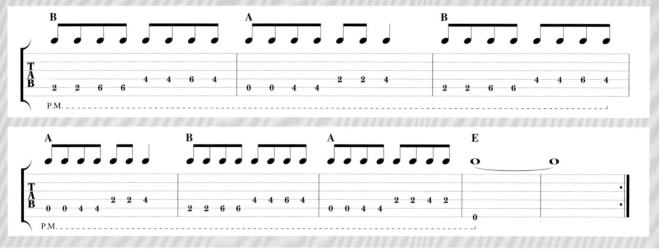

The full chorus accompaniment

Now it's time to join together the three versions of this rock'n'roll riff based on the chords of A, E and B major. The entire section should be palm muted, and you'll find that finger 1 can remain at fret 2 on the A string as you move into bar 5, which makes the change to the B chord riff simpler. Use alternating down- and upstrums, and notice the different endings in the 1st and 2nd time bars.

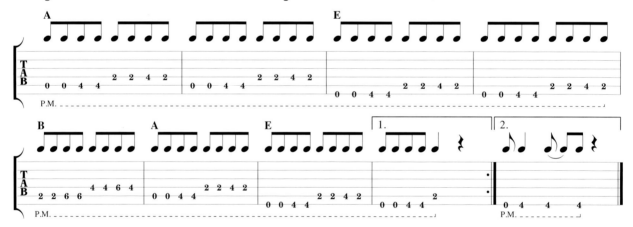

Beginning the solo

The first part of the solo revolves around a two-string chord with finger 1 at fret 8 on the B string and finger 4 at fret 12 on the top E string. Although it's a five-fret stretch, the frets are quite narrow at this point of the neck, which should allow you to connect these two notes comfortably. Use a downstroke each time, and keep your finger contact firm so that the sound sustains through the tied rhythm values. Try to create the quaver rests by either releasing the left finger pressure slightly or dropping the side of the right hand onto the strings.

The opening two-string chord of the solo.

The unison bend

The word unison describes sounds played together at the same pitch. The effect can be created by bending the pitch of one string up to the pitch of another. Here, finger 1 remains fixed at fret 9 on the B string, while fingers 2 and 3 line up along frets 10 and 11 on the G string. Strike the two strings together and simultaneously bend the G string to imitate a fret 13 note. Repeat the process for the 2nd chord, then play the remaining notes in bars 1 and 2 with a permanent full bend of the G string. Acoustic players can use half bends from fret 12 throughout.

Both strings sound at the same pitch.

Muting the B and G string chord.

The first half of the solo

This piece links the phrases studied in the previous two exercises. At the end of bar 2, move finger 1 a fret up the B string, and observe the quaver rests by lowering the right hand onto the strings. The thumb needs to be low for the left hand to cope with the stretch between frets 8 and 12 in bars 1 and 2. It's also advantageous to keep the thumb low as you move into the string bends of bars 3 and 4. The final B5 chord is a useful preparation for the full B major barre chord that follows the unison bends.

After the repeat, a B5 chord ends the piece.

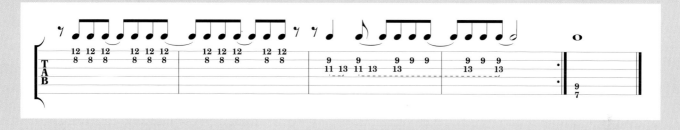

The B major barre chord

You played B major as an A shape barre chord earlier on, but here B major is relocated to 7th position using the E barre chord shape as its template. Just like F and A major, this chord needs a full finger barre across all six strings, with fingers 2, 3 and 4 forming the E major chord shape above. Strum all six strings, followed by two strikes of the bottom three strings and then another six-string strum. Wait for the tie, then lightly strum the bottom three strings two more times. At this point, reduce your barre chord to a power chord, and shift down to 4th position for the G#5 chord. Slide G#5 up one fret to create the first of six A5 chords that fill the 2nd bar.

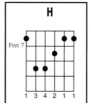

The B major barre chord in 7th position.

The welcome return of the power chord shape.

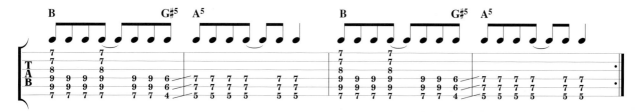

A quick shift of position

The last phrase of the song's solo involves a leap from the A5 chords down to E major in 1st position. After the opening chord, play downstrums of the D and G strings only, but leave the E major fingering in place. Add finger 4 at fret 2 on the G string where marked to give a sus4 feel to the harmony. In bar 2, you have only a quaver rest in which to fly back up to the 6th position D# major chord played much earlier. The 2nd E chord shape of the piece is the 7th position equivalent of the D# chord.

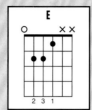

E major in 1st position. Do not play strings 1 and 2.

The E chord plus finger 4 at fret 2 on the G string.

The complete solo

There's a lot to think about as you merge the four phrases of the solo. Use downstrokes throughout and keep your plectrum work light. The link between bars 2 and 3 was rehearsed in the first half of the solo, although the tempo is quicker this time. One of the most difficult moments is the change to the full B major barre chord on the last quaver beat of bar 4. Bars 7 to 10 are identical to the previous piece, providing another chance to practise the return to 6th position and the D# and E chords that accompany the verse.

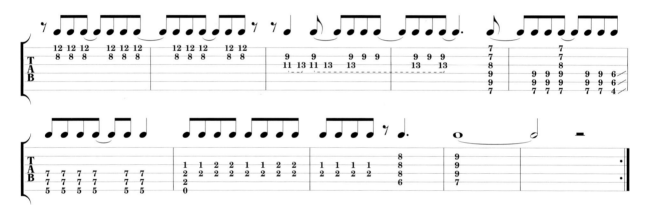

The conclusion

The original Elvis recording ends with a fade out of the chorus riff, but we've taken the liberty of giving the song a solid ending using D# and E chords. Start with the palm-muted E chord riff, with your left hand in 2nd position and using fingers 3 and 1 for the fretted notes. After three bars, mute the bottom two strings with the right hand, and run finger 1 swiftly up to the 6th fret on the same string. The D# and E chords return in bar 4, but this time they need to be played on different beats of the bar.

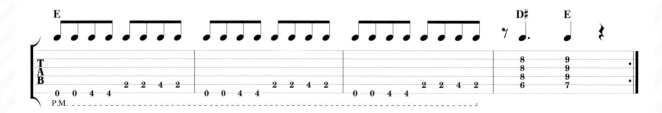

POLISHING YOUR LEAD AND RHYTHM SKILLS

Jangling strummed guitars and chiming lead lines abound as you turn your attention to mastering this session based on There She Goes by The La's.

The absence of any string bends or high fret work makes this an ideal song to play on an acoustic as well as an electric guitar. We've broken up the lead part by switching over to strummed chords for the bridge section. This provides an opportunity to brush up on several important chords covered in previous sessions.

Beginning the principal riff

Before you start, place fingers 2 and 3 at fret 3 on the B and top E strings, respectively (you should leave finger 2 in place throughout the piece). This hand position best allows the release of finger 3 after the 2nd note so that you can reach up to fret 5 with your 4th finger. Use finger 1 for the 2nd fret note, while finger 3 returns to fret 3 on the 7th quaver. After an identical approach to bars 2 and 3, the left hand is also set for the final three crotchets.

Place fingers 2 and 3 before beginning.

Finger 4 replaces the 3rd finger.

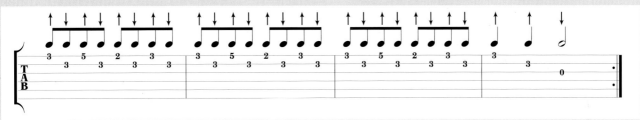

More over-ringing strings

The second half of the riff is easier as it involves none of the top string finger movement of the previous piece. Keep the top E string open and leave finger 2 at fret 3 on the B string throughout. Use alternate up- and downstrokes for easier string crossing. The over-ringing of the notes is an integral part of the riff's sound, so make sure that the underside of finger 2 never collapses onto the top E string.

Finger 2 stays in place for the whole piece.

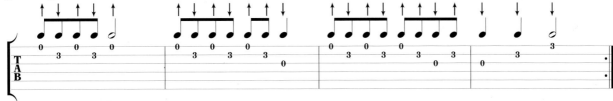

Linking the two sections

The piece starts with a quaver upbeat, so begin with a downstroke of the 2nd string note before moving into a bar identical to that rehearsed in the very first exercise. At the end of the 1st full bar, release finger 3 from the top E string and your left hand is ready to deal with the 2nd bar. The inclusion of the open G string gives rise to a variation of plectrum stroke direction. Although a little confusing at first, concentration on the plectrum work will help you achieve a more flowing performance.

Use small plectrum strokes and a low right wrist.

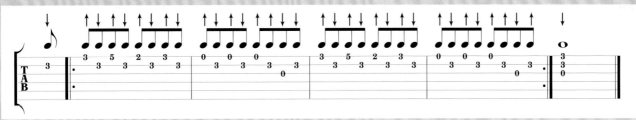

Moving up to 3rd position

Keep the left hand in 3rd position, using finger 3 for any fret 5 notes and finger 1 for fret 3. In bar 1, place each finger separately to prevent over-ringing of the strings. In bar 2, however, aim for the opposite effect and allow both strings to ring by leaving the 3rd and 1st fingers on their respective strings.

The opening note with the 3rd finger.

Change to finger 1 on the top E string.

Fingers 3 and 1 placed together in bars 2 and 4.

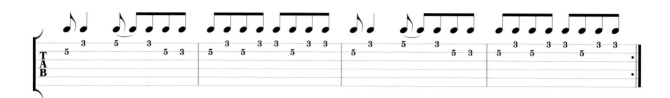

Two-string chords

Use fingers 1 and 3 in 5th position for the 1st chord. Next, shift the shape down two frets to 3rd position, but aim to avoid a sliding effect by releasing the finger pressure as you move. Play frets 2 and 3 together with fingers 1 and 2 in bar 2. The remaining 2nd and 3rd bar chords use these three patterns, but the shifts are much faster at the end of bar 3. For the final chord, retain finger 2 on the B string and add finger 3 at the same fret on the top E string.

Start with fingers 1 and 3 in 5th position.

Shift to 2nd position for the 3rd chord.

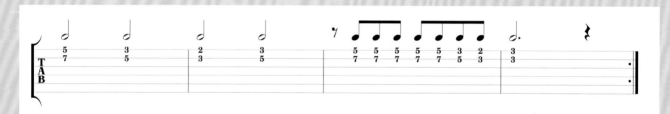

The accompaniment takes shape

By connecting all the previously rehearsed sections, most of the lead guitar part will be covered. Play the main riff three times before linking the 3rd position phrase from the piece above to form bars 7 and 8. This involves a quick move up the B string from finger 2 at fret 3 to the 3rd finger at fret 5. Aim to shift your left thumb up a fret at the same time to eliminate the finger stretch. Damp the right hand onto the strings at the quaver rest, and follow this with the sequence of two-string chords practised in the previous exercise.

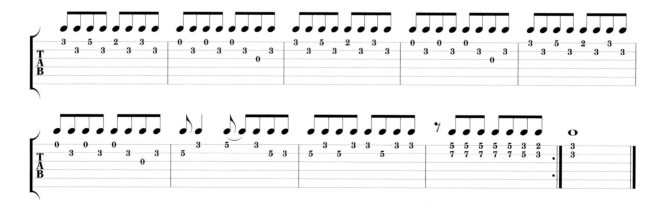

An extended passage of syncopation

Beginning with an upbeat, this piece develops the opening from the first piece on the previous page into a much longer syncopated idea used in the accompaniment of *There She Goes*. After the opening 2nd finger note, place the remaining 3rd and 5th fret notes with fingers 1 and 3, respectively. Leave both fingers in place throughout the 4th full bar to allow the strings to over-ring. During the 1st quaver rest, shift the same finger shape up from 3rd to 5th position for the two-string chords in the 5th full bar.

Begin with your 2nd finger at fret 3.

Quickly shift to fret 5 with your 3rd finger.

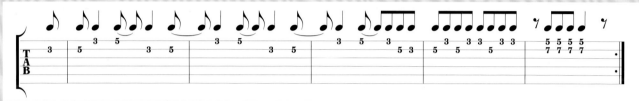

Starting the strummed bridge

For this piece, E minor alternates with the C major chord. By using fingers 1 and 2 to place E minor, you can keep finger 2 in the same place as you shift to C major. Complete the C major shape by adding finger 1 to the B string at fret 1 and finger 3 to the A string at fret 3. Bars 2 and 4 end with an upstrum of the open top three strings, which allows you to remove fingers 1 and 3 from the C chord in preparation for the shift back to E minor.

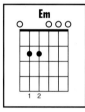

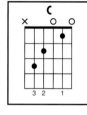

A reminder of E minor.

C major is another familiar chord.

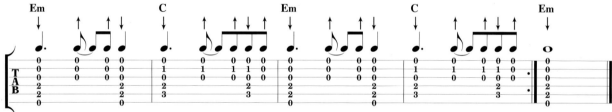

Adding the D major chord

Bars 1, 3 and 5 are the same as in the previous piece. Use the two-beat length of the C chord in bars 2 and 4 to shift to D major, although the longer you leave the fingers on the strings, the smoother your playing will be. C to D is one of those chord changes where there is no common fingering to ease the shift. The best you can do is glide your fingers close over the strings by the most direct route to their new locations. Avoid sizeable movements away from the strings or dramatic shifts of the hand and thumb position.

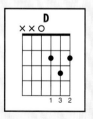

D major in bars 2 and 4.

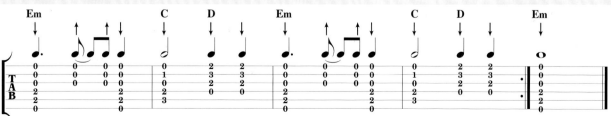

A smooth change between G and D major

G major has featured so often that you're likely to be able to place the fingering instinctively by now. However, a quick check of the photo and chord box is always a good idea if you're in any doubt. After two full downstrums of the G chord, release all but the 3rd finger as you play the three-string upstrum. While playing the upstrum, pull your 1st and 2nd fingers over towards the G and top E strings to maximize the speed of the shift to D major. A down-up-down sequence of D strums follows with the D chord fingers remaining firmly in place.

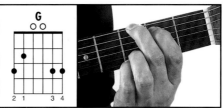

The four-fingered version of G major.

Leave finger 3 only as you prepare D major.

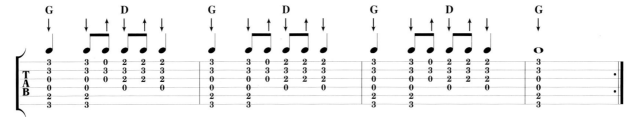

Incorporating Cadd9

The symbol Cadd9 might be familiar from an earlier session. On this occasion, however, the chord is subtly altered, with an open top E string instead of a fret 3 highest note. In every other respect it is the same, with fingers 2, 1 and 3 placed on the A, D and B strings. Bar 1 differs from the previous piece in that an extra upstrum is added at the end of the bar. For this, return to the finger-3-only shape played earlier in the bar. This process eases the way into the Cadd9 chord in bar 2. As you move between the three chord shapes, notice that finger 3 remains at fret 3 on the B string.

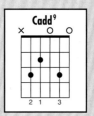

Keep finger 3 in place as you change to Cadd9.

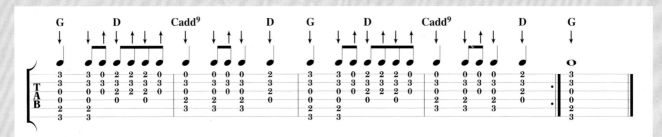

A minor and another rhythm pattern

A minor is a chord that dates back to the very first session of *Play Guitar*, where it was played together with E minor, as is the case here. Both chord shapes fall nicely under the fingers, so aim for a really neat result as you shift between the two. You can make this even smoother by releasing your 1st and 3rd fingers for the last upstrum of bars 1 and 3. This leaves finger 2 in place, meaning that a simple addition of finger 1 at fret 2 on the A string creates the E minor chord which is played throughout bars 2 and 4.

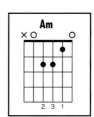

The last new chord is A minor.

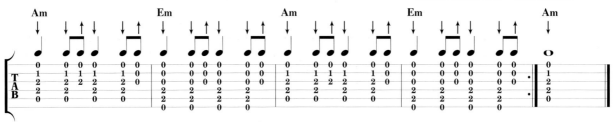

The end of the bridge

The shift from E minor to C major benefits from leaving finger 2 in place as you play the open string upstrum that ends bar 2. To capitalize on this short cut, make sure you twist fingers 1 and 3 into a C chord shape as soon as you release finger 1 from E minor. Watch out for the quaver rests in the 1st and 2nd time bars and notice that the D chords are all downstrummed.

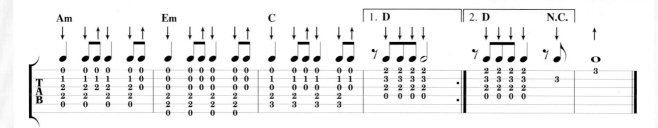

The entire bridge

Now that you've worked on each of the bridge chord changes separately, it's time to join the content of the previous six practice pieces together. This is never as easy as it seems, since the musical material now appears in a much more condensed form. In this particular instance, you also have to deal with several rhythm changes alongside the use of six regularly shifting chords. Initially, the previously discussed short cuts will require a little more thought, but the long-term results will more than make up for the extra effort.

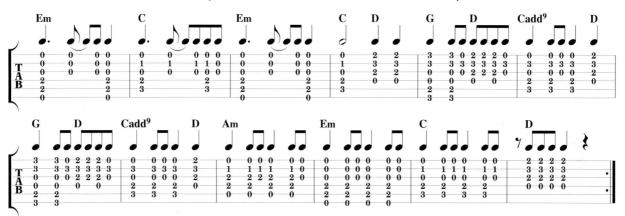

Final exercise

Bars 1 and 3 use part of the top E and B string phrase from the intro and verses. The 2nd and 4th bars repeat the two-string chord sequence studied earlier. As before, observe the half-beat rests by muting the strings with the right hand before launching into this series of downstrummed mini-chords. At the end of bars 2 and 4, leave finger 2 in place as a neat way of linking to the next bar. For the final chord, use fingers 2 and 3 on the top two strings at fret 3 and add an open G string.

The ideal place to mute the strings.

Fingers 2 and 3 form the final three-string chord.

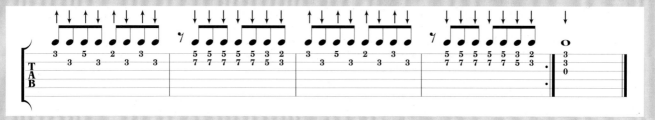

OPEN G TUNING

It's time to try out a dramatic re-tuning for Start Me Up *by The Rolling Stones.*

By dropping the pitch of your bottom and top E strings to D, as well as flattening the A string to G, it's possible to play a major chord using open strings only. Since the chord in question is G major, this system of tuning is referred to as open G tuning. Before playing these pieces, be sure to re-tune your guitar accordingly.

C major using the finger barre

To form C major, place finger 1 across the top five strings at fret 5. For the other chord (Fadd2/C), keep the barre in place and add finger 2 to the B string at fret 6 and finger 3 to the D string at fret 7. The two chords combine to form a rock'n'roll shuffle. Play all downstrums and mute the staccato notes crisply with the right hand.

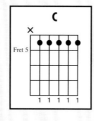

The finger barre at fret 5.

Add fingers 2 and 3.

Developing the rhythm figure

The same two chords are used again here, only this time the repeated three-strum figure from the exercise above is extended by extra quaver strums in bars 2 and 4. Work at producing a softer top-string note by focusing the main plectrum contact on the lower four strings. Count your bars in half-beat quavers to ensure a tight rhythm and a precise first entry on the upbeat before bar 1.

Finger tip

DEALING WITH THE BOTTOM STRING
To avoid striking the bottom string, Keith Richards removes it from his guitar when using this tuning. Since you'll need this string for the solo pieces, mute its sound with the tip of the finger barre, and then try to be as tidy as possible with your strumming.

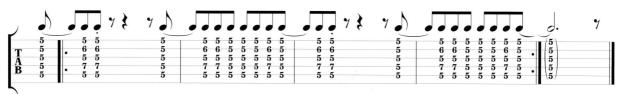

Shifting to 3rd position

Start with the C major chord using the finger barre at fret 5, then add fingers 2 and 3 after two beats. Release all three fingers for the open 3rd, 4th and 5th string chord, then shift the barre down to fret 3 for the three-string chord in bar 2. Although you have a full B♭ major chord in place, only strum the three strings shown on the TAB. Use the crotchet rest to move the barre back to fret 5. Bars 3 and 4 are then a replica of the first two bars.

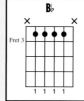

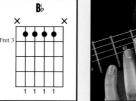

Prepare the barre during the open string chord.

B♭ major using the finger barre at fret 3.

The B♭ chord shape

This piece explores the effect of the chord shuffle in 3rd position. The approach is similar to the 5th position sequence already rehearsed. By moving the finger barre back to 3rd position, your starting chord is now B♭. Only play strings 3, 4 and 5, but keep the barre across strings 1 and 2 as well. The staccato dots under the quaver note values tell you to mute these chords with the right hand, a process that gives your playing extra punch. Wherever fret 5 is included in the chord, add finger 2 at fret 4 on the B string as well as finger 3. In later pieces you'll need this full E♭/B♭ chord, as shown in the chord box and photo.

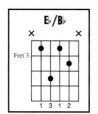

The E♭/B♭ chord shape in 3rd position.

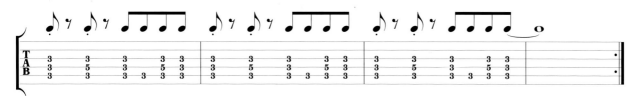

A more intricate shuffle pattern

Most of the groundwork for this exercise has already been covered in the previous exercise. However, the interchange between the B♭ and E♭/B♭ works as follows in bars 2 and 4: keep the finger barre at fret 3 in place and add the 2nd and 3rd fingers, as in the piece above, for the 2nd chord; then remove these fingers again for the three fret 3 chords that follow. Aim to include the 2nd string in your strum at the end of the bar. As with all these practice pieces, downstrums create the best effect.

The right hand implements the rests.

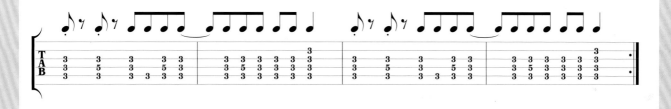

Putting the changes together

On this occasion, you need to join up the 5th position shuffle, from the rhythm figure exercise, with the 3rd position sequence practised above. The two sections are linked via the open 3rd, 4th and 5th string chord at the end of bars 2 and 6. This open chord provides you with a moment to achieve the 3rd position shift. At the end of bar 4 you are afforded no such luxury, as the B♭ chord at fret 3 is followed immediately by a two-fret shift up to the C chord in 5th position. The rests are crucial to the feel of the song, so try to implement them.

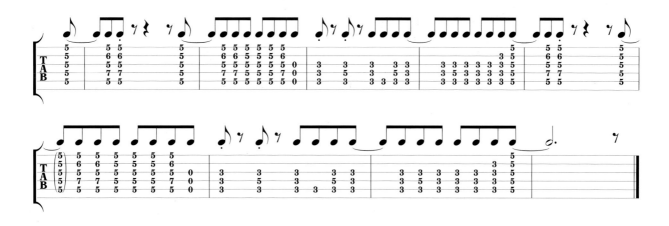

A variation on the opening sequence

There are many similarities between this phrase and the previous piece. However, you'll need to be alert to the variations of rhythm and the number of strings strummed within the same four-chord sequence. This is the first piece to include the fret 4 note on the B string that you've been adding 'unnecessarily' up until now. Its inclusion at all times gives you the option of playing this string as a part of the 3rd position chords. Watch out for the single 3rd string note in bar 4, picked out of the B♭ chord while the finger barre remains from bar 3.

Strike the G string only in the 4th full bar.

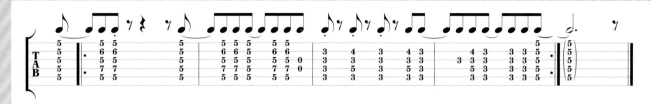

Another subtle adaptation

Although the chords and rhythm patterns are similar to those used before, some subtle alterations prevent the guitar part from becoming dull. These are the main differences to watch out for: the 1st chord is on beat 1 of the bar; an extra strum of C major keeps the quavers regular in the middle of bar 2; bar 3 uses thinned-out forms of the 3rd position chords; the single 3rd string note in bar 4 is replaced by a four-string B♭ major chord; finally, a quarter rest is introduced in the middle of bar 4.

AUTHENTICITY vs ACCESSIBILITY
On the original recording of *Start Me Up*, Keith Richards varies the verse-chord sequence so that no four-bar phrase is the same. To make the song accessible, we've repeated the phrase rehearsed in this piece throughout the session.

Beginning the chorus

The finger barre also has a central role to play in the song's chorus. Play the C major chord, formed in open G tuning by barring the top five strings at fret 5, three times. Release the barre and make a quick shift up to fret 10. As you shift the left hand, strike the open G and D strings together, then mute them with the right hand to create the quaver rest. Place the five-string barre at fret 10, but only strike the 3rd, 4th and 5th strings to play a series of five F5 chords. A slight release of the 1st finger pressure enables the percussive muted chord shown on the TAB by the block of crosses.

The F5 chord at fret 10.

Release finger pressure for the percussive muted chord.

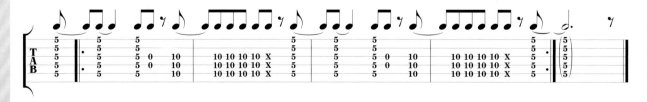

Sliding the barre

The chorus develops courtesy of some rhythm variation in bars 3 and 4 and a slide of the finger barre. Bars 1 and 2 are almost identical to the last exercise. Try to master the rhythm pattern that follows, built around predominantly offbeat strums. In bar 3, play the clipped open-string chord as you shift the barre up to fret 10, then transfer the barre to fret 8 during the quaver rest in bar 4. After one strum of strings 3, 4 and 5 in this position, slide the barre down to fret 7, without re-striking the strings. A further shift down two frets sets up the final 5th fret C chord before the repeat.

The 1st finger barre at fret 8.

Slide the barre down to fret 7.

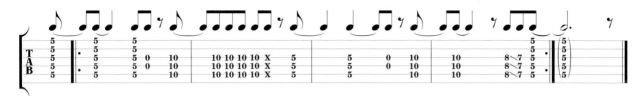

An involved figure

This brief but important passage combines a slide of the finger barre with some neat right hand work. Although the TAB indicates two-string chords sliding from fret 8 to fret 7, try to stay consistent and place the finger barre across the top five strings. The slide is followed by an open G string, which presents a moment to send the barre down to fret 5. Play this open G with an upstroke to take your plectrum back towards the 5th string. As you move into the 1st full bar, place the finger barre at fret 5 but only play the 5th string. The familiar sight of alternating C and Fadd2/C chords completes the phrase, which repeats for the rest of this excerpt.

Pick the G string on its own with an upstroke...

...then barre fret 5 but only play string 5.

Barring with the 3rd finger

Here's a neat way of dealing with the fret 8 two-string chords in bars 1 and 3. Since these chords are only fleeting decorations of the mainly C major-based material, it's a good idea to keep the five-string barre in place at fret 5. Extend finger 3 and drop it flat across the D and G strings at fret 8 to cover both the notes needed. A quick release of finger 3 straight after the fret 8 chord leaves your 1st finger still in position for the five-string C chord that follows. The rhythm is rather complex, so try to count carefully in half-beat quavers as you practise.

Finger 3 barring the D and G strings.

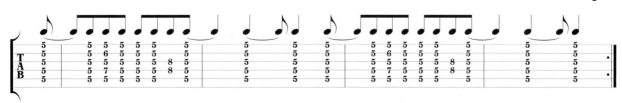

A welcome diversion

It's refreshing to get away from the C chords for a few moments to take a look at a quick combination of two-string chords. Barre finger 1 across the top five strings at fret 8, ensuring that your thumb is also behind fret 8. Strike the 4th and 5th strings, then swiftly shift the barre to fret 7 and strum the same two strings again. Release the left hand finger just enough to allow a clear strum together of the open G and D strings. As before, shift the left hand during the open string chord. Repeat the entire process again, mute the strings at the quaver rest, then end the 1st bar with a single open D.

Get the barre ready over fret 8 during the open string chord.

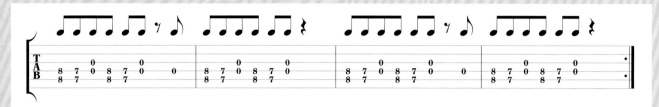

The second half of the chorus

Here's a chance to link up some concepts covered in the previous three pieces, as well as introduce yet another slight variation on the verse chords in bars 5 to 8. Remember that the opening note should be placed with the 1st finger barre, and to have fingers 2 and 3 shaped up for the chord shuffle that immediately follows. At the end of bar 3, an open D string presents a fractional space for the left hand to move up to fret 8.

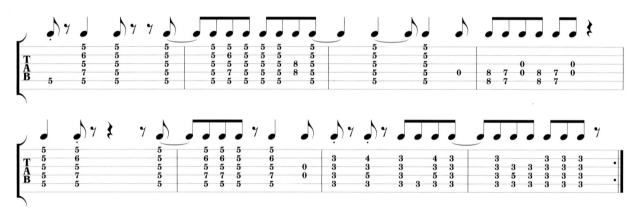

Final exercise

Tied rhythm values throw the downbeats into confusion in this final practice piece, so be ready to count very carefully. The good news is that the majority of the chords are simply the barre at fret 3, which you'll recall is the chord of B♭ major. The only change occurs on the first new strum of bars 2 and 4, where the addition of fingers 2 and 3 results in a brief E♭/B♭ colouring. After the repeat of bars 1 to 4, shift the finger barre up to the 5th fret for a sustained final C major chord.

A reminder of the finger barre at fret 3.

The E♭/B♭ chord returns in bars 2 and 4.

EXPANDING YOUR RHYTHM GUITAR SKILLS

Discover an elegantly crafted accompaniment to On And On *by The Longpigs as you work through this session's exercises.*

Throughout the practice pieces, you'll find examples of an accompanying style built on strummed chords in partnership with decorative single-note lines. These melodic strands take the chord shape as their starting point and often use hammer-ons from open strings as an effective embellishment.

Getting started with G major

This session features the four-fingered version of G major. Place the chord and hold it throughout this piece. Concentrate on the plectrum work; use light, wristy strokes and make contact only with the strings marked on the TAB. Play the bottom two strings at the start of bar 1, then follow this with a pair of five-string downstrums. The three-string upstrums take the plectrum back to the bass string for the next stroke.

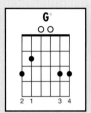

The key chord of G major.

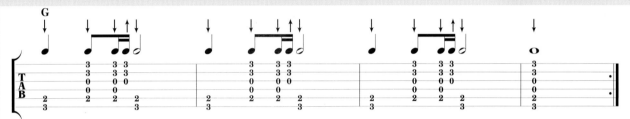

Adding hammer-ons

During the hammer-ons, aim to leave as much of the G chord in place as you can. For the A string hammer-on, release finger 1, then play the open string. Hammer finger 1 back into place at fret 2, then strike the open D string. As you play the 2nd open D, release finger 1 and move it across to hammer-on at fret 2 on the D string. A downstrum of the B and G strings together completes each of bars 1 to 3, while bar 4 ends with a full G major strum.

Remove finger 1 to begin each hammer-on.

Hammer finger 1 onto the D string.

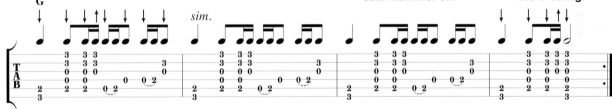

Introducing D minor

For the D minor chord, a low, vertical thumb positioned behind finger 2 should help you to achieve a good shape. Start by downpicking the 4th and 3rd string notes of D minor, before moving into a down-down-upstrum of the top three strings. This time it's the turn of your 2nd finger to create the hammer-ons, but remember to keep fingers 1 and 3 in the same place. Return to a full G chord shape for the notes in bar 4.

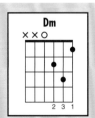

The D minor chord.

Integrating G and D minor

In this exercise you need to alternate between G major and D minor chords. We have covered most of the content already, apart from the opening of bar 3, where the G major chord is given a slightly different treatment. At this point, continue to place the full chord shape, then stroke the bottom E and D strings separately. The two G chords that follow require four strings instead of the five used on previous occasions. The strum directions are the same as before.

Hammer-on finger 2 in bars 2 and 4.

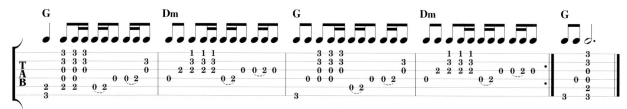

Preparing the D minor chord change

The shift from G major to D minor is prepared in a way you have studied before. For the last strum in bar 1, and again in bar 3, release finger 4 for an open top E string. If, at the same time, you release all but finger 3, you can give yourself a little extra time to shape the fingers for the D minor chord in bars 2 and 4. Otherwise, be sure to keep a G major chord in place throughout bars 1 and 3, but this time pay particular attention to the altered strum and picking pattern.

Finger tip

A STATIC 3RD FINGER

The shift between G major and D minor chords is simplified if you always keep finger 3 at fret 3 on the B string. This helps you to achieve sustain, as well as giving the left hand a useful point of reference while the other fingers change position.

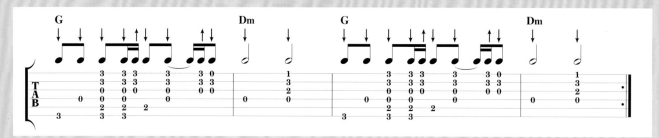

An inventive link to G major

The link referred to, which takes you from D minor to G major, occurs only twice in the session but it's a moment of creativity that's worth storing up for the future. As you play the open D string on the 4th beat of bar 2, release the D minor shape. Always be sure to keep the fingers hovering near to the strings, ready for new tasks. Swiftly place finger 1 on the B string at fret 1. By keeping your 3rd finger stretched out over fret 3, the replacement of this finger for the final strum of bar 2 should present no major problems. Use a down-up-down-up plectrum combination for these four semiquavers of bar 2.

Move finger 1 to the B string at the end of bar 2.

Change to finger 3 for the last chord of bar 2.

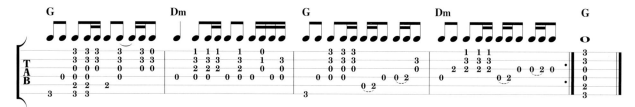

136

Shifting to C major

Play the notes and strums built on a fixed G chord in bar 1. There are two ways of approaching the chord change in bar 2. If you are confident of your ability, the best option is to place the full C chord as a unit. However, since the first two notes of bar 2 are picked separately, you can instead build the shape one finger at a time. The hammer-ons work in the same way as for the D minor chord, but notice the B string pull-off at the end of bar 2. As you release finger 1, make sure that you also release the rest of the C chord.

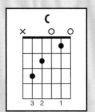

The C major chord in bars 2 and 4.

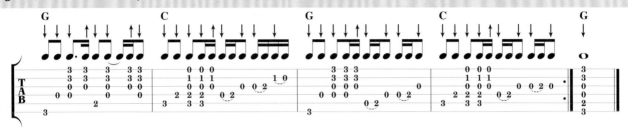

The end of the verse

Most of bar 1 is based on the G chord, with finger 1 providing the first hammer-on and finger 2 the second. The bar ends with a change to finger 1 at fret 1 on the B string. For F major, add fingers 3 and 2 to the D and G strings, and collapse finger 1 to cover both the top E and B strings. A minor is an old favourite, but check the photo and chord box if in doubt.

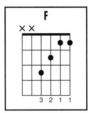

The four-string F major chord begins bar 2.

A minor also features briefly in bar 2.

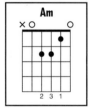

More new chord shapes

G6/B is formed by releasing fingers 2 and 4 of the G chord. B is the bass note, so avoid contact with the bottom E string. The next new chord is Cadd9, for which you can leave finger 3 in place. The upstrum of Cadd9 contains only three strings, as do all the upstrummed chords in this exercise. Continue to hold finger 3 in place as you lift fingers 1 and 2 back onto the bottom two strings, also adding finger 4 to return to G major.

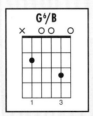

G6/B is closely related to the G chord.

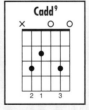

Cadd9 with an open top E string.

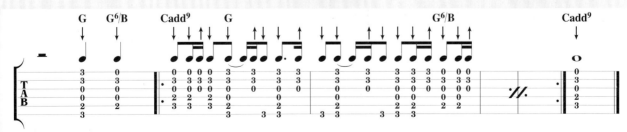

Incorporating D major

Finger 3 can remain in position throughout.
Another consistent feature is to use an upstrum
wherever a three-string chord is written and
downstrums for all other chords. A single G6/B
breaks up the Cadd9 chords in bar 1, while the
first half of bar 2 is built on the familiar D major
chord shape. The full downstrum of G major in
bar 2 is anticipated by the formation of the top
part of the chord on the preceding upstrum.

Release all but finger 3 at
the end of bars 1 and 3.

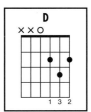

D major is used for
the first time in bar 2.

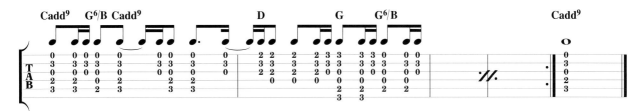

First chorus exercise

Provided the last two breakdowns felt comfortable,
you should experience few problems linking them
together to form most of the chorus. Bars 1 to 5
are identical to the new chord shape exercise,
followed by a straightforward join to the above

sequence. The fun starts with the extraordinary
single $\frac{5}{8}$ bar, almost unheard of in rock music. Try
to count in quavers as you make swift changes
between Cadd9, an isolated appearance of E minor
using fingers 1 and 2, and a single strum of D major.

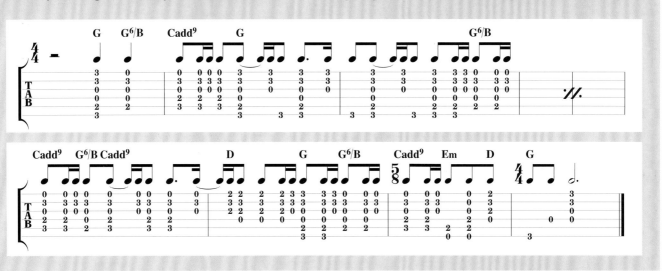

A change of harmony

After the first chorus, the accompaniment reverts to a repeated two-bar
phrase from the intro followed by eight bars identical to those used in
verse 1. The second half of verse 2, however, is supported by a different
sequence of chords altogether. The good news is that all four chords,
including the new A7sus4, should fall nicely under your fingers provided
you keep finger 3 static. Don't forget to release finger 4 for the D chords,
to add a 4th finger to the top of the Cadd9 chords and to pre-empt the
return to G major at the end of bars 2 and 4.

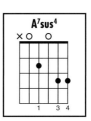

A7sus4 in bars 1 and 3.

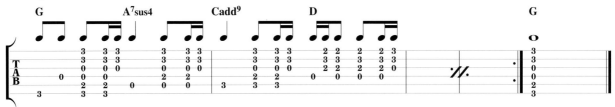

Second chorus exercise

There are similarities between this altered second chorus accompaniment and the music rehearsed in the previous piece. One difference is the two semiquavers followed by a quaver figure on beats 1 and 3 of bars 1 to 4. Keep the single bass notes light and always aim to let the right arm swing evenly down and up to help achieve a precise rhythm.

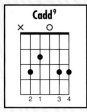

Cadd9 with finger 4 on the top E string.

Prepare for G major at the end of bars 2 and 4.

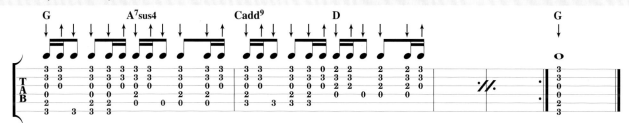

Fattening up the sound

The second chorus is extended by a barrage of fully strummed chords. D major from previous pieces is altered to include fret 3 on the top E string, turning the chord into Dsus4. This means that fingers 3 and 4 can stay in the same place for the entire section. The best strum pattern is that used above, but be careful not to upstrum through bass strings that are not part of the chord. Where necessary, you could wrap the thumb over the top of the neck to mute these unwanted bottom strings.

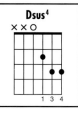

Dsus4 keeps fingers 3 and 4 on the top two strings.

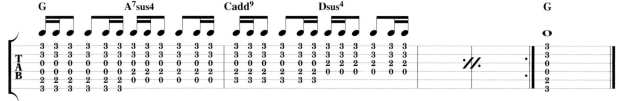

Double pull-offs

Release fingers 1 and 2 of G major as you move into the A7sus4 half of bar 1, and use finger 1 for the D string hammer-on. In bar 2, adding finger 2 on the A string gives you Cadd9. As you strike the open D string in bar 2, release all except finger 3. Use finger 2 for the hammer-on, giving you the fingering for the two-note chord that follows. As you play this, move finger 1 to the B string at fret 1, then release finger 3 for the pull-off. For the double pull-offs, marked with curved, dotted lines above and below, simply release fingers 1 and 2 after the plectrum stroke. The result should be a pair of open string notes.

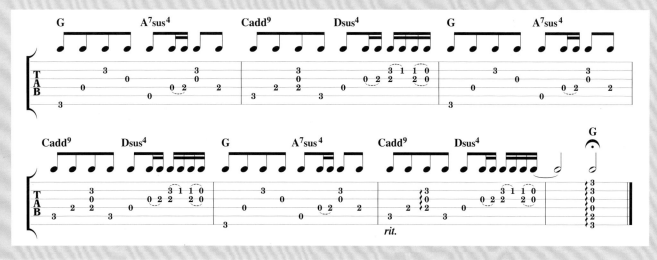

139

STRENGTHENING THE FINGER BARRE

The one-finger power chord introduced earlier returns to dominate a gutsy accompaniment to The Bartender And The Thief *by Stereophonics.*

This session's practice pieces use dropped D tuning. Dropped tuning involves lowering the pitch of the bottom string down to D.

Power chords can be played in this tuning as well: all you need to do is simply barring finger 1 across the lower strings.

Moving between 5th and 3rd position

For G5add11, barre finger 1 across fret 5 and strike the four lowest strings. Release the barre but use finger 1 again for the fret 3 notes on the bottom string. From here, if you have the correct hand shape, finger 3 should be ideally situated for the fret 5 notes, while the open strings help you to return the barre to 5th position.

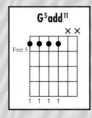

For G5add11, lie finger 1 across fret 5.

Lift the barre as you play fret 3.

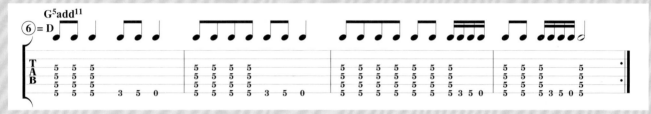

An extraordinary-sounding chord

F5#11 is based on the standard three-string power chord, albeit placed with a finger barre rather than with fingers 1, 3 and 4. This was also true of G5add11 in the previous piece, but the clash of the sharpened 11th degree above the bottom string note makes for an intentionally brutal clash of sound this time. Use finger 1 as a barre across fret 3 and place finger 2 at fret 4 on the G string. The top two strings should not be heard.

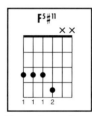

F5#11 is easier to play than its name suggests.

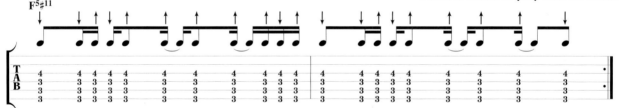

Preparing the riff

One of the main features of *The Bartender And The Thief* is the riff that regularly punctuates the vocal lines of the verses. With the aid of a couple of pull-offs, it's actually easier to play than it might sound. For now, you have to use only finger 1 for the 3rd fret notes, while the others are all open strings.

Start the pull-off at fret 3.

The last note of bar 2.

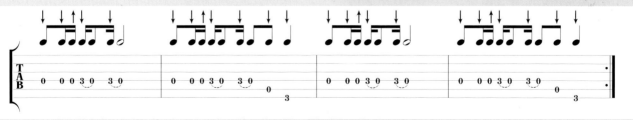

The complete riff

To finish off the riff started in the previous piece, you need two open A notes instead of just the one before falling to fret 3 on the de-tuned bottom string. Since these are now semiquavers, the 5th string notes follow swiftly on from the second pull-off. As before, use finger 1 for the 3rd fret note on the lowest string and leave it in place as you add finger 3 at fret 5 – you'll find this the easiest method of returning to fret 3 for the next note. An open bottom D string completes bar 1, while bar 2 is the same but without the final open D.

The plectrum strokes the open D string.

Leave finger 1 in place and add finger 3.

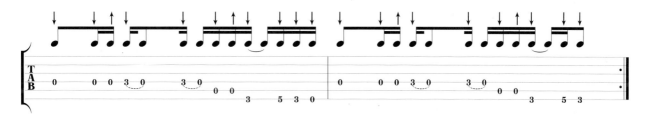

Pure power chords

So far, the song's verse switches between F5#11 and the riff from the exercise above. Now it's time to introduce a new idea for the pre-chorus. Three-string power chords are the driving force, with the dropped D tuning resulting in a straightforward fingering. Every note can be placed by finger 1, barring either fret 8 for Bb5 or fret 5 for G5. As on earlier pieces, a lighter contact with the upper strings has a muting effect, allowing you to go for your strums of the regular, half-bar repeating rhythm pattern.

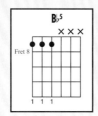

The Bb5 chord using only your 1st finger.

Shift the barre down three frets for G5.

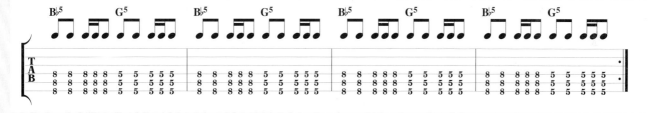

Setting up the chorus

Just before the chorus, the Bb and G power chords give way to a chunky sequence of 4th string pull-offs. There are five pull-offs in all, still occurring between the 1st finger at fret 3 and the open string, as on earlier tracks. Each pair of notes is followed by another open 4th string, this time struck with the plectrum, while the rhythm stays in even semiquavers. After four repeats of bars 1 and 2, the piece closes on the first chord of the chorus, an open strum of the bottom three strings, which equates to D5.

Finger tip

A DUAL ROLE FOR THE FINGER BARRE

Make a firm contact with the strings you want to hear, but aim for lighter finger pressure across the remaining strings. You can now go for your strums, confident that the unwanted strings are muted.

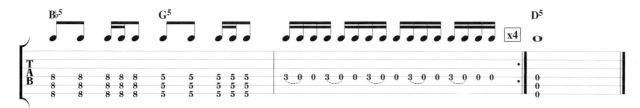

Open string power chords

An open strum of the bottom three strings results in a D power chord. D5 pairs up with the G5 shape of the pre-chorus, so keep the finger barre close over fret 5 when it's not in use. It's worth muting the top three strings of D5 with the left hand in case you strum too far. As you work through this chorus sequence, you should recognize the rhythm figure you played in the session's second exercise.

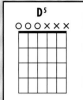

Strum the three open bottom strings for D5.

The barre is ready over fret 5 for G5.

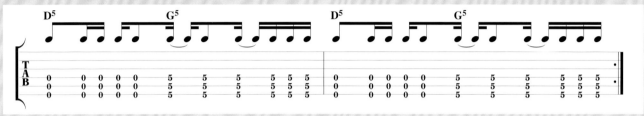

Starting the solo

The solo adds a new idea with falling B string notes providing a simple melody. Keep the finger barre at fret 3 for most of the piece, including the single fret 3 notes that begin each bar. Add fingers 2 and 4 for the chord on beat 2, switching the 4th finger for finger 3 on the 3rd beat. With the barre and finger 2 still in place, release finger 3 and you have the last chord shape for each of bars 1 to 3. At the end of bar 4, use finger 1 to slide quickly down the bottom string from fret 12.

Start with a barre at fret 3. **Add fingers 2 and 4.**

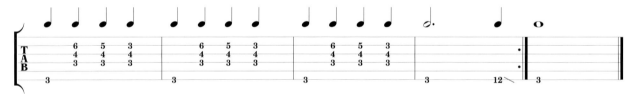

Adding the appropriate rhythm

The crotchet movement of the previous piece is replaced by the authentic rhythm of the solo. Like the chorus, it's very much based on a pattern first used in the verse earlier on, only this time the first and last notes of the one-bar figure are more sustained. The note values look different due to the inclusion of short rests, which can be achieved by slightly releasing the string pressure under the left fingers. Apart from this, the left hand approach is virtually the same as for the previous piece.

Finger 3 replaces finger 4 on the B string at fret 5.

The finger barre takes care of the fret 3 notes on the B string.

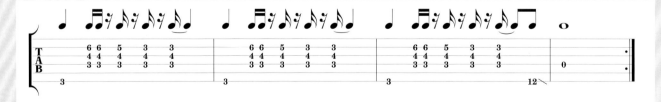

142

Two variations of the riff

This exercise isolates the two slight variants of the riff. The first difference occurs at the end of bar 1, where the fret 3 note on the A string is best played with finger 1. In bar 2, follow the two open A notes with a rapid slide of finger 1 from fret 3 up to fret 12. Leave the fret 12 note ringing for most of the 4th beat before sliding the finger back down the string. Reduce the finger pressure as you slide back down so that the note appears to run smoothly into the open 4th string as you repeat.

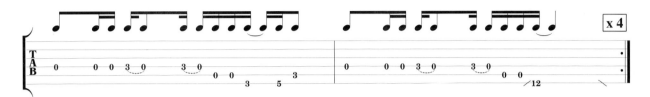

The entire solo

This piece brings together the 3rd fret barre chords with the riff and its variations rehearsed above. Remember that it's best not to remove the barre in bars 1 and 2, but if you can adjust the finger pressure to mute in turn the bottom string and then the three-string chords, this should create some space and clarity. Finger 4 can help by muting the top string as it frets the B string. Look out for a new development at the end, as the fret 12 slide falls onto a finger-barred fret 8 power chord.

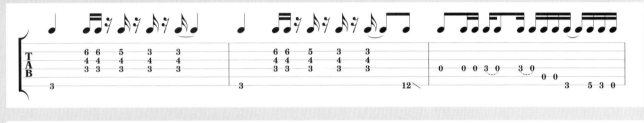

One last lead figure

There's a tasty bit of lead playing through the outro, as the guitar pretty much follows the vocal line. It's an opportunity to step away from using the finger barre in favour of a one-finger-per-note policy. With your left hand in 5th position, use finger 3 for any fret 7 notes and finger 1 at fret 5 on both the top E and B strings. The plectrum directions marked should help you deal with the fast tempo, while the rhythm is borrowed from earlier material.

The outro solo begins at fret 7.

Use finger 1 for the top string notes.

The finished outro

To complete the outro, all that remains is to adjust the second half of bars 2 and 4. Use finger 3 to play a single 7th fret note on the G string, followed by finger 1 at fret 4 on the same string. This requires a temporary extension of the hand shape down one fret further than normal, but try to keep your hand movement to a minimum. Follow the fret 4 note with a return of finger 3 to fret 7, only this time on the D string. The rhythm of these notes in bars 2 and 4 is tricky, especially as there is a subtle difference in the placement of the final note each time.

Reach back with finger 1 to fret 4.

Use finger 3 to return at fret 7 on the D string.

The final bar

The last notes of this piece are unrelated to anything that has come before but make for an inventive conclusion. You'll be jumping down from fret 7 to fret 3 for the opening note, so it's easiest to use finger 1 for all the fretted action. The last plectrum stroke of each bar is on the fret 3 chord – after this, you should just let the finger slide and the pull-off create the other sounds.

Begin with finger 1 at fret 3.

Sliding the finger barre up to fret 12.

Stereophonics, from l to r: Kelly Jones, Stuart Cable and Richard Jones.

THE INFLUENTIAL STYLE OF BUDDY HOLLY

Put together a blend of country, pop and R&B to mimic the style of Buddy Holly.

This session's practice pieces, preparing for *That'll Be The Day* by Buddy Holly, have a swinging jazz/Blues rhythm and require a capo at fret 5. For neatness, the capo position and swing rhythm symbols occur on the TAB only for the very first exercise, but you should apply them to all the practice pieces.

A vintage lick

With the capo at fret 5, slide finger 3 from fret 3 above the capo up to fret 4 on the G string. Leave this note ringing as you play the two open strings that follow using upstrokes. Slip finger 3 back to fret 3 on beat 3, which leaves finger 2 as the best choice for the 2nd fret note. Listen for the Bluesy effect of the open two-string chord that ends bar 1 as you place fingers 1 and 2 together for the E chords of bar 2.

Slide finger 3 to fret 4 above the capo.

The four-string E chord shape in bar 2.

The B7 chord

You can complete the intro by adding the B7 chord shape to the end of the figure rehearsed above. After the two-string E chord at the start of bar 2, release the left hand fingers and play the open D and G strings together. Make the B7 chord by lifting the E chord shape up one string and adding finger 3 at fret 2 on the G string. An open B string completes the chord, which is strummed three times.

Finger 2 at fret 2 on the G string.

The B7 chord.

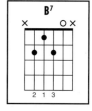

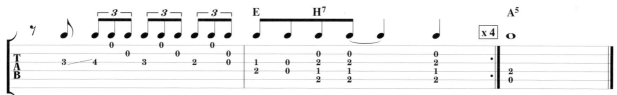

A boogie-woogie back-up

Originally synonymous with the left hand work of boogie-woogie pianists, this style of accompaniment is often used to support the vocal line in rock'n'roll music. You played the notes of this piece in an earlier session, so you should find it straightforward. It's easier and smoother if you leave finger 1 in place and then add and release finger 3 from the 4th fret notes.

The opening A5 position.

E5 with finger 3 added for a boogie-woogie shuffle.

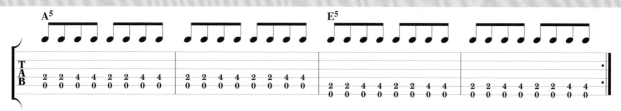

Palm muting the accompaniment

The lightness of Buddy Holly's accompaniment comes from palm muting the shuffling chords. Drop the right side of the right hand lightly onto the strings just before the bridge to achieve a muffled sound that still allows the pitch of the notes to be heard. Only lift the right hand from this position to play the bar 4 chords. After a quaver rest, strum B7 twice, avoiding the top string. Follow this with the conventional open position form of E major, although the associated two open top strings are not included.

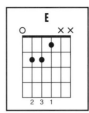

The E chord but the two top strings are not played.

The right hand palm mutes the strings.

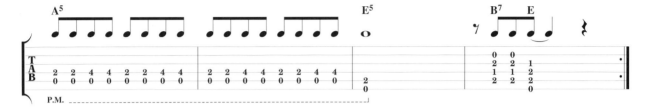

The F# major chord

Most of the guitar part is built around the swinging quavers that dominate the two previous pieces. The other important rhythm figure is the even stream of triplet quavers featured in this exercise and in the intro, which results in faster strums. To form F# major, place a full E barre chord shape in 2nd position. Avoid the top string when strumming because it's not possible on this occasion to mute the string.

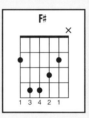

F# major uses the E barre chord shape.

More triplet strumming

The palm muted chords based on A5 and E5 in the first two bars are straightforward enough. However, the F# and B7 chords combine to give you a tricky shift of hand position to deal with. Aim for a neat release of the right hand from the bridge to allow the chords in bars 3 and 4 to ring fully. With finger 1 already positioned over fret 2, placing the F# chord is not too hard. There are no common fingerings as you shift to B7, so the best you can do is focus on the position you wish to shift to and then go for it.

Finger tip

SIMPLIFYING A QUICK CHORD CHANGE
At the end of bar 2 of this exercise, release finger 1 from fret 2 as you place finger 3 at fret 4 on the A string. You can now stretch out the barre in readiness for the F# chord. Keep the common 3rd finger location as you place the rest of F# major.

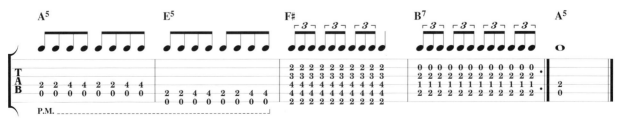

Triplet crotchets

The 'repeat previous bar' sign relates to the first play-through of this bar, while the floating triplet rhythm pattern should be adopted when you return to it after the guitar solo. It's a memorable moment in the song, as the rhythm apparently drags its heels due to the use of slower triplet crotchets instead of swinging quavers. Listening to the original should give you the idea, particularly as you are helped by the rest of the band, who play along with you using the same rhythm.

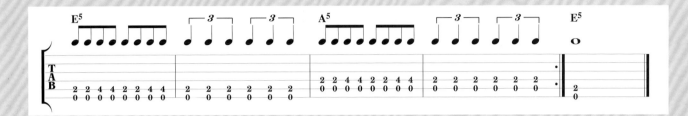

Solo, part one

Things hot up as you begin a demanding solo, made more complex by the speed of the triplet notes in the opening bars. You begin on the 6th quaver beat of the bar with a series of three-string E major chords. After these, it's single notes all the way, starting with finger 3 at fret 3 on the top E string. From the 3rd beat of the first full bar, use finger 2 as you slide swiftly from fret 2 up to fret 4 and then slide in measured fashion back down again to fret 2 a few notes later.

Start with finger 1 on the G string.

Finger 2 slides up to fret 4.

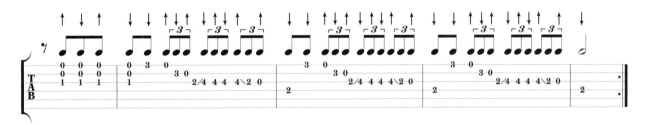

Adding weight to the solo

Start bar 1 with finger 2 on the D string. Aim to have finger 3 pulled back towards the top E string in preparation for the following 3rd fret note. Instead of sliding back down the G string, as in the previous piece, you should leave finger 2 at fret 4 and also place finger 1 at fret 3 on the B string. Further weight is given to the solo as you add finger 3 to the top string at fret 4. Count your strums carefully in the 4th time bar so that you release the chord in time to play the open D string that precedes the final A5 chord.

Finger 2 is best for the opening note.

The three-string E7 shape in bars 2 and 3.

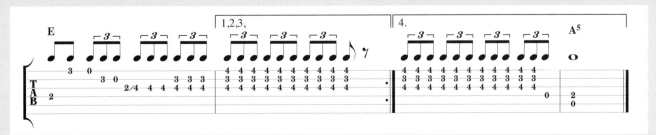

Sliding the three-string chords

Here's a chance to link together the parts of the solo covered so far. This involves no new material until the start of the 4th full bar. At this point, you can see that there are finger slide lines before each group of triplets. Although these aren't essential, they do give a touch of panache and authenticity to your performance. The effect is created by starting each triplet with the left hand fingers a fret lower, and then very quickly sliding them into the marked position. The last four bars are virtually a note-for-note repeat of the fourth piece.

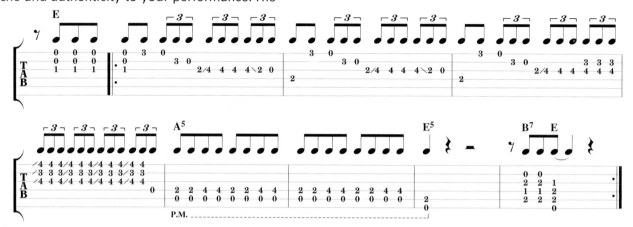

Alternating bass and treble strings

The alternate switching between bass and treble notes in bar 4 of this piece is a technique Buddy Holly borrowed from country and western music. With finger 2 on the A string and finger 3 on the top E string, both at fret 2, the plectrum alternates between down- and upstrokes for these last four notes. Despite the continuation of the P.M. bracket beneath the notes, mute only the bass notes and let the top strings ring fully.

The open A string with finger 1 kept close above.

Swap to finger 2 from the last note of bar 3.

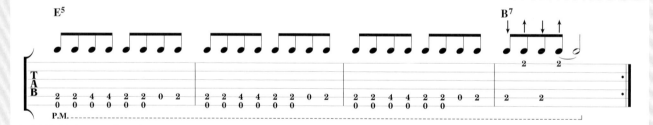

More country picking

The alternating bass and treble string style introduced in the previous piece is often referred to as 'country picking'. After beginning with the same four notes that ended the piece above, replace these with finger 1 on the D string. The photo shows fingers 1, 2 and 4 in position for the notes of the broken A7 chord in bar 2. Continue to alternate between up- and downstrokes to help with the string crossing, except for the pair of downstrokes that end bars 2 and 4.

Finger 1 on the D string at fret 1.

Hold the A7 shape throughout bars 2 and 4.

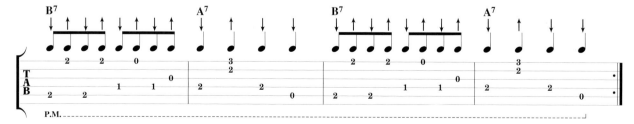

Completing the solo

Use the single open A string in bar 4 to prepare finger 2 for the next 2nd fret note. This sets you up for the country picking of bar 5. The A7 bar continues in swing quavers, and the three left hand fingers release half way through bar 6 for the open A and B string notes. Fingers 1 and 2 are best for the 2nd fret chord that follows, while the open strings then give you time to prepare the turnaround, which is similar to that used in the intro.

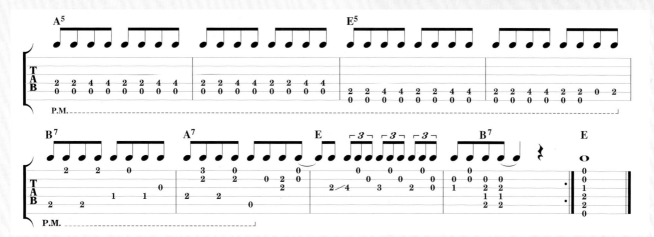

Barring the A shape

The closing stages of *That'll Be The Day* move from shuffling two-string chords to more solid A and E chord shapes. After the first two chords, release finger 1 from the G string and use it to barre the top four strings at fret 2. At the end of bar 2, move the barre to fret 1 in order to slide back up to the A chord shape without re-striking it with the plectrum.

The A chord shape using the 1st finger barre.

A single fret 3 note in bar 5.

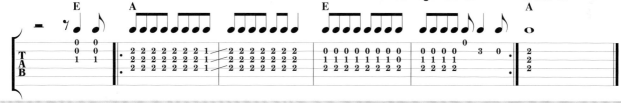

A classic Blues ending

Bars 1 to 3 are modelled on the A and E chord shapes of the previous piece. In bar 2, finger 2 makes for the easiest change to the top string at fret 3. The chromatic fall of fingers 1 and 2 in the 1st and 2nd time bars is pure Blues and wraps up the song nicely when followed by a full strum of E major.

Slide fingers 1 and 2 from 3rd position...

...through 2nd position to 1st position.

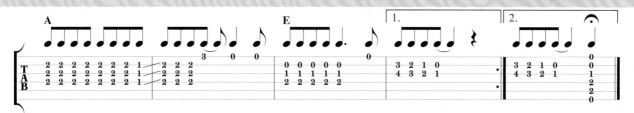

149

RIFFING AND STRUMMING

Fine-tune a host of playing techniques as you work your way through the practice pieces for one of Sheryl Crow's Grammy-winning hits.

The intricate riffing used to accompany the verses of *There Goes The Neighborhood* by Sheryl Crow puts plenty of skills through their paces, including muting with either hand, hammer-ons, pull-offs and slides. As a capo is used, so attach yours at fret 1 for all the relevant exercises.

Percussive muting

For the early practice pieces in this session, it's not the notes themselves that will require most of your attention. Instead, the difficulty lies in the different right hand muting techniques you need to employ. The E major chord notes in this introductory piece are no exception. The staccato marking on the 1st beat of each of the first three bars makes it necessary to damp the sound swiftly with the side of the right hand.

The percussive muting on the 2nd beat, indicated by the crosses on the bottom two strings, is best achieved by keeping the right hand firmly across the strings as you strike them with the plectrum. You should release the right hand from the strings for a clean two-string chord on beat 3, but then damp the chord to observe the rest on the 4th beat.

Percussive muting with the right hand.

Leave the E major chord in place.

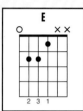

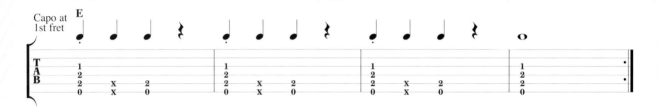

Developing the riff

To continue building the E chord riff, you need to condense the above material from three beats to two. To do this, simply change the percussive mute and two-string chord into quavers. For the hammer-on that follows this condensed material, retain fingers 1 and 3 of the E chord and lift finger 2 off the A string. After the open A is struck, hammer finger 2 back into position and then strike the D and A strings together. Observe the quaver rest by stopping any string sound using the side of the right hand. With the full E major shape still in place, play the bottom E string only. Repeat the process in bars 2 and 3, but with open D and A strings to end bar 3. At this point, release the E chord fingering in favour of a fret 3 bottom string played with finger 3.

Preparing the hammer-on.

Use finger 3 in bar 4.

WHY USE A CAPO?

You may wonder why people bother to use a capo to make a song just one semitone higher. The answer usually lies with the singer, for whom that slight rise in pitch can make all the difference to their interpretation.

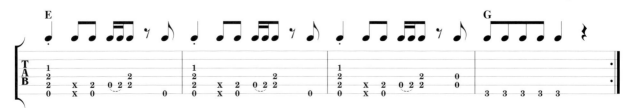

A variety of G chord shapes

There are three different G related chords in this piece, but none of them is the standard G major that you are familiar with. Begin with finger 3 on the bottom E string, played together with the open D and G strings. Allow finger 3 to fall across the A string to damp out its sound. Leave finger 3 in place as you hammer finger 2 onto fret 2, and also as you replace finger 2 with finger 1 on the B string for the Gsus4 shape. For G/F#, use your 2nd finger to place the bottom string note and to mute the A string.

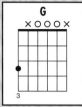
The G chord.

Finger 2 hammers-on.

The G/F# shape.

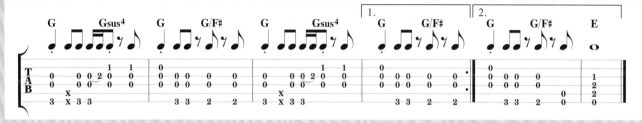

Another G chord treatment

This exercise focuses on a variation of the musical content of the previous piece. It begins in exactly the same way, but watch out for the additional open B strings on the central chords in bars 1 and 3. Release finger 1 as you move into bars 2 and 4, leaving just your 3rd finger on the bottom E string at fret 3. Briefly release finger 3 for the open strings that end bars 2 and 4, but keep the finger close to the bottom string so that it is easy to replace again.

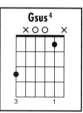
Gsus4 as it is used in the 1st and 3rd bars.

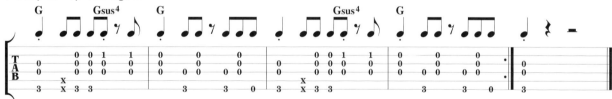

Putting the verse together

This piece combines the verse segments rehearsed so far. To start off, slide finger 1 down the bottom E string from fret 16 to a lightly struck open string. Quickly land the E shape for bars 2 and 3, then link up as smoothly as you can to the sequence rehearsed above. When tackling the Gsus4 shapes, it's worth collapsing finger 1 across the top E string to stop this string sounding accidentally. Also, keeping your left thumb high will help the fingers to lie flatter across the strings, which aids the muting process.

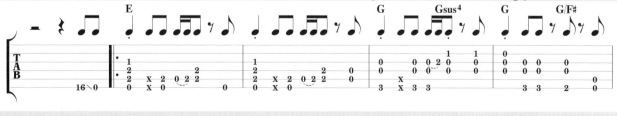

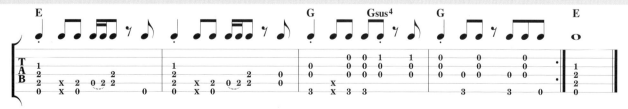

A new phase

A major and Asus(9) dominate the remainder of the verse. The TAB for A major should look familiar, despite the lack of a top-string note, since it's a pattern you've used before in *Play Guitar*. What is more unusual is the use of a finger barre to place all the fretted notes. The reason becomes clear when you add fingers 2 and 3 to the B and G strings to form Asus(9). In contrast to all that has come before, aim for a smooth sound with no muting.

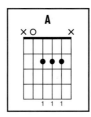

Place the A chord by barring fret 2.

Keep the barre for Asus(9).

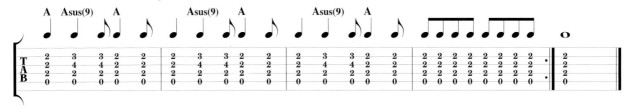

Decorating C major

As with many of the shapes in this session, C major does not include the top string. This concentration on a range that is lower than usual emphasizes the G and A chord suspensions and contrasts well with the full chords strummed in the forthcoming chorus. As you place C major, try to mute the top E string with a collapsed 1st finger. It's also helpful to mute the bottom E string by wrapping the thumb over the top of the neck. Release finger 2 where open D strings are used to add colour to the C chords.

A standard C major shape.

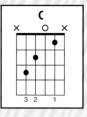

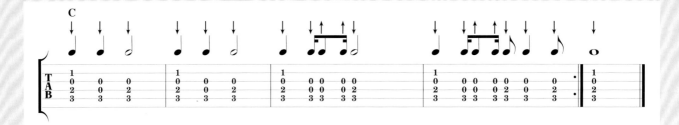

A fiddly C chord lick

The opening bar combines A and C chords, effectively pasting together material from Tracks the new phase exercise and the previous piece. The shift from the barred A shape to C major is not easy, so you might need to spend a little time practising the left hand moves without adding any of the right hand rhythm complications. In bar 2, your 2nd finger skips between strings 4 and 3, while fingers 1 and 3 hold the C chord shape firm. The last of these fret 2 hops begins the only pull-off. The open-string chord that ends bar 2 is the point at which you should release fingers 1 and 3 in readiness for another barred A shape.

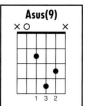

In bar 2, finger 2 moves over to the G string.

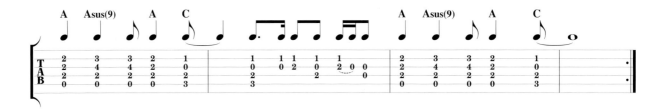

Completing the verse

Passages of the previous three pieces are forged together into the missing section of the verse. The combination of A, Asus(9) and C chords in bar 1 is a direct copy from the chord lick piece, while bar 2 is the same as the 4th bar of the C major one. Downstrums are ideal for most of the notes, but using upstrums on the 3rd and 4th chords in bar 2 and on the 2nd chord in bar 4 will help the right hand work remain relaxed. After a repeat of bars 1 to 4, use fingers 2 and 3 for the final E shape, which sets the scene for the start of the chorus.

Release finger 2 of C major in bar 2.

Use fingers 2 and 3 for the final chord.

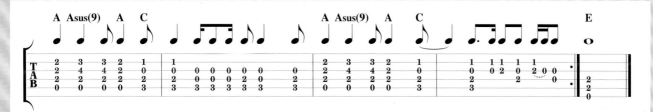

Constructing the chorus

The chorus is based on quite simple rhythms and chord shapes. To get you started, here's an alternate sequence of E and G shapes. The E major chord includes all six strings on the 3rd and 4th quavers of bars 1 and 3, so keep the fingers arched. Finger 3 makes a quick change across to the lowest note of the G chord. As in the verse, the same finger mutes the A string, allowing you to strum through the chord. Add finger 1 briefly for a sus4 colouring of the 5th quaver in bars 2 and 4.

The chorus uses full E strums.

A reminder of the G shape.

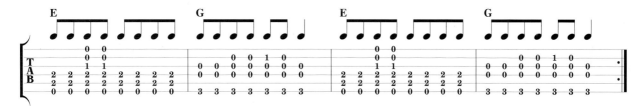

The Asus2 chord

The selection of an open B string instead of a fret 2 note turns A major into the more exotic Asus2 chord. To form Asus2 from the preceding C major chord, remove finger 1 and transfer finger 3 to the G string at fret 2. Create some melodic interest in bars 2 and 4

by strumming differing numbers of strings as marked on the TAB. Also, be alert to the release of finger 3 for the final two-string chords of bars 2 and 4. Use this moment to shape up the 3rd finger shift back to the A string for another volley of C chords.

Asus2 in bars 2 and 4.

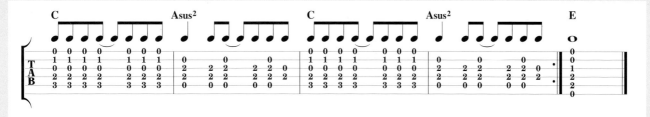

Tying up the chorus

Use smooth downstrums throughout the chorus, picking out the written number of strings carefully for the optimum effect. Although much of the rhythm is based on driving quavers, watch out for a few tied notes and the occasional crotchet. The abbreviated form of G chord needed in bar 2 makes for an easier change to C major, particularly as finger 1 ought to be hovering over the B string at fret 1 after its brief sus4 action on the 5th quaver of bar 2. For bar 6, quickly switch to a finger barre or the Asus(9) will be stranded.

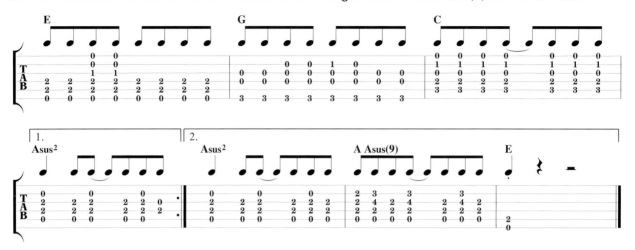

A touch of wah-wah

This brief two-bar phrase features in the instrumental break at the centre of *There Goes The Neighborhood*. Place the left hand in 4th position, from where fingers 1 and 3 can comfortably place the notes at frets 4 and 6. Although it's only a subtle difference, see if you can put more weight behind the second hammer-on of finger 3 to help emphasize the first beat of bars 2 and 4. If you play electric guitar and happen to have a wah-wah pedal at your disposal, try using it here.

Finger 1 plays the opening note.

Use finger 3 for the fret 6 notes.

A variant of the verse riff

This session ends with a pared-down version of the verse riff studied earlier. A slide of finger 1 down from fret 10 frees up fingers 2 and 3 to form the E shape required at the start of bar 2. Observe the staccato markings by stifling the sound of the opening chords in bars 2 to 6, but make a point of letting the open bottom E, hammered-on A string note and fret 2 D string note overlap. A right hand mute creates the quaver rest that follows. Remember to add finger 1 for the final chord.

Start with a slide down from fret 10.

Release finger 2 of the E shape to begin the hammer-ons.

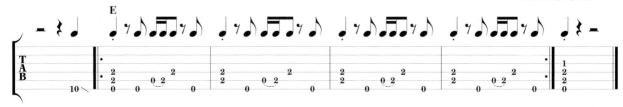

DOUBLE STRING BENDS

Liven up your lead playing by bending two strings at the same time.

The arrangement of *Staying Out For The Summer* by Dodgy takes sections of both the lead and rhythm guitars from the original song and fuses them into a single part of great diversity. A swinging riff, solid strumming and two contrasting solos are broken down into easy exercise pieces in this session.

Setting up the main riff

Notice the rhythm symbol at the start of this piece – it indicates that your quavers will have to swing in this and all of the exercises that follow. The riff begins with fingers 2 and 3 at fret 2. After the 3rd downstroke, release finger 3 for the open G upstroke. Keep finger 2 in place as you shift finger 3 to fret 3 on the A string, where it remains throughout bar 2. Bar 4 starts with finger 3, now on the bottom string at fret 3.

Fingers 2 and 3 together in bar 1.

Finger 3 moves to the A string in bar 2.

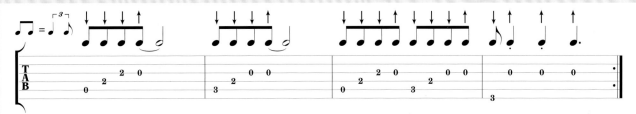

A new idea for the intro

After two bars identical to those practised above, return fingers 2 and 3 to the D and G strings for the notes that begin bar 3. Release the shape as finger 3 moves to the A string. It sounds better if you let this note ring as you play the open G and B strings. As you switch to your 2nd finger for the last note of bar 3, watch out for the tied note that carries over into bar 4.

G on the 6th string throughout bar 2.

Use the plectrum to mute the open strings in bar 2.

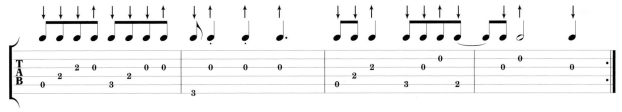

Revisiting the A minor chord

This chord shape ought to fall comfortably under your fingers by now. Use a high thumb to mute out the bottom E string. Provided you can still make the other five strings ring clearly, this hand position insures against accidental plectrum contact, and is bound to tidy up your performance. The strumming action should flow evenly down and up throughout – don't be tempted to stop the regular motion of the arm, particularly during the tied chords.

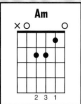
Hold A minor throughout this exercise.

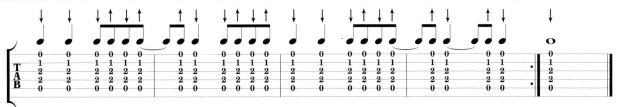

Adding C major to the strum pattern

For this exercise, you need to keep the strum pattern and rhythm of the previous piece, but add C major chords to the A minor shape. This is one of the easiest chord changes you'll come across. From A minor, simply release finger 3 from the G string and transfer it to the A string at the 3rd fret. Try to shift between the two chords without moving the thumb from its high position, where it mutes the bottom string.

Release finger 3 from A minor...

...and place it at fret 3 on the A string for C major.

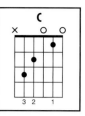

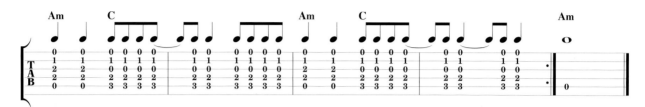

G major completes the sequence

This piece focuses on the change to the three-finger version of G major. For the final chord of bars 1 and 3, the left hand has to make a complex shift from C major to G major. The two chords have no common fingering, so you'll need pinpoint accuracy of hand movement for a swift change. The open string chord that ends bar 2 allows you to shape the A minor chord in readiness for bar 3. Bar 5 prepares the return in the Songbook to the riff rehearsed in the second piece, so use fingers 2 and 3 for the fretted notes.

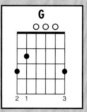

The three-fingered G major shape.

Prepare A minor at the end of bar 2.

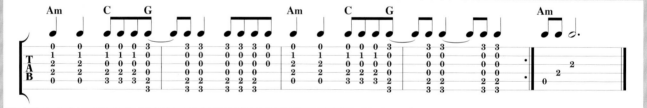

A variation on the opening riff

This repeating two-bar phrase is very similar to the first two bars of the second practice piece, although small differences set the phrases apart. First of all, there's no bottom E string note at the start of bar 2; and second, there's an extra open G on the last quaver of bar 2. This adds a third staccato note to bar 2 – remember to touch the pick quickly against the underside of the string for these notes.

Finger tip

SQUEAK-FREE SHIFTS
A common problem, particularly on acoustic guitars, is the high-pitched squeak that can accompany left hand finger shifts. It's hard to eliminate this entirely, but the effect can be reduced by lifting the fingers fractionally out from the strings as you move between notes.

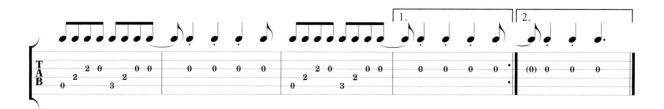

Introducing D minor 7

An extra strum of G major keeps the quavers going in bar 2, and more consecutive G strums fill in most of bar 4. A single strum of D minor 7 ends bar 4, where you might need to drop the thumb down so that both fret 1 notes can be placed with finger 1. Finger 2 is the conventional finger to use for the 3rd string note, but finger 3 can be used instead if it helps improve the sound of the chord.

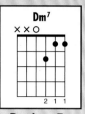

Barre finger 1 across fret 1 for D minor 7.

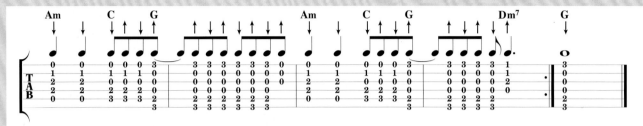

Alternating between G and D minor 7

The original song's chorus centres on these two chord shapes. Hold G major throughout bars 1 and 2, while concentrating on the new strum pattern. A crotchet beat at the end of bar 2 gives you a moment to change to D minor 7. Straight one-count strums of D minor 7 fill bar 7, while a sustained A minor strum in bars 8 and 9 rounds things off. Most of the chord work uses full up- as well as downstrums to create a stronger effect.

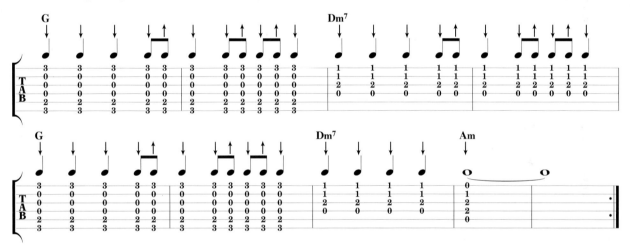

Octaves

D minor 7 now includes the open A string as its bass note, hence the new label of Dm7/A. In bars 3 and 4, you have to play a repeated three-string shape consisting of three D notes at different octaves. Use fingers 1 and 4, muting the B string with the underside of finger 1 so that you can strum through the top four strings.

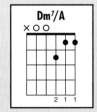

Dm7/A is strummed from the 5th string.

Octave Ds with the muted B string.

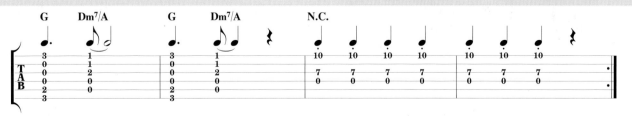

157

The first solo

The two solos that feature in *Staying Out For The Summer* could not be in sharper contrast to each other. The first one is a simple stream of single, held notes that work well on an acoustic but rely on the sustain of an overdriven electric guitar sound for their full impact. Start with finger 1 on the B string at fret 8. Slide the same finger down to fret 5 just before the opening beat of the 2nd bar. The easiest fingering option is to use finger 1 for most of the remaining notes, bearing in mind the slides that are an important trait of the solo. The exceptions are the 4th fret notes, which work well with finger 3.

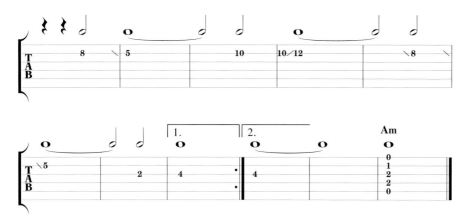

The opening note with finger 1.

A brief linking idea

The first chorus ends with an A minor chord, which is held for two bars. The end of the second chorus is extended by two bars, leaving just enough room for the understated solo figure that follows the A minor chord in this piece. One quaver rest is all the time you have to shift up to 8th position in bar 2. After playing fret 8 on the B string with finger 1, swiftly hammer-on then pull-off your 3rd finger. In bar 3, add finger 2 to the G string at fret 9. An open top E completes this higher-pitched form of the A minor chord.

Hammer finger 3 onto fret 10.

Add finger 2 after the pull-off for the bar 3 chord.

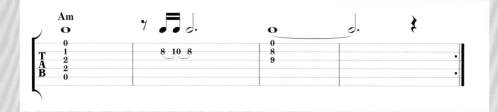

Fast triplet strumming

Despite the swing beat of this session's arrangement, triplet quavers feature only occasionally. The effect is even more dramatic because of this, and the rapid, alternately strummed G major chords of bar 3 make for a fine musical moment. The triplets are quick, but you should find them attainable, if you keep the right wrist loose and relaxed as you strum. Clip the final chord so that silence fills most of bar 4.

Mute all six strings to clip the final G chord.

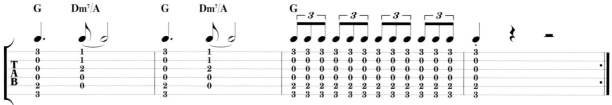

Double string bends

This new technique, which works on both electric and acoustic, involves bending two fretted notes at the same time. A double dotted bracket indicates the two-string bends, which are best executed using fingers 2 and 3 on the G and B strings, respectively. Strike the two strings, then push both of them upwards until their pitch is one semitone higher. As soon as this is achieved, damp the strings with the right hand and then release the bend. Use a barre at fret 5 for the two-string chords that follow, and finger 3 for the fret 7 notes on the D string.

Use fingers 2 and 3 to half-bend the strings.

Barre the B and G strings at fret 5.

A fiendish series of unison bends

This is the most demanding piece you've come up against so far in *Play Guitar*. Full bends, played with fingers 2 and 3 together for added strength, alternate with fret 10 notes on the B string played with finger 1. Apart from the opening D string bend, each of the others occurs on the G string. With finger 1 in place throughout, the bends result in a unison effect.

With finger 1 at the 10th fret...

...add a full bend of the G string for a unison effect.

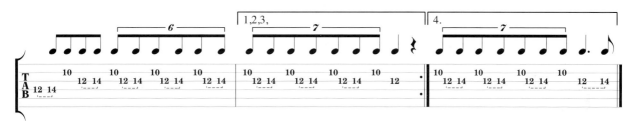

The downward bend

Although this piece is easy compared to the previous one, there's still a lot to think about. String bends and hammer-ons combine in the 1st bar, as well as a downward bend, also known as a pre-bend. The opening bend starts at the higher 14th fret and falls to fret 12. This is done by bending the string at fret 12 up to a 14th fret pitch before you strike the string. A quick release of the bend just after the string is struck results in a highly effective fall of the note. At the end of the 4th time bar, slide finger 1 down the D string. Neatly drop the finger across the B and G strings for the 5th fret notes that follow.

Start with a pre-bend of the G string at fret 12.

Follow the release bend with finger 1 at fret 9.

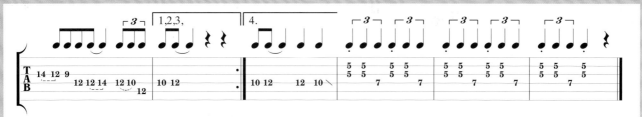

SHAPING A SOLO

Structure and development are vital aspects of a good guitar solo. This session's practice pieces will help you get to grips with a classic by Free.

One of the things you will learn with experience as a guitarist is how to build a long solo. *All Right Now* by Free perfectly demonstrates the art of soloing, starting low and sustained before building to a flurry of high notes at the climax. It also contains one of rock's best known riffs. There's no capo or swing rhythm to worry about in this session, which makes things fairly straightforward for the first few exercises.

The barred A chord shape

To get you started, this piece introduces the two left hand shapes that the riff is built on. Begin with an A major chord played by forming a barre with finger 1 across the top four strings at the 2nd fret. Strum down from the open A but make sure that you avoid striking the 1st string. Damp the sound after one beat – use right hand muting for all of this exercise's rests, which are crucial to the riff. With the barre still in place, play an open A, then add fingers 2 and 3 for the D shape that ends bar 1.

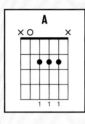

The opening A major chord.

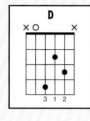

The D major shape.

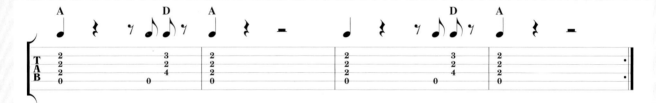

An exacting passage of right hand work

This piece continues to use the left hand shapes practised in the previous exercise. Positioning your hand as shown in the photos above will help to mute the two outer E strings. The main concern of this exercise is right hand control as you mix down- and upstrums of the 2nd, 3rd and 4th strings. Aim for a light, wristy action as you play the alternating semiquaver-quaver rhythm. A slight release of the left hand shape creates the quaver rests in bars 1 to 3, while allowing the open strings to carry on ringing.

About to strike the open A string.

Muting the A chords.

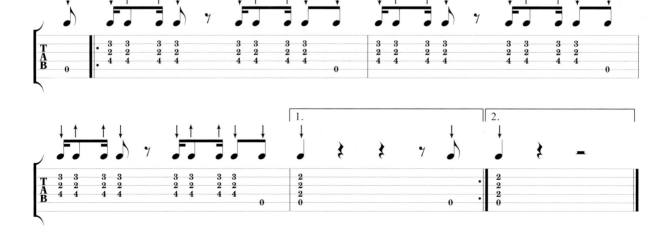

A classic riff

It's now time to have a go at playing one of the greatest rock riffs around. You might find that it's harder to play well than it looks on the page. The neater you are with the strumming and observation of the rests, the better your performance will be.

The tempo of this piece is slower than that of the original song, which will help you cope with the demands of the rhythm. Finally, remember to play this exercise four times (as shown by the 'x4' symbol) to help get the riff fully under control.

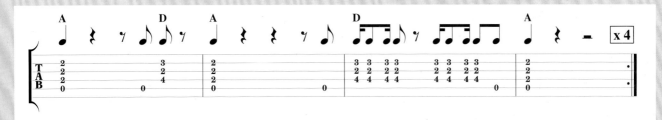

Beginning the chorus accompaniment

This exercise moves into a new phase with a shift of the left hand up to 7th position. Unusually, the fingering we recommend for the opening three-string A5 chords is fingers 1 and 4 for the fret 7 and fret 9 notes. This selection leaves finger 3 free to play fret 9 on the A string. The staccato dots indicate clipped chords, which are best executed with the side of the right hand. Move finger 1 across to the A string for the 4th beat of bars 1 to 3, and shift fingers 1 and 4 down to 5th position for the two-string G5 chords in bar 4.

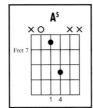

Fingers 1 and 4 in 7th position for A5.

Use finger 3 at fret 9 on the A string.

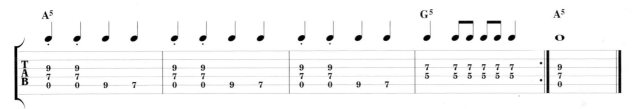

Muting the B string

For the second D chord shape of the session, it's important to make sure that you don't strum through to the B string – something that's all too easy to do. To insure against this, use finger 1 for the 4th string note and let this finger fall lightly against the B string. You might also find that the 4th finger automatically does the muting job for you as it places the fret 7 note on the G string. You should recognize the percussive mute symbols in bars 1 and 2 – for the purposes of this exercise, strike the B string on beats 3 and 4 to produce a definite click. Slip fingers 1 and 4 back up to 7th position for the final chord.

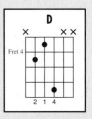

Another form of D major.

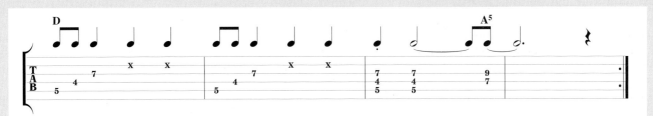

The first half of the chorus

Use fingers 1 and 4 for the D and G string notes, and fingers 3 then 1 for the fretted A string notes in bar 1. You'll notice the changes speeding up in the opening bar, now that four quavers occupy beats 3 and 4. Use the right hand to effect the crotchet rest at the end of bar 2, during which time the 1st finger extends back to fret 4 for the D major shape played in bar 3.

A quick shift from fret 7 on the A string...

...to G5 in bar 1.

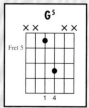

A5/E in 7th position

A5/E is closely related to the A5 chord encountered previously, only instead of an open A at the bottom you need to play fret 7 on the 5th string. This exercise prepares you for another part of the chorus, so it's a good idea to keep the same left hand shape you used before, barring the top five strings at fret 7 with finger 1 and keeping finger 4 at fret 9 on the G string. The staccato markings are important, so try to damp the strings swiftly whenever you find a small dot under a note value.

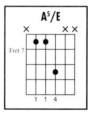

The A5/E shape.

The entire chorus

Another section can now be joined together. You've played most of the material in the previous four pieces, and long, tied notes and rests give you time to consider your next fingering. The one new shape to feature is the final A5 chord, which requires a smooth shift down from D major in 4th position. The simplest fingering option for this chord is a 1st finger barre across the D and G strings at fret 2.

Finger tip

4TH FINGER POWER CHORDS
The selection of finger 4, rather than finger 3, for all but the last chord of the chorus makes for a more economical use of the left hand. Also, the extra stretch this gives you comes into its own when you have to reach across four frets for the D chords.

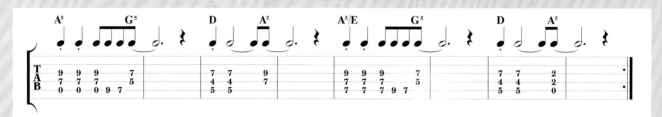

Low and slow

The remainder of this session is given up to an in-depth look at a great rock guitar solo. Aware that he has plenty of bars in which to develop his ideas, Free's guitarist, Paul Kossoff, starts the solo with this figure on the lower frets of the G string. It's a simple opening that uses only three notes – open G, fret 2 A and fret 4 B. The notes are given plenty of space, but to prevent any feeling of dullness he embellishes the phrase using a swift hammer-on in bar 1 and finger slides.

Finger 2 hammers onto the G string.

Slide the finger to fret 4 in bar 2.

Combining slide and open string

To ensure continuity, the next four bars of the solo use similar rhythm figures to those played in the previous piece. However, the notes are higher pitched, which automatically gives the solo an injection of excitement. After a quick slide of finger 3 from fret 3 up to fret 5 on the B string at the start of bar 1, the piece continues with notes on frets 5 and 7 using finger 3. The most compelling feature of this section is the simultaneous strike of the open top E string as your finger slides up to fret 7 on the B string in bars 1 and 3.

The 3rd finger slides up to fret 7...

...and the plectrum strikes the open 1st string.

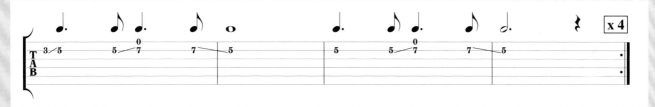

Wide intervals and a string bend

The third part of the solo from *All Right Now* continues to use finger slides but also weaves in two more classic devices. The first break from the smooth ebb and flow of consecutive notes occurs in bar 1 as you hold onto fret 4 on the G string with your 3rd finger and add your 4th finger almost an octave higher at fret 5 on the top E string. In bar 3, release the 4th finger from fret 5, leaving finger 3 still on the G string. With fingers 1 and 2 added for control, half-bend then return the G string to fret 4. Finish with a flamboyant slide of finger 2 from fret 3 up to fret 10.

A half-bend of the G string at fret 4.

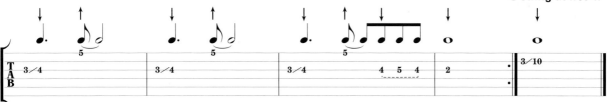

Semiquaver hammer-ons

The solo heats up with streams of semiquavers all played in the same 9th fret hand position. This combination of higher and quicker notes is great to play, and isn't as hard as it might sound. This is largely due to the 3rd string hammer-ons and the fact that finger 2 can stay placed at fret 10 on the B string. Use right hand muting to observe the staccato markings, and shift fingers 1, 2 and 3 up to frets 10, 11 and 12 to make the final full bend.

Hammer finger 3 onto fret 11.

Add finger 2 on the B string.

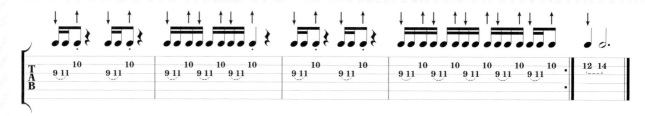

Linking the semiquaver runs

It's time to put the flurries of 9th position notes into their context. A semibreve B string note at fret 10 gives you time to prepare for the sequence of hammer-ons and B string notes in bar 2. Remember to leave finger 1 on the B string throughout the semiquaver passages, and notice that the bend in bar 3 is much quicker than before. Bars 4 and 5 are identical to the equivalent bars from the previous piece.

A full bend of fret 12 on the B string.

The end of the solo

A big sequence of bends and releases, topped by the highest notes you've ever played in *Play Guitar*, brings the solo of *All Right Now* to a climax.

Using three fingers to execute the full tone bends gives you the necessary extra strength and added finger control, which is vital for playing a solo of this type. From this position, the fret 11 and 10 notes that end bars 1, 3 and 5 can be placed with fingers 2 and 1, respectively.

The left hand in 17th position in bar 6.

DE-TUNING EVERY STRING

A first look at a tuning system preferred by many rock guitarists.

Flattening all six strings by one semitone is a common guitar technique. The looser strings are easier to bend and also produce a slightly darker tone that many bands favour. *Lump* by The Presidents Of The USA adopts this approach and goes even further, dropping the bottom string down another tone to D flat.

Barred power chords

Despite the dramatic de-tuning needed for this session, the chord shapes are easy to understand. Most simply involve barring a left hand finger across the bottom three strings, as is the case with the C5 and D5 chords in this piece. A conventional 1st finger barre is ideal for C5 at fret 10, but try adding a finger 3 barre at fret 12 for D5, as this will help avoid many unnecessary hand shifts.

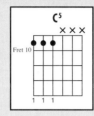

C5 with a fret 10 barre.

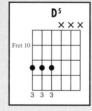

Add finger 3 for D5.

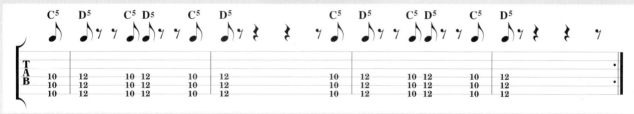

Sliding the finger barre

After opening in the same way as above, use the rests in bar 2 to shift finger 3 up to fret 16. Play this note, then slide down to connect with the three-string F5 chord that begins bar 3. Having used finger 1 for F5, keep a firm contact and slide the finger up two frets to play the three G5 chords. Return to fret 3 after the quaver rest for another F5 chord on the last half-beat of bar 3.

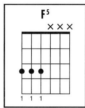

The F5 chord.

Stretch up to fret 16...

...then slide down to 3rd position F5.

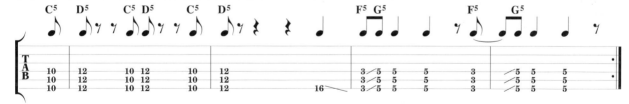

A comfortable 1st finger bend

Because of the de-tuning, it's relatively easy to make the half-bends in this piece, even if you play an acoustic. Try to use finger 1 only for the fret 5 bend, since this will perfectly position finger 3 for the quick slide in bar 3 from fret 7 up to fret 12. A fast push upwards begins each sequence of bends, denoted by the dotted brackets on the TAB. Hold the bend for the fret 6 pitch notes, then release the bend as you strike the return to fret 5.

Half-bend the D string at fret 5.

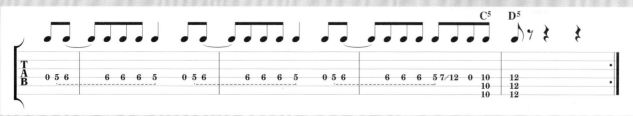

Controlled release of a full bend

The main lead guitar figure appears in two forms. The first is dominated by the half-bends practised in the previous piece while the second uses a full bend of the same fret 5 note on the 4th string. Even with the lower string tension, it's worth using three fingers for the full bend. Release the bend partially for the fret 6 note in the 2nd bar, before returning the string to its normal position on the 3rd beat of bar 2.

For the full bend, use all three fingers.

Slide finger 3 up to fret 10 in bar 3.

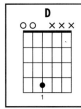

The final D chord.

An acoustic alternative to the full bend

The lessons of the first four pieces come together to build the chorus. However, we have removed the full bend rehearsed above and replaced it with a slide of finger 3 up from fret 5 to fret 7. This makes the chorus playable on an acoustic, and should be used in place of the full bend. The fret 6 and fret 5 notes that follow can be played with fingers 2 and 1, respectively. Acoustic players should continue with a finger 1 slide up to fret 10, whereas electric players should follow the full bend with finger 3.

Slide up to fret 7 in bar 7.

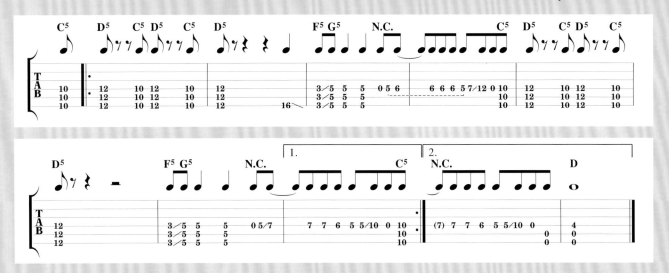

Tidying the chord shifts

Streams of quaver power chords dominate this accompaniment to verse two of the song. You have to shift the 4th position D major shape right up to 10th position for the barred C5 chords, before plummeting back down to F5 in 3rd position. Making these changes cleanly would tax the most accomplished player, so try adding an open-string D5 chord where marked to ease the shifts.

The D major shape.

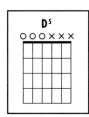

Open D5 chord.

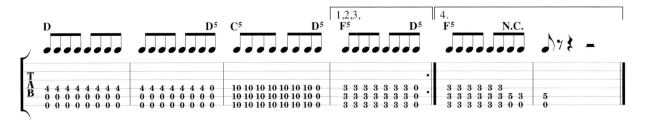

Barring with the 2nd finger

This practice piece starts with D5 and C5 barre chords using fingers 3 and 1, respectively. Using finger 3 to form the D5 barre will make it easier to shift finger 1 down to 3rd position in bar 2. Once there, try using a 2nd finger barre for the 4th fret chord, followed by finger 3 for G5. The result is a more static left hand, which, with practice, can only improve your performance.

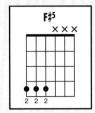

F#5 using the 2nd finger barre.

Damp the staccato strums with the right hand.

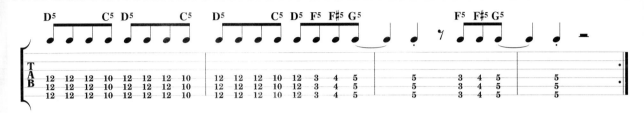

Another busy power chord sequence

As in the previous piece, use fingers 1, 2 and 3 to barre the power chords. For the sake of continuity, start with finger 3 barring fret 5. After two strums of G5, slide finger 3 up to C5 at fret 10 without a further stroke of the plectrum. The finger arrives at fret 10 on the 4th quaver of bars 1 and 3, and you should then quickly mute the strings with the right hand. You are now perfectly positioned to play the Bb5, B5 and C5 chords with a barred 1st, 2nd and then 3rd finger.

Finger tip

BARRING WITH FINGER 1 ONLY
If you don't feel suited to 2nd and 3rd finger barring, it is possible to play this session's exercises with 1st finger power chords only. However, this one-finger approach will result in some loss of accuracy and smoothness in the frequently rapid shifts.

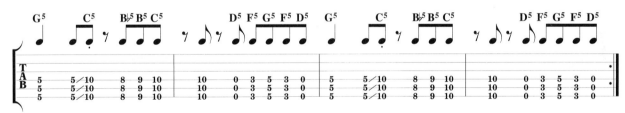

A rare lead line

This short phrase of lead playing is restricted to the lower notes of the 4th and 5th strings and uses a lively hammer-on and pull-off figure. In bar 1, aim to damp out the lower two strings of the opening D5 chord with the heel of your right hand as you strike the fret 5 note that follows. Leave finger 1 in place as you hammer-on and then pull-off at fret 7 using finger 3. Quickly shift back to 3rd position for the remaining notes of bars 1 and 2.

Hammer-on finger 3 at fret 7.

Use finger 1 for the 3rd fret notes.

167

Measured slides

Four varied challenges make this piece harder to play than you might think. First, there are the gradual slides of the 1st finger barre between 10th and 3rd positions. Next is the importance of the right hand not only to strike the strings accurately but also to implement the rests. The leap up to 10th position at the end of bar 3 also deserves your attention, as does the introduction of the syncopated (or off-beat) rhythm as you move from bar 3 into bar 4. Remember to use a 3rd finger barre to eliminate a shift on the G5 chord in bar 4.

Finger tip
MUTING THE TREBLE STRINGS

Not one note of *Lump* is played on the top three strings, so it's essential to keep these muted when strumming the power chords. When barring, your left hand fingers will inevitably fall across the top three strings – try to lighten the finger pressure at this end so that accidental plectrum contact is muted.

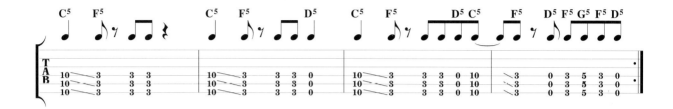

A chance to link two passages

Sections of the previous two pieces come together to form quite a tricky section. Use the fingering suggested in the lead line piece for the opening two bars and keep the fingers spread as you shift down to 3rd position. You'll get a tidier effect if you release finger 1 from the 4th string when you play fret 5 at the end of bar 1. Don't be caught out by the C5 chord at the end of bar 2 – use the preceding quaver rest to move your 1st finger quickly from 3rd up to 10th position. Bar 4 is another direct lift from the exercise above.

Mute the bottom two strings after the opening chord.

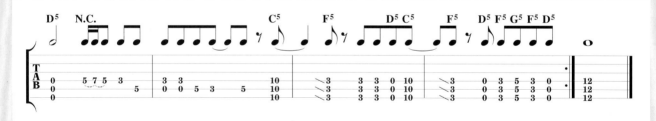

A lighter verse accompaniment

There are parallels between this verse three accompaniment and the verse two accompaniment practised earlier on. The difference lies in the use of 12th fret D5 chords instead of the fuller-sounding D major shape used earlier. These repeated D5 chords must remain firmly in position for two whole bars, which makes it preferable to use the stronger 1st finger to place them. However, if you play acoustic and find this awkward because of the closeness of the left hand to the guitar's body, feel free to use a 3rd finger barre instead.

Finger 1 can play the 12th fret D5 chord.

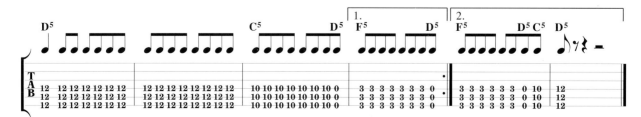

A touch of percussive muting

Bar 1 uses octave Ds with an occasional shuffle to fret 3 on string 5. Barred power chords return in bar 2, which are best played with fingers 1, 2 and then 3. For the percussive muting in bar 3, slide your 3rd finger up to fret 10 and also lie fingers 1 and 2 lightly across frets 8 and 9. You should hear a pitchless click as you strike the bottom three strings. Use finger 3 for the fret 5 notes at the end of bar 4 to gain position for the repeat.

The opening octave.

Mute the strings at 8th position in bar 3.

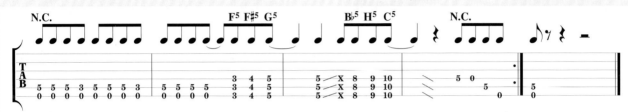

Tracks 56, 57, 58 and 59 – One last lead lick

Slide the 3rd finger barre down from 10th position, releasing the finger pressure at around fret 5 so that the barre mutes the sound of the chord. Quickly slide finger 3 up from fret 8 to fret 12, before using fingers 1 and 3 on the 4th string to end bar 1. In bar 4, half-bend the 3rd string using fingers 2 and 3, and then add finger 1 on the top string at fret 10. A quick release of the bend is followed by finger 1 at fret 10 on the 3rd string.

Quickly slide finger 3 from fret 8 up to fret 12.

Hold the half-bend and add finger 1 in bar 4.

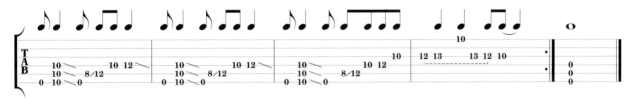

The conclusion

The content of this final practice piece draws heavily on the percussive muting exercise, but there are a few differences worth noting. The piece begins with a crotchet, so count the space carefully, then notice that the 3rd fret shuffle on the 5th string pops up on the 2nd quaver of bar 2. F5, G5 and D5 chords replace the lead lick in bar 4. The only other change occurs right at the very end, where barred D, C# and C power chords with fingers 3, 2 and then 1 bring the exercise to a grinding halt.

Barring the C#5 chord with finger 2.

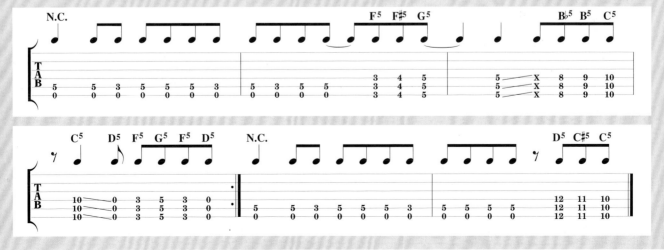

A NEW TIME SIGNATURE

Lightly strummed rhythm guitar dominates your preparations of **Why Does It Always Rain On Me?** ***by Travis. You will need a capo at fret 2 for every practice piece.***

This session's practice pieces are written out in $\frac{12}{8}$ – a time signature with 12 quaver beats in a bar. The quavers are divided into four groups of three. It's often used as an alternative to $\frac{4}{4}$ time with a swing rhythm symbol. Although a little more awkward to read, $\frac{12}{8}$ allows the swing rhythm to be written out literally.

Introducing $\frac{12}{8}$

Before you start playing, spare a couple of moments for some rhythm theory. Dotted crotchets are common in $\frac{12}{8}$ because the 12 quaver beats divide naturally into four groups of three, each worth a dotted crotchet. A crotchet followed by a quaver also features frequently, creating the swing in the rhythm. Hold the D major chord throughout, except for a brief release of the shape on the last quaver of bar 3.

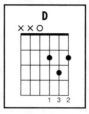

D major with a capo at the 2nd fret.

Release the D chord briefly at the end of bar 3.

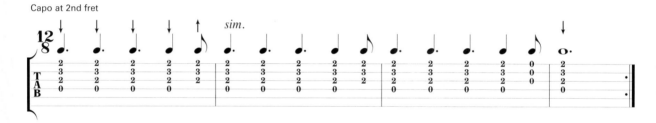

Shifting between D and A minor

Once you have come to terms with reading the new time signature, there are many sections that are quite straightforward. For example, you should be able to switch easily between D and A minor using the same three fingers and minimal hand movement. Further help is provided by the open chords that end bars 1 and 3, which give you the chance to prepare the A minor hand shape. As in the previous piece, try to use lighter upstrums for the quaver beat chords.

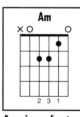

A minor features in bars 2 and 4.

Travis, l to r: Neil Primrose, Andy Dunlop, Doug Payne and Fran Healy.

A return to the bass-strum style

You might recall the bass-strum right hand technique from *Fake Plastic Trees* by Radiohead. This technique involves playing the bass note of a chord on its own followed by a full strum, and it's used on both the G and G/F# chords featured here. Begin with a full G chord in place and simply switch your 1st finger to fret 2 on the bottom string in the second half of bars 1 and 3 to form G/F#. Notice that the 5th string should be muted by finger 1 for the G/F# shape.

 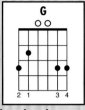

Start with the familiar G major chord.

 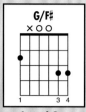

The G/F# chord is used in bars 1 and 3.

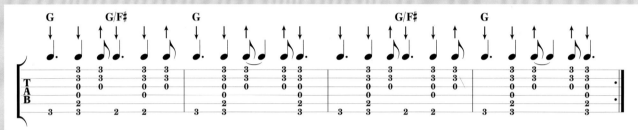

Spreading strums

Usually, you strum swiftly through a chord to create the effect of all the strings being struck simultaneously. On occasions, however, it's more stylish to spread the notes of a chord by opting for a slower strum. In this piece, the wavy, vertical lines to the left of some of the E minor 7 strums instruct you to do just that. As before, use upstrums for the three-string chords.

 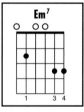

E minor 7 uses fingers 1, 3 and 4.

Begin bars 1 to 3 with an open 6th string.

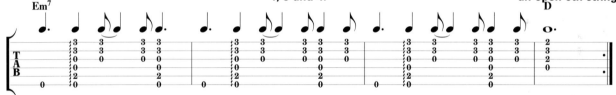

Linking the five chords

Having tried out some of the chord changes, it's now time to pull the various sections of the intro together. This involves connecting A minor to G major for the first time at the end of bar 2. This difficult shift is simplified by the placement of the G chord in two halves, starting with fingers 3 and 4 on the top two strings. After this upstrum, the remainder of the chord is added to the 5th and 6th strings in time for the full strum at the start of bar 3. G/F# to Em7 is another new change that's easy provided you leave fingers 3 and 4 in place as you take finger 1 across to the 5th string at the 2nd fret.

Prepare G major at the end of bar 2.

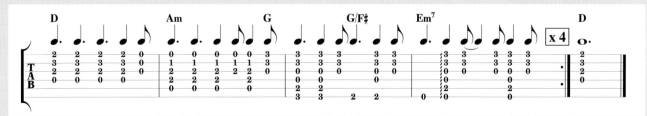

A lighter verse treatment

Here, we use three-string chords in higher fret positions, in contrast to the full-strummed approach adopted up until now. Locate the opening D major shape in 5th position using the fingering shown in the photo, including a 1st finger half-barre. This fingering simplifies the two-fret shift up to B minor, which needs only the half-barre. For D major 7 (or Dmaj7 for short), add finger 3 to the top string at fret 9 above the capo.

The three-string D shape.

Dmaj7 in 7th position above the capo.

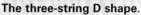

An over-ringing lead idea

This simple mix of held fret 7 and open-string notes creates a highly effective lead fill. Before you begin, place finger 3 at fret 7 on the G string. Keep the finger curved so as not to block the open B notes, and leave it in place until the end. For the 2nd bar, add finger 2 at fret 7 on the D string, once again allowing each note to ring over the last. Even though the tempo is steady, aim to play each note with the marked down- or upstroke, and be wary of the tied rhythm values.

Begin on the G string with finger 3.

Add finger 2 in bars 2 and 4.

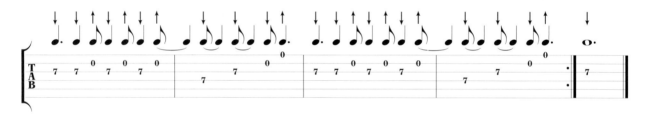

Moving the lead pattern down to fret 2

Bars 1 and 2 are modelled on the opening bar of the previous piece. The end of the pre-chorus requires a simple shift of the left hand from fret 7 down to fret 2. As you play the open B string that ends bar 2, release finger 3 for a clean, comfortable shift down to fret 2 on the same string. In bar 3, add finger 2 at the same fret on the D string. If you haven't already done so, try starting to think in terms of four dotted crotchet beats per bar rather than 12 single quavers.

Shift finger 3 down to fret 2 in the 3rd bar.

The 2nd finger is added.

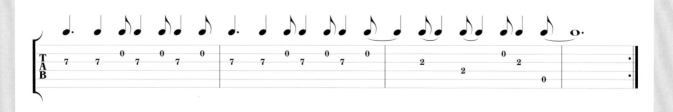

Substituting A major for A minor

The song's chorus is based on the intro chords, but with A minor being replaced by A major. This subtle alteration to a 'happier' chord helps to counteract the obviously gloomy lyrics, thus avoiding too downcast a mood for the song's crucial chorus. In this piece, you should concentrate on a controlled shift between the D and A chords. As in the second practice piece, an upstrum of the top three open strings precedes the shift to the A chord, giving you time to reshape your hand.

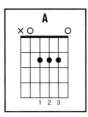

A major is played in the chorus.

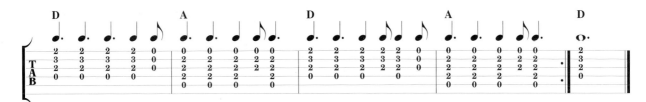

Tidying up another chord change

This exercise focuses on the change in the chorus from A to G. The approach is just the same as in the linking five chords exercise, only this time A major rather than A minor is replaced by fingers 3 and 4 of the G chord shape on the last quaver of bar 2. Add the remainder of G major on the first beat of bar 3. Remove the entire G chord for the last strum of bar 3, and reshape the hand ready for the four strums of A major in bar 4. Remember that the upstrums use three strings only to give a lighter effect to the upbeats.

Finger tip

AN EASIER CHANGE FROM A TO G MAJOR
As well as breaking up the G chord placement into two halves, this shift can be simplified further by keeping your 3rd finger in contact with the B string as you slip out of fret 2 and across into fret 3.

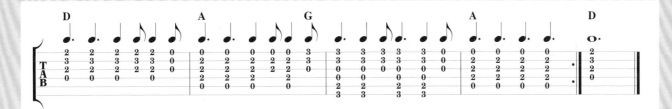

Adding B minor

Another new shape is introduced in the bridge section. B minor is a barred A chord shape played at the 2nd fret, which involves placing finger 1 across the top five strings at fret 2. The other three fingers are added as shown in the photo. The shift from Em7 is divided by an open-string strum, but keep your 1st finger on the A string at fret 2 above the capo to help you land the difficult barre chord.

Keep finger 1 on the A string...

...as you change to B minor in bars 2 and 4.

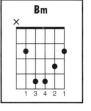

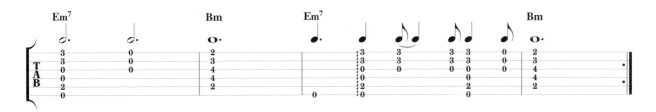

173

A quick shift of the finger barre

The B minor chord rehearsed in the previous piece returns, this time in alternation with the D/A shape. D/A is a full D major chord with an open A string added at the base of the chord. However, the conjunction with the barred B minor shape makes the use of a half-barre for the D/A chord a better option than the standard D major fingering. It also means that finger 2 can stay in the same place for both chords.

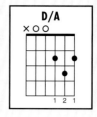

A half-barred D/A chord.

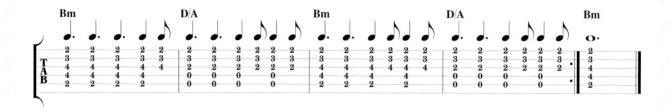

A falling lead line

Another lead line appears towards the end of the bridge. Based on three-note broken chords, the fingering holds no surprises. It's good to let the sounds overlap, so keep fingers 3 and 2 in place throughout the first three notes. Transfer finger 2 to the A string at fret 2 for the second half of bar 1. Finger 2 moves back to the D string in bar 2, leaving finger 3 as the obvious choice for the bottom string. To avoid an ugly clash of sound, it's better to damp out the open A string with the underside of finger 3 as you play the bottom string at fret 3.

The opening note.

Finger 2 on the D string in bars 2 and 4.

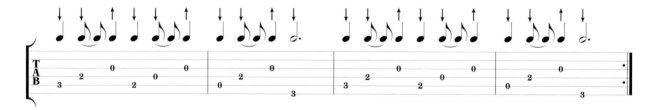

Asus4 to A

The final exercise of this session brings one more chord shape into play, as Asus4 follows an opening two bars that are identical to those above. The sus4 chord has cropped up on a number of occasions in previous sessions of *Play Guitar*, but here it is used in a classic fashion. The notes of Asus4 are almost the same as A major, but the 2nd string note is one fret higher, replacing the 3rd of the major chord with a suspended 4th. At the end of bar 3, the 4th finger suspension falls back to fret 2 with the 3rd finger.

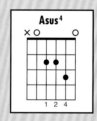

Asus4 is this session's final new shape.

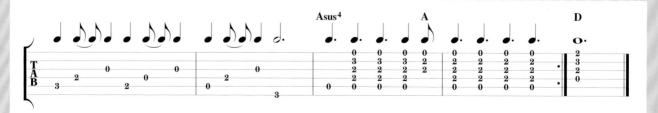

174

FLATPICKING

Exploring the distinctive style of country guitar playing.

The main feature of this session is flatpicking, a combination of strummed chords in alternation with single-string bass notes. What sets this style apart from the bass-strum used previously is the regular alternation of the bass between the root note and the 5th of the chord. Every exercise is played with a capo at fret 1.

Setting up the country rhythm style

This session's practice pieces all have a familiar four crotchet beats in a bar. To keep your music looking as uncluttered as possible, this is the only piece to indicate the need for a capo at fret 1, but you should leave it in place for all of the pieces. Hold the B7 shape for bars 1 to 3, before changing to E major for the whole of bar 4. When making this shift, leave finger 2 at fret 2 on the A string.

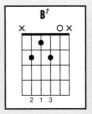

The B7 shape used in bars 1 to 3.

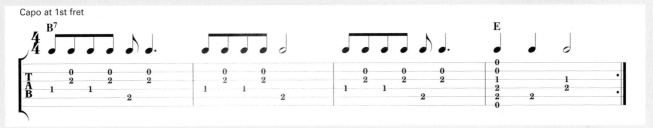

Flatpicking

For this simple introduction to flatpicking, hold an E major shape and concentrate on the plectrum work. Begin with the root note of the chord, which is an open bottom E string. Then strike the D and G strings together, while the bottom E keeps ringing. Next, play the 5th of the E chord at fret 2, followed, once again, by the D and G strings together. Continue this flatpicking pattern for the remainder of the piece.

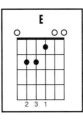

Hold E major throughout the exercise.

Adding light upstrums

Try to think of the notes of this exercise in terms of a broken E chord. The flatpicked bass notes and paired D and G strings are retained from the previous piece, but two new ideas give the music a lift. First, a quick upstrum is added within the 2nd and 4th beats of each bar. This should be very gently struck to give the right feel to your strumming. Also, you need momentarily to release finger 1 to produce the open G string notes.

Release finger 1 for an open 3rd string.

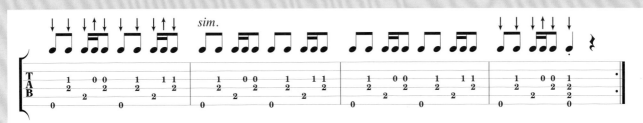

Heavy palm muting

Another trait of much country guitar playing is a heavily palm muted sound. You've used palm muting (P.M.) before, but on this occasion it's important to press the right hand more firmly against the bridge. This results in a punchier attack and shorter sustain of the notes. The half-bends that follow the flatpicked E chord work also have a country flavour. For these, release the chord shape and bend the bottom string down towards the 5th string with your 2nd finger.

Palm mute everything except for the note bends.

Use finger 2 for the half-bends.

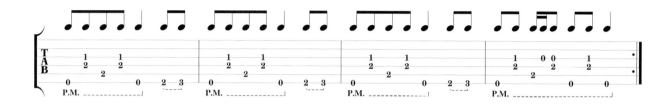

The intro

All the techniques dealt with so far in the session are contained within this busy opening. The notes are principally taken from the B7 and E major chord shapes, the exceptions being the open G string notes that lend a Blues flavour to the harmony, and the string bend in the 1st full bar. Have the B7 chord placed before you begin and leave it in position until the string bend. The flatpicking starts at the same time as the palm muting in the second half of the music.

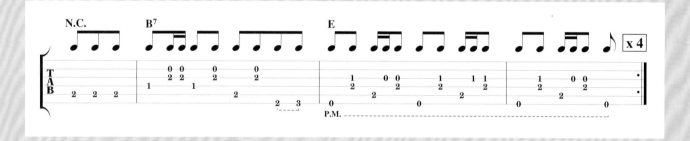

Linking chords with a bass run

A classic characteristic of country music is the use of short runs of bass notes to join two chord shapes together. The short scale-based runs of 2nd and 4th fret notes, played with fingers 2 and 4, smooth out the progression between the root notes of the E and A5 chords. The flatpicking approach is used again and the entire piece is palm muted, but notice that the bass notes of the newly introduced A5 chord move from the root note on the A string to 5th on the bottom E string. This is a common flatpicking variation that makes best use of the full bass range of notes.

Finger 4 on the 6th string.

The A5 chord shape played in bars 2 and 4.

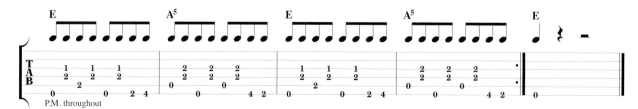

A subtle hammer-on

There are a few variations to flatpicking, one of which is this sequence of notes based around the E major chord. You covered most of this pattern in the third exercise, and the only difference is the swift hammer-on of finger 1, which returns the chord to its full E major shape. The effect is subtle, simply adding a small decoration to the existing pattern. Keep the chord placed for most of the piece, but release the fingers at the open A string in bar 2.

Replace only finger 2 at the end of bar 2.

Taking shape

Here are the first eight bars of the verse, which bring together the E and A5 chords, flatpicking, heavy palm muting, a bass run at the end of bar 4 and the Bluesy hammer-ons of the previous piece. Keep the E chord in place for most of the first four bars, but remember to release finger 1 for the last chord of bars 1 and 2. E major gives way to the 2nd and 4th finger bass run that ends bar 4. Use the 1st and 2nd fingers for the A5 chord, and a light upstroke for the 2nd semiquaver at the end of bar 5.

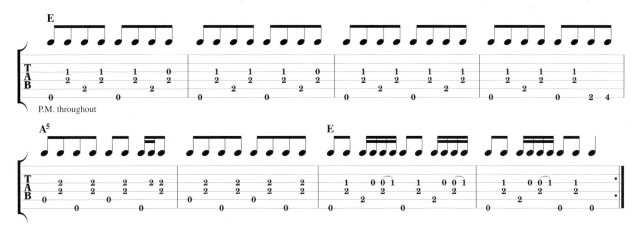

A different use of B7

The string selection for this B7 shape is different to that used in the very first piece. On this occasion, there's no open B string and the two-string strums are on the D and G strings. A consistent flatpicked pattern is also used, which involves you switching finger 2 between the fret 2 notes on the A and bottom E strings. The pick-up bar contains a short bass run that will link this part to the end of the piece above. For the 1st fret note in the pick-up bar, the obvious and best choice is to use finger 1.

Finger 1 at fret 1 in the pick-up bar.

Swap finger 2 of B7 to the 6th string.

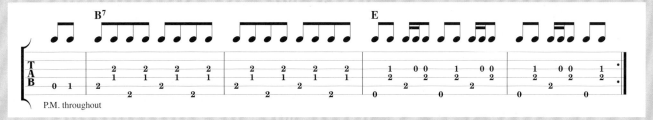

177

Starting the solo

Although a fair amount of the solo is chord based, the opening features a single line of notes played on the top two strings. You can play most of these in 7th position, but it's best to use finger 3 for the slide between frets 8 and 9. Release the B string note as you move onto the top string, then place finger 1 and leave it at fret 7 until the next 3rd finger slide. Add your 4th finger at fret 10, before gently pulling the same finger off the string to create a light return to fret 7.

Slide finger 3 from fret 8 above the capo.

Fingers 1 and 4 in place for the pull-off.

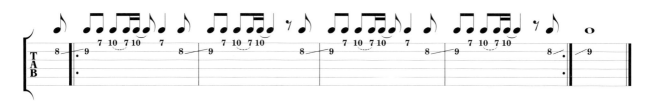

Developing the lead line

Much of this exercise's content was contained in the previous piece, but the slide up to fret 9 has been removed, and a short pull-off idea at the end of bars 1 and 3 takes the solo on a stage further. The hardest part of this particular shift back across to the B string stems from a need to place both fingers 3 and 1 simultaneously in readiness for the fast pull-off. A dramatic shift is required in bar 4, as the open A string gives you a moment to set up the finger-barred 2nd fret chord that follows on the G and B strings.

Finger 3 ready to pull-off the B string.

Use a half-barre for the final A chord shape.

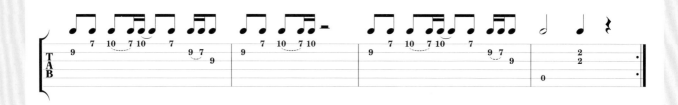

An elaborate broken chord figure

The reason for the finger-barre at the end of the previous piece becomes clear as you continue the solo. By barring the top three strings of this new A chord shape at fret 2, your 4th finger can reach the fret 5 notes. You will need to release the fingers slightly for the open B and G string strums, but aim to retain the hand shape for a comfortable return to the same notes moments later. Let the open A bass notes ring at all times and persevere with the marked plectrum directions so that your hand movement stays smooth and relaxed.

The half-barre is joined by finger 4.

Another A major shape

One of the hardest parts in this session is a shift up the neck from A major in 2nd position to another form of the same chord at frets 9 and 10. The distance between the two shapes, the difference in the hand positions and the lively speed of the song all contribute to the difficulty. One saving grace is the consistent use of finger 1 on the G string, so be sure to focus your shift on this finger and also as you drop back down to fret 1 for E major in bars 3 and 4.

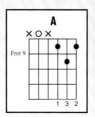

A new form of A major.

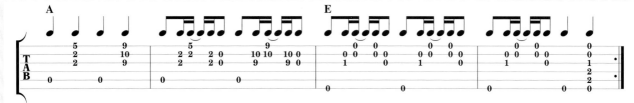

B7 as a barre chord

The final slice of the solo requires another version of B7, this time played in 2nd position with a 1st finger barre across the top five strings. This is the first time that this frequently used barre chord shape has appeared in *Play Guitar*. Release B7 on the 3rd beat of bar 2, slipping finger 1 back a fret for the A string note at fret 1. The same 2nd finger half-bend from earlier pieces returns as a link to the key chord of E major and yet more flatpicking. This is a good opportunity to practise the return to palm muting after a cleanly played solo.

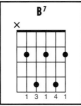

The frequently used barre chord version of B7.

Finger tip

PLACING THE FULL B7 SHAPE
It's worth placing all of the fingers for the B7 barre chord in this exercise, even though you won't be playing the 3rd finger note on the D string. This approach will encourage you to think of the pattern as a single chord shape, making it easier to remember as well as safeguarding against an accidental strike of the D string.

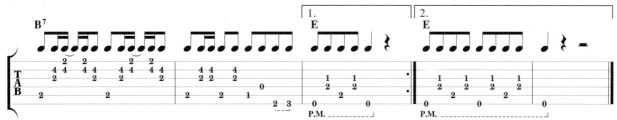

The final phrase

The session ends very much as it began, with a short phrase constructed from B7 and E chord shapes. However, there are a few small changes to the piece played earlier. To make the guitar ring through over the band there is no palm muting, and the pick-up bar contains two instead of three B notes on the 5th string. Another slight variation sees the top strings of the E chord used in the 2nd and 3rd bars of the line, once again projecting the sound for a big finish. You might find it less confusing to place the full E major shape immediately after the open bottom E note in bars 2 and 3.

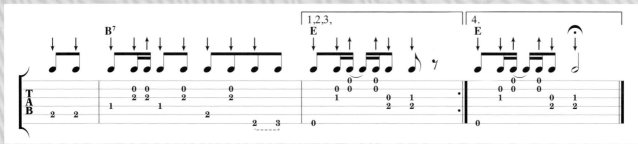

TOTAL LEAD

Put chord shapes and strums to one side to prepare a 100 per cent lead guitar part.

There are plenty of lead techniques on display in *Hanging On The Telephone* by Blondie, including finger slides, hammer-ons, string bends and vibrato.

Although each of these techniques has been covered to some degree in previous sessions, their combined use will require lots of practice.

Neat finger slides

The nearest thing to a chord in this session occurs right at the start of this piece, where you have to combine frets 4 and 6 on the top two strings. It's best to place these notes with fingers 1 and 4, leaving finger 3 poised for the fret 6 note on the G string that follows. A one-fret, downward slide of finger 3 creates the fret 5 pitch, with finger 1 then positioned to deal with the 3rd fret note that ends each bar.

Fingers 1 and 4 in 4th position.

Use finger 3 at fret 6 on the G string.

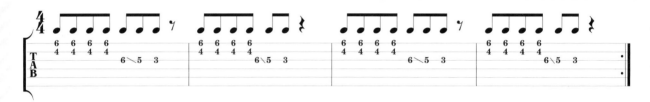

A subtle bend

The string bends, marked by the usual dotted brackets, are achieved by a quick nudge of finger 1 at fret 3 up towards the D string. Although a one-fret rise in pitch is marked on the TAB, your bend will sound even more like the Blondie original if you use a touch less than that. As soon as you've made the bend, damp the string smartly with the heel of the right hand to kill the sound. The other notes are straightforward, and can be achieved by remaining in 3rd position and using fingers 1 and 3.

Nudge finger 1 up towards the D string for the bends.

Light vibrato

You will probably recall the wavy line that indicates vibrato. On this occasion, placing fingers 1, 2 and 3 at frets 6, 7 and 8 gives you the greatest amount of control as you lightly wobble the B string to and fro for the long fret 8 notes in bars 2 and 4.

Slide finger 3 to fret 8.

Aim for a light fret 15 note.

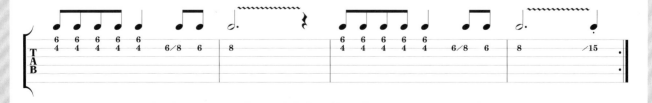

Hammer-ons and falling slides

This two-bar, repeating phrase is made up of several tricky manoeuvres. Start with a very fast slide of finger 3 from fret 6 down to fret 5 on the G string. Finger 1 plays the fret 3 note that follows before skipping across to the D string for the hammer-on. Bars 2 and 4 begin with a slide of finger 3 down two frets, followed by finger 1 for the fret 1 notes. Throughout the piece, the first TAB number of each slide or hammer-on has no fixed time value, which means that the first note is purely a quick decoration of the second.

Hammer-on finger 3 at fret 5.

A two-fret, downward slide in bars 2 and 4.

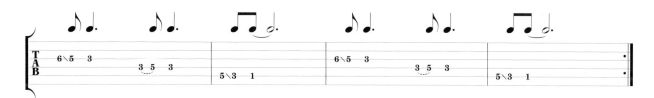

The verse

Now it's time for your first real taste of the song, as the techniques and fingerings of the opening four pieces are merged into a single demanding line of lead playing. Remember to begin by using the more unorthodox 4th finger on the top E string, as this will make the transfer to the G string notes as smooth and inconspicuous as possible.

A welcome, two-beat rest follows the string bend in bar 2, giving you a little extra time to relocate the two-string chords. In bar 3, pay particular attention to the small leap from 1st finger at fret 3 to 3rd finger at fret 6. And keep practising!

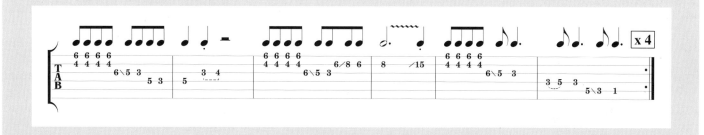

Clean shifts

This exercise focuses on another important sequence of notes. With its simpler rhythm pattern and lack of left hand techniques, you should find this piece easier to play than the previous one. Using finger 4 for the fret 6 note helps to share the workload and to simplify a leap. However, if you prefer, you can use finger 3 to place both this and the following 5th fret note. Shift finger 1 smoothly between strings 5 and 6 in bar 2, and neatly slip the same finger up to fret 3 for bar 3.

A quick shift from fret 5...

...down to fret 1 on the A string.

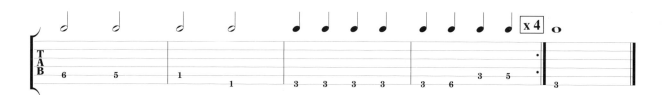

G minor as a broken chord

The first three notes of this piece are the component parts of G minor – in other words G, B♭ and D. Played one after the other, they result in a broken chord. You don't want these notes to ring over each other, so release finger 3 from the bottom E string and replace it with finger 1 on the A string at fret 1. Similarly, release finger 1 in order to sound the open D string cleanly. As you return to fret 1 on the A string, let the underside of finger 1 damp out the previous D string note. A quick, neat transfer of finger 1 between the bottom two strings follows, with a measured hammer-on of finger 3 taking you into bar 2.

Finger 1 damps the D string in bars 1 and 3.

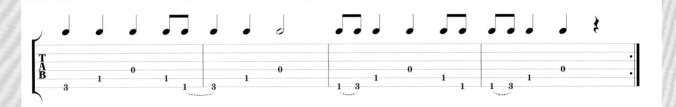

Putting together the chorus

The previous two pieces should have gone a long way towards preparing this next part. Avoid the temptation to slide heavily down from fret 5 to fret 1 on the A string. Instead, slightly release the 3rd finger pressure and leave the shift to 1st position as late as you can. As you play these eight bars, listen out for over-ringing strings and the kind of harmonics mentioned in the Finger tip box.

Finger tip
MUTING THE STRINGS

You might be noticing unwanted harmonics and sympathetic background noises coming from the unused strings. Try muting out this untidy over-ringing using either the heel of the right hand or the left hand fingers.

Verse lick variations

This pair of closely related two-bar phrases are nearly identical to the first two bars of the verse exercise. In bar 1 of the first phrase, the notes remain more firmly on the G string, with finger 3 returning to fret 5 while the 1st finger remains at fret 3. The simple alteration at the end of phrase two involves holding a semibreve fret 5 note on the D string.

Add finger 3 at fret 5 in bar 1.

The right hand quickly damps the string bend.

The palm muted bridge

The bridge is the only section to employ palm muting, a technique you should feel at home with by now. Stretch fingers 1 and 4 apart to cover the 3rd and 6th fret notes, leaving finger 3 well placed to cope with the action at fret 5. Even though the palm muting will ensure a lack of sustain, be sure to place only one finger at a time to avoid any messy over-ringing. Lastly, watch out for the slight variation in the pattern of the notes at the end of the final bar.

The opening note.

Palm mute throughout.

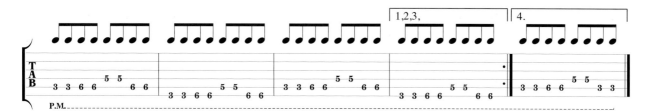

Beginning the solo

The pieces rehearsed so far come from the accompaniment, despite the fact that many of them could easily be sections of a solo. The guitar actually takes centre stage for the first time in this exercise, with a solid, melodic phrase based in 8th position on the B and G strings. Use finger 1 for the opening pair of notes, then add fingers 2 and 3 for a comfortable half-bend and release before returning to finger 1 only at fret 8. Although slightly unusual, try using finger 2 for the 10th fret notes in bars 2 and 4. The reason for this will become clear in the next part of the solo.

The half-bend in bars 1 and 3.

Use finger 2 on the G string.

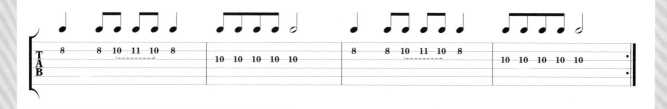

Extending the left fingers

The frequent use of quick finger slides to embellish the lead work in this song raises the technical stakes considerably. With a forthcoming link to the previous piece in mind, it's worth persevering with finger 2 for the opening series of fret 10 notes. Next, extend finger 3 to fret 12 for the rapid downward finger slide, and finish off bar 1 with finger 1 at fret 8. In bar 3, drop finger 3 and then finger 1 onto the A string, before ending the piece with a tricky leap of finger 1 across to the B string.

Begin the slide at fret 12.

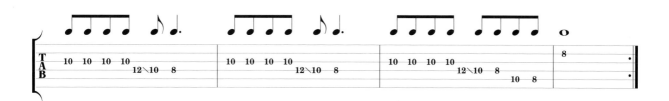

Shifting a phrase up an octave

If you recognize the sound of these notes, it's because you have already played them an octave lower in your chorus exercise. The higher range of the notes immediately gives them the greater prominence needed for a solo, while at the same time helping to unify the song's musical material. Use finger 2 for the first note, followed by finger 1 at fret 7. Slide your 1st finger down the G string to fret 3, where the note is held for three beats instead of two as played earlier.

Begin with finger 2.

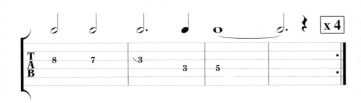

Finger tip

FINGER SELECTION
Always try to choose your fingering carefully, bearing in mind the context of each note. Remember that your fingering should always be selected to help create the best musical effect.

The complete solo

Although there are no new notes to learn, the process of spinning the opening pair of bars round several times in a row is quite a finger-twister. The extension of fingers 1, 2 and 3 across frets 8, 10 and 12 also takes some getting used to, but gives the best results if you are prepared to work at it. Use finger 2 at the start of bar 8, as this allows for a smoother change from the preceding 1st finger note at the same fret on the A string.

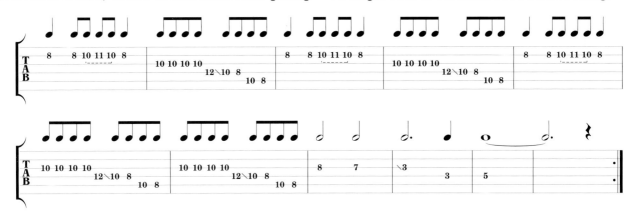

Rounding things off

The final piece of this session is based on the song's conclusion. The G minor broken chord idea returns in bar 1, while a comfortable shift of the 3rd finger up to fret 6 is aided by the open D string minim that ends bar 1. Finger 3 is preferable to finger 4 at the start of bar 2 because it is an easier finger to control for the slide to fret 3. However, the cleanly played fret 6 note in bar 3 is best placed with finger 4, since it reduces the size of the hand shift up from fret 1.

Slide finger 3 down from fret 6.

Finger 4 on the same note in bar 3.

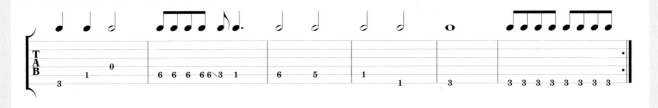

TIDY PLECTRUM WORK

Chord shapes are the starting point for a fluid, picked accompaniment.

The notes of familiar and new chord shapes are often picked out individually in these practice pieces to make for a light, busy guitar part. Strummed passages, some regularly featured lead techniques and the $\frac{12}{8}$ time signature introduced earlier mean there's never a dull moment in *Marblehead Johnson* by The Bluetones.

A reminder of $\frac{12}{8}$

The time signature introduced earlier returns for this session's exercises. The 12 quaver beats are divided into four dotted crotchet groups, making the long streams of notes in each bar easier to read. Use finger 2 for the hammer-ons and also for the fret 2 notes on the D string. Leave the finger in place wherever it is possible and aim to let the notes of the different strings ring over each other.

Hammer-on finger 2 at fret 2.

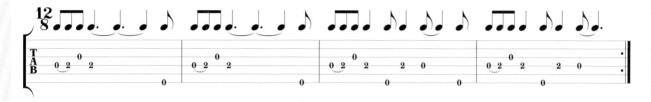

Completing the intro

In the previous piece, it was easy enough to use down-picks for all the notes. This time, however, try to follow the stroke directions above the note values, as these will help you deal with a quicker tempo. The first three bars are related to the content of the previous piece, but you'll need to move the hammer-on of finger 2 across to the A string in bar 4. Also, at the end of bar 4 you need to add a slight bend of the bottom E string with finger 3 down towards string 5.

Hammer-on at fret 2 on the A string in bar 4.

A slight bend of the bottom E string.

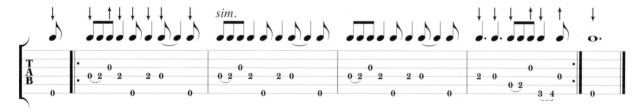

Forming a riff from E minor 7

E minor 7 (Em7) was introduced in one of the first sessions. Here, the four fingers are never placed at the same time. Strike the open D and A strings and quickly hammer-on the 1st and 2nd fingers at fret 2. Release fingers 1 and 2 before you play the four-string strums at the end of each bar. This piece works best with constant downstrums, and as the rests are crucial to the overall effect, damp the sound where marked with the side of the right hand.

Place fingers 1 and 2 together.

End each bar with the top four strings of Em7.

Linking the Asus2 chord

Asus2 is the five-string chord strummed at the start of bar 3. Think of it as an A major chord with finger 3 removed to give an open B string, which is the suspended 2nd of its title. The opening two bars are identical to those played on the previous piece, and using fingers 1 and 2 makes for an easy transfer across to the Asus2 chord. Play bars 3 and 4 with the Asus2 shape firmly in place, until you reach the final open G note. The static left hand should allow you to give your undivided attention to the neatness of your picking and the marked stroke directions.

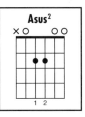

Strum Asus2 in bar 3.

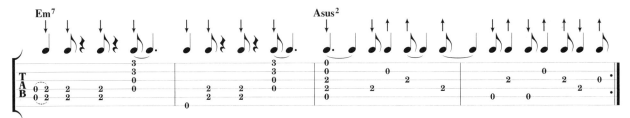

Adding C and Dsus2

These five bars pick up where the previous piece left off. Once again, the best policy is to place full chords and then pick out the notes separately. Place all three C major chord fingers, even though the D string note is not played in bar 1 – you'll see that it does feature in bar 3. Use fingers 1 and 3 for the fretted Dsus2 notes. This shape resembles D major with an open E on top. An open B string at the end of bar 4 is your cue to release the Dsus2 chord and either repeat or move into bar 5 with a single D string hammer-on.

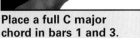

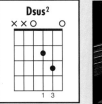

Place a full C major chord in bars 1 and 3.

The Dsus2 shape used in bars 2 and 4.

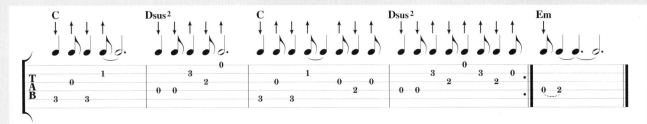

A busy left hand passage

The first two bars are straightforward enough, using the Asus2 chord as the basis for a delicate piece of plectrum work. Leave finger 1 at fret 2 on the D string as you release finger 2 for the hammer-on and open G string notes in bar 2. In bar 3, the shift from C to Cmaj7 is achieved simply by removing finger 1 from the B string. In bar 4, slide finger 3 up to fret 5, then add the 4th fret note with finger 2. Drop to 2nd position for the elaborately named Bmadd6 shape.

Add finger 2 after the slide in bar 4.

A shift to 2nd position completes bar 4.

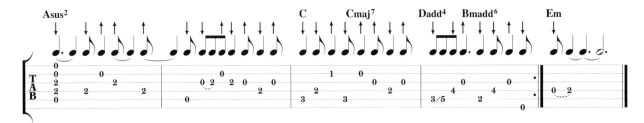

186

Beginning the chorus

The piece starts with spacious, full-bar, spread strums of Dsus2 and the new D9 chord. You might remember that spread chords need to begin a little early in order to end on the beat they are written on. These strums contrast well with the broken-chord approach of the last few bars.

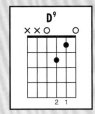

The D9 chord in bar 2.

Bottom G in bars 4 and 5.

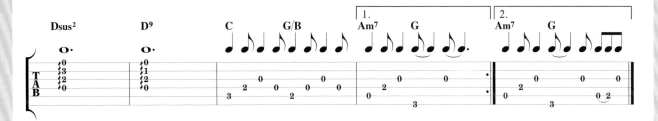

A couple of barre chords

This full-strummed piece opens with the barre chord form of G7, played in 3rd position. The addition of finger 4 to the G string in bar 2 creates the first of three G7sus4 strums. Bars 3 and 4 centre on the A chord with three subtly different harmonic flavours. A7sus4 comes first, using fingers 1 and 3, followed by the A7 shape with fingers 1 and 2. Single-string picking returns at the end of the piece, including a broken chord version of A7sus2.

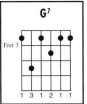

The G7 barre chord shape in bar 1.

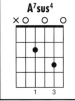

Use fingers 1 and 3 for A7sus4 in bar 3.

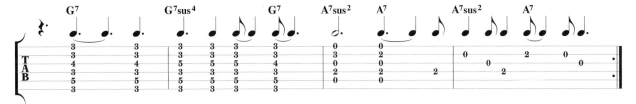

Double string slides

Place fingers 1 and 2 on the bottom two strings at fret 2. Don't re-strike the strings as you slide the fingers up to fret 3. Transfer finger 1 to the D string in time for the fret 2 notes in bars 1 and 2. The use of fingers 1 and 2 makes placing B7 more straightforward. For this chord, shift fingers 1 and 2 down a fret and add finger 3.

Slide fingers 1 and 2 to fret 3.

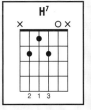

Avoid the top string as you play B7.

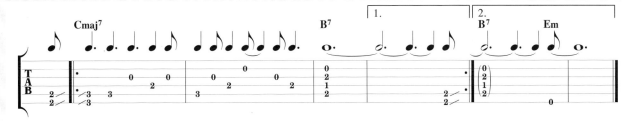

Developing the intro figure

There are similarities between the first four notes of the very first exercise and the repeating idea that forms the majority of this piece. On this occasion, however, the 4th note is dropped down an octave to an open bottom E string, instead of E at fret 2 on the 4th string. On each occasion in bars 1 and 2, use finger 2 for the hammer-ons, and allow all the strings to ring over each other. The Asus2 bars are much the same, but with the addition of finger 3 at fret 2 on the G string.

Fingers 2 and 3 together in bars 3 and 4.

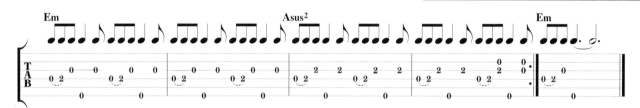

Further use of the hammer-on

Most of the pieces featured so far have included at least one example of this characteristic guitar technique. More examples are found here, with two hammer-ons in close succession in bar 1, followed by a fret 1 hammer-on from an open D string in bar 2. Keep your fingers just above the strings and these should be easy enough to place. Bars 3 and 4 are a more straightforward version of the Em7 material covered in the third exercise.

The Bm7 shape that starts bar 2.

Hammer-on finger 1 to form B7.

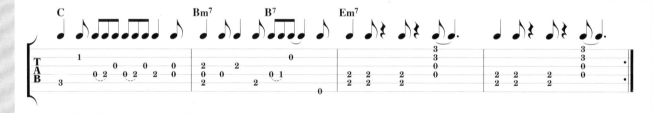

More finger barre practice

Start with an A minor chord shape in 5th position. Let this chord ring into bar 2, before removing the 3rd finger and re-striking the top three strings. Slide the half-barre up two frets to end bar 2, and observe the rest that starts bar 3. Keep the half-barre in place for the three-string chords in bar 3, and extend finger 1 to cover the D string at fret 7 in bar 4.

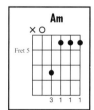

The opening A minor chord.

Slide finger 1 up to fret 7 in bar 2.

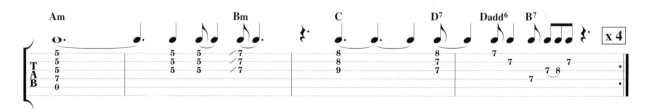

A powerful moment

There is an overall lightness of texture in *Marblehead Johnson*, but this passage briefly shakes off the delicate treatment. The notes of bars 2 and 3 are concentrated on the G string in a much more lead solo manner than anything that has come before. Slide finger 3 from fret 9 down to fret 7 in bar 2, and use finger 3 again, together with finger 2, on the B string to place the two-string chords in the same bar.

Begin with this 7th position D7 shape.

Slide finger 3 to fret 7 in bar 2.

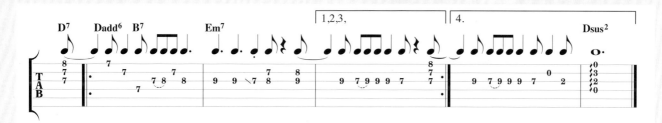

More chord shapes

A five-string G5 chord makes an impact in bar 1, for which you must mute out string 5 with the underside of finger 2. This unusual form of G5 provides all the notes to get you through to the end of the 2nd bar, at which point the emphasis swings towards a clutch of D chords. Dsus4 can be placed smoothly if you take advantage of the same finger 3 placement as for G5. Only the top E string notes change until you release all the left hand fingers for an open strum at the end of bar 4.

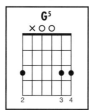

G5 in bar 1.

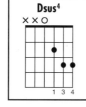

Dsus4 begins bar 3.

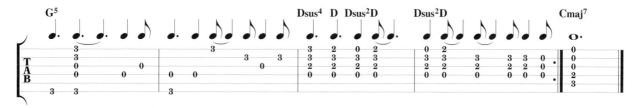

Winding down

The tempo slows down during the closing stages of *Marblehead Johnson*. The effectiveness of gradually slowing down just before the end of a song has been explored in earlier sessions. Traditionally, the Italian word *ritenuto*, abbreviated to *rit.*, is used to signify this change of tempo. Try to make the speed change gradual, otherwise you will end up with a jerky effect that destroys the final moments of the song. Make the hammer-ons quick but light, and ripple through the final E minor chord. The pause sign above this chord gives you the freedom to hold the chord for as long as you wish.

FIVE-FRET STRETCHES

This session's classic riff will test the endurance of your left hand.

The famous guitar riff in *Message In A Bottle* by The Police demands a high degree of left hand skill and a relaxed technique. Built on a repeating sequence of four add9 chord shapes, the riff virtually locks your hand into a five-fret stretch throughout the first pieces. Power chords, barre chords and some tasty Bluesy background licks contribute to the remainder of quite a busy session.

Stretching across five frets

This opening exercise introduces the finger pattern used throughout the riff. It is essential that you keep your thumb in a low, central location behind the guitar neck as you place fingers 1 and 3 in a conventional 4th position power chord shape. C#5 is transformed into C#madd9 by also placing finger 4 two frets up on the G string at fret 8. Take some of the pressure off the left hand by lying finger 1 lightly across the other strings. Keep the change to fret 5 on the bottom E string as smooth as you can in bar 3, then add fingers 3 and 4 to the A and D strings in bar 4 to form Aadd9.

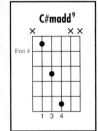

C#madd9 involves a five-fret stretch.

Smoothly shift finger 1 to fret 5 in bar 3.

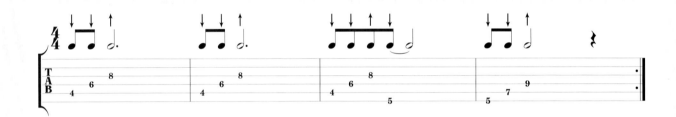

More add9 chord shifts

This piece provides some more practice of the extended add9 shape. Get used to placing the three notes of the opening Aadd9 chord separately, piling up the sounds from the different strings. The third note in each bar has a staccato mark, allowing the early release of the three fingers as you move finger 1 up to fret 7. Keep the other fingers fully extended in preparation for the return to Aadd9 in bar 2. Although the plectrum stroke directions are not yet essential, following them will make the riff easier to play at faster speed.

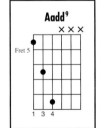

Aadd9 on the bottom three strings.

Move to 7th position for Badd9 in bars 2 and 4.

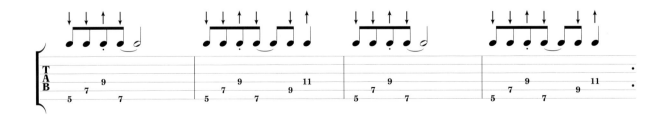

The four add9 chords

The 4th, 5th and 7th position add9 chords of bars 1 to 3 have been covered in the two previous pieces. Bar 4 introduces F#madd9, which is a five-fret shape in 2nd position on the bottom three strings. As you place fret 6 on the D string in bar 4, release fingers 1 and 3. You can now slide the 4th finger up to fret 7, before returning to C#madd9 in 4th position. Take note of the staccato markings – they are necessary when you come to play the full riff – and always keep the fingers spread.

The opening note of bar 4.

The finger slide in bar 4 starts at fret 6.

The riff

The notes, fingerings and shifts that make up this superb riff were dealt with in the first three exercises. The challenge of this piece is to link the four add9 chords together using the correct rhythm pattern. Tied note values break up the flow of quaver beats, and also give you a valuable, if brief, gap to think ahead as well as to make sure that your fingers are fully extended across five frets. Keep the fingers spread as you move between the chords, and always skim close over the frets to help you make the quick left hand changes.

Finger tip
THINKING AHEAD

The add9 chord changes come thick and fast in this riff, so always focus on the fret your 1st finger is moving to. The tempo also makes it essential to maintain the five-fret stretch of the left fingers at all times.

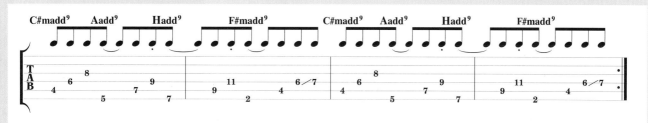

Palm muted power chords

The chorus moves away from add9 chords in favour of more straightforward, two-string power chord shapes. Work on this piece to make sure you can shift fluently from the final F#madd9 of the verse to the A5 shape in 5th position. The power chords are palm muted, but aim for a light contact of the palm against the bridge to allow a decent amount of the notes to sound. Bars 2 and 4 are played cleanly, using the heel of the right hand to effect the quaver rests.

Lightly palm mute the power chords.

A5 in bars 1 and 3.

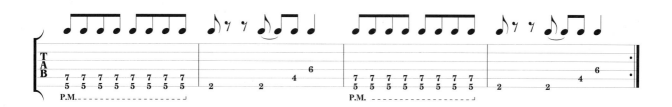

191

Adding D5 and E5

The actual chorus opens with a repeating two-bar phrase formed from A5, D5 and E5 chords. Two-string power chord shifts have featured frequently in *Play Guitar*, so your left hand should be comfortable with its role in these six bars. The palm muting might create the rests in bars 2 and 4, but if the chords ring for too long you can also slightly release the left finger pressure.

D5 on the A and D strings.

The same shape two frets higher forms E5.

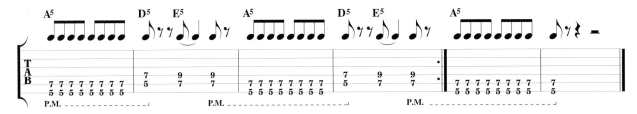

Shifting position using an open A string

Instead of imposing a lightning-quick left hand shift, it is often possible to integrate an open string, freeing up just enough time for a seamless change of position. The approach is used here to link F#5 and D5 via an open A on the last quaver of bars 1, 2 and 3. After streams of two-string chords, be sure to strike only the 5th string at the end of the first three bars.

F#5 in bars 1 and 3.

Use the open A to move up to 5th position.

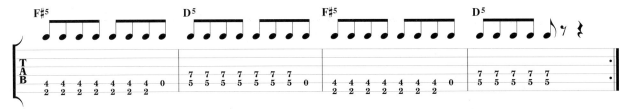

The entire power chord section

Here, you put together the power chord passages rehearsed in the two previous exercises. It involves only two small adjustments. First, at the end of bar 4, watch out for the link between E5 and F#5 in 2nd position. As you make this shift, retain the palm muted right hand location. The second difference is the longer sequence of alternating F#5 and D5 bars, with a minim chord on the third beat of bar 10.

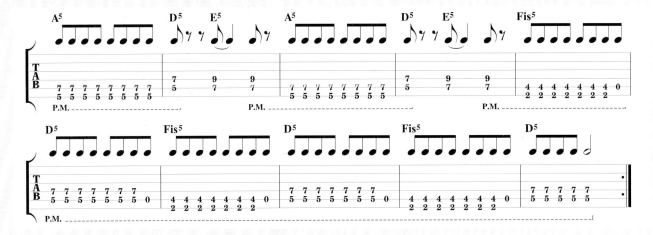

Tidy barre chords

The broken chord shapes in this exercise mark the beginning of a new stage of preparations.
Although the notes are played separately in bars 1 to 3, aim to place the full C# minor and
A chords at the beginning of each bar. By picking out the notes one at a time, you'll find it easier to hear any weak or blocked notes. Let the strings ring throughout each bar and aim to make the shift to the next shape as late as possible.

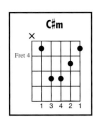

C#m in 4th position.

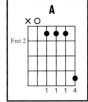

Use a barre for the A chords.

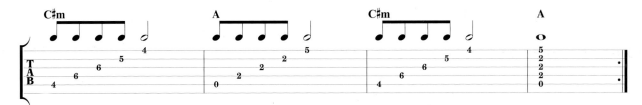

Another barre chord shape

A spacious accompaniment to the latter stages of the chorus is achieved by using long, sustained, strummed chords. C# minor and A major are joined by the F# minor barre chord shape. Success with these changes is very much dependent on the accuracy with which your finger barre shifts from five strings in C# minor, to four strings for the A chord, and finally extends across all six strings for F# minor. Notice that the F# minor chord is held for a full two bars before each repeat.

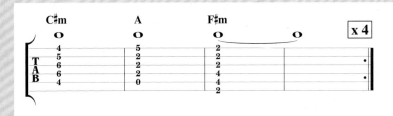

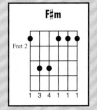

The F# minor barre chord.

The C# minor pentatonic scale

Background licks can add a subtle yet crucial element to the musical effect of the chorus. Without exception, these licks are created from the notes of a C# minor pentatonic scale. The pentatonic is presented here in an elaborated form, enhanced by a varied rhythm pattern, hammer-ons and finger slides. Use the 3rd finger for the slides and finger 1 for the final note of the 1st bar.

Start by hammering-on finger 3.

The top note of the C# minor pentatonic scale.

Bends and pre-bends

If you play an electric guitar, you can replace the slides between frets 7 and 9 in the previous exercise with string bends. This lick, based on the notes of the C# minor pentatonic scale, uses swift, full bends of the B string in bars 1 and 4. Bar 2 also contains a descending bend, sometimes referred to as a pre-bend, which gives the effect of the note falling. To achieve this, bend the string to a fret 9 pitch before you play, then swiftly strike it and release the bend, making sure that your three fingers remain in firm contact with the string.

Play a full bend in bar 1.   **Hammer-on at fret 6.**

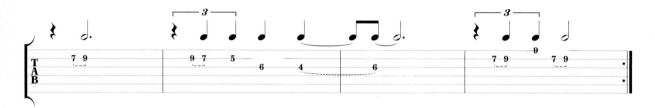

A rhythmically challenging lick

In addition to the technical demands of hammer-ons, slides and string bends, this piece contains awkward note lengths. Listening to the original song will improve your chances of successfully coping with the unusual combination of note values. Begin with finger 2 and stay in 5th position until you shift to finger 1 at fret 4 in bar 2. Quickly slide your 3rd finger down from fret 6 to fret 4. If you're playing acoustic, the bend in bar 1 can be replaced with a rapid 3rd finger slide up to fret 9. Watch out for the tricky timing at the start of bar 4.

Begin at fret 6 with finger 2.   **Quickly slide finger 3 down in bar 2.**

A new form of unison bend

This is the first time in *Play Guitar* that you have had to combine a note on one string with a pre-bend on another. It sounds difficult, and it is, but with plenty of practice it is sure to become second nature. Before you strike any notes, place finger 1 firmly on the top

E string at fret 4 and add a full bend of the 7th fret on the B string. After a crotchet rest, play the two strings together, then effect a gradual release of the B string bend. Use fingers 1 and then 2 for the 5th and 6th fret notes that complete the two-bar phrase.

Pre-bend fret 7 on the B string.

194

ALTERNATIVE TUNING

A host of new chord shapes are inspired by Joni Mitchell's inquisitive musical mind and fascination for uncommon tunings.

Rhythm guitar is the sole concern of this session as you prepare *Free Man In Paris* by Joni Mitchell. Mitchell has explored the potential of the guitar through the use of dozens of different tunings spanning her 30-year career.

The guitar part for this song is written with the top and bottom strings tuned down a tone to D. Make sure your instrument is tuned accordingly before trying any of these practice pieces.

Half-barred major chords

The unconventional de-tuning of the top string to D means that you can place the three notes of a major chord using just a 1st finger half-barre. The C and D major chords in this piece are an important component of the intro, as are the percussive mutes, which are marked, as always, by crosses on the TAB. To achieve the mutes, strum the three strings with the half-barre resting lightly across the 5th fret. Much of the plectrum work in the session follows the regular down-up pattern adopted in each of these four bars.

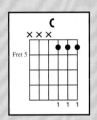

The opening C major chord.

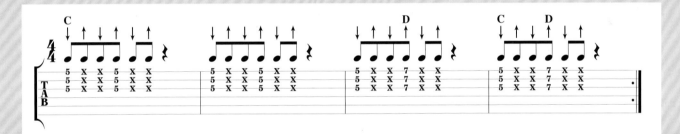

Adding F major

Now it's time to add another left hand position as you shift to the F chord. Extend the finger barre to cover four strings as you move up to the 10th fret. Although this chord is literally F major with a C in the bass, the simple F major label is adopted because most of the F chords played in this piece contain the top three strings only. Make a firm 1st finger contact at frets 5, 7 and then 10 for the C, D and F major strums respectively. As you shift between chords, loosen the finger pressure to produce percussive-muted strums.

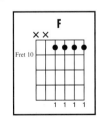

The F shape using a finger barre.

Finger tip

PERCUSSIVE MUTING

The damped strum is a crucial element of *Free Man In Paris*, and can be clearly heard on the original recording. This technique encourages a continuous alternate strum pattern, as well as providing a distinctive, percussive effect.

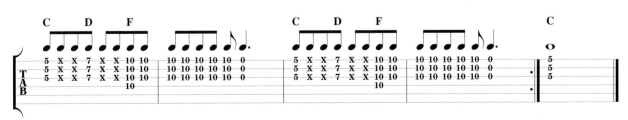

Open string colouring

Here, the most important chord of the song is the Aadd9 shape used throughout these five bars. As the key chord, it forms the backbone of the song's harmony and features in the intro, verse, chorus and instrumental bridge sections. The dropped bottom-string tuning creates this unusual major shape, with the open B string providing the add9 note. Aim to mute the top string by raising the left thumb and collapsing the hand shape slightly.

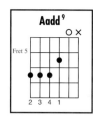

Use all four fingers to form Aadd9.

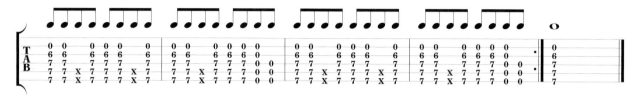

Varying the time signature

This exercise introduces a new idea by featuring bars containing different numbers of beats. An exciting, intentional juddering of the rhythm is the result of alternating three and then four crotchet beats in a bar. The concept is another example of Mitchell's enthusiasm for the unconventional within the framework of her songs. The C and G major shapes in bars 1 and 3 share the same finger pattern as Aadd9, the chord introduced in the previous piece, but they lack an open B string.

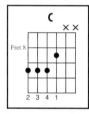

C major with a dropped D bottom string.

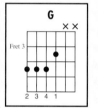

The same shape in 4th position makes G major.

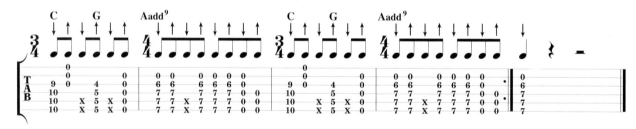

The complete intro

These opening bars, which bring together the major chords played on the upper strings and those based on the de-tuned bottom string. Remember to extend the finger barre across the 4th string for the first F chord in bar 1, and use the open-string strums that end bar 2 to shape up the piece's second version of C major. The 3rd bar has three beats, but provided you keep the quavers at the same speed as the preceding four-beat bars, this touch of rhythm variation should be manageable.

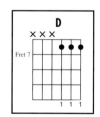

D major at fret 7.

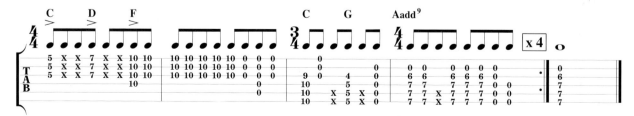

Another vital chord shape

The six-string D/A barre chord only achieves a pure major harmony when the hammer-on at fret 9 produces the necessary major 3rd. The 5th of the D major chord is at the bottom, hence the D/A label. It's interesting to think that, if the guitar was tuned with standard E notes on the outer strings, this shape's sound would be utterly transformed to that of a B minor 7 chord. Leave the barre in place for the whole piece, using finger 3 to hammer-on and then release to liven up this strum pattern.

Finger 1 barring all six strings.

Hammer-on finger 3 for D/A.

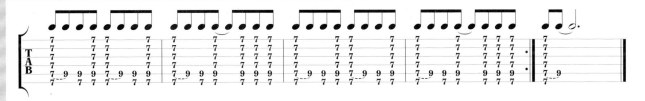

Shifting the same pattern

Try to maintain a regular down-up-down-up strumming action by moving the right arm back up during the execution of the hammer-ons, and remember to reduce the depth of your strums for the lighter two-string chords. The first two bars are almost identical to those of the previous piece. Carefully release the left hand shape for the open strings that end bar 2, at which point you should move the D/A chord down two frets. Bars 3 and 4 are then 5th position replicas of the opening two bars, the chord shape now becoming C/G.

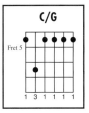

C/G in 5th position.

Repeating the previous bar

The sign that fills bars 2 and 3 has featured before in *Play Guitar*. It signifies a repeat of the bar before, and is a useful means of making the music easier to read. The repeating bar uses the four-fingered G major shape played in the Song's intro, but with an additional open B string. This fills out the sound of the chord and allows a full strum, so long as you are able to mute out the top string with the inside of the left hand. Keep finger 1 as straight as possible while you barre all six strings to make the brand new Fadd2/C in bar 4.

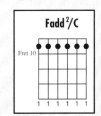

A full barre at fret 10.

The verse

Two chord shapes dominate the verse of *Free Man In Paris*. First, there is the Aadd9 pattern, which, when dropped to frets 4 and 5, also forms G major in bar 7. Second, there is the full barre chord shape plus 3rd finger hammer-on, which gives you both D/A and C/G when placed in 7th and 5th positions respectively. Try to make the muted notes as percussive as you can, without resorting to forced strokes, and use the open strings that end bar 2 to drop the thumb in time for the D/A barre chord that follows.

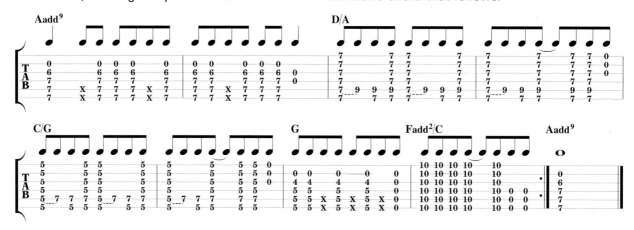

Accenting the offbeats

As a song pushes towards its chorus, the rhythm guitarist often invents a more elaborate strum pattern to mark the occasion. This series of Aadd9 bars isolates and repeats the two-bar rhythm fill that rounds off the verse. The upstrums marked with arrows (>) should be given a bit of extra weight in order to make these offbeats sound a little louder than the other chords. At the end of each pair of bars, release the left hand shape momentarily. The fingers return to the same locations after the open string chord.

Release Aadd9 slightly at the end of bars 2 and 4.

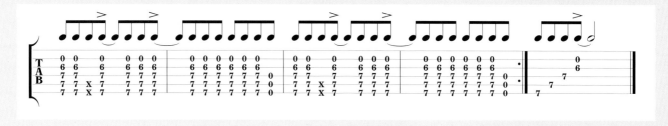

Creating a fuller sound

This piece introduces a new location for the D/A and C/G shape. You can produce an F/C chord by placing the barre across fret 10 and hammering-on finger 3 at fret 12 on the A string. The creases at the finger joints are a common source of weaker placement when barring, so it's worth checking from time to time that every string is sounding true by listening to each one separately. There are no muted strikes in this exercise and every strum produces a six-string chord. This results in a fuller sound.

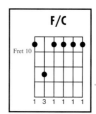

F/C is the third use of this shape in the song.

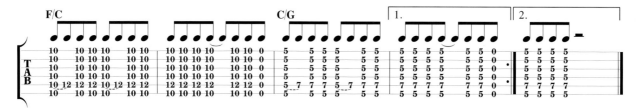

A splash of open top string

Full-strummed D/A and Aadd9 shapes make up the second half of the chorus chord sequence. As you hammer-on finger 3, keep the finger arched to avoid blocking the sound of string 4. Also, notice the subtle difference between these D/A bars and those in the complete intro piece. On this occasion, there are only two hammer-ons, followed by straight strums in the 2nd bar. The open top string in the 1st and 2nd time bars adds a touch of colour to Aadd9.

Arch Aadd9 to allow the open 1st string.

A SENSE OF ADVENTURE

Take a leaf out of Joni Mitchell's book and try dabbling with unusual string tunings. You might find the unconventional sounds this experimentation produces a great short cut to writing original songs.

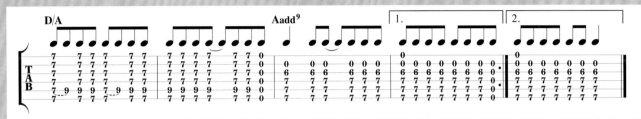

An uncommon chord

The use of unconventional tuning systems allows Joni Mitchell to create original-sounding chords, such as this Em11/A pattern. Without the dropped 1st string pitch, this particular chord voicing would be impossible to achieve. Also, pay attention to the deceptively tricky rhythm of this repeated two-bar phrase. Use fingers 2, 3 and 4 to place the fret 7 notes, and be as tidy as you can with the right hand work to emphasize the addition of the open top two strings for the upstrums.

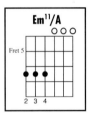

Em11/A using fingers 2, 3 and 4.

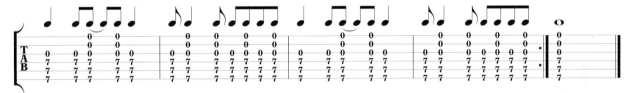

The instrumental bridge

The final section of *Free Man In Paris* combines the material used in the previous piece with bars of Aadd9 strums. The difference between the two chord shapes is minimal, the simple addition or release of finger 1 being all that is needed to make the switch. This instrumental bridge is followed by a return to the intro idea, so place the half-barre again as you start the final bar.

FAST SOLOING

Prepare for your playing to be pushed to the limits by the mighty riff and blistering solo of this session's arrangements.

Master the opening bar of *Place Your Hands* by Reef and you are well on your way to playing the whole song, such is the importance of this repetitive, chord-based riff. Although the song's solo is only six bars long, it contains relentless streams of hammer-ons and slides that would challenge even the most talented player. The session features dropped D tuning, so adjust your 6th string before starting to play.

Preparing the riff

The de-tuning symbol at the top left of the music instructs you to drop the bottom E string down a tone to D. This tuning applies to all the practice pieces, and each exercise features a standard four beats in a bar. Play an open 6th string, then use finger 1 to barre the top four strings at fret 7. With a low right wrist, strum down from string 4, then up again while avoiding contact with the top E string. A slight release of left finger pressure sets up the damped strum marked by crosses in bars 2 and 4. With the 1st finger barre firmly in place, hammer-on fingers 2 and 3 to create the G/D chords.

The opening D chord hand position.

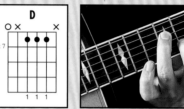

Hammer-on fingers 2 and 3 for G/D.

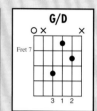

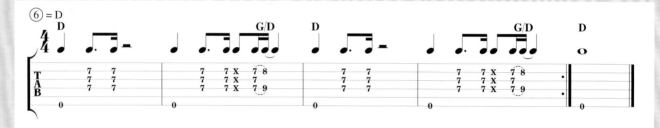

Completing the vital riff

The previous piece ought to have laid the foundations for a perfect performance of the song's all-important riff. Bars 1 and 2 of this exercise edge you ever closer to the finished product, with the addition of a further percussive strum before each hammer-on. Try to tidy up the over-ringing bottom D string by muting it with the heel of the right hand as you strum the first of the damped chords in each bar. Bars 3 and 4 present the definitive riff, which includes a further pair of percussive strums and a downstrummed G/D chord.

Strike the de-tuned D string first in each bar.

Release the pressure for the percussive strums.

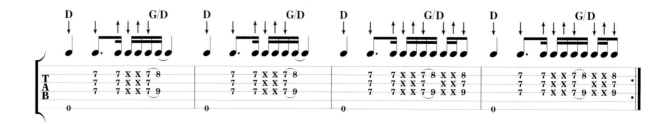

200

3rd finger barring

G major in 10th position features in one of the rare verse/chorus phrases that moves away from the riff. The frets are smaller at this end of the neck, so we suggest you barre all three fret 12 notes with finger 3 while also barring fret 10 with finger 1. Leave these fingers very lightly placed as you strike the percussive chords in the first two bars. Move the 1st finger barre up to fret 12, and use finger 3 for the hammer-ons in bar 3.

G major with a 3rd finger barre.

Shift up to 12th position in bar 3.

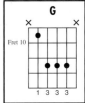

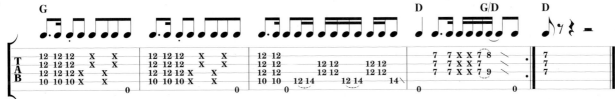

Incorporating subtle bends

This phrase from the end of the verse uses two string bends as part of a great Bluesy lick. After the initial open-string chord, barre finger 1 across strings 5 and 6. Release the barre as you strike the open G string. Place finger 1 at fret 3 on the D string for the half-bend in bar 2. Pull down towards the G string to make the one-fret bend, then follow with an open D. Bend the last note of bar 4 in the same manner, but this time aim for only the slightest bend, as indicated by the quarter symbol.

G5 in bar 2.

A half-bend of the D string in bars 2 and 4.

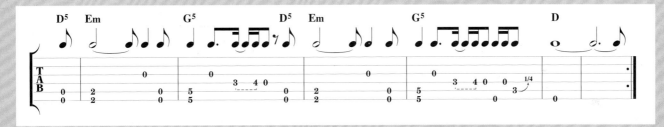

7th and power chord shapes

The bridge section of *Place Your Hands* features the 9th fret B5 chord. Play the chord with a 3rd finger barre, as this leaves finger 1 free to barre the fret 7 notes that follow. Block the A string as you play the G5 chords in bars 1 and 2 with finger 1. A conventional 2nd position

B5 shape dominates bar 3. This is decorated by a single fret 3 note on the D string, and then expanded to include finger 4 on the G string. At the end of bar 3, use your 3rd finger for the G5 fretted note, as this enables finger 1 to reach the abbreviated G7 chord.

Linking B minor and G major

Use finger 1 for the quick two-string slide up from 5th to 7th fret. Return this shortened barre chord to fret 5 after the tied note in bar 1, which also positions your hand for the 3rd finger pull-off and the subsequent move of the same finger across to the G string. Stay in 5th position as you connect the G chord shape in bar 2, using finger 1 on the lowest string.

The opening left hand position.

Another form of G major.

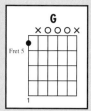

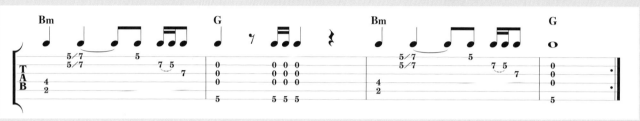

The entire bridge section

To complete the bridge, you need to add some extra G major strums and to join up the material covered in the previous two pieces. A 3rd finger on the G5 chord that ends bar 5 allows fingers 1 and 2 to shape up for

the three-string G7 chord in bar 6. The G major rhythm pattern rehearsed above is extended to fill bars 8 and 9, while the rests in these bars are best achieved using the side of the right hand.

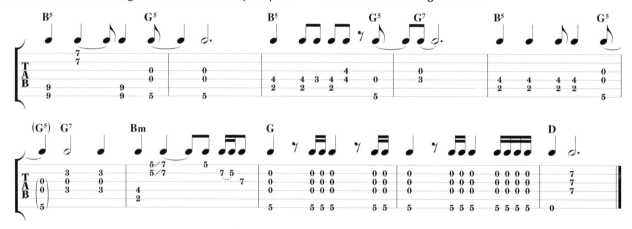

More D chord licks

In the middle of *Place Your Hands* there is a drum-break (drum solo) that includes brief snippets of guitar playing. Here, we have condensed the three guitar fills into a compact exercise based on the barred fret 7 chord, two-fingered hammer-on and open bottom D string from the main riff. Leave the 1st finger across fret 7 for the lick in bars 2 and 4, and use the 3rd finger for the hammer-on and pull-off that completes the picture.

Use the right hand to create the rests.

Variations on the riff

The riff also occurs in two slightly altered forms. Bar 3 of this exercise features the version used twice just after the drum-break. Bar 4 is a substitute for the standard riff, as played by Reef throughout the second and third verses. The lack of percussive strums makes both variations smoother than the original riff.

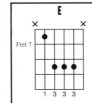

Barring the E chord with finger 3.

Finger tip

TO BARRE OR NOT TO BARRE?
There are two possible fingerings for the E and G chords in this exercise. You could try the standard A barre shape using fingers 1, 2, 3 and 4. However, squeezing three fingers into one of these small, higher fret positions can make barring all three strings with finger 3 a better option. Try out both ways and go for the one that works best for you.

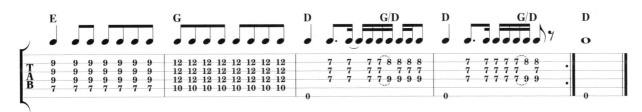

Beginning the solo

We have broken the six bars of the solo down into manageable, two-bar chunks. Quick moves between the D and G strings are eliminated by barring fret 7 with your 1st finger, while finger 3 is perfectly placed to deal with all the fret 9 notes. The slides that end each bar are to no fixed fret, so gradually release the finger pressure as it slips down the string.

Start by barring the D string at fret 7.

Use finger 3 for the fret 9 notes.

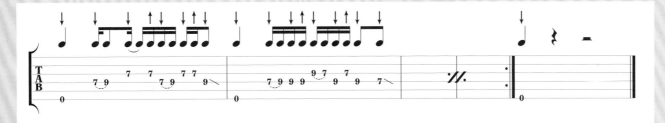

More hammer-on and pull-off combinations

The middle section of the solo persists with predominantly 7th position work, broadening to take in A string notes as well as those on the D and G strings. As in the previous exercise, hammer-ons and pull-offs are used regularly, making it easier to play so many notes at a fast speed. However, the downside is that this results in a more complicated plectrum stroke pattern. Persevere with the recommended stroke directions to prepare for eventually playing the pieces faster.

About to pull-off fret 7 in bar 2...

...followed by a fret 2 pull-off with finger 1.

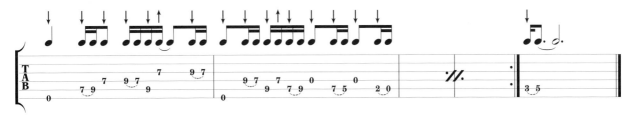

The toughest bar

Constant semiquavers and a brief shift up to 5th position put your technique firmly under the spotlight in bars 2 and 4. Hammer-ons, pull-offs, slides and the correct choice of stroke direction are the keys to success, along with the use of only fingers 1 and 3. Watch out, in particular, for the fast shift down to 3rd position for the series of three pull-offs that ends bars 2 and 4.

Begin with finger 1 in 3rd position.

Slide finger 3 to fret 7 in bars 2 and 4.

The full solo

String together the phrases practised in the previous three pieces to form an impressive solo. The links are not too tricky, but a high level of concentration is required to keep these six bars running along at the right tempo. You might find that memorizing the notes helps, rather than trying to read from the page.

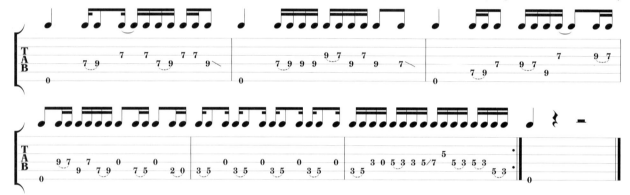

The closing stages

In bar 1, the notes and rhythm are essentially the same as the main riff, but the damped clicks have given way to firmly placed notes. Also, traces of the solo are evident in the D string hammer-on and the falling finger slide. In bar 2, slide the finger barre from fret 7 up to fret 12, remembering to place it across five strings in readiness for the A string hammer-on.

Finger 3 about to slide down from fret 14.

Finger tip

AN ACOUSTIC ALTERNATIVE TO 12TH POSITION

12th position passages, such as those in this piece and in the third exercise, are awkward to play on an acoustic guitar. These phrases can be dropped down to 7th position and played with the same fingerings on the D and G strings, plus finger 2 at fret 8 on the B string.

RELENTLESS RIFFING

The exacting riffs of Blur's guitar maestro dominate this session.

This session's exercises inspired by *There's No Other Way* by Blur feature two powerful and highly imaginative riffs. Guitarist Graham Coxon tears up the rule book to create these from finger-barred chords that swoop up and down the full length of the neck. He adds a liberal sprinkling of hammer-ons and pull-offs, plus a dash of percussiveness provided by damped strums to complete an electrifying piece of playing. All the practice pieces are played in standard tuning and have a time signature of four beats in a bar.

Sliding the finger barre

The technical demands of the opening riff are considerable, so take advantage of these slowed-down practice pieces to gain a full understanding of the fingerings, rhythm and plectrum work. Even though the opening chord contains just two 5th fret notes, use your 1st finger to barre the top four strings for this and every chord in the piece. Firmly slide the barre up to fret 12 where the percussive chord, marked with crosses, is achieved by muting the strings with the side of the right hand as you strike them with the plectrum. Repeat the muting process at fret 3 after sliding the finger barre down from the 12th fret chord.

A 1st finger barre at fret 5.

Mute the strings as you strike the damped chords.

Hammering-on a 3rd finger barre

Begin in the same manner as above, but this time add a downstroke of the D and G strings on the 2nd crotchet beat of bar 1. Use the side of the right hand to make the quaver rest, then repeat the whole process and add a 3rd finger hammer-on at fret 14. As you hammer-on again in bar 2, collapse finger 3 to also barre the G and B strings in readiness for the upstroke that follows. After another clicked chord, release finger 3, leaving finger 1 still in place for the three-string chord at fret 12 that ends bar 2.

Slide the barre up to fret 12.

Hammer-on a 3rd finger barre at fret 14.

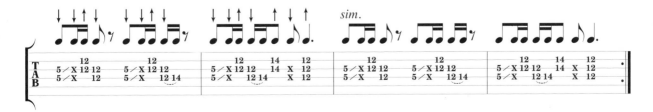

Adding Asus4 and A chords

Start with a 1st finger barre across the top four strings at fret 3 and be careful to avoid strumming the 1st string with the plectrum. The fret 5 chord should be played with a 3rd finger barre, and the crossed notes should be created by striking the D and G strings while keeping the side of the right hand in firm contact with the strings. This gives you a moment to shift the 1st finger barre up to fret 5 for the Asus4 and A chords that end bar 1. Return to 3rd position as you begin bar 2, and keep finger 1 in place as you hammer-on a 3rd finger barre at fret 5.

The Asus4 shape.

Asus4 resolves to A major.

The complete opening riff

Here are four repeats of the two-bar riff that begins *There's No Other Way* and recurs frequently during the course of the song. You played bars 1 and 3 in their entirety back in the second exercise, and you should use the recommended plectrum stroke directions from that earlier piece. The 2nd bar of the riff connects the bold slide down from fret 12 to 3rd position with the hammer-on and A chord material of the previous exercise. Keep the 1st finger barre across fret 5 as you play the Asus4 and A chord shapes that end bars 2 and 4.

Finger tip

ALL BARRE NONE

1st and 3rd finger barres should be used at all stages of the first riff. This combination promotes smooth chord placement by reducing the number of position shifts.

Starting the next riff

The second riff is used to accompany the verses and the backwards guitar solo. It also merits an instrumental appearance just before Blur's Damon Albarn starts to sing. Keep the 1st finger barre at fret 2 throughout bars 1 to 3. The photos show the two main shapes used, while the 5th position Asus4 and A chords return in bar 4. Count carefully to observe the quaver rest that begins the final bar.

The opening E5 chord.

The D major shape.

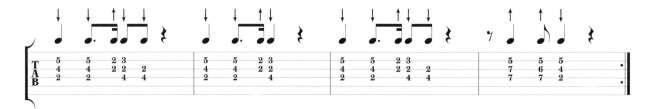

Sliding the 3rd finger

Start by taking the unusual step of sliding the barred 3rd finger between fret 4 and fret 7. This finger choice keeps the left hand shifts to a minimum. Always strike the chord following the finger slide with the plectrum. Use a more conventional 1st finger barre for the return to fret 4 on the staccato-marked 3rd beat of bars 1 to 4. This clipped chord gives the 1st finger barre time to drop to 2nd position for the hammer-on and pull-off figure of bars 1 to 3 and the slightly busier end to bar 4.

Use a 3rd finger barre for the 1st beat chords.

Hammer-on finger 2 at the 3rd fret.

Putting together the second riff

If the previous two pieces are sounding good, you should find it straightforward to link the sections of the verse riff together. Keep finger 1 barred across the top four strings throughout bar 1 and aim for smooth changes of the other fingers.

At the start of bar 2, release finger 1 and place your 3rd finger across the 4th fret. After the staccato 4th fret chord, return to 2nd position and hammer finger 3 onto the D string. Follow this with a hammer-on and pull-off of finger 2 on the B string.

The staccato fret 4 chord.

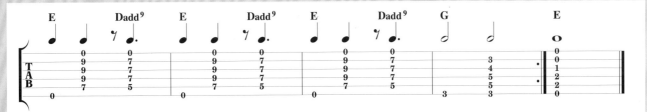

A rest from riffing

After the intricate riffs, you'll be glad to see the more sustained full chords of the chorus section. E major in 7th position is virtually the A barre chord shape, but the open top string removes the need for a barre. Allow the open E in bars 1, 2 and 3 to carry on ringing as you strike the five remaining strings together on beat 2. Dadd9 is the same shape again, only this time down two frets, in 5th position. The G major chord in bar 4 requires a standard six-string barred shape in 3rd position.

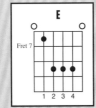

E major in 7th position.

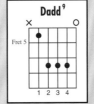

Shift down 2 frets for Dadd9.

Two more versions of A major

A three-string form of A major featured in the first riff. The three notes of that chord are also present in the six-string A major shape that ends bars 2 and 4 of this piece. The extra notes are achieved by shifting the G barre chord of the previous piece up two frets to 5th position. A major also appears in bars 1 and 3 as a four-string shape, with a 1st finger barre taking care of the fret 2 notes. Avoid the top string in bars 1 and 3.

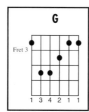

The G major barre chord.

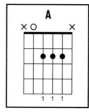

A major in 2nd position.

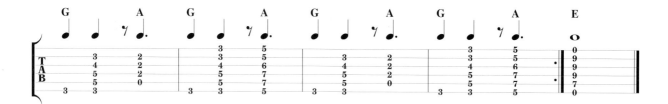

A slow trill

Trills (hammer-on and pull-off combinations) are needed in bars 2 and 4 of this exercise, although the speed of the notes is fairly slow. The E chord requires a 1st finger barre across strings 1 to 4, which should be held in place as the trill is made using finger 2 at fret 10. Another major shape forms both the G and A chords in bars 1 and 3. As with so much of the left hand work in this session so far, these require a 1st finger barre across the top four strings.

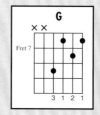

G major in 7th position.

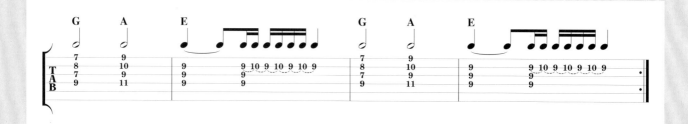

A novel form of finger slide

The chorus ends with this brief solo guitar phrase. After a minim rest, the 1st finger slides from fret 7 down to fret 4, then immediately back up to fret 7 again. Strike only the first of these three notes if you wish to recreate the original effect. Drop finger 1 to fret 4 for the last note of bar 1, which positions finger 2 for the 5th fret notes on the D string. The 2nd finger slides up to fret 7 in bar 2, from where fingers 1 and 2 can deal with the swift hammer-on and pull-off combination that follows.

Finger 1 at fret 7.

Slide finger 2 up to fret 7.

The chorus

There's plenty to bear in mind as you play the full chorus. Concentrate on landing the 1st note of bar 2 before worrying about the rest of the G barre chord fingers. Also, see if you can mute the strings on beat 3 of the opening two bars, to help you shift neatly to the next chord position. Think ahead as you approach the 7th position G chord that starts bar 3, and keep your fingers close to the strings as you shift.

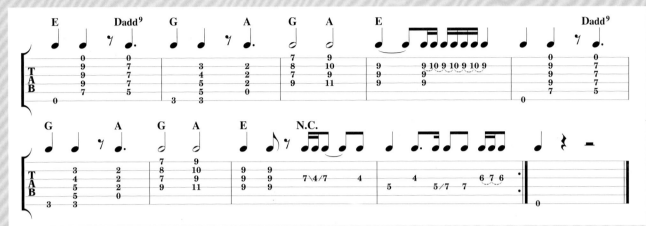

High-position strumming

One more riff comes at the very end of the song. It is based on the fast strumming of a four-string major chord shape in 12th, 10th and 7th positions. These chords are tricky to play (particularly on an acoustic) and the 2nd finger hammer-ons need to be firm to have any real impact. The shift down to D major is extremely fast, so stay alert and notice the touch of 4th finger sus4 colouring in the three-string chord near the end of bar 2.

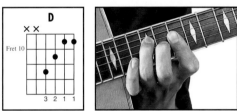

D major in 10th position.

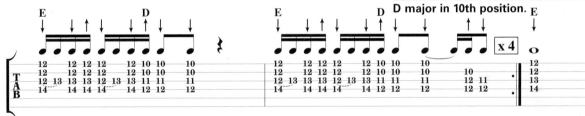

B major joins the D and E chords

In this final piece, you practice the finished outro, a development of the four-string chords that dominated the previous exercise. Drop the shape to 7th position for B major before returning to D major in 10th position. Make sure you shift on the right beat, and use a light, relaxed alternate strum to cope with the quick tempo.

Ready to start in 12th position.

Finger tip

If you play acoustic, try this adaptation

for the 12th position E chords.

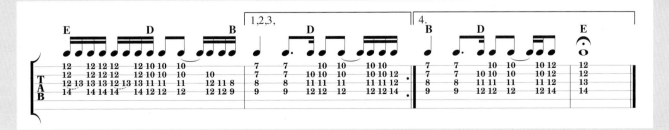

REFINING YOUR RHYTHM SKILLS

Our final session's arrangement, Crazy Little Thing Called Love by Queen, is a perfect balance between strummed chords and vintage rock'n'roll lead guitar.

Somewhat unusually, Freddie Mercury played acoustic, 12-string rhythm guitar on this classic song, while Brian May put his famous home-made guitar to one side and used a Telecaster for the lead fills and solo.

Although our adaptation concentrates on the rhythm guitar work, it also includes the central solo, which is modelled on the playing style of rock'n'roll greats such as Scotty Moore and Chet Atkins.

A touch of Dsus4 colour

Crazy Little Thing Called Love has a swinging rhythm that is written out using a 12/8 time signature. You will remember that you have had some previous experience of this timing. In this exercise, most of the chords are D major, with an occasional 3rd fret note added to the top string to lend a touch more musical interest. Use finger 4 for the extra 3rd fret note, which changes D major to Dsus4. However, the chord quickly returns to D major, so leave finger 2 at fret 2 throughout.

The key chord of D major.

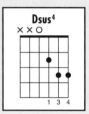

Add finger 4 for Dsus4.

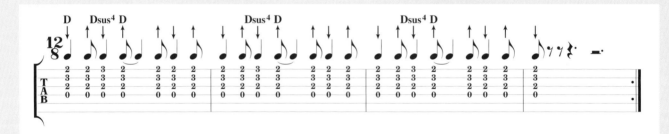

A new G major chord fingering

Most of the chords in this issue's exercises have featured before in *Play Guitar*. Many, such as D major and the C chord in bars 2 and 4, have been regulars since early in the series. However, the G major chord here is slightly altered since it lacks a note on the A string. Also, a smoother change to C major can generally be achieved by using fingers 3 and 4 for the two fretted notes of this G chord shape. The stretch can take a little getting used to, but you will probably find that the A string is automatically damped by this finger selection.

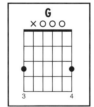

G major with a damped A string.

Follow C major with this G/B shape.

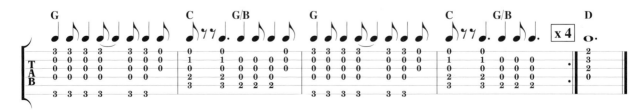

Smooth B♭ to C major changes

The shift between B♭ major and the C chord from the previous piece is not easy. The thumb has to drop down behind the neck for the B♭ major barre chord shape, then move up higher for a comfortable C chord position. Also, the 1st finger barre has to release in favour of a B string only placement and the 3rd finger is poorly positioned for a smooth change. Bar 2 shows how the C chord can be placed in stages during the song, starting with finger 1 only on the lighter, three-string upstrum.

B♭ major in 1st position.

A standard C major chord.

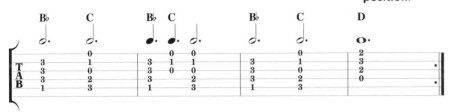
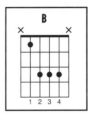
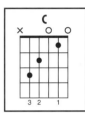

Putting the verse sequence together

Take full advantage of the open-string upstrums that end bars 2, 3 and 5 to shape the next chord. Use the side of the right hand to quickly smother the C chord at the start of bar 4, while a smooth switch to finger 2 for the G/B chords is your objective in the remainder of the bar. Both the down- and upstrums generally contain the same number of strings, which encourages a positive approach.

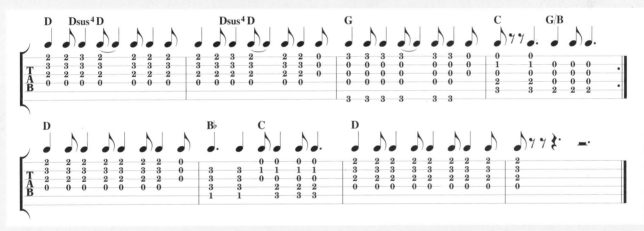

Adding three more chords

The bridge contains a few different rhythm figures as well as three more chords. Clipped C chords on the first three beats of bar 1 lead to the G chord with fingers 3 and 4. Prepare the finger barre above fret 1 during the G strums for a neat transfer to B♭ major, which, as before, does not include the top string. The E, A and F chords of bars 3 and 4 use their standard fingerings, while a pronounced silence precedes the single-note fill.

E major in bar 3.

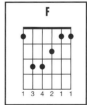

The F barre chord in 1st position.

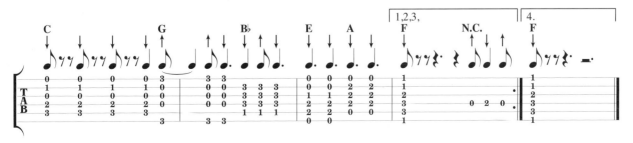

211

An effective single-note passage

Two three-note bars begin this excerpt from the bridge. The sudden sense of space and the ambiguity of the rhythm have a potent effect, emphasized by the return of hammered-out strums across the beats of bar 3. Use fingers 3, 2 and then 1 for the single notes of bars 1 and 2, and use the same three fingers to shape both the E and A major chords in bars 3 and 4.

Use finger 3 for the opening note.

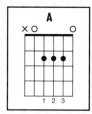

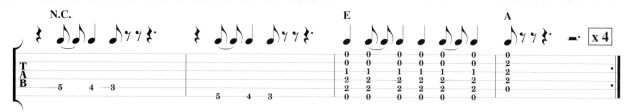

Play a clipped A chord in bar 4.

Double-stopping

The high proportion of string bends in the solo makes it a nightmare to play on an acoustic guitar. Something of a compromise can be achieved by sliding finger 3 between the 13th and 15th fret notes of this piece, although this is by no means easy so far up the neck of the guitar. Start with a 1st finger barre across the top two strings at fret 9, then strike both strings and slide quickly up to fret 10. The series of two-string chords in bar 1 are examples of double-stopping, a term used to describe the playing of two fretted notes at the same time.

Swiftly slide a two-string barre up to fret 10.

> ## Finger tip
>
> **A SMOOTH LINK TO THE FULL BEND**
>
> As finger 1 is busy right to the end of bar 1 of this piece, use only fingers 2 and 3 to produce the full bend at the start of bar 2. You then have until beat 3 to position your 1st finger at fret 11, ready for the pull-off.

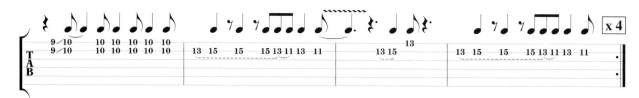

Barring the 3rd finger

This piece starts with the same 1st finger double-stopping as the previous piece, but this time watch out for the single B string note that follows the slide. Use a 3rd finger barre for the two-string fret 12 chord towards the end of bar 1, as this allows you to remain in 10th position. A lively run of fret 10, 11 and 12 notes comes next, including a swift 1st to 2nd finger hammer-on. Take a close look at the note values above the TAB and try to hear the rhythm in your head before attempting to play.

Barre the 12th fret chord with finger 3.

Finger 2 at fret 11 on the G string.

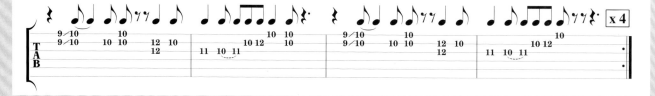

A series of full bends

Start with fingers 1, 2 and 3 all placed along the B string at frets 11, 12 and 13. This gives you all the leverage you need to bend the string up to a fret 15 pitch. Mute the bend and add finger 4 at fret 13 on the top E string. Now remove finger 4 from the 1st string and quickly prepare the B string for another full bend. Remove fingers 2 and 3 together to make the pull-off to fret 11. The left hand remains in 11th position throughout.

A full bend at fret 13.

Hold the bend and add finger 4 in bars 1, 2 and 3.

Another bend and pull-off combination

Begin by sliding a double-stopped chord up the top two strings from fret 11 to fret 12. Leave finger 1 at fret 12 and reach to fret 15 on the B string with finger 3. Release finger 1 as you half-bend string 2 at fret 13 using only finger 2. Extend fingers 3 and 1 for the series of five notes that follows at frets 14 and 11, then shift up to 14th position for a bend and pull-off combination just like that played in the previous piece, only three frets higher.

Keep the barre firm and reach up to fret 15.

Use finger 2 only for the half bend in bar 1.

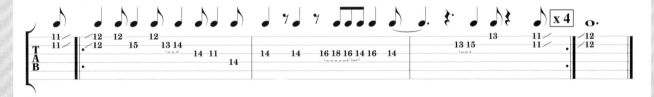

The complete solo

Take care to wait for the crotchet rest before coming in with the opening, double-stopped slide. As you work your way through the nine bars that follow, notice how your left hand operates mainly within a tight fret 10 to fret 13 zone. This just goes to show that you don't need to be flying up and down the guitar neck to turn in an impressive, inventive solo. For practice purposes, there's a repeat at the end of bar 9, and you'll need to be alert if you are to make it back to fret 9 in time for the second play-through.

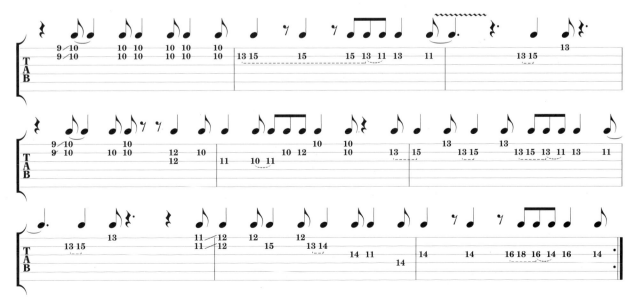

PLAY LIKE THE GUITAR GREATS

Have you ever wanted to play like Jimi Hendrix, Kurt Cobain, Chet Atkins or Django Reinhardt but you didn't know how? Well, in this section you can learn exactly that: how to play the great guitarists' songs in their own signature styles.

With biographies of 36 featured guitarists covering many years of popular music and introductory essays on each featured style from folk to country to jazz to blues and rock and pop, this section guides you through a song or more from each guitarist, showing you the musical notation and how to master the fingering.

In addition there is supporting text on each guitarist's preferred guitar, amplifier, accessories and playing style. From finger-picking acoustic work to slide guitar, from stratocasters to dobros and effects achieved with fuzz boxes, bottlenecks or violin bows, you will find it all explained in the following pages.

PLAY LIKE THE GUITAR GREATS

Over the last fifty years one instrument has come to dominate

popular music: the guitar. Whether it's the electric guitar, as

wielded by rock legends from Jimmy Page to Kurt Cobain, and

blues legends from BB King to Stevie Ray Vaughan, or the

acoustic guitar as strummed by folk artists from Woody

Guthrie to Nick Drake, it's the instrument that

defines the sound of our times.

RIGHT *The hollow-bodied acoustic guitar remains a popular and practical instrument for guitar students and professionals.*

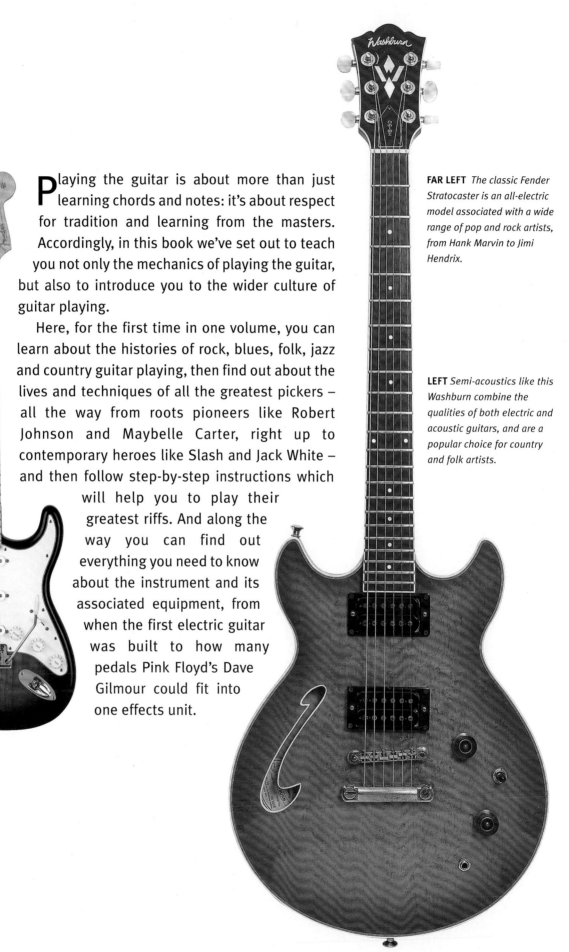

Playing the guitar is about more than just learning chords and notes: it's about respect for tradition and learning from the masters. Accordingly, in this book we've set out to teach you not only the mechanics of playing the guitar, but also to introduce you to the wider culture of guitar playing.

Here, for the first time in one volume, you can learn about the histories of rock, blues, folk, jazz and country guitar playing, then find out about the lives and techniques of all the greatest pickers – all the way from roots pioneers like Robert Johnson and Maybelle Carter, right up to contemporary heroes like Slash and Jack White – and then follow step-by-step instructions which will help you to play their greatest riffs. And along the way you can find out everything you need to know about the instrument and its associated equipment, from when the first electric guitar was built to how many pedals Pink Floyd's Dave Gilmour could fit into one effects unit.

FAR LEFT *The classic Fender Stratocaster is an all-electric model associated with a wide range of pop and rock artists, from Hank Marvin to Jimi Hendrix.*

LEFT *Semi-acoustics like this Washburn combine the qualities of both electric and acoustic guitars, and are a popular choice for country and folk artists.*

ROCK AND POP GUITARISTS

Just as rock music itself evolved out of other pre-existing musical forms – rhythm & blues and country music in particular – so rock guitar emerged from a variety of sources. The dominant influence may have been electric blues guitar playing, but there are also definite influences from country guitar playing and from mainstream pop.

BELOW: *Carlos Santana lays into a guitar riff. Santana began learning the guitar at age eight, entering professional music just after he finished high school.*

Above all, though, the rise of rock guitar is intimately connected with technology. Rock was the first music to grow up with the electric, rather than the acoustic, guitar as the standard instrument. The first electric guitars had been around since the 1920s, but it was only with T-Bone Walker's adoption of the electric guitar in a blues context, in the early 1940s, that the roots of rock guitar playing can really begin to be seen. Walker and his successors – bluesmen like B.B. King, John Lee Hooker and Muddy Waters – began to demonstrate the awesome power and volume the electric guitar could offer.

Meanwhile, in the field of country music, players like Merle Travis and Chet Atkins were developing a more melodic finger-picked electric style. Gradually, during the 1950s, the two styles began to come together. You can hear them both at work in the guitar playing of Scotty Moore with Elvis Presley. Moore was a country picker raised in the Merle Travis school, but he was recording in the same Sun Studios where a host of electric bluesmen had worked, and their influence most certainly rubbed off on him.

Another key player in the development of rock guitar was Bo Diddley. Bo Diddley came out of a rhythm & blues background, but his idiosyncratic additions of Cuban rhythm and full-on showmanship, plus a knack for the catchy nursery rhyme-simple song, proved a huge influence on rockers to come.

Then there was Chuck Berry. If there's a single inventor of rock guitar playing, it has to be Chuck Berry. He took blues and country and melded them together in a defiantly original, deceptively simple, style that was to provide the building blocks for everything that was to follow. All the early rock guitarists – from Buddy Holly to Cliff Gallup to James Burton – were disciples of the great Berry.

The flame of rock died down considerably in the USA during the late 1950s. For a while rock guitar seemed to appear only on instrumental recordings – Link Wray's sinister 'Rumble', Lonnie Mack's 'Memphis', a whole heap of Duane Eddy records – before surf music arrived in the early 1960s, and the likes of Jan And Dean and The Beach Boys once more raided Chuck Berry's riff larder.

SOUNDTRACK TO A GENERATION

For most of the next decade rock guitar – and rock music generally – would be dominated by musicians from across the Atlantic. Rock 'n' roll had a huge impact in the UK, and a generation of teenagers started learning Chuck Berry riffs – among them the likes of George Harrison, Keith Richards, Jimmy Page and Ritchie Blackmore. They all started out playing Chuck Berry covers in local bands, and by the early 1960s, they had started to get pretty good at it. Gradually, too, they started to write their own material.

Leaders in the field were, of course, The Beatles. Prior to The Beatles, rock 'n' roll and teen pop had always featured a pretty boy standing at the front, with the musicians kept well in the background. The Beatles ushered in the era of the band. Typical bands were four- or five-piece combos with vocalist, bassist and drummer plus either one or two guitarists. Steadily the role of the guitarist began to rival that of the singer in importance.

Despite their fame, The Beatles may not be thought of as a guitar band, but the guitar playing of John Lennon and particularly George Harrison was to become hugely influential. Harrison's knack for a catchy riff or an interesting fill inspired thousands of guitarists to follow in his wake.

The guitar became even more prominent in the work of The Beatles' great rivals, The Rolling Stones. Signature Stones' songs

ABOVE: *Chuck Berry performs his legendary 'duck walk' guitar step. He said he created the step in 1956, originally to hide the creases in a rayon suit.*

like 'Satisfaction' were driven by the guitar riffs, and Keith Richards was seen by many fans as the real heart of the band.

While the likes of Harrison and Richards tried to combine their love of R&B and blues with the demands of a pop career, other young British guitar players were getting ever deeper into the blues. The first of these to really make a name for himself was Eric Clapton, though others, like Peter Green, soon followed. The original guitar hero, Clapton was inspired by American bluesmen like Freddie King, and his virtuosity on his instrument made him the star of every band he was in. As the 1960s moved on, and the album market began to develop, Clapton and his followers were able to stretch out and solo for as long as they liked.

If Clapton's playing sometimes veered towards the self-indulgent, and was certainly angled more at his fellow musicians than the mass of pop fans, the next great guitarist to emerge showed that technical brilliance could be allied to rock 'n' roll showmanship. His name was Jimi Hendrix and his impact on rock guitar playing is unrivalled. Here was a man who understood that the electric guitar was not just an acoustic guitar with a pickup, but an instrument in its own right with its own extraordinary sonic potential.

Other guitar players were quick to exploit the new sonic territory that Hendrix opened up. Jimmy Page, a versatile former session musician, formed Led Zeppelin and combined delicate folk-derived playing with fiery full-on electric assaults. Jeff Beck, thought by many to be the most technically gifted of all the classic rock guitarists, gradually fused jazz influences into his playing. Others, like Ritchie Blackmore of Deep Purple and Tony Iommi of Black Sabbath, opted for a simplified style known as heavy metal, in which the riff was king.

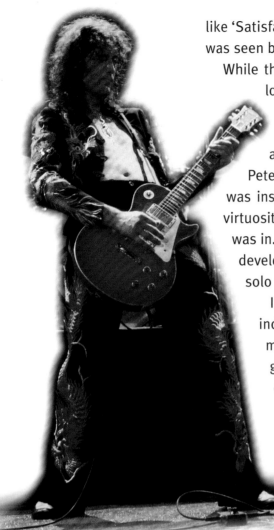

ABOVE: *Jimmy Page joined forces with singer Robert Plant to create legendary riffs such as 'Whole Lotta Love' and student guitarists' all-time favourite, 'Stairway to Heaven'.*

A NEW BREED OF GUITAR HEROES

By the late 1960s American guitarists had responded convincingly to the British invasion. The Grateful Dead's Jerry Garcia developed a style of psychedelic rock playing that drew heavily on the folk and country tradition. The Allman Brothers' Duane Allman and Dickey Betts brought soul and jazz influences into a southern rock style. Texan Johnny Winter offered a blistering blues attack, while California's Carlos Santana fused Latin American influences into his melodic post-Hendrix style.

In the late 1970s rock music went through a period of re-evaluation. The rock gods of the previous decade had become increasingly self-indulgent and punk rock came along to take rock back to basics. The new breed of rock guitar heroes to emerge in the next decade were typically disciplined, focused players who understood the demands of the song. Such players included the supreme hard rock technician Eddie Van Halen, and the much more technically limited, but undeniably effective, The Edge from U2. Nile Rodgers also demonstrated that the guitar had a place at the heart of funk, while Prince showed that boundaries between funk, rock, pop and psychedelia were all imaginary if you had the nerve – and the talent – to cross them.

Perhaps the definitive late 1980s guitar hero was Slash from Guns n' Roses. His riff for 'Sweet Child O' Mine', along with his wholesale appropriation of the Keith Richards rock 'n' roll swagger, marked something of a last hurrah for the traditional guitar hero.

During the 1990s the music business became increasingly diffuse. It was no longer possible to talk of rock as being a single entity. Different strands – punk, metal, nu-metal, country-rock, post-rock, roots-rock – all flourished alongside each other, their followers barely aware of each other's existence. So, too, the styles of rock guitar became more varied. At one extreme a new kind of 'guitar player's guitar player' emerged – phenomenally gifted musicians like Steve Vai and Joe Satriani who have huge followings among guitar buffs, yet are almost unknown to the general public. At the other extreme were musicians like Kurt Cobain and The White Stripes' Jack White who proudly displayed their punk credentials and disdain for musical snobbery. Meanwhile guitarists like Sonic Youth's Thurston Moore tried their utmost to take sonic exploration to its outer limits.

With such a wide breadth of guitar styles to choose from today, one might feel that there is not a whole lot of new territory to explore. However, all aspiring guitarists have to begin by choosing a style or styles to imitate; then, if they

BELOW: *Keith Richards of the Rolling Stones studied the work of early blues guitarists in the early 1960s to develop his distinctive style and tunings.*

have the talent, they will go on to create their own style. If they do, they will find that even today, there is always room for that indefinable element that makes a 'guitar great': originality.

KEEPING IN THE BACKGROUND

Playing rock guitar isn't always about taking centre stage and pulling dramatic poses. Rock and pop music are ultimately song-based and some of the form's consummate craftspeople are those guitarists who would hate for you to be distracted by their playing, and who put all their talent at the service of expressing the song. Perhaps the ultimate example of this type of musician is the guitarist from the all-time definitive pop/rock group, The Beatles. As a guitarist George Harrison was the ultimate team player. Lennon and McCartney may have hogged the limelight but without George's support they wouldn't have been nearly so successful. Time and time again, Harrison crafted intros, fills and lead lines that were as hook-laden as the songs themselves. He opened John Lennon's rocker 'A Hard Day's Night' with a single ringing G7sus4 chord, in the process creating one of the most celebrated introductions in rock. Throughout 1964 and 1965, Harrison uncorked one Rickenbacker riff after another, from the descending fills of 'Help' to the ear-grabbing opening in 'Ticket to Ride'. It's hard to imagine those songs without the sections George created. Divorce any one of them from the track, and the song just doesn't sound right.

When rock took a more aggressive turn in 1966, Harrison once again switched instruments, acquiring a Gibson SG and announcing his presence with authority on McCartney's 'Paperback Writer', the toughest-sounding A-side in The Beatles' collection. On *Revolver*, Harrison's experimental nature led to yet another new wrinkle: backwards guitar.

Even as the artistic and personal distance between Lennon and McCartney increased in later years, Harrison's guitar work continued to create the impression of a unified group. From *Sgt. Pepper* forward, the music was really Lennon songs or McCartney songs, but George helped keep the cohesion because he'd put his signature parts in all of them. Unlike most guitar heroes, more often than not the whole point of George Harrison's playing was not to be noticed.

THE CLASSIC ROCK SET-UP

So you want to play rock guitar? Well you'll need a guitar and an amp. Now the first thing to remember is that these two purchases need to go together. Not all amps sound great with every guitar, and vice versa. So let's start with the guitar first.

ABOVE: *The modern electric guitar has, in general terms, developed little from the best guitars of the 1950s and 1960s, although the range of ancillary electronic effects has hugely expanded.*

Very crudely, there are three types of classic rock guitar. There's the Gibson Les Paul and SG, great riff guitars popular with hard rockers. There's the Fender Stratocaster and Telecaster, popular with bluesier players from Jimi Hendrix to Stevie Ray Vaughan. Finally there are the Rickenbackers and the Gretsches, popular with bands from the Beatles to REM who are looking for something a little twangier. If you're not sure which camp you fit into, try a few out; there's no one guitar that fits every player's style.

Next step is to choose the right amp for your guitar. If you're looking to play classic rock then you're likely to be interested in a vintage-style amp. There are three main types: Marshall style, Fender style and Vox style. Essentially what makes these amps 'vintage' is the lack of a pre-amp section to generate distortion. This means that to generate overdrive or distortion, you either have to turn them all the way up to 11 or, better, use a distortion pedal. The advantage of a pedal/vintage amp situation, especially for live work, is that you only have one volume control to worry about.

So which style of vintage amp should you go for? Well it's worth looking at what has worked for the guitar greats. The classic rock 'n' roll guitar/amp combinations are Gibson into a Marshall amp, Fender into a Fender amp and Rickenbacker or Gretsch into a Vox amp (there are of course exceptions – Hendrix, for instance, played his Fender Strat through a Marshall amp). Don't take these principles as given, however, but bear in mind that these are well tried and tested combos.

The guitar and vintage amp combo, with effects pedals as required, is the choice of most working musicians. It's simple, relatively cheap and versatile. However, if you're more confident with your sound you might want a modern style guitar amplifier like a Mesa Boogie or a Peavey Classic. These amps offer a lot more features than the vintage amps. Great if you know exactly what sound you're looking for, but confusing for a beginner. Finally, though it's between you and your ears (and the patience of the staff in your local music shop). Experiment and enjoy.

BELOW: *Prince was at the forefront of funk guitar playing, developing the style during the 1980s with tracks such as ' When Doves Cry' and ' Purple Rain'.*

BO DIDDLEY

1928–2008
BAND: **SOLO ARTIST**
HEIGHT OF FAME: **1950s–60s**

Bo Diddley is one of the most influential of all rock guitar players. However, his style is not one you're going to pick up simply by reading the sheet music. With Bo Diddley's guitar playing it's all about the rhythm. This is a guitar player whose two most famous songs, 'Bo Diddley' and 'Who Do You Love', each feature only a single chord.

Bo Diddley was born in Mississippi on 30 December 1928. He was inspired to become a blues artist after seeing John Lee Hooker in action. In the early 1950s, he began working with maraca player Jerome Green, giving his music even more of a rhythmic drive, and he also signed to Chess Records of Chicago. His first single, the self-titled 'Bo Diddley' sported one of the key rock 'n' roll rhythms, one later used by Buddy Holly, the Rolling Stones and hordes of lesser-known imitators.

The extraordinarily catchy, African-derived rhythm was backed up by equally remarkable guitar playing. What Bo Diddley was doing in terms of using treble and an overdriven amplifier to create a fuzz tone was years ahead of its time, foreshadowing the likes of Jimi Hendrix. Subsequent Bo Diddley hits like 'Who Do You Love' and 'You Can't Judge A Book By The Cover' made it clear that Bo Diddley was much more than a one-trick pony. However, he will always be remembered for that one extraordinary riff-cum-rhythm played on a custom-made square-shaped guitar that looked and sounded as if it came from outer space.

RIGHT: *The great Bo Diddley poses with his custom-made guitar, notable for its peculiar shape as much as for the distinctive sound he created with it.*

AFRICAN RHYTHM – DRUM BEAT ON A GUITAR

'Bo Diddley' is a one-chord monster riff built on a rhythm that few listeners, back in the 1950s, realized actually originated in West Africa. Even Bo Diddley would have been surprised to know that.

For between Africa and Bo Diddley the rhythm had been on quite a journey. It had travelled with African slaves to Cuba where it was known as the clave, the rhythm of the bass line in Cuban song, allied to the rhumba. It can also be traced in New Orleans music too, New Orleans being the only American city in which African slaves were allowed to keep their drums, and then it made its way into African-American street culture as a rhythm known as the 'hambone'. This was used by street performers who would play out the beat by slapping and patting their arms, legs, chest and cheeks while chanting rhymes over the top of it.

As for how exactly Bo Diddley got the rhythm, it's hard to say. The man himself claims, tongue very likely in cheek, that he got it from trying to play a cowboy song by Gene Autry and messing up the beat. What he does admit to, and which is at the heart of his innovation, is that he decided to play the rhythm on the full six strings of the guitar. Thus, at a stroke, he invented a style of pure rhythm guitar playing so up front that the guitar was also effectively a lead instrument.

RIGHT: *Bo Diddley built traditional African rhythms into the heart of his music, using these to push along tracks such as 'Bo Diddley'.*

Who Do You Love?

ALBUMS: **BO DIDDLEY; BO DIDDLEY'S A TWISTER; SUPER BLUES**
SONGWRITER: **ELIAS MCDANIEL**
RECORDED: **CHESS STUDIOS**
PRODUCER: **LEONARD CHESS, PHIL CHESS, BO DIDDLEY**

Alternating between E, A and B chords is the basis of the 'Bo Diddley sound'. Experiment with dampening the strings on the fret board between the chords, but still keep the rhythm going, using the guitar in a percussive way. Generate extra rhythm by playing the full chord on the down stroke, then just clip the strings on the up stroke. Practise the rhythm on just one chord – muting then releasing. Mastering this technique will improve your rhythm playing generally.

BASIC SONG RIFF

HERE'S HOW

1 The E chord forms the basis of the riff and provides the central pulse for the rhythm. Mute and release the strings to let the sound out.

2 Use your second right finger across the top four strings at the second fret. Finally, strike all the strings open before returning to the E chord.

The key is keeping the rhythm bouncing along. Practise that unmistakable 'shuffle sound' that is produced by muting or dampening the strings.

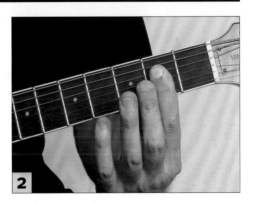

KEITH RICHARDS

1943–
BAND: THE **ROLLING STONES**
HEIGHT OF FAME: **1960s–PRESENT**

It's easy to see Keith Richards as simply the cartoon version of the rock guitarist – the rats' nest hair, the cigarette permanently in the corner of the mouth, the bottle of Jack Daniel's perched on the amp, the 'any cooler and I'd be dead' attitude. However, important as his pose may have been to his success, one should never let it obscure the fact that he is one of the half-dozen most significant guitar players of all time in popular music. What marks him out from most of his rivals is that he is essentially a rhythm guitarist. It's not that he never plays lead, it's rather that his rhythm playing, producing classic riff after classic riff, has defined the role of the guitar in the rock 'n' roll band.

Keith Richards was born on 18 December 1943, in Dartford, Kent, just outside London. While at art school in London he formed The Rolling Stones with childhood friend Mick Jagger. At first performing R&B and blues covers, the band really hit their stride with an original song, 'Satisfaction', based on an inordinately catchy distorted guitar riff played by Richards.

From this point on, it was the guitar riffs that would mark out the Stones' most successful songs – 'Honky Tonk Women', 'Jumpin' Jack Flash', 'Brown Sugar', 'Start Me Up' and others. Deceptively simple, the riffs actually owed their lasting appeal to Richards' subtle use of blues tunings – open G and open E in particular – and the habit of taking the top string off his Telecasters.

Over the years the excesses of his lifestyle have kept Richards in the headlines, but it's the intricacies of his playing that have made him a true role model for successive generations of guitar players.

RIGHT: *Keith Richards (right) performs an early acoustic set with the Rolling Stones' Mick Jagger. Richards was more typically seen playing with his electric Telecasters.*

FIVE-STRING TELECASTERS

In 1968 The Rolling Stones were at a watershed in their career. Their ambitious *Satanic Majesties* album had been a relative flop and they needed to revitalize their sound. Keith Richards came to the rescue with some new guitar tunings and a bunch of killer riffs, beginning with 'Jumpin' Jack Flash'.

Fellow guitar players were mystified as to how he got his distinctive droning sound on the lower strings. Part of the answer was in the tunings, particularly the open G. The other part lay in Keith's innovation of removing the top string from his guitars while playing in open G, and tuning the remaining strings DBGDG (high to low). Keith was so happy with the result that he began to use it constantly, using a whole range of customized five-string butterscotch Fender Telecasters, all dating from 1952 to 1954, with maple necks and black pickguards. So fond is Keith of these guitars that he gives them their own names. The best known of Richards' guitars is 'Micawber'. It has a brass replacement bridge with the nut cut to accommodate five strings, not evenly spaced across the fingerboard, but the first string moved over a little. Keith uses it live to play 'Brown Sugar' and 'Honky Tonk Women'.

His other main Telecaster is known as 'Malcolm'. The pickups and mods are the same as Micawber but this Tele stays capoed at the 4th fret and is tuned in B: BF#BD#F#. It's a little louder than Micawber and can be heard on stage for 'Tumbling Dice' and 'Jumpin' Jack Flash'.

RIGHT: *Keith Richards has had a long-standing love affair with the Telecaster. The Telecaster was Fender's first solid-body electric guitar, first produced in 1951.*

Jumpin' Jack Flash

ALBUM: **HOT ROCKS**
SONGWRITERS: **MICK JAGGER, KEITH RICHARDS**
RECORDED: **OLYMPIC SOUND STUDIOS, LONDON**
PRODUCER: **JIMMY MILLER**

This has to be one of the most famous guitar riffs of all time. It combines some great double note parts with single notes on the A and D strings. The notes on the A string can be played as a hammer-on. Practise moving between the double notes and single notes in the riff. Play big down strokes with your plectrum for the double notes, then position ready to play notes on the A and D strings.

BASIC SONG RIFF

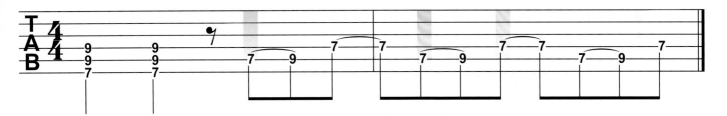

HERE'S HOW

1 The first finger plays the B note at the 7th fret on the E string and the ring and little fingers play the A and D strings.

2 On the A string play a hammer-on between the 7th and 9th fret; practise repeating this phrase including the note on the D string.

3 Play the A note on the D string with the first finger; it forms the rest of the phrase when played straight after the hammer-on.

OPEN G TUNING

Keith Richards began experimenting with alternate tunings around 1967/68 when the Stones took a break from the non-stop touring of their early years. Keith started studying early blues guitarists, people like Blind Willie McTell and Mississippi Fred McDowell. Particular inspiration, however, came from a young American guitar player named Ry Cooder. Cooder was drafted in as a possible replacement for Brian Jones and contributed to the Stones' *Let It Bleed* album, but his most important contribution was to teach Richards the open G tuning. This involves retuning the guitar to DGDGBG. Keith refined the tuning by removing the bottom D string entirely to leave five strings tuned GDGBG. The result was a formula he succinctly summed up as 'Five strings, three notes, two fingers and an asshole, and you've got it'.

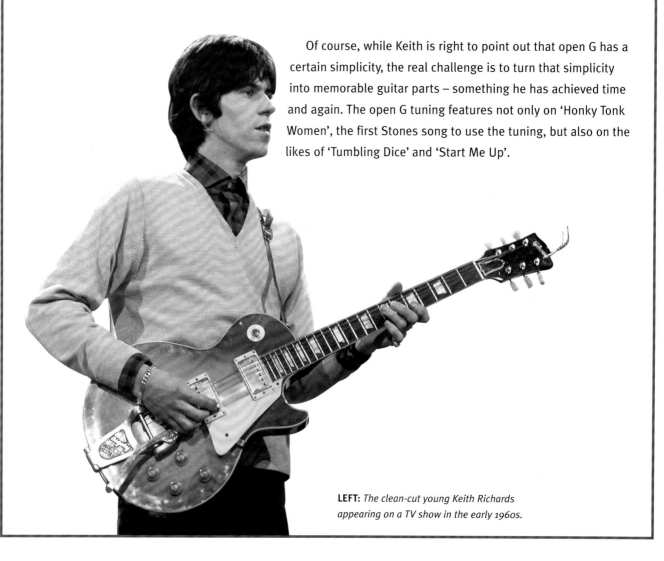

Of course, while Keith is right to point out that open G has a certain simplicity, the real challenge is to turn that simplicity into memorable guitar parts – something he has achieved time and again. The open G tuning features not only on 'Honky Tonk Women', the first Stones song to use the tuning, but also on the likes of 'Tumbling Dice' and 'Start Me Up'.

LEFT: *The clean-cut young Keith Richards appearing on a TV show in the early 1960s.*

Brown Sugar

ALBUM: **STICKY FINGERS**
SONGWRITERS: **MICK JAGGER, KEITH RICHARDS**
RECORDED: **OLYMPIC STUDIOS, LONDON**
PRODUCER: **JIMMY MILLER**

This is a great opening riff to a great rock song. Keith Richards uses open tunings a lot and for this riff the guitar needs to be retuned to DGDGBD. The tab shows the first chords of the intro. The chords are played high up the neck so practise getting your fingering accurate. Experiment with other open tunings. Always use a guitar tuner as you'll be very likely to break strings when de-tuning.

BASIC SONG RIFF

HERE'S HOW

1. Your first finger plays the 12th fret of the G string, your middle finger plays the B string and the ring finger plays the D string.

2. This is a straight first finger across the D, G and B strings at the 12th fret. Try to only hit the fretted strings.

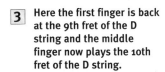

3. Here the first finger is back at the 9th fret of the D string and the middle finger now plays the 10th fret of the D string.

4. Simply add your ring finger to the 10th fret on the G string and keep your middle finger where it was.

LEAD OR RHYTHM?

Star guitarists almost always play lead – it's the guitar solos that allow you to show off your speed and dexterity (and pull ridiculous faces). Rhythm players, on the other hand, are generally the hardworking guys in the background who lay down the foundation for the star to solo all over. Keith Richards knows that as well as anyone, but he just doesn't care. As he says himself: 'It doesn't matter about the B.B. Kings, Eric Claptons and Mick Taylors, 'cause they do what they do – but I know they can't do what I do. They can play as many notes as there are under the sun but they just can't hold that rhythm down, baby. I know what I can do and what I can't. Everything I do is strongly based on rhythm 'cause that's what I'm best at. I've tried being a great guitar player and, like Chuck Berry, I have failed."

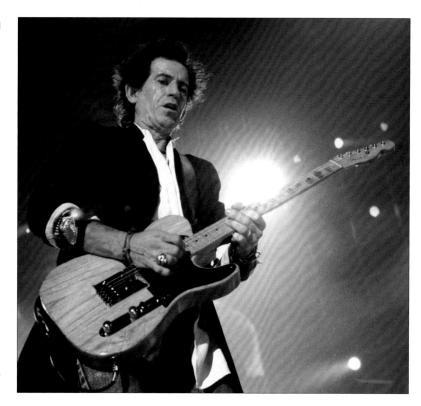

ABOVE: *Keith Richards is still performing with the Stones four decades after they were first formed, and shows no signs of losing his love for the electric guitar.*

Of course the joke here is that Berry and Richards between them have more or less defined rock 'n' roll guitar. After all, at its heart the music is not about fast solos or complex jazz-derived chord structures – its real foundation is the mighty riff. Guitar figures in rock 'n' roll need to anchor a song rhythmically and at the same time have a melodic component that makes them instantly memorable. Chuck Berry did it with 'Johnny B Goode' et al; Richards did it with 'Satisfaction', 'Brown Sugar' and all the rest. It is sometimes useful to remember that a great lead player playing alone is basically a showman, while a great rhythm player is rock 'n' roll incarnate.

Satisfaction

ALBUM: **BIG HITS (HIGH TIDE AND GREEN GRASS); OUT OF OUR HEADS**
SONGWRITERS: **MICK JAGGER, KEITH RICHARDS**
RECORDED: **RCA STUDIOS, HOLLYWOOD, CA**
PRODUCER: **ANDREW LOOG OLDHAM**

This is a classic Stones riff played along the A string. Use big solid notes to create that driving rock sound. You'll need to use your first finger at the B note on the A string as your middle and ring fingers will be needed at the 4th and 5th frets. Practise up and down strokes with your plectrum on the notes at the 5th fret to give you speed.

BASIC SONG RIFF

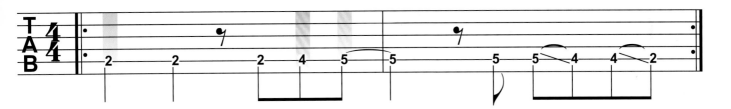

HERE'S HOW

1 The riff starts on the B note with your first finger, use down strokes here to get a good steady rhythm going.

2 Your ring finger should be waiting to hit the C# on the 4th fret of the B string. Get your little finger positioned.

3 Your little finger hits this D note – try some up and down strokes with the plectrum on these D notes at the 5th fret.

PLAYING BEHIND THE BEAT

Crucial to the process of The Rolling Stones mutating from a bunch of English kids doing their best to imitate black American blues, and then developing their own distinctive sound, was

Keith Richards' determination to dig into the foundations of the blues. What he realized was that really playing the blues was not simply about playing the right notes, it was also about the notes you didn't play and, crucially, it was about rhythm and timing.

Most white blues bands strove to keep in time, but Richards watched Muddy Waters and absorbed the way in which Waters would deliberately sing and play just behind the beat, giving his music an organic looseness. That looseness was something Richards was determined to incorporate into The Rolling Stones and, in partnership with Ronnie Wood over the last 20 plus years, he has done exactly that. Sometimes that looseness can descend into sloppiness, but listen hard to Richards' guitar playing, especially on live recordings, and you can see how he will deliberately drop behind the beat during the course of a song, letting the rhythms shift and breathe. It is of course advisable to master playing in time before you start experimenting with this technique!

LEFT: *By his own admission, Richards is more of a rhythm guitarist than a soloist, although he has an acute feel for blues-oriented melodies.*

Start Me Up

ALBUM: **TATTOO YOU**
SONGWRITERS: **MICK JAGGER, KEITH RICHARDS**
RECORDED: **COMPASS POINT STUDIOS, NASSAU**
PRODUCERS: **MICK JAGGER, KEITH RICHARDS**

This song is in open G tuning. Remember that Keith Richards often plays with his bottom E string removed, so to really get that authentic Stones sound you'll have to do the same. The tuning is as it was for 'Brown Sugar'. Hit these chords hard to get a good driving rock sound. Vary your strumming technique with the plectrum and experiment with different rhythms on these big open tuned chords.

BASIC SONG RIFF

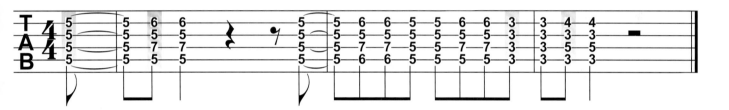

HERE'S HOW

1 We can just use the first finger across the 5th frets of G, D, G and B strings. Now get your middle and ring fingers poised ready for the next chord.

2 Use your first finger across the 5th frets of all the strings, add your middle finger to 6th fret of the B string and your ring finger will play the D string.

3 Use your first finger, this time at the 3rd fret across four strings: G, D, G and B. Be sure to place the finger in the middle of the fret to get a nice clear sound.

4 This is the same pattern two frets back. Use your first finger across three frets with your middle and ring fingers ready to come down on D and B strings.

DAVE DAVIES

1947–
BAND: **THE KINKS**
HEIGHT OF FAME: **1960s**

The Kinks, perhaps the quirkiest of all the great British bands of the 1960s, are remembered for two very different reasons. One is the quirky, typically English songwriting of Ray Davies; the other is the ferocious guitar riffing of younger brother Dave, whose influence was seminal. Many critics believe that Dave Davies' guitar riff on the band's first hit 'You Really Got Me' provided the template for what would later become heavy metal.

Dave Davies was born in Muswell Hill, London on 3 February 1947, three years after his brother Ray. In their teens, the brothers formed a rock 'n' roll group with a schoolmate of Ray's, Peter Quaife, on bass. By the summer of 1963, the group had decided to call itself the Ravens and had recruited a new drummer, Mickey Willet. Eventually, their demo tape reached Shel Talmy, an American record producer, who helped them land a contract with Pye in 1964. Before signing to the label, the Ravens replaced Willet with Mick Avory and changed their name to the Kinks. Their first two singles failed to chart, but the band's third release, 'You Really Got Me', reached number one within a month of its release. It was the first British hit to be built on a simple power-chorded guitar riff. The follow up, 'All Day and All of the Night', made number two on the charts.

Non-stop touring provoked tension in the band and Dave started releasing solo singles. Brother Ray, meanwhile, began to move away from straight-ahead rock to more unusual songs like 'Sunny Afternoon', 'Waterloo Sunset', 'Autumn Almanac' and 'Lola'. All were big hits but, by the early 1970s the band's star was on the wane. Gradually the Kinks reverted to a harder rock sound with Dave's guitar once more to the fore, and they became a popular live act in America through the late 1970s and early 1980s.

The Kinks were inducted into the Rock 'n' Roll Hall of Fame in 1990, but split up soon after. Since then, Dave Davies has released several solo albums and written his autobiography.

RIGHT: *Dave Davies performing with The Kinks on the British TV show* Supersonic *in March 1977. With his songwriting brother Ray, Davies created some of the most memorable pop riffs of the 1960s.*

THE ORIGINAL MONSTER RIFF

Ray Davies wrote 'You Really Got Me' in the front room of his parents' house with help from Dave. Ray first played the riff on a piano. Dave tried it on the guitar, and Ray shifted the tone a couple of times. Ray wanted the song to be a live showstopper and the riff to be as simple and repetitive as possible, 'like an African tribal chant,' he once said. A more obvious influence is the Kingsmen's classic 'Louie Louie,' which the Kinks used to cover.

The song was selected to be the group's make-or-break third single. The recording was a rushed, bad-tempered affair with ferocious drumming and a truly extraordinary guitar sound: fuzzed, distorted and utterly primitive. It was five years before heavy metal and twelve years before punk, but Dave Davies had anticipated both these movements in two minutes of pop revolution. In later years cynics would claim that Jimmy Page really played guitar on the song – as he did on so many 1960s pop hits – but it's hard to believe that a master craftsman like Page could ever have come up with something quite so gloriously dumb yet utterly right as the two-chord monster that is 'You Really Got Me'.

LEFT *Dave Davies, sporting a wig, in the late 1970s. Despite the changing fortunes of The Kinks as a group, their unforgettable riffs have remained ever popular. 'You Really Got Me' has been covered by many different artists including Iggy Pop and Van Halen.*

You Really Got Me

ALBUM: **KINKS**
SONGWRITER: **RAY DAVIES**
RECORDED: **IBC STUDIOS, LONDON**
PRODUCER: **SHEL TALMY**

This great Ray Davies song uses power chords to underpin the vocal line. You'll need to practise the rhythm with your strumming hand to get it absolutely right. Hit the chords hard on the down stroke and sing the verse as you play to practise your timing. Concentrate on getting a good clean hit across all the strings being held down. Listen to the record to check out the rhythm.

BASIC SONG RIFF

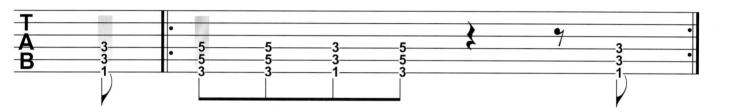

HERE'S HOW

1 This shows the first finger holding down the F note on the E string with the middle and little fingers holding down the A & D strings.

2 This is the same shape moved up 3 frets to the 3rd and 5th. Practise keeping the shape solid as you move around the fret board.

ELPICO – THE GREEN AMP

The ElPico was a small, green, 8–10 watt amplifier that Dave Davies found in a radio spares shop in Muswell Hill in 1962. At the time he was determined to get a dirtier, more distorted guitar sound than he could achieve with his AC30 but he couldn't afford a Watkins Dominator, which was a popular alternative at the time. Instead, he bought the little green amp and went home and started to experiment.

The ElPico had a cheap, fuzzy sound he liked, but it wasn't nearly loud enough. His first experiment involved plugging the guitar into the ElPico, the ElPico into a hi-fi amp, which was in turn plugged into a radiogram, which was finally plugged into his Vox AC30. As soon as he switched on there was a surge of electricity that sent Davies flying across the room. Clearly this was overdoing things. He simplified matters and simply plugged the ElPico into the Vox AC30. There was almost as much hum from the larger amp as there was signal from the smaller, but the tone was getting there. Still not quite satisfied, his next experiment was to slash the speaker cone of the ElPico with a razor. As it vibrated it produced a wickedly distorted sound. According to brother Ray Davies, Dave also stuck knitting needles into the speaker cone. Be that as it may, what is certain is that a sound was born. Dave Davies started using this unorthodox set-up on stage, and when it came to recording 'You Really Got Me,' there was no question what he would use...

RIGHT *The Kinks were a popular live act in the United States during the early 1980s.*

All Day and All of the Night

ALBUM: **KINDA KINKS**
SONGWRITER: **RAY DAVIES**
RECORDED: **IBC STUDIOS, LONDON**
PRODUCER: **SHEL TALMY**

This is a great Kinks tune with a guitar sound that wouldn't have sounded out of place in some of the punk bands that came along around 10 or 12 years later. Again hit these chords loud and hard but practise getting the rhythm right. These shapes move around the fret board a fair bit so practise moving between each shape quickly and accurately.

BASIC SONG RIFF

HERE'S HOW

1 The first finger is on the F note on the E string, the middle and little fingers take the A & D strings, the middle finger plays the G string.

2 The same shape 2 frets up, the finger positions are exactly the same with the first finger starting at the G note on the E string.

3 Here the tab shows the same chord shape at the 6th fret, keep these shapes nice and firm and practise sliding up and down the neck.

THE MANY GUITARS OF DAVE DAVIES

Some guitar players stick with more or less the same instrument throughout their careers; others make a decisive switch, such as when Eric Clapton abandoned the Gibson Les Paul in favour of the Fender Stratocaster. Dave Davies, unusually, seems to be a man ready and willing to play whatever he can get his hands on. Here are just some of the guitars with which he has been associated.

The guitar on which he played 'You Really Got Me' was his first ever electric guitar, a 1962 Harmony Meteor. His next guitar was a 1964 Epiphone which he used on early package tours with The Hollies and the Dave Clark Five, and on the album *Kinda Kinks*. Then came a Fender Electric XII, which he used on 'I'm Not Like Everybody Else'. He also used a custom-built Guild on several of the early hits, but when it was lost in transit to the USA he went to the nearest pawnshop and bought a Gibson Flying V. He didn't find it particularly easy to play, but used it on the TV show *Shindig* because he thought it looked cool!

In the late 1960s Davies switched, like so many others, to a Fender Stratocaster, which he used a lot during the *Everybody's In Showbiz* and *Preservation* period from 1972–74. At around the same time he also played a 1952 Telecaster, which he later replaced with a 1983 Fender Elite Telecaster. In between, however, he used a 1960 Gibson Les Paul 'Gold Top'.

In more recent times Davies has returned to Fender and currently uses a sunburst 1994 Telecaster for electric work and a couple of different Ovation guitars – a Custom Legend and A Custom Balladeer – for acoustic work.

LEFT *The Kinks on the BBC TV show Shindig in 1965. Dave Davies (left) looks a little uncomfortable playing the Gibson Flying V which he had recently purchased in a local pawnbrokers.*

Tired of Waiting For You

ALBUM: **KINDA KINKS**
SONGWRITER: **RAY DAVIES**
RECORDED: **IBC STUDIOS, LONDON**
PRODUCER: **SHEL TALMY**

This is a slower Kinks tune with a wonderful melody. The tab shows the arpeggio guitar line played by Ray which complements the rocky chords played by Dave. The chords to go with the arpeggio are G and F. Try playing with another guitarist for the full effect. Practise picking out arpeggios on other riffs to vary your playing style, then slip between strummed chords and picking in the same song.

BASIC SONG RIFF

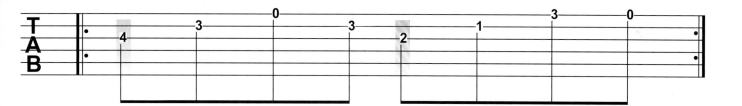

HERE'S HOW

1. The picture shows the first finger playing the B string and the middle finger playing the G string. You can try finger picking without using a plectrum.

2. For this part slide your first two fingers back 2 frets and use your little finger to play the 3rd fret of the G string.

JIMI HENDRIX

1942–1970
BAND: **THE JIMI HENDRIX EXPERIENCE**
HEIGHT OF FAME: **1960s–70s**

Just as Elvis Presley is the king of rock 'n' roll, Jimi Hendrix is the king of electric guitar.

Other great guitarists have come along in his wake, but they will never match his originality.

He was the first musician to understand fully the implications of a guitar's electrical

possibilities. As well as playing the strings, he used effects, volume and feedback in ways

that no one had ever done before. Almost everyone has copied elements of Hendrix's sound.

Hendrix was born on 27 November 1942 in Seattle, Washington. When he was 16 his father Al gave him a ukulele, and later bought him an acoustic guitar. It was clear that he had great talent, and as a young man began playing guitar for the likes of Curtis Knight, Little Richard and The Isley Brothers. By 1966 he had his own band, Jimmy James and the Blue Flames, based in New York City. There he was discovered by Chas Chandler, who brought him to England and helped him form a new band, The Jimi Hendrix Experience.

His first three singles – the incendiary 'Hey Joe', 'Purple Haze' and 'The Wind Cries Mary' – were all Top 10 hits, as was the group's first album, *Are You Experienced?* Suddenly, Hendrix was a big star. He performed at two of the seminal 1960s festivals, Monterey Pop and Woodstock; both were filmed and helped ensure Hendrix's fame. Monterey showcased his routine of burning and smashing his guitar, while at Woodstock he played an unforgettable instrumental version of 'The Star Spangled Banner'. No one had heard guitar playing like it before. Interestingly enough, Jimi's sound was achieved with quite basic equipment: he simply plugged a Fender Stratocaster into a wah wah pedal, a Fuzz Face, a Uni Vibe, or – occasionally – an Octavia, and amplified it all through a Marshall stack.

RIGHT: *Hendrix raised the status of the electric-guitar player to new heights, promoting the instrument through stunning riffs combined with outright showmanship.*

After his third album, *Electric Ladyland*, Hendrix disbanded the Experience and formed a new group, Band Of Gypsies, intending to take his music further in a jazzier direction. However, before he could fully realize his new direction, he died from choking on his own vomit after taking sleeping pills on 18 September 1970.

MARSHALL STACKS

Jimi Hendrix's guitar style, the volume he used, and his onstage pyrotechnics, demanded robust, powerful amplifiers. At first he used Vox and Fender amps, but wasn't happy with them. He then discovered the new range of high-powered guitar amps being made by London audio engineer Jim Marshall and used by The Who. Finally, he had an amp strong enough for his music. His Marshall stacks helped shape his heavily overdriven sound, and, above all, gave him the opportunity to use feedback as a musical effect. Of course, Jimi's patronage soon meant that the Marshall amp was the only one for any new rock band to be seen with.

All of which was a triumph for Jim Marshall, the man behind the amp. A former drummer, he'd

PYROTECHNICS

An essential part of what made Jimi Hendrix the enduring star he is was his showmanship. Before Hendrix rock guitar heroes were mostly studious musicianly types like Eric Clapton, whose idea of showmanship was to close their eyes during a solo. Hendrix came out of a different world, that of soul and blues, where artists were expected to have a stage act.

So British audiences gazed on in amazement when Hendrix performed tricks like playing the guitar with his teeth or behind his head; when he set it on fire they could scarcely believe their eyes. Here was not just another guy who could play the guitar well, but a fully-fledged entertainer.

This talent for showmanship also manifested itself in Hendrix's playing, with his extravagant use of effects to make his guitar sound that much more bizarre than anything anyone had heard before. It's an approach that reached its apotheosis in the classic footage from Woodstock of Hendrix playing 'The Star Spangled Banner.' Here Hendrix ran through the full gamut of his effects pedals – the UniVibe, Octavia, Cry Baby and Fuzz Face, plus copious feedback – first one at a time and then all together, to create an extraordinary array of noises evoking the sounds of the Vietnam War, such as machine-gun fire and bombs dropping. Here Hendrix demonstrated that showmanship and pyrotechnics were not trivial distractions, but vital parts of a guitarist's armoury.

LEFT: *Hendrix pushed guitar playing to its absolute limits both in terms of tonal quality and melodic experimentation, all using his 'left-handed' Stratocasters.*

Hey Joe

ALBUM: **ARE YOU EXPERIENCED**
SONGWRITER: **BILLY ROBERTS**
RECORDED: **OLYMPIC STUDIOS, LONDON**
PRODUCER: **CHAS CHANDLER**

This is the part of the song where the guitar and bass play a climbing scale. It comes in just after Hendrix takes the main solo. Use your first three fingers and play nice big chunky notes. Listening to the record will help you improve your timing on this section. Use this song to practise climbing riffs on the bass strings of your guitar. Try to play along with the band.

BASIC SONG RIFF

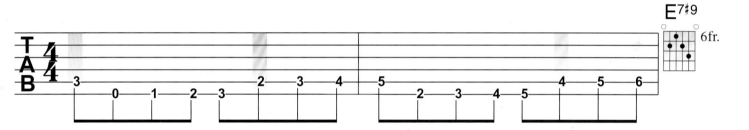

HERE'S HOW

1 The riff starts on the C note on the 3rd fret of the A string. Use your ring finger to play this note and hold it firm.

2 This is the start of the ascending climb along the A string from the 2nd fret to the 5th. Once you've played this, play the same frets on the E string.

3 Here we go back to the A string to play an ascending scale from the 4th fret to the 6th fret. Use all fingers here.

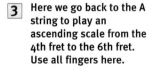

4 The riff finishes with this E7#9 chord – known as the Hendrix chord because he used it so often.

LEFT-HANDED STRAT

Thanks to Jimi Hendrix, the Stratocaster is the biggest-selling electric guitar in history. Before Hendrix, most top guitar players in the UK used Gibsons and Rickenbackers. After he appeared, almost all of the leading guitarists, including Jeff Beck and Clapton, switched to the Stratocaster.

ABOVE: *Hendrix in action with his Strat.*

Hendrix bought his first Strat from Manny's Music in New York, in 1966. The left-handed Hendrix bought right-handed Strats because he preferred to have the controls on top. This set-up created a totally different tension to the standard feel of the guitar. Also out of its usual position was the patented Fender tremolo arm which enabled him to bend notes and entire chords without the guitar going out of tune. The Strat's low action and narrow neck were also ideally suited to Hendrix's style as, he had very large hands to start off with, and he was able to fret across all six strings with the top joint of his thumb alone.

Despite Hendrix owning dozens of Strats at one time or another, only six are still known to be in circulation. The best known of these is the white 1968 Strat that Hendrix played at Woodstock, which was resold in 1993 for £750,000. It is now on display at the Experience Music Project in Seattle, built by Microsoft billionaire Paul Allen, a Hendrix fan.

opened his own London music shop in 1960. His customers often asked for louder amplifiers, so Marshall started making them himself, having enlisted the help of Ken Bran, an electrical technician and former customer. They built a prototype and immediately received orders for 50 more. By 1964 Marshall Amplifiers had their own factory in west London. Among their customers was Pete Townshend of the Who, who asked for a still more powerful amp. In response to this request, the company developed the first 100-Watt amps. Townshend also asked for a larger 8x12 cabinet for the speakers. The impracticality of this cabinet led to a 'stacked' version, one 4x12 on top of another. The Marshall stack was born, and it only needed Hendrix to take it to the next level.

FUZZ BOXES

A fuzz box is essentially a unit designed to increase the instrument's volume, while simultaneously increasing the 'overdriven' quality of the tone – to give it the 'fuzz' if you like. It allows the guitar to sustain and feed back with the touch of a button. Hendrix started using a fuzz box, the Maestro Fuzz Tone, almost as soon as they became available, while playing with Curtis Knight. On moving to London he found a new favourite, The Fuzz Face. This was originally manufactured by Arbiter and sported a distinctive round shape inspired by a microphone-stand base. Hendrix used the device a great deal, though as the sound of a fuzz box so closely resembles that of an overdriven amplifier it is not always easy to detect its use on record.

Later on, Hendrix acquired a personal effects guru, Roger Mayer, who built a variety of custom effects units for him, including the Octavia. This was a unique combination of fuzz box and octave doubler. It produces a sound that is an octave higher than the note that the guitarist is playing, as well as creating some otherworldly noises all its own. Hendrix can be heard using the Octavia on songs such as 'Purple Haze'.

All Along the Watchtower

ALBUM: **ELECTRIC LADYLAND**
SONGWRITER: **BOB DYLAN**
RECORDED: **RECORD PLANT, NEW YORK**
PRODUCER: **JIMI HENDRIX**

A great Jimi Hendrix lead solo from the intro of 'All Along the Watchtower'. This solo uses some great bends to express the melody. It's amazing how much feeling Hendrix managed to squeeze into so few notes. Use bending techniques to really let those high notes scream. Practise pulling some big bends after coming off a run to get more melody from your lead solos.

BASIC SONG RIFF

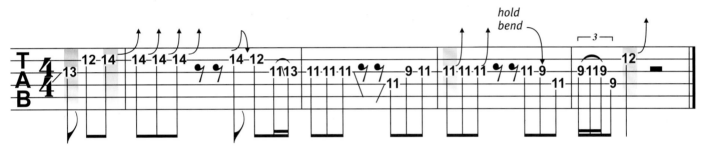

HERE'S HOW

1 Start on the G# at the 13th fret of the G string with the middle finger, this allows your first finger to play the B string.

2 This is the bend up from the 14th fret of the B string, use your ring finger to pull a nice big bend here.

3 This shows a down pull on the G string at the 11th fret; again use your ring finger to get maximum downward pull on the string.

4 The last note of the riff is a bend at the 12th fret on the B string. Use all your fingers to support the bend.

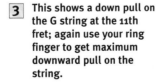

JIMMY PAGE

1944–
BAND: **THE YARDBIRDS; LED ZEPPELIN**
HEIGHT OF FAME: **1970s**

Often thought of as simply the prototypical heavy-metal axe hero – all monster riffs and epic solos – Jimmy Page is actually one of the most versatile guitarists to appear during the rock era. He was a renowned session man before emerging as an artist in his own right and, even within his work with Led Zeppelin, he incorporated subtle acoustic playing and modal experimentation, not to mention playing with a violin bow, alongside the familiar heroics.

RIGHT: *Jimmy Page here seen with his trademark Gibson twin-neck guitar. One neck had 12 strings, the other six.*

Jimmy Page was born in London in January 1944. He started playing guitar aged 12, inspired by Elvis' guitarist Scotty Moore. In his teens he toured with rock 'n' roll band Neil Christian and the Crusaders, before giving up music temporarily in favour of painting. He soon returned to guitar playing, however, and during the 1960s established himself as Britain's number one session guitarist, playing on records by everyone from The Kinks to The Rolling Stones, before finally agreeing to join The Yardbirds, where he briefly formed a partnership with fellow guitar legend Jeff Beck. Following The Yardbirds' split, he formed Led Zeppelin and moved, once and for all, to centre stage.

With Led Zeppelin Page was able to show off his entire box of tricks, whether creating archetypal heavy metal riffs like 'Whole Lotta Love', mystical but still thunderous modal riffs like 'Kashmir', or delicate acoustic constructions like 'Black Mountain Side', where he first revealed the influence of folk guitar great Bert Jansch. Then, with 'Stairway To Heaven', he put it all together to create a rock epic that started out with acoustic delicacy and then built to a majestic electric climax. It's the ultimate guitar anthem, and learning to play it is a rite of passage for budding guitar players (though one discouraged by guitar shop employees worldwide, who tire of

ROGER MAYER FUZZ BOX

Back in 1964, when Jimmy Page was a young session guitarist, his friend Roger Mayer was working for the British Admiralty in the field of vibration and acoustic research, to aid with underwater warfare. Jimmy Page was already interested in stretching the sonic capabilities of his electric guitar and he encouraged Mayer to build him an effects unit. The result was one of the first ever fuzz boxes, featuring germanium transistors.

The unique sound was an immediate hit. Producers clamoured for Page to use the effect on records they were making – for instance the fuzz guitar on the 'Who's 'My Generation' was played by Page rather then Pete Townshend. Popular demand soon meant that Mayer made further units for the other great studio guitarists of the time, Jeff Beck and Big Jim Sullivan, who used it on pop hits like 'Hold Me' by P.J. Proby, which may have contributed to the effect becoming seen as essentially a novelty. Mayer went on to build more sophisticated fuzz boxes that would become part of Jimi Hendrix' signature sound. Page, however, still believed in the potential of the original box, and when he started making his own music with Led Zeppelin, its true potential was unleashed.

BELOW: *Jimmy Page with the band that made him famous, Led Zeppelin. Zeppelin remain one of the biggest selling rock bands in history.*

Whole Lotta Love

ALBUM: **LED ZEPPELIN II**
SONGWRITERS: **JIMMY PAGE, ROBERT PLANT, JOHN BONHAM, JOHN PAUL JONES, WILLIE DIXON**
RECORDED: **OLYMPIC STUDIOS, LONDON**
PRODUCERS: **PETER GRANT, JIMMY PAGE**

Also known as the theme to BBC TV's weekly chart show Top of the Pops, *this is one of the most famous rock riffs ever. The key to getting it right is in the rhythm; the fret board finger movement is minimal but you will need to get the rhythm right. Practise playing single heavy notes on the bass strings and sliding into the chord at the 7th and 8th frets.*

BASIC SONG RIFF

P.M = Palm Muting

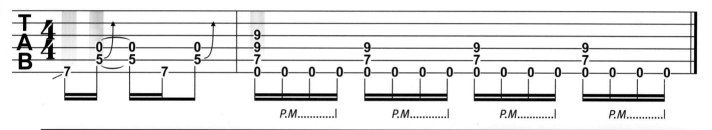

HERE'S HOW

1 This shows the ring finger at the 7th fret of the E string, your first finger will be back at the 5th fret of the A string.

2 Practise this part of the riff, rocking between the E and A strings. Get the timing right before moving to the next chord.

3 Slide into this chord to complete the riff, first finger on the A string and ring and little fingers on the D and G strings.

THE VIOLIN BOW

At the heart of *The Song Remains The Same*, the epic concert and fantasy film capturing Led Zep in their pomp and splendour, is a 28-minute version of 'Dazed And Confused', a showcase for Page's amazing guitar skills. At the song's dramatic highpoint Page brings out a violin bow and uses it on his Les Paul, coaxing out some quite extraordinary sounds.

Though an undeniably effective piece of showmanship, the use of the violin bow was more than a simple stunt. Page first recorded with a violin bow while still with The Yardbirds, and used it regularly on record with Led Zep. He didn't simply bow the guitar either, but combined it with wah wah and echo. As for where he got the inspiration for it, accounts differ. Page claimed that the idea was put to him by a classical string player while he was doing studio work. Others, however, have pointed out that Eddie Phillips, guitarist with another 1960s band, The Creation, used the bow before Page. Whatever the truth of it, if you're thinking of trying this yourself a key tip is to make sure you put rosin on the bow, as the rosin sticks to the string and makes it vibrate.

RIGHT: *The violin bow and the guitar are not a typical combination, but Jimmy Page used them together to create eerie musical effects.*

THE GIBSON DOUBLENECK

When it came to live work Jimmy Page's versatility provided some logistical problems – most obviously on 'Stairway To Heaven'. On record the song began with Page playing a Martin Acoustic, then he switched to a Fender XII 12-string for the rockier section, while the solo was played on a Fender Telecaster. Clearly, switching guitar repeatedly in the course of single song wasn't an option, yet the song, an instant classic, demanded to be played live. Then Page came up with a solution. He remembered that Gibson had briefly produced a twin neck guitar in the late 1950s. The Gibson EDS 1275 had one neck with twelve strings and another with six, both using the same body.

LEFT: *Jimmy Page was a true showman. He is still heavily involved in music, and has remastered the Zep back catalogue.*

Heartbreaker

ALBUM: **LED ZEPPELIN II**

SONGWRITERS: **ROBERT PLANT, JIMMY PAGE, JOHN PAUL JONES, JOHN BONHAM**

RECORDED: **A&R STUDIOS, NEW YORK**

PRODUCERS: **PETER GRANT, JIMMY PAGE**

This is another great Led Zeppelin rock riff all on the bass strings to get a nice heavy sound. The riff starts with a bend at the G note on the E string before falling into the main riff. There are some quick notes on the A string in the second part. Practise changing pace from the faster double notes to the main notes in the riff, and use up and down strokes with the plectrum to get speed.

BASIC SONG RIFF

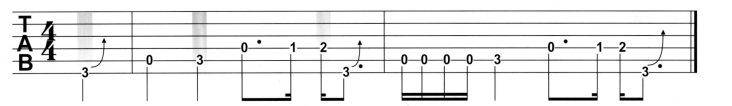

<table>
<tr>
<td style="background:black;color:white">HERE'S HOW</td>
</tr>
</table>

1 This is the bend on the E string. Use your ring finger here then drop down to the A string for the next part of the riff.

2 Hit the open A then bring your ring finger down on the C note at the 3rd fret of the A string.

3 This three-note run is on the D string. Play open then use your first and middle fingers to play the 1st and 2nd frets.

The guitar was out of production, but Page custom ordered one from Gibson. Now he was able to perform the crucial sound change, midway through 'Stairway', live with just one guitar. Soon afterwards other 1970s guitar heroes, including Steve Howe of Yes and jazz-rock supremo John McLaughlin, ordered their own doublenecks. However, it wasn't simply the live convenience that interested Page. He noticed that if you leave the 12-string neck switched on and play on the six-string neck, the 12-strings start vibrating in sympathy to produce an Indian sitar-like effect.

MAESTRO ECHOPLEX

Jimmy Page is one of the great pioneers when it comes to electric guitar effects. His role in developing the fuzz box is only the most influential example.

Similarly innovative was his championing of the Maestro Echoplex. This was a mid 1970s solid-state circuitry tape-based echo machine. Essentially the guitar part went on the machine, was recorded on tape, and played back a fraction of a second later to provide an echo. Jimmy Page used the straightforward echo effect a lot, but his urge to experiment also unearthed new possibilities in the machine. He would play a note or even a chord, clean or with edge, and give it a long delay rate, then he'd add the sustain which made the echo repeat, and adjust the frequency so that the echoes sped up like a plane taking off, before reaching an almighty crescendo. It's an effect he used to breathtaking effect on 'Whole Lotta Love', and which was crucial in establishing the Led Zep sound as more powerful than anything previously heard. Modern digital effects units can, of course, offer far longer lasting and infinitely tweakable echoes, but purists will assure you that they can never match the analogue warmth of the original Echoplex.

LEFT: *Here Page is playing with a sunburst Gibson Les Paul. Page tended to use his double-necked guitar only in stage performances rather than during recordings.*

Kashmir

ALBUM: **PHYSICAL GRAFFITI**

SONGWRITERS: **ROBERT PLANT, JIMMY PAGE, JOHN BONHAM**

RECORDED: **STARGROVES; OLYMPIC STUDIOS, LONDON**

PRODUCER: **JIMMY PAGE**

This is a great driving Jimmy Page riff that runs up the fret board. To play this riff, tune the bottom E string down to a D – check that it's in tune by comparing it with the open D string. Make sure you include the bottom D in this riff for maximum effect. Listen to the record to practise the rhythm. Practise using and varying up and down strokes with the plectrum to achieve that stuttering sound on the rhythm guitar.

BASIC SONG RIFF

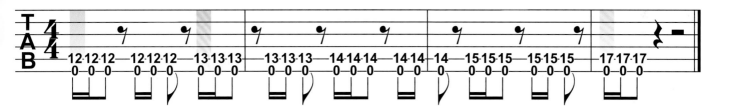

HERE'S HOW

1 The tab picture shows the first finger at the 12th fret on the A string. Remember you only need to hit the bottom two strings.

2 By adding the middle finger at the 13th fret of the A string we start the ascending riff. Work on your up and down strokes, you'll soon get that great rhythm.

3 This is a two-fret jump up to the 17th fret, it's easiest to slide the little finger up to here. Remember to take care detuning and tuning your strings.

Stairway to Heaven

ALBUM: **LED ZEPPELIN IV**
SONGWRITERS: **ROBERT PLANT, JIMMY PAGE**
RECORDED: **ISLAND STUDIOS, LONDON**
PRODUCER: **ANDY JOHNS**

The tab shows the lovely arpeggio pattern at the start of 'Stairway to Heaven'. It does require some practice, but it is rewarding to play once you've nailed it – this is why it's such a popular practice tune in guitar shops around the world. It's probably best to only play this one at home! Split each section of the tab to practise until you are comfortable, then put them all together.

BASIC SONG RIFF

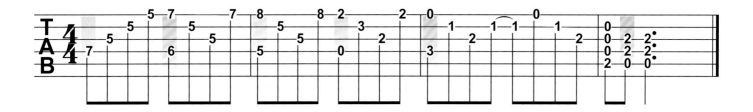

HERE'S HOW

1. Your first finger covers all 5th fret notes on the G, B and E strings whilst your ring finger plays the 7th fret of the D string.

2. Keep your first finger in position, but now your little finger plays the E string and your middle finger plays the 6th fret of the D string.

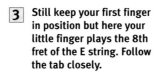

3. Still keep your first finger in position but here your little finger plays the 8th fret of the E string. Follow the tab closely.

4. The first finger is on the G string, middle finger on the E string and the ring finger is on the B string.

Famous Albums

Led Zeppelin's first four albums were officially untitled. They are usually known as Led Zeppelin I, II, III *and* IV, *although the latter is also referred to as 'Four Symbols'. Six Zeppelin albums appear in the listing of the top selling albums of the 1970s, with Led Zeppelin IV selling a remarkable 22 million copies in the United States alone.*

ALBUM: **LED ZEPPELIN II**
YEAR: **1969**
RECORDED AT: **OLYMPIC, LONDON**
PRODUCED BY: **JIMMY PAGE**

ALBUM: **LED ZEPPELIN III**
YEAR: **1970**
RECORDED AT: **HENLEY GRANGE**
PRODUCED BY: **JIMMY PAGE**

ALBUM: **LED ZEPPELIN IV**
YEAR: **1971**
RECORDED AT: **HENLEY GRANGE**
PRODUCED BY: **JIMMY PAGE**

5   First finger is at the 1st fret of the B string, the middle finger is at the 2nd fret of the G string and the ring finger is at 3rd fret of the D string.

6   The final shape is the middle finger on the 2nd fret of the D string and the ring finger on the 2nd fret of the G string.

BAND INFO

LED ZEPPELIN
BAND FORMED: **1968**
ALBUMS: **12 including reissues**
TOTAL ALBUM SALES: **more than 40 million**

ORIGINAL LINE-UP
LEAD: **ROBERT PLANT**
GUITAR: **JIMMY PAGE**
BASS: **JOHN PAUL JONES**
DRUMMER: **JOHN BONHAM**

THE ALLMAN BROTHERS

1946–1971 AND 1943–
GUITARISTS: **DUANE ALLMAN, DICKEY BETTS**
HEIGHT OF FAME: **LATE 1960s–EARLY 1970s**

Most bands would be happy to have one great guitarist in their ranks. The Allman Brothers were lucky enough, for a time, to have two, Duane Allman and Dickey Betts.

In the late 1960s Duane Allman was already a highly rated session player who had appeared on a whole range of Atlantic soul classics. Determined, however, to make his own music, he put a band together with his brother Greg on vocals and organ, Dickey Betts on joint lead guitar, Berry Oakley on bass, plus both Butch Trucks and Jaimoe Johanson on drums. They combined a love of R&B and rock 'n' roll with the improvising ability of a top-flight jazz group, and their incendiary live shows soon won then a devoted following.

They hit their stride with their second album, 1970's *Idlewild South*, which added a softer acoustic texture to their music and included the classics 'Midnight Rider' and 'In Memory of Elizabeth Reed', an instrumental tribute to Miles Davis, written by Betts.

In March 1971, the band, always at their best on stage, recorded a live album, *At Fillmore East*, which became an instant classic.

Duane Allman, meanwhile, took time out to moonlight with Eric Clapton's Derek & The Dominoes project, contributing the lead riff and classic slide guitar part to 'Layla'. Then, in October 1971, tragedy struck as he was killed in a motorcycle accident. The Allmans had been midway through work on their next album, *Eat A Peach*, at the time. They completed it as a five-piece, with Dickey Betts playing all of the lead and slide guitar parts. This was their first album to reach the Top 10.

From then on Betts and Greg Allman shared leadership of the band, with Betts writing and singing the group's biggest hit, 'Ramblin' Man', and the instrumental classic 'Jessica'. The Allmans split up in 1976, and after several abortive reunions came back together properly in 1989.

RIGHT: *Duane Allman was a true guitar hero who achieved legendary status in only two years of performing, before his untimely death in 1971.*

THE CORICIDIN BOTTLENECK

Guitar players have used the necks from glass bottles since slide guitar playing began, back in the early days of the blues. However, only Duane Allman has been identified with one particular brand of bottle. This was the Coricidin bottle. Coricidin was a cold medicine and Allman happened to have a cold and to be taking the medicine just at the time he started to learn to play slide. He then discovered that this particular medicine bottle just happened to be the perfect size and length to fit on most people's second or third fingers, and to be just about exactly the width of a standard-issue Les Paul electric guitar's neck.

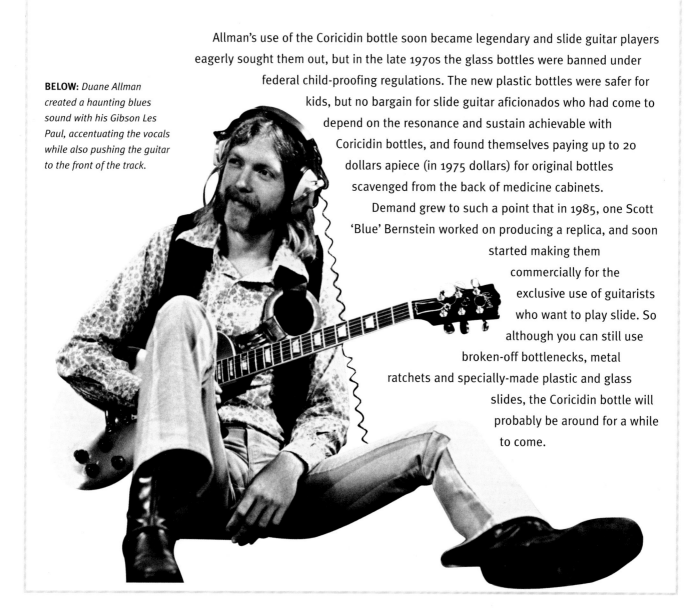

BELOW: *Duane Allman created a haunting blues sound with his Gibson Les Paul, accentuating the vocals while also pushing the guitar to the front of the track.*

Allman's use of the Coricidin bottle soon became legendary and slide guitar players eagerly sought them out, but in the late 1970s the glass bottles were banned under federal child-proofing regulations. The new plastic bottles were safer for kids, but no bargain for slide guitar aficionados who had come to depend on the resonance and sustain achievable with Coricidin bottles, and found themselves paying up to 20 dollars apiece (in 1975 dollars) for original bottles scavenged from the back of medicine cabinets.

Demand grew to such a point that in 1985, one Scott 'Blue' Bernstein worked on producing a replica, and soon started making them commercially for the exclusive use of guitarists who want to play slide. So although you can still use broken-off bottlenecks, metal ratchets and specially-made plastic and glass slides, the Coricidin bottle will probably be around for a while to come.

Jessica

ALBUM: **BROTHERS AND SISTERS**
SONGWRITER: **FORREST RICHARD BETTS**
RECORDED: **CAPRICORN SOUND STUDIOS, GA**
PRODUCER: **JOHNNY SANDLIN**

A nice acoustic guitar intro. The riff starts with an open A before going into the A chord. Listen to the recorded version to help with the rhythm. Use up and down strokes with the plectrum and practise moving between the G bass note and the chord shape. Try to make the chords play out clearly and avoid touching the open strings with your fretting fingers.

BASIC SONG RIFF

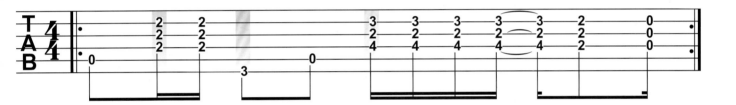

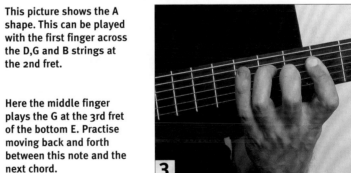

1 This picture shows the A shape. This can be played with the first finger across the D,G and B strings at the 2nd fret.

2 Here the middle finger plays the G at the 3rd fret of the bottom E. Practise moving back and forth between this note and the next chord.

3 In this picture the first finger plays the G string, the middle finger plays the B string and the ring finger plays the D string.

PETE TOWNSHEND

1945–
BAND: **THE WHO**
HEIGHT OF FAME: **1960s–70s**

Pete Townshend is up there with Keith Richards as one of the all time great rock rhythm-guitar players. Unlike most rock bands, The Who based their rhythm on Townshend's guitar, letting drummer Keith Moon and bassist John Entwistle improvise over his foundation, while singer Daltrey belted out his vocals. That formula gave their records a unique power and momentum, while in live performances Townshend took the band into even wilder sonic territory with his fondness for ending songs in a flat-out cacophony of noise as he destroyed his guitars on stage.

RIGHT: *Pete Townshend's on-stage guitar demolitions with The Who have sometimes distracted attention from his formidable talents as a rock musician.*

He was born Peter Dennis Blandford Townshend on 19 May 1945 in Chiswick, London, England, the son of singer Betty Dennis and saxophonist Cliff Townshend. In his teens he started playing banjo in a Dixieland jazz band, before joining The Detours as rhythm guitarist, alongside Roger Daltrey and John Entwistle. Soon the Detours evolved into The Who, and a string of classic Townshend compositions like 'I Can't Explain', 'My Generation' and 'Substitute' established the group not just as a great rock band, but one that explicitly confronted the turmoil of the times.

Townshend's song writing became ever more complex, leading to the rock opera *Tommy*, before switching to a simpler, but still blisteringly effective, hard-rock style for the classic albums *Who's Next* and *Live At Leeds*. During the 1970s Townshend began to develop a solo career but the resulting, more personal, material never gained the mass audience that the band continued to enjoy, boosted by the live film *The Kids Are Alright* and the feature films based on the rock operas *Tommy* and *Quadrophenia*. In recent years

Townshend has been heavily involved in writing books and working on an epic multimedia work called *Lifehouse*.

GUITAR SMASHING

The first time Pete Townshend smashed a guitar on stage was during an autumn 1964 Who gig at north London's Railway Tavern. During the show Pete Townshend repeatedly smacked his Rickenbacker against the ceiling while trying to shake off some feedback whistles. The band's fans loved it, and they dared him to abuse his guitar again for the band's second set. 'The guitar broke,' Townshend recalled, 'and the audience was waiting for me to sob over it — like, "Hey, that'll teach you to jump around like a lunatic."' However, Townshend decided to act as if the destruction had been deliberate. 'So I smashed up the guitar even more and jumped all over the bits, which gave me a fantastic buzz.' The crowd, of course, went wild. Unfortunately, from then on fans expected The Who to destroy their gear at every gig – a situation that at one time threatened to drive the group into bankruptcy, especially as their fortunes dipped after the huge success of their first few singles. However, the success of *Tommy* later gave Townshend the financial leeway to destroy as many guitars as he liked (and drummer Keith Moon the opportunity to drive as many Rolls-Royces into swimming pools as he wanted!).

GIBSON SG

The Gibson SG is the model of guitar with which Townshend is most associated. He used this model almost exclusively on stage between 1968 and 1973. He tended to use SGs dating between 1966 and 1970, which are identified by their full black wraparound pickguard.

ABOVE *Townshend playing one of his favourite Gibson SG guitars.*

In fact, when Gibson changed the SG's specification in 1971, it caused Townshend major upset. In an interview with *Guitar Player* magazine in 1972 he confided that 'They took the old SG off the market like about a year ago, so we used up every old SG in the country...I raided every music store in the country practically, looking for old SGs.' This was of course a particular problem for Townshend, with his penchant for destroying his guitars at the end of gigs. So when supplies of 1966–1970 models did finally dry up, he then briefly switched to pre-1966 models. As well as the classic red SGs he also appears to have owned at least two, or possibly three, Polaris White Gibson SG Specials. Then, at the end of 1973, he switched permanently to using a Gibson Les Paul Deluxe.

Recently, though, Gibson have introduced a Pete Townshend-endorsed Gibson SG. According to Gibson, Townshend's SG possessed 'the most recognizable Gibson electric guitar style of the 1960s.' The new Signature model is a replica of that guitar, with its bold, pointed horns, a Townshend signature decal on the back of the peghead and a Pete Townshend Signature SG hardshell case. Townshend himself has commented that 'This guitar is amazing. It looks, sounds, and feels exactly like the SG I used during *Live At Leeds*.'

Pinball Wizard

ALBUM: **TOMMY**

SONGWRITER: **PETE TOWNSHEND**

RECORDED: **IBC STUDIOS, LONDON**

PRODUCERS: **CHRIS STAMP, KIT LAMBERT**

This song has some great big power chords to practise your 'windmill swings' with your strumming arm ! The tab shows the main guitar riff as chords. Practise your timing with these chords it has to be spot on if you're to come even close to sounding like Pete Townshend from The Who. Play these chords big and loud using only down strokes with the plectrum, and listen to the song to help you with timing.

BASIC SONG RIFF

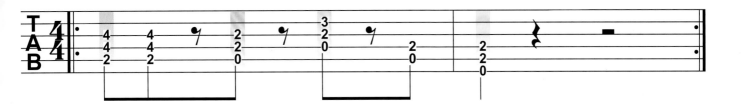

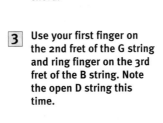

1. Your first finger plays the B note on the A string; ring and little fingers play the F# and B notes on the D and G strings.

2. Let your first finger slide down to cover the second frets on the D and G strings, remember to include the open A in this chord.

3. Use your first finger on the 2nd fret of the G string and ring finger on the 3rd fret of the B string. Note the open D string this time.

4. The riff finishes with this E5 chord; use your middle finger at the second fret on the A string and your ring finger at the second fret on the D string.

JERRY GARCIA

1942–1995
BAND: THE **GRATEFUL DEAD**
HEIGHT OF FAME: **1960s–70s**

Jerry Garcia is a guitarist who spans the extremes. On the one hand he's famous for epic electric-guitar solos, improvising around classic Grateful Dead tunes like 'Dark Star' for anything up to an hour. On the other hand he's also known for tight, focused acoustic playing on his trusty Martin Dreadnought, as featured on the two definitive Dead studio albums *Workingman's Dead* and *American Beauty*.

He's also the man who played perhaps the first pedal steel-guitar solo rock fans had ever heard – when he guested on CSNY's classic 'Teach Your Children'. All this despite having a mutilated right hand – he lost his right middle finger just below the first knuckle while chopping wood in his youth.

Jerry Garcia was born in San Francisco on 1 August 1942. He learned to play guitar when he was 15 years old, originally playing folk and rock 'n' roll. He dropped out of school aged 16 and spent a brief time in the army. After leaving the military he moved to Palo Alto where he met future Dead lyricist Robert Hunter. Garcia bought a banjo and began playing in local bluegrass bands. One of these, Mother McCree's Uptown Jug Champions, eventually evolved into the Grateful Dead in 1966, with Garcia switching to electric guitar.

Jerry Garcia's electric-guitar playing incorporated aspects of a whole range of music: bluegrass and Chuck Berry, country & western, and modern jazz could all be heard in the mix. During the band's early years Garcia played a Guild, then an assortment of Gibsons, mainly Les Pauls, plus the occasional Strat. From the late 1970s onwards, however, he mostly played custom-made guitars. For many years, these were made for him by Doug Irwin. One, nicknamed 'Tiger', was to remain Garcia's main instrument for an unprecedented

RIGHT: *Jerry Garcia was a true legend of American guitar playing. On his death in 1995 President Bill Clinton remembered Garcia as 'an American icon'.*

11 years. In the 1990s he also used guitars made by a remarkable talented novice guitar maker named Stephen Cripe.

The Grateful Dead, with their combination of roots influences and psychedelic sensibilities, became a colourful American institution and a massive live draw right up until 1995 when Garcia's hard living finally caught up with him and he died of a heart attack while attending a drug rehabilitation clinic.

GUITAR VERSUS BANJO

'I put my first real energy in music into the five-string banjos,' said Garcia. "I slowed the records down and painstakingly listened to every lick and worked them out. Having gone through that process with banjo, when I went to electric guitar I knew how to learn it.'

Garcia had actually started out by playing a Danelectro electric guitar during his mid teens. However. by 1960 he was caught up in the folk and bluegrass revival of the time and switched his instrumental focus to the more traditional banjo. He soon mastered the basic techniques of bluegrass banjo, playing clawhammer and two-finger picking, and at first took an orthodox approach, trying to sound as much as possible like an old-time Kentucky mountain picker. All that changed though with the influence of Bill Keith, who, through his work with Bill Monroe, revolutionized bluegrass banjo. Keith used dazzling 'chromatics' (melodic arpeggios, strings of notes or 'runs' up and down the musical scale) and new chordal complexity. Garcia was immediately inspired by Keith's playing. He

appreciated and extended Keith's subtle rhythmic accents, and in particular he worked on learning Keith's mastery of the whole of the fretboard, often playing higher notes on a lower string, and using this facility to produce arpeggiated passages that swooped dramatically up and down the neck. Garcia particularly liked producing long ascending lines in this fashion. All of this exerted an obvious influence when, from 1964 onwards, Garcia turned his attention back to the electric guitar.

LEFT: *Garcia brought together multiple musical influences, from heavy rock to gentle folk tunes.*

Dark Star

ALBUM: **LIVE DEAD**

SONGWRITERS: **JERRY GARCIA, ROBERT HUNTER**

RECORDED: **THE FILLMORE WEST; AVALON BALLROOM, SAN FRANCISCO**

PRODUCERS: **THE GRATEFUL DEAD**

This is a lovely riff to improvise over from The Grateful Dead, the masters of rock improvisation. The tab shows the riff starting on the G string, but once you've mastered the tune fingering it sounds good anywhere on the guitar. Experiment with some bends to add expression to the tune. It's a fairly slow riff so it's a good time to practise some up and down strokes with the plectrum.

BASIC SONG RIFF

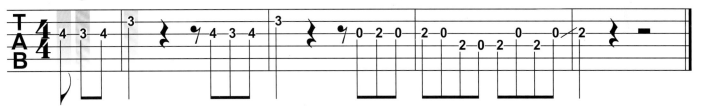

swing

HERE'S HOW

1 Try the first part of the riff with your middle finger on the 4th fret of the G string; get used to dropping down to the B string for that D note.

2 Here you can use your first finger to play the 3rd fret on the G string. Split the riff into sections and repeat them.

3 The first finger is playing the D note at the 3rd fret of the B string. Experiment with the riff and improvise playing some of your own notes.

DOUG IRWIN GUITARS

During the early 1970s Garcia became increasingly dissatisfied with mass-produced guitars. In 1972 he came across a guitar maker from Sonoma, California, called Doug Irwin, who had just made his first electric guitar (known as 001). Garcia bought it for $850 and ordered another one custom-made. In May 1973 he received the custom–made guitar, known as 'Wolf', for which he paid $1500. He gave Irwin's 001 to original Dead road crew member Ramrod. Wolf sported a maple neck, 24-fret ebony fingerboard, a blonde Western 'quilted' maple body and a core made from purpleheart. Its electronics were broadly similar to a Strat but with an Alembic Stratoblaster installed.

At the same time Irwin delivered Wolf, Garcia commissioned another guitar and told him time and money were no object. Irwin evidently took him at his word, as he spent seven years making the new guitar. However, the effort

was well worth it as the new guitar, christened 'Tiger', became Garcia's main axe from 1979 right up to 1990. Tiger was an unusually heavy 6kg (13$\frac{1}{2}$lb) guitar with a pearl coverplate, an ebony fingerboard on maple neck, an arched cocobola top and back, vermilion neck and body striping, and a flamed-maple body core.

Garcia's final Doug Irwin guitar took an epic 11 years to make. Delivered in 1990 it was nicknamed Rosebud (after the inlaid dancing skeleton on the ebony cover plate) and cost $11,000. Irwin saw it as his masterpiece, a beautifully made electric guitar that also doubled as a guitar synthesizer, with MIDI controls built in. It is almost a twin of Tiger, but is lighter at 5.2kg (11$\frac{1}{2}$lb), as its core had been hollowed out to house a gutted out Roland GK-2 guitar synthesizer interface. It soon replaced Tiger as Garcia's regular guitar.

LEFT *Jerry Garcia crafting an extended solo on Tiger during a 1988 concert. The guitar was christened Tiger because of the inlay on the battery/preamp compartment cover.*

St. Stephen

ALBUM: **AOXOMOXOA**

SONGWRITERS: **JERRY GARCIA, ROBERT HUNTER, PHIL LESH**

RECORDED: **PACIFIC RECORDERS, CA**

PRODUCERS: **THE GRATEFUL DEAD**

This is a gentle lead guitar intro. The sound is a lovely mix of jazzy improvisation and rock that was a trademark of the band. All the notes are around the top end of the neck and around the top three strings. Try improvising with other notes around this area of the guitar neck – see what happens when you start to trust your own ear.

BASIC SONG RIFF

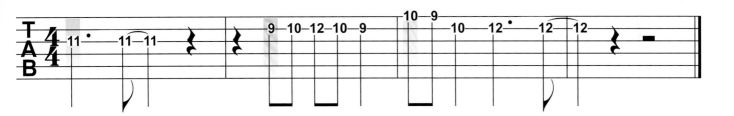

HERE'S HOW

1 This shows the ring finger at the 11th fret kicking off the solo. The other fingers are well placed behind to play notes on the lower frets.

2 Play this note at the 9th fret of the B string with your first finger leaving your middle and ring finger free. Play gently.

3 For this note let your middle finger drop down to the E string to play the D note at the 10th fret.

275

JEFF BECK

1944–
BAND: **YARDBIRDS**
HEIGHT OF FAME: **1960s**

Jeff Beck is the guitarists' guitarist par excellence. He may not be a household name like his contemporaries Eric Clapton and Jimmy Page, but ask any of the greats and they'll tell you that when he's on there's no one to touch Jeff Beck. He's a man who makes the electric guitar do the apparently impossible. The secret is the extent to which he plays the entire guitar: using his fingers instead of a guitar pick for greater speed and control over the fretboard, Beck adds constant twists of the volume and tone knobs to shape the notes as he's playing them, and then further bends the sounds with his expert use of the whammy bar.

RIGHT: *Jeff Beck was a true innovator on the electric guitar. He not only experimented with style but also with sound, being one of the earliest exponents of distortion.*

Beck was born in Wallington, England, on 24 June 1944, just before the end of World War II. He took up the guitar in his teens, inspired as much by jazz as rock. A fast learner, he was soon in demand as a session player, before he replaced Eric Clapton as the Yardbirds' lead guitarist in 1965. Beck's innovative style on hits like 'Heart Full of Soul' and 'Shapes of Things' helped influence the psychedelic sound of the 1960s.

In 1967 he formed The Jeff Beck Group, releasing two albums which ploughed a similar furrow to early Led Zeppelin, though with rather less commercial success. Increasingly impatient with the rock format, Beck switched gears in 1975 with the groundbreaking instrumental jazz-fusion album *Blow By Blow*, which surprisingly became the biggest hit of his career. Produced by Sir George Martin, the album fused the complexity of progressive rock with jazz and thus opened up the horizon for future guitar instrumentalists like Steve Vai and Joe Satriani.

THE WHAMMY BAR

The whammy bar or tremolo arm is a very powerful sound-altering tool for the guitar. As a string bending vibrato unit it actually physically changes the sound the guitar makes as it is played rather than simple transforming the sound after the fact. The development of the whammy bar goes back to the early 1950s when a cumbersome unit called the Bigsby was developed for the Epiphone ES-295, and used by Scotty Moore. The first integral whammy bar came with Leo Fender's 1954 introduction of the Stratocaster. Initially it was intended to be a tool to add some slight vibrato to single notes and chords.

It was only in the mid 1960s that guitarists started fully to experiment with its possibilities. Jimi Hendrix was perhaps the most flamboyant proponent of the whammy bar (just listen to his version of 'The Star Spangled Banner'), but it is Jeff Beck that most thoroughly explored its capabilities. Beck managed to play whole melodies using only the whammy bar and would even combine finger- and bar-vibrato, thereby shaping the notes in remarkable ways, sometimes even creating an almost human voice. His early work on the whammy bar was all the more extraordinary when you realize that these early units tended to make the guitar go out of tune very quickly.

In the late 1970s, Floyd Rose came up with a double locking system which largely solved the tuning problems and has allowed guitar virtuosos (and Beck disciples) like Steve Vai and Joe Satriani to conjure extraordinary effects from the whammy bar. See Steve Vai's appearance in the movie *Crossroads* for an awesome demonstration of the technique.

LEFT: *Jeff Beck can truly make a guitar sing, and the whammy bar is just one tool in his box of tricks.*

I Ain't Superstitious

ALBUM: **TRUTH**
SONGWRITER: **WILLIE DIXON**
RECORDED: **ABBEY ROAD STUDIOS, LONDON**
PRODUCER: **MICKIE MOST**

A great blues riff that uses nice thick and solid notes on the bass strings. Starting off on the 8th fret of the A string the riff moves to a nice alternating pattern on the D string before finishing with double notes at the 3rd fret on the A and D string. Play these notes slow and hard to give you that heavy blues sound. Practise the alternating notes on the D string.

BASIC SONG RIFF

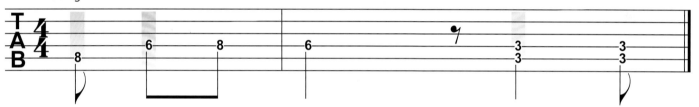

HERE'S HOW

1 It sounds great if you use your ring finger to slide into this F note on the A string just before you play it out.

2 This alternating part rocks between the 6th and 8th frets; use your first and ring fingers for these notes. Tap a beat with your foot to keep time.

3 Back at the 3rd fret on the A and D strings, use your middle and ring fingers to hold the C and F notes. Keep the whole riff steady.

279

THE TELE-GIB

Jeff Beck's most unusual guitar was the so-called Tele-Gib, built for him by noted guitar maker and pickup specialist Seymour Duncan. In 1974 Duncan was working in the repairs and modifications section of the Fender Soundhouse. After watching Beck play, Duncan had the notion that what Beck needed was a guitar that played like a Fender but which had the tone of a Les Paul. As no such instrument existed Duncan set out to make one. He began with the carcass of a 1959 Fender, gave it a new maple fingerboard and cut the fret slots by hand, before putting in Gibson Les Paul frets. Then he went through the tortuous job of rewinding a broken pair of old Gibson 1959 humbuckers. The pickups came from an old 1959 Gibson Flying V that once belonged to Lonnie Mack. The finishing touches included a lever switch knob from an old telephone switchboard, while the volume and tone control knobs and control plate are from an early 50's Telecaster. Jeff liked the instrument immediately and used the 'Tele-Gib' on the seminal *Blow By Blow* album, which included arguably the finest Beck guitar performance, on 'Cause We've Ended As Lovers'.

RIGHT: *Crafted by Seymour Duncan, the Tele-Gib guitar was a unique fusion of Fender and Les Paul. This is a copy of Jeff Beck's guitar, also made by Duncan.*

Where Were You?

ALBUM: **GUITAR SHOP**

SONGWRITERS: **JEFF BECK, TERRY BOZZIO, TONY HYMAS**

RECORDED: **THE SOL STUDIO, ENGLAND**

PRODUCERS: **JEFF BECK, TERRY BOZZIO, TONY HYMAS, LEIF MASES**

This riff is all played along the the B string using the first, middle, ring and little finger. This is great for practising moving up and down the fret board on one string and improving accuracy in your lead playing. Try to get fluency between notes with all your fingers. Get used to climbing the fret board using one finger after another, then descend using the same technique.

BASIC SONG RIFF

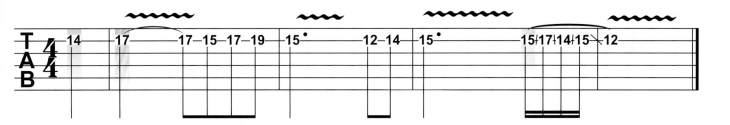

HERE'S HOW

1. The tab shows the first finger playing the C# note at the 14th fret with the ring finger about to play the F# at the 17th fret.

2. Simply slide the first finger up one fret to the D, again use your ring finger to play the F# at the 17th fret.

3. This is a lovely descending passage that you can play between the 17th and 12th frets. Try using different fingers to find which suits you best.

MARC BOLAN

1947–1977
BAND: TYRANNOSAURUS REX, T REX
HEIGHT OF FAME: **1970s**

Marc Bolan, lead singer and guitarist with T Rex, was one of the original glam rock stars. For a couple of years during the early seventies, T Rex were greeted by the wildest scenes of mass hysteria since Beatlemania. And while Marc is more often thought of as a lead vocalist and songwriter, it's his distinctive way with a guitar riff, played on his signature white Stratocaster, that underpinned the band's hit singles – pop classics like 'Get It On' and 'Telegram Sam'.

Although he appeared to many to be an overnight sensation, Marc Bolan had actually been around the pop scene for a while before his time finally came. He was born Mark Feld in Hackney, East London, on 30th September 1947. Leaving school at 14, Bolan went on to form his first band, Suzie And The Hula-Hoops, in 1959.

After recording some early demos, Bolan signed to Decca Records as a solo artist in August 1965. A song called 'The Wizard' was released as a single, but failed to chart. The follow-up singles met a similar fate. Then, after a brief stint in a band called John's Children, Bolan formed his own band, Tyrannosaurus Rex, in July 1967. The band released several psychedelic folk-tinged albums, attracting a firm fan in DJ John Peel and scoring a minor hit with 'Deborah', but still remaining a cult act.

All that changed in 1970 when the band changed their name to the catchier T Rex and released a single, 'Ride A White Swan'. This saw them switching to a tighter, poppier sound, underpinned by Marc's switch to electric guitar. Hit single followed hit single for the next two years. Unfortunately, however, from 1974 onwards their popularity nosedived, and three years later Marc Bolan died in a car accident. Yet today, while many of his contemporaries are forgotten, Marc Bolan's string of hit singles remain classics of riff-based pop-rock.

RIGHT: *During the early 1970s, Marc Bolan's appearances on TV shows such as the BBC TV chart rundown* Top of the Pops *helped to promote his image as a teen icon and glam rock superstar.*

BOLAN'S WHITE FENDER STRATOCASTER

The guitar with which Marc Bolan is most closely associated is undoubtedly his white late-'60s Fender Stratocaster. He actually had two of these guitars, one of them marked out by a teardrop-shaped paisley enamelled sticker on the upper body horn. He bought the first of the guitars in 1969 and used it on his next album *Beard Of Stars*, released in March 1970. It is rumoured that 'Ride a White Swan', the single that finally launched him into the big time, was actually a tribute to his beloved white Strat.

BELOW: *Bolan performs on a T Rex Christmas TV special in December 1972. Note the enamelled teardrop sticker on his white Stratocaster.*

Bolan was a friend of Eric Clapton during the late 1960s, so it's more than likely that it was Clapton's example that persuaded him to buy a Strat. Bolan's Stratocaster sound, though, is distinctively his own. In part this is due to his use of the capo. On some of his earlier songs, the capo can be seen as high as the sixth or even seventh fret, giving the guitar an almost mandolin-like sound. He also preferred to fingerpick rather than use a plectrum. According to Bolan's long-time producer, the legendary Tony Visconti, one of Marc's two white Stratocasters was given to David Bowie after they'd done a TV show together, just weeks before Bolan's death. The other, sadly, was stolen when his house was burgled shortly after he died.

Get it On

ALBUM: **ACOUSTIC WARRIOR**

SONGWRITER: **MARC BOLAN**

RECORDED: **WALLY HEIDER, LOS ANGELES, CA; ADVISION, LONDON; TRIDENT, LONDON**

PRODUCER: **TONY VISCONTI**

Also known as 'Bang a Gong (Get it On)' this song starts with a great boogie riff in E at the 2nd fret of the A string. Listen to the record to get the rhythm exactly right. Practise playing the C# note at the 4th fret with your ring or little finger, keep your index in position at the 2nd fret of the A string. Try this same shape and movement on the D string, then come back to E.

BASIC SONG RIFF

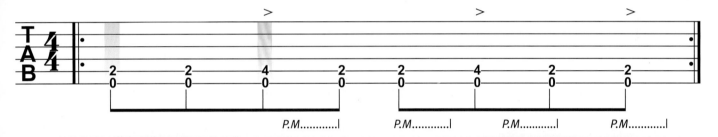

HERE'S HOW

1. Use your index finger to play the B note at the 2nd fret of the A string, then use your middle or ring finger to play the alternating note at the 4th fret of the A string.

2. This shows the C# note being played at the 4th fret of the A string, practise your rhythm playing with this riff to get that classic T Rex boogie feel.

THE DALLAS RANGEMASTER

The British-built Dallas Rangemaster was an effects pedal that Marc Bolan used frequently. This was an early example of a booster unit, designed to give a treble boost to the dark British amps of the time.

Demand for such a unit had grown as the guitar began to figure as a lead instrument, rather than as just part of the rhythm section. The Rangemaster supplied a new, punchier sound. This kind of booster pedal is subtly different to a distortion pedal, although it does not offer an altogether clean boost, but modifies the sound quite a bit. It excites certain frequencies and pushes the amp to allow it to create rich tube distortion. The pedal gives the tone a crunchy overdrive and warms it thanks to the use of germanium transistors.

One classic early use of the Rangemaster was on the epochal John Mayall and the Bluesbreakers album. On that record, Eric Clapton famously used the Les Paul and Marshall amp combination. Less well known is that on several of the tracks his sound was boosted by the use of a Dallas Rangemaster. The original Rangemaster was not a pedal at all, but a tabletop unit with just an on/off switch and a volume knob.

Clapton's example inspired many other guitarist to experiment with the Rangemaster: Brian May used a modified version on nearly all his guitar parts with Queen, which is how he got such a distinctive tone out of his Red Special through walls of AC30s.

Early heavy metal guitarists were particular fans of the unit. Ritchie Blackmore of Deep Purple used it often, and another key user was Tony Iommi of Black Sabbath. He used the Rangemaster to boost the signal from his Gibson SGs into his Laney amps, and created what is perhaps the definitive heavy metal guitar sound.

RIGHT: *As an artist, Bolan appealed to both the older fans who appreciated his earlier, more mystical material, as well as new listeners attracted by the poppy riffs of tracks like 'Twentieth Century Boy'.*

Ride a White Swan

ALBUM: **VARIOUS COMPILATIONS**
SONGWRITER: **MARC BOLAN**
RECORDED: **N/A**
PRODUCER: **TONY VISCONTI**

This is a nice lead riff that plays under the rhythm at the start of the song. Pick out these notes individually and remember to use hammer ons between the notes at the 4th and 6th frets. Try playing with the record to get your lead playing locked in with the rhythm. Playing this lick is good practice for playing between bass and high strings and will improve your lead playing generally.

BASIC SONG RIFF

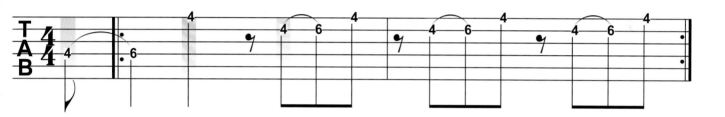

| HERE'S HOW |

1 The first part of the riff shows the index finger playing the 4th fret of the D string and the hammer on with the ring or little finger at the 6th fret.

2 Bring your index finger down to the A flat note at the 4th fret of the top E to play the next part of the riff, let this note ring out.

3 Finally use your index finger to play the 4th fret of the B string and your ring or little finger to hammer on to the 6th fret of the B string.

JAMES TAYLOR

1948–
BAND: **SOLO ARTIST**
HEIGHT OF FAME: **LATE 1960s–EARLY 1970s**

James Taylor invented the modern day singer-songwriter genre: the introspective balladeers with just an acoustic guitar for company. There had been singers accompanying themselves on the guitar before, of course, but generally they'd been out-and-out folk singers in the Woody Guthrie tradition.

What James Taylor did was to take the instrumental style of the folksinger and turn it inwards, rejecting protest songs in favour of love songs. With 'Fire and Rain' and 'Sweet Baby James', Taylor succeeded in soundtracking the lives and loves of the post-Woodstock early 1970s generation. While it's his classic songwriting and smooth voice that are the first things most people associate with James Taylor, his fingerpicked acoustic accompaniments have also been an enormous influence on generations of guitar-playing songwriters.

James Taylor was born 12 March 1948 in Boston, the second son of a wealthy, musical family. Later the family moved to Chapel Hill, North Carolina, where James' father was dean of the medical school. Taylor studied cello as a child, but first took up the guitar when he was 12. After suffering teenage stints at boarding school and in a psychiatric hospital following a bout of depression, he moved to Greenwich Village where he started performing.

His first break came when he was signed to The Beatles' Apple label in 1968. His big breakthrough came with his second album *Sweet Baby James* released on Warners in 1969. Since then, his musical career has never looked back. Album after album has gone gold or platinum with his *Greatest Hits* collection selling over 10 million copies. He continues to sell records consistently, having discovered the knack of growing old gracefully.

RIGHT: *James Taylor is a master of intricate blues and rock melodies, and his fingerpicking style makes him difficult to imitate.*

JAMES TAYLOR'S GUITAR STYLE

James Taylor's guitar playing is all about fingerpicking, He scarcely ever plays block chords. Instead he uses complex right-hand picking patterns with distinctive bass lines picked out with his thumb.

His style is based on the classic Merle Travis two fingers and thumb picking style, though over the years he's customized it considerably and always uses three fingers instead of two. Unlike many fingerpickers, Taylor doesn't use a thumb-pick either. Instead he simply grows his thumbnails along with the rest of his fingernails, though while he keeps his other nails about an eighth of an inch beyond the tip of the finger, he grows the thumbnail a little longer and files it straight across rather then curved around the line of the quick. In this way, it acts more like a thumbpick. Such is Taylor's aversion to picks that if he breaks a nail he'll glue on an artificial nail rather than use a pick.

Thankfully while Taylor's right-hand work is deceptively complex and difficult to imitate, his left-hand work is relatively straightforward. He almost always uses standard tuning, with the occasional excursion into G (DGDGBD), and with particular fondness for open chords (especially since an accident resulted in him severing a nerve in his left index finger, thus making chord barring difficult). Taylor relies heavily on the capo, sometimes even using different capo positions within a single song. 'One, Your Smiling Face' actually has three separate capo positions so when playing it live the capo would start on the second fret, move to the fourth and end up on the sixth. Asked why he used the capo so much, the endearingly modest Taylor once commented, 'It's really the thing that shows how rudimentary a player I am.'

BELOW: *James Taylor delivers an acoustic set. Taylor's favoured acoustic is the Olsen SJ.*

You've Got a Friend

ALBUM: **MUD SLIDE SLIM & THE BLUE HORIZON**
SONGWRITER: **CAROLE KING**
RECORDED: **CRYSTAL STUDIOS, HOLLYWOOD, CA**
PRODUCER: **PETER ASHER**

For this song we've used a capo on the 2nd fret to bring the tuning up a tone. This tune sounds lovely strummed or picked-finger style on an acoustic guitar. Move gently between chords for a nice relaxed feel and experiment mixing strumming with finger style. Try a capo on other songs to find the key that suits you best. Practise picking arpeggios on other chords.

BASIC SONG CHORDS

G   C   D⁷sus⁴

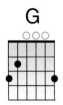 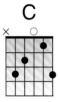 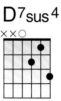

Capo 2nd fret

HERE'S HOW

1. Use your middle, ring and little fingers to keep your first finger free for the 1st fret on the B string in the next chord.

2. This picture shows a C chord shape. Notice the little finger playing the G note on the E string; this gives the chord a lovely melodic ring.

3. Play this chord by using the first, middle and little finger on the E string. Practise using your little finger on other chords.

JAMES TAYLOR'S OLSON SJ

In his early days, James Taylor favoured Gibson guitars, using a J-50 on much of his material. Then John McLaughlin introduced him to a luthier named Mark Whitebook who made him a series of acoustic guitars, modelled on the Martin dreadnought style and generally equipped with Takamine pickups.

However, Whitebook retired from the guitar-building business and since 1989 Taylor has found himself a new luthier, Minnesota guitar-maker James Olson. Olson left a guitar in James Taylor's dressing room, when he was playing a gig locally, and Taylor called him the next day.

Taylor loved the guitar, but he wanted a non-cutaway version with the same neck dimensions. Taylor took the cutaway guitar on the spot with the understanding that he would exchange it when the new guitar was completed. Once the new guitar was finished, however, Taylor decided to keep the cutaway guitar as well, and while he was at it, he ordered an Olson dreadnought to round out his collection. All three guitars remain active in Taylor's stage setup, but he considers the SJ to be his main instrument and has used it on every CD he's recorded since he purchased it.

For the SJ, Olson decided to use East Indian rosewood on the guitar's back and sides. It sports an abalone rosette and purfling, but simple fingerboard inlays give it an understated look. The only thing different about James Taylor's personal SJ from Olson's standard design is that the guitar's neck is laminated using rosewood instead of mahogany. Taylor had the guitar set up with an L.R. Baggs LB-6 pickup and John Pearse strings.

LEFT: *James Taylor and Carole King had a close working relationship, collaborating on several projects.*

Sweet Baby James

ALBUM: **SWEET BABY JAMES**
SONGWRITER: **JAMES TAYLOR**
RECORDED: **SUNSET SOUND STUDIOS, LOS ANGELES**
PRODUCER: **PETER ASHER**

These are the main chords used in James Taylor's classic 'Sweet Baby James'. Get used to moving between different chords fluently, and don't be afraid to experiment by adding or taking away a note here and there. Use a nice relaxed strumming style on an acoustic guitar for this tune. Practise moving between these chords fluently and integrate them into your repertoire. Try singing along as you play.

BASIC SONG CHORDS

G

Em^7

A^{7}sus^4

HERE'S HOW

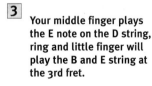

1 Use your first finger for the B note at fret 2 of the A string. Your middle finger should play the G note on the top E string.

2 For this chord cascade your fingers down the fret board from first to little to play the four notes shown on the chord diagram. Keep G open.

3 Your middle finger plays the E note on the D string, ring and little finger will play the B and E string at the 3rd fret.

CARLOS SANTANA

1947–
BAND: **SANTANA BLUES BAND**
HEIGHT OF FAME: **1970s–PRESENT**

Carlos Santana is the most purely melodic of the great rock guitarists. His controlled, fluid technique makes a uniquely smooth ride, as in his classic interpretation of 'Black Magic Woman' or his huge recent hit, the aptly titled 'Smooth'. At other times, he uses it to keep the listener engaged while he works through some exceedingly complex jazz rock – as on the John Coltrane-inspired duo album he made with fellow guitar legend John McLaughlin, *Love Devotion Surrender*.

Carlos Santana was born on 20 July 1947 in Autlan De Navarro, Mexico where he spent his early years. His father was a mariachi violinist and Carlos took up the violin at five, but at eight switched to the guitar. Later the family moved to Tijuana, where he began playing in clubs and bars. Then, in the early 1960s, the family moved to San Francisco where he finished high school in 1965. The following year he formed The Santana Blues Band, a collective of Bay Area musicians. While nominally a blues band, it stood out from the competition by incorporating elements of Latin music and jazz into its sound. Soon they were signed to Columbia Records and released their first album in 1969. It became an instant hit following the band's performance at Woodstock, and proved the template for several more hit albums, peaking with 1970's *Abraxas*.

This album showed the full range of Santana's abilities. The material mixed rock, jazz, salsa and blues, but whether the band were playing salsa tunes like 'Oye Como Va', Latin-flavoured jazz-rock as on 'Samba Pa Ti', or moody blues-rock with their classic version of Fleetwood Mac's 'Black Magic Woman', what kept things together was the utterly distinctive sound and tone of Carlos Santana's lead guitar.

RIGHT: *Carlos Santana is the archetype of the smooth Latin guitar sound, although his musical influences stretch well beyond indigenous Latin-American music.*

THE RED GUITAR

During the 1970s the electric-guitar market had more or less boiled down to a war between the two big players, Gibson and Fender. These two big manufacturers made a fine job of producing mass-market guitars, but for players looking for something classier, but without wanting to pay the fortune needed for a fully custom-made guitar, there wasn't much choice out there. Then along came Paul Reed Smith. A young man with a vision, he started manufacturing guitars in his attic in Annapolis, Maryland. He produced several prototypes and did his best to talk visiting musicians into trying them out. The first person to take him seriously was Carlos Santana, who was thrilled with the extraordinary attention to detail and overall quality of Smith's guitars. His endorsement helped Smith set up PRS guitars as an increasingly flourishing business at the high end of the market.

Santana himself has had any number of PRS guitars over the years, but his clear favourite is the so-called Red Guitar made in the original PRS factory in Annapolis. It sports a Brazilian rosewood neck and mahogany body plus an East Coast Curly Maple top. You can see its photo on the back of Santana's multi-platinum *Supernatural* album.

There are also several Santana-endorsed PRS models available to the general public – just don't expect them to feature Smith's private stash of Brazilian rosewood. PRS also supply Santana-endorsed pickups carefully designed to offer devotees the chance to recreate Santana's signature smoothness of sound.

RIGHT: *The Red Guitar is a beautiful instrument from PRS guitars, made from the finest rosewood, mahogany and maple. It is easy to see why it is Santana's favourite guitar.*

She's Not There

ALBUM: **MOONFLOWER**
SONGWRITER: **ROD ARGENT**
RECORDED: **CBS STUDIOS, SAN FRANCISCO, CA**
PRODUCER: **CARLOS SANTANA**

This is a great little repetitive riff played over four strings. You can try up and down strokes with the plectrum on this one to vary the speed of the riff. Try to move easily between the different strings to give the riff a nice fluid sound. Listen to the song to check your timing. Once you feel relaxed and confident playing this riff use a few slides into the notes to accentuate the melody.

BASIC SONG RIFF

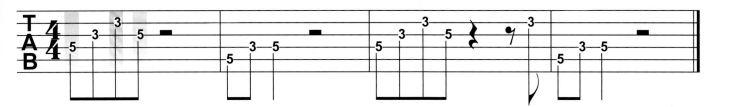

HERE'S HOW

1 The ring finger plays the 5th fret of the D string and the first finger is back to play the 3rd fret of the G string.

2 Here the first finger has dropped down to the B string to play the D note on the 3rd fret.

3 Bring the ring finger up to play the C note which is at the 5th fret of the G string.

Famous Albums

The Santana Band's debut self-titled album was among the bigger splashes made by San Francisco's second wave of acid rock artists, buoyed by the group's incendiary live shows, including Woodstock. Abraxas *features two of Santana's better known tracks,* 'Black Magic Woman' *and* 'Oye Como Va', *while* Supernatural *saw Carlos Santana top the charts a remarkable 29 years later.*

ALBUM: **SANTANA**
YEAR: **1969**
RECORDED: **PACIFIC RECORDING, CA**
PRODUCERS: **SANTANA**

ALBUM: **ABRAXAS**
YEAR: **1970**
RECORDED: **PACIFIC RECORDING, CA**
PRODUCERS: **SANTANA**

ALBUM: **SUPERNATURAL**
YEAR: **1999**
RECORDED: **FANTASY STUDIOS, CA**
PRODUCERS: **SANTANA**

RIGHT: *Carlos Santana is still going strong. To date he has sold over 50 million albums and in concert he had entertained nearly 30 million fans.*

BAND INFO

THE SANTANA BAND
BAND FORMED: **1966**
ALBUMS: **36**
TOTAL ALBUM SALES:
50 MILLION

ORIGINAL LINE-UP
LEAD: **CARLOS SANTANA**
KEYBOARDS: **GREGG ROLIE**
BASS: **GUS RODRIGUES**
VOCALS: **GREGG ROLIE**
DRUMMER: **ROD HARPER**
More than 60 musicians have played with the band since 1966

Smooth

ALBUM: **SUPERNATURAL**

SONGWRITERS: **ROB THOMAS, ITAAL SHUR**

RECORDED: **FANTASY RECORDING STUDIOS, BERKELEY, CA**

PRODUCERS: **CARLOS SANTANA, CLIVE DAVIS**

The higher up the neck you go the more narrow the distance between each fret. Playing riffs high up the neck will get you used to the differences in fret width. You may need to slightly adjust your body position when moving between high and low frets, find out what position is most comfortable for you. Use hammer-on technique with first and ring finger for this riff. First finger can cover notes at the 12th fret.

BASIC SONG RIFF

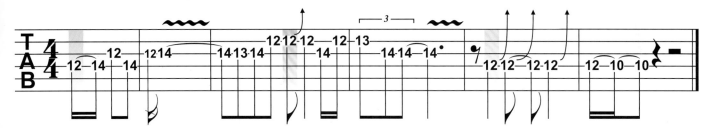

HERE'S HOW

1 Try to make the hammer-on sound smooth by holding the original note firm with the first finger and hitting the 14th fret with the ring finger.

2 Use the first finger on the B string and make sure your ring finger is poised ready to hit the A note at the 14th fret of the G string.

3 Practise moving between the high strings down to the bass strings. Use your first finger to play the D ocatve at the 12th fret of the D string.

RITCHIE BLACKMORE

1945–
BAND: **DEEP PURPLE, RAINBOW**
HEIGHT OF FAME: **1970s**

Ritchie Blackmore is the epitome of the heavy-rock guitar god – a mean, moody Strat-slinger dressed in black. His claim to fame may be having written the ultimate rock guitar riff in 'Smoke on the Water', but his real importance as a guitarist lies in the way he incorporated classical and even country influences into his playing to create a heavy-rock style. This style is entirely original, and sounds quite different from that purveyed by blues-oriented guitarists such as Clapton and Hendrix.

RIGHT: *With Deep Purple Ritchie Blackmore pioneered the heavy metal sound, combining powerhouse rhythms with the nimblest of solos and melodies.*

Blackmore was born on 14 April 1945, in Weston-super-Mare, UK. His first guitar was a Framus, a Spanish guitar made in Germany. He took classical guitar lessons for a while, but the influence of rock 'n' roll soon convinced him to trade up to an electric. His early influences included Duane Eddy, Big Jim Sullivan – Britain's premier session guitar player during the 1960s – and Hank Marvin, who fronted legendary '60s British group The Shadows. The real turning point, though, was his discovery of country pickers like Chet Atkins. He was amazed by the speed and dexterity of Atkins' playing and started to practise for eight hours a day in order to acquire quick-picking and double-note riffing techniques that form the bedrock of his style to this day.

Ritchie played with several groups during his early teens. He left school when he was 15, worked as an apprentice radio mechanic at nearby London Airport, and then played with Screaming Lord Sutch. By the time he reached 16, his devotion to and subsequent mastery of fast, complex riffing led to plenty of session work, often sharing studio dates with Jimmy Page. Finally, in March 1968, Blackmore became a founder member of Deep Purple.

At first the band played psychedelic pop, but with the addition of new vocalist Ian Gillan they soon became hard rockers, providing a new generation with monster riffs like 'Black Night'. Blackmore once described the song as 'A total rip-off. I stole the riff from Ricky Nelson's record of "Summertime".' Another classic was 'Smoke On The Water', written after the band went to see Frank Zappa playing in Montreux and the venue caught fire.

AIWA TAPE DECK

Ritchie's best known effects unit is the Aiwa open-reel tape deck used both in the studio and live, which acts as an echo unit and a preamp. He introduced the Aiwa on the 1974 Burn tour. The tape deck was originally intended to act as a delay unit, as the use of open-reel tape decks for echo was a fairly common technique at the time. Mike Oldfield notably used an Akai open-reel machine

ENGL AMPS

For many years Blackmore played his guitars – first the Gibson then the Fender Strat – through Marshall amplifiers. He even persuaded Jim Marshall to build him a custom amp, alleged to be the most powerful Marshall amplifier ever made. Most guitarists might have been satisfied with that, but Blackmore is a restless soul, and was still not entirely happy.

He felt the sound only worked at full volume; anything less and he thought it sounded thin. He compensated for this perceived deficiency by using his Akai tape deck preamp which fattened up the mid-range sound, but he still felt a lurking dissatisfaction. Then, in the early 1990s, while playing some smaller club dates, he tried out a German made Engl amplifier, which used the traditional tube valve technology, and was amazed to realize that he'd

found the amplifier of his dreams. This was a huge boost to the small German company founded in the 1980s. Since then they've gone on to produce a Ritchie Blackmore signature model based on a classic, proven design also equipped with a number of innovative features. For instance, you can vary the amount of crunch for the two channels Clean and Lead via the Gain-Boost switch. Also, each of the two Gain stages (Lo and Hi) is equipped with a dedicated master volume control, or you can activate Master A and Master B via footswitch.

LEFT: *Richie Blackmore had a long journey to find his ideal amp system, discovering it in the Engl tube valve amp.*

Smoke On The Water

ALBUM: **MACHINE HEAD**

SONGWRITERS: **IAN GILLAN, RITCHIE BLACKMORE, IAN PAICE, JON LORD, ROGER GLOVER**

RECORDED: **MONTREUX CASINO, THE GRAND HOTEL, SWITZERLAND**

PRODUCERS: **DEEP PURPLE**

These are fantastic power chords frequently used in heavy-metal tunes. Like the 12-bar chords in rock ' n ' roll, you can move these shapes around the fret board to hear echoes of many great rock songs. Crank the amp up to ' 11' and enjoy! Power chords need to be very solid; learn to slide them up and down the fret board. Use the sliding sound to accentuate the tune.

BASIC SONG RIFF

HERE'S HOW

1 Use your first, ring and little finger on this shape. The basic shape stays the same throughout. Keep the chord rigid as you move up and down.

2 This is the shape up five frets from the first shape. Try to include the slide as part of the riff, and experiment with different rhythms with your plectrum.

3 The shape is now at the 8th fret; from here use the sound sliding down to the 7th fret as part of the tune.

WAH WAH

The wah-wah pedal is the gizmo that created the 'wakka wakka' effect beloved of Jimi Hendrix and most early 1970s guitarists. Ritchie Blackmore was at the forefront of this sound, though it has become somewhat less fashionable now.

ABOVE: *An array of pedals beneath a guitarist's feet can be more of a distraction than an asset, but Ritchie Blackmore used his sounds only to enhance the piece being played.*

The first wah-type sounds could be found on country albums in the late 1950s and early 1960s. However, these were not obtained by a separate effects unit but simply by the player working the tone knob. Vox was the first company to have commercial success with the Wah. It came about accidentally, when testing an oscillator for an amp. The sound created brought people running to find out what on earth the effect was, and Vox knew they were on to a winner.

Soon afterwards Vox introduced the classic Cry Baby Wah to the US market and guitar playing was never quite the same again. Over the next few years Vox also tried different variations on the wah theme, such as the bass wah and the fuzz wah. A legion of imitators also sprang up. By the late 1960s there were probably 40 or 50 different manufactures making wah-wah pedals on both sides of the Atlantic. Some of the more familiar names were Marshall, DeArmond, Sound City, Colorsound, Gibson, Fender, Gretsch and Kay. Many of these devices offered extra sounds like fuzz, sirens, surf, tornado, etc. As the late 1970s approached, the wah effect was becoming unhip, and the number of manufacturers dropped accordingly. To hear definitive use of the wah-wah in a hard-rock setting, listen to Ritchie Blackmore's playing on *Deep Purple In Rock*.

on *Tubular Bells*. The echo effect comes from the delay between the record head and the playback head with the recorder in monitor mode to produce a delay. If the deck can do it, plug the guitar in and set the left channel to monitor the recorded signal and the right channel to the original signal. The faster the tape is run, the shorter the echo/delay. However, as Blackmore discovered, these open-reel tape decks with valve electronics can be used as guitar preamps as well an echo units. Lindsey Buckingham used a Sony tape deck as a preamp with Fleetwood Mac. At various times Ritchie used both effects. The preamp he used to give his sound an altogether fuzzier effect. Having tried it successfully in the recording studio, he decided to use it on stage as well and the Aiwa tape deck has become a familiar sight to anyone who has been fortunate to see Blackmore play live over the subsequent 30 years. He plugs the Aiwa in between his guitar and the amp and uses a foot pedal to control how much effect it has.

Black Night

ALBUM: **DEEP PURPLE IN ROCK**

SONGWRITERS: **IAN GILLAN, RITCHIE BLACKMORE, IAN PAICE, JON LORD, ROGER GLOVER**

RECORDED AT: **N/A**

PRODUCED BY: **DEEP PURPLE**

This tab shows the riff picked out on the bass strings – this gives a great heavy metal sound. Use your first and ring finger to hit the notes on the fret board. Practise moving between the three bass strings (E, A and D). Play slowly then speed up once you feel comfortable. Alternate use of first and ring finger, and get used to moving between bass strings. Every note in this riff counts, so play them solidly.

BASIC SONG RIFF

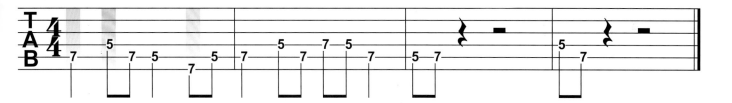

1 Use muting to cut notes off before playing the next one. This technique will help to accentuate heavy-metal riffs. Use it on other songs.

2 Drop down to the D string with your first finger; with practice you'll be able to move easily between these notes that are only two frets apart.

3 Your ring finger should play this note on the E string, every note should sound loud and bold, remember the guitar and bass lead the band on this riff.

RIGHT: *Ritchie Blackmore became one of the most recognizable figures of Deep Purple, proving how much the status of lead guitarists had changed since the 1950s. He would, however, have an emotionally troubled relationship with other band members and finally left in 1994.*

Since You've Been Gone

ALBUM: **DOWN TO EARTH (RAINBOW)**
WRITTEN BY: **RUSS BALLARD**
RECORDED AT: **LE CHATEAU, PARIS, FRANCE**
PRODUCED BY: **ROGER GLOVER**

This tune uses some nice big power chords at the intro – notice again the two-fret distance between the notes to give that solid power chord sound. Practise using up and down strumming techniques to create interesting rhythm patterns. You'll need to get comfortable moving these shapes around the fret board. Use big down strokes with the plectrum for power and combine with up strokes to vary the rhythm.

BASIC SONG RIFF

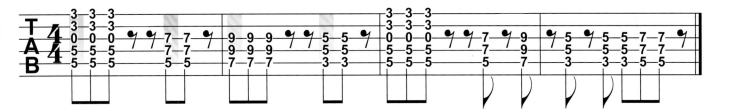

HERE'S HOW

1 This chord uses the first finger to play the B and E strings, so you'll need to stretch your ring and little fingers to play the A and D strings.

2 Change shape here, your first finger plays the D note on the A string and your ring and little finger plays the D and G strings.

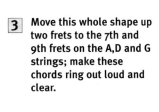

3 Move this whole shape up two frets to the 7th and 9th frets on the A,D and G strings; make these chords ring out loud and clear.

4 Back at the 3rd and 5th frets use the first finger for the A string and ring and little fingers for the D and G strings.

TONY IOMMI

1948–
BAND: BLACK SABBATH
HEIGHT OF FAME: **1970s**

Tony Iommi has a good claim to be the heaviest of all heavy-rock guitarists. After all, he more or less invented heavy metal single-handedly with Black Sabbath. Sabbath's classic songs – 'Paranoid', 'War Pigs', 'Iron Man' and many others – combined brutally simple, yet monstrously effective, riffs with banshee vocals courtesy of Ozzy Osbourne and relentlessly dark lyrical imagery. With Black Sabbath, a genre was born.

Tony Iommi was born on 19 February 1948, in Birmingham, England, He started playing guitar as a teenager, inspired by the likes of Hank Marvin & the Shadows. By the late 1960s, Iommi had formed a group called Earth with three old school friends — bassist Terry 'Geezer' Butler, drummer Bill Ward, and singer John 'Ozzy' Osbourne. Iommi's musical career was nearly over before it began after an accident at work led to the loss of the tips of the fingers on his right hand. However, he managed to recover and adapt his style.

Iommi briefly joined Jethro Tull in 1968, but quickly rejoined Earth, now renamed Black Sabbath. They quickly developed their new direction – dark lyrical subjects backed by repetitive heavy riffs. They got the mix perfected right from the start. Their self-titled debut album was an immediate hit as were its follow-ups, 1971's *Paranoid* and *Master of Reality*, 1972's *Vol. 4*, and 1973's *Sabbath Bloody Sabbath*. By that time they were one of the world's top hard-rock bands, with Iommi's guitar playing at the heart of their sound, pumping out some of the most recognizable guitar riffs in rock history.

But by the late 1970s, constant touring and drug abuse began to fracture the band, leading to Osbourne's exit in 1979. Iommi kept the band going and it triumphantly re-formed in the late 1990s, their music acknowledged as uniquely influential.

RIGHT: *Tony Iommi was fundamental to heavy-rock history; indeed, some music critics have claimed that Iommi and Black Sabbath were the sole creators of the genre.*

TONY'S FINGERS

The pivotal moment in Tony Iommi's guitar-playing history was almost his last. It happened when he was 18 and the band he played in had just landed a tour of Germany. On Tony's very last day at work in a sheet-metal factory, he caught his right hand in a machine press. He instinctively pulled his hand away and as he did so, ripped off the ends of his middle and ring fingers, which were caught in the machine. Ironically enough, Iommi had actually planned on skipping work that day but his mother had insisted he go, telling him it was the right thing to do.

At first, Iommi was close to giving up on ever playing again, Then a friend gave him a record by legendary gypsy jazz guitarist Django Reinhardt, who had suffered a burn to his left hand that left him with only two working fingers. This inspired Tony to start playing again. First he experimented with playing the guitar with his other hand, but without much success. Then he came up with the rather brilliant idea of making himself thimbles for the tips of his two damaged fingers. He made them by melting down plastic bottles of Fairy Liquid (an English brand of washing-up liquid), shaping them, and then putting leather ends on them so he could grip the strings better. Then, despite not being able to feel the ends of his 'thimble' wearing fingers, Tony set about relearning how to play. Whether he would have come up with the revolutionary style he eventually arrived at without the accident we shall never know.

RIGHT: *Iommi is most identified with Black Sabbath in the late ' 60s and early ' 70s, but he has also built a successful solo career in the 2000s.*

Iron Man

ALBUM: **PARANOID**

SONGWRITERS: **TONY IOMMI, BILL WARD, GEEZER BUTLER, OZZY OSBORNE**

RECORDED: **REGENT SOUND, ISLAND STUDIOS, LONDON**

PRODUCER: **RODGER BAIN**

This is a chunky rock riff played with a two-fret gap at all times. Try to keep the notes solid and heavy; practise accuracy moving the shape around. Be careful to avoid hitting the open E bass string when bringing the plectrum down on the notes in the chord. Try to practise holding the chord shape steady, especially as you move it up and down the fret board.

BASIC SONG RIFF

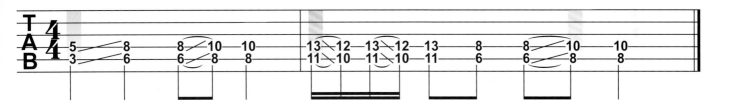

HERE'S HOW

1 With the first finger at the 3rd fret of the A string and ring finger at the 5th fret of the D string hold this shape firm.

2 The riff has climbed to the 11th and 13th frets and now jumps back and forth between two frets. Keep time with the beat.

3 This is exactly the same shape back on the 8th and 10th frets of the A and D strings. Repeat the riff slowly until you feel comfortable.

TONY IOMMI'S SGs

Being left-handed, Iommi had a lot of trouble finding a guitar that suited him when he was starting out. At that time, the early 1960s, electric guitars weren't easy to get hold of at all, let alone left-handed ones.

His first guitar was a Watkins, a popular, inexpensive British copy of a Fender Stratocaster. As he moved on to a Burns (another British brand) and then to a real Strat, his choices were limited by his left-handed playing style. He did find a left-handed Strat eventually, but he preferred the sound of the Gibson SGs he'd heard, so he bit on the bullet, bought a right handed SG, and strung it upside down, just as Hendrix did with his Strat. Then, by chance, he ran into another guitarist who was right-handed but, bizarrely, happened to be playing a left-handed SG strung upside down. Tony Iommi suggested they swap, and it was this SG he played on most of the classic Black Sabbath albums. As he became successful, he was able to get custom-made left-handed guitars, all modelled on the SG shape. The best known of these are the ones made by Jaydee guitars, a company started by Iommi's sometime guitar tech John Diggins and, later on, a signature model made by British company Patrick Eggle Guitars. More recently a Tony Iommi signature model has also been manufactured by Gibson themselves – so anyone interested in reinventing heavy metal today is spoilt for choice.

RIGHT: *The Gibson SG provided Tony Iommi's ideal guitar shape, and his custom-built guitars are made to this pattern.*

Paranoid

ALBUM: **PARANOID**

SONGWRITERS: **TONY IOMMI, BILL WARD, GEEZER BUTLER, OZZY OSBORNE**

RECORDED: **REGENT SOUND, ISLAND STUDIOS, LONDON**

PRODUCER: **RODGER BAIN**

Another classic early heavy metal riff using that familiar two-fret distance between each string. You need to ensure these notes are played hard and accurately when dropping down from your E to D string. To create speed this riff also uses the hammer on technique. Use the two finger shape to create a heavy rock sound. The hammer on will increase speed and can be used to accentuate the tune.

BASIC SONG RIFF

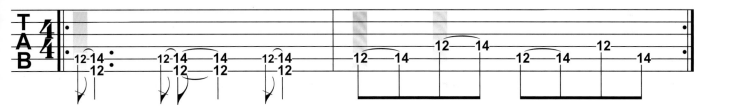

HERE'S HOW

1. First and ring fingers are used together, the first finger playing notes on two strings at the 12th fret and the ring to hammer on.

2. Here the riff only requires you to play the A string, again use the hammer on technique but be careful to avoid hitting the E string.

3. Bring your first finger down to the D string ready to play the 12th fret, once again use the hammer on to create speed.

MICK RONSON

1946–1993

BAND: **THE SPIDERS FROM MARS, HUNTER AND RONSON**

HEIGHT OF FAME: **1970s**

Mick Ronson was the undisputed king of the glam-rock guitarists. For three tumultuous years he played a stack-heeled Keith Richards to David Bowie's preening Jagger. His riffs powered Bowie rockers like 'Jean Genie' and 'Rebel Rebel', while his melodic lead playing turned songs like 'Ziggy Stardust' into classics. What marked Ronson's style out was its mixture of simplicity and sophistication. When a straightforward catchy riff was needed, that was just what he supplied, but he was also able to supply the avant-garde sound textures which still make those 30-year-old Bowie recordings sound contemporary.

RIGHT: Mick Ronson was a major influence on the sound of David Bowie, and played on some of Bowie's most popular tracks.

Mick Ronson was born in Hull, Yorkshire, on 26 May 1946. He received both piano and violin lessons as a child and also played the harmonium in church before taking up guitar in his late teens. He played in various local bands, including The Rats, who would later provide the nucleus of Bowie's backing band The Spiders From Mars. But Ronson's real preparation for working with Bowie came when he added electric guitar to an album by folkie Mike Chapman, full of string-bends and unusual rhythmic sequences. Hearing this inspired Bowie, then recording the acoustic-based 'Space Oddity', to hire Ronson to add some rock edge to his material. Their combination was spectacularly successful through the early 1970s. Then, in 1974, Bowie split up the band and Ronson tried a brief solo career before teaming up with Mott The Hoople's Ian Hunter. The next decades saw Ronson working with an extraordinary variety of artists from Bob Dylan to Morrissey, via John Mellencamp and Meatloaf. He had a brief reunion with David Bowie shortly before he died of liver cancer on 30 April 1993, aged 46.

RONSON'S LES PAUL

Whenever people talk about the 1970s' guitar sound, chances are they mean something not far removed from Ronson's signature '58 Les Paul/100-Watt Marshall sound. As a member of Bowie's Spiders from Mars, Ronson gave the Les Paul an image overhaul and a thrilling new sound. It certainly didn't sound like the same Les Paul that had been played by Clapton and his fellow blues rockers. This Les Paul had an edgier, punkier sound. To get his particular sound Ronson used his Dunlop CryBaby wah as a tone shaper, working the pedal until he found the desired mid-range bite, then leaving it in that position. He was also a master at using the wah to push a solo to its squealing, wailing climax.

BELOW: *Ronson helped put the Gibson Les Paul on the map by combining it with a Dunlop CryBaby. All of Ronson's recordings in his Spiders period were made using a Marshall Major 200W amp nicknamed 'the pig'.*

The actual age and model of Ronson's much-photographed Les Paul Custom, however, remains unclear. Ronson was famously uninterested in his equipment. In a December 1976 feature in *Guitar Player* magazine, it is identified as a '58, but other articles suggest that it was actually a '68. One thing is sure: the famous Paul didn't start out with its blonde colouring.

When he was playing with Michael Chapman in 1969, Ronson admired the natural wood on the folk singer's Gibson J-200. Chapman explained that he had stripped the original finish to improve his acoustic's high-end response. Impressed, Ronson immediately directed one of Chapman's roadies to remove the black finish from his Les Paul. By the late 1970s, however, Ronson had moved on to playing Stratocasters and had sold the Les Paul to Steve Jones of The Sex Pistols – a guitarist whose sound was clearly shaped by Ronson's knack with a heavy yet poppy riff.

Rebel Rebel

ALBUM: **DIAMOND DOGS**
SONGWRITER: **DAVID BOWIE**
RECORDED: **OLYMPIC STUDIOS; ISLAND STUDIOS, LONDON**
PRODUCER: **DAVID BOWIE**

This is a lovely descending riff from David Bowie's 'Rebel Rebel'. Following the single E note intro on the D string use your ring finger to slide into the E note at the 5th fret on the B string. Practise using your first three fingers to play descending runs down the fret board. Play the riff slowly with feeling, hit the notes hard with the plectrum to get that great Mick Ronson sound.

BASIC SONG RIFF

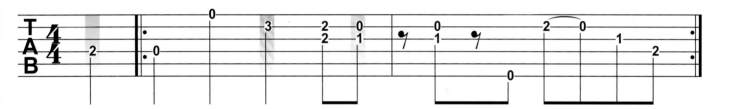

HERE'S HOW

1 This shows the long E note on the D string – hold this note with the first finger while you find position to start the descending run.

2 Play this D note on the B string with your middle finger to allow your first finger to fall behind and hit the 2nd fret.

3 Position your first finger on the first fret of the G string and your middle finger can hit the final E note on the D string.

THE ANTI-GEAR GUITARIST

Most of the guitar greats are gear obsessives, musicians who are constantly tweaking their guitars and amps and effects to find that killer distortion sound, that perfect fretboard, or super-sensitive pickup. Others are collectors always on the lookout for that pre-war Gibson or that perfect Martin. Mick Ronson, however, was most definitely the exception to the rule.

Ronson's attitude comes over clearly in his description of playing a guest spot with David Bowie in the 1980s. He borrowed a guitar from Bowie's regular axeman, Earl Slick, and started thrashing out 'Jean Genie', whirling the guitar around his head. He couldn't understand why Slick was looking so horrified. 'Later on I found it was his special guitar. I didn't know it was his special guitar, I just though it was a guitar, a lump of wood with 6 strings.' That's certainly the attitude Ronson had to his own guitars.

'I've always been the same way with guitars, they've always got something wrong with them. I'm really lazy about getting things fixed and I tend to sort of leave them. But at the same time I kind of leave them on purpose, for some psychological reason I leave them like that so I have to wrestle with them. Then it feels real to me.' And as for amplifiers, 'Often I wouldn't even think of what I was plugging into...it doesn't matter to me at all as long as it works.' Without taking Ronson's attitude to extremes, it's worth taking in the crucial fact that what really matters is what you play, not what kind of guitar you're playing it on.

LEFT: *Mick Ronson was a rock guitarist who focused all his efforts on playing, not on his equipment.*

Ziggy Stardust

ALBUM: **THE RISE AND FALL OF ZIGGY STARDUST AND THE SPIDERS FROM MARS**
SONGWRITER: **DAVID BOWIE**
RECORDED: **TRIDENT STUDIOS, LONDON**
PRODUCERS: **DAVID BOWIE, KEN SCOTT**

Here is a great example of using regular chords to create a classic riff. The intro to 'Ziggy Stardust' is based around the G and D chords with a few extra notes to make it more interesting. Listen to how Mick Ronson plays around the D chord during the intro. You can use the chords in this song to experiment using single chords as a melodic intro to a tune.

BASIC SONG RIFF

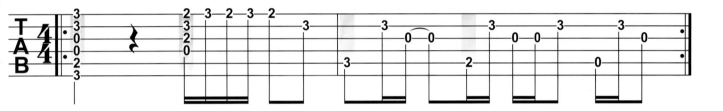

HERE'S HOW

1 The middle finger holds down the bass note G on the E string, the ring and little fingers play notes on the B and E strings.

2 D chord – you can either play this with your middle, ring and little finger or first finger across three strings with your little finger on the D note.

3 Your middle finger should play the C note on the A string and your third finger plays the D note on the B string.

4 Your first finger plays the B note on the A string; release your middle finger and play the D note on the B string.

DAVID GILMOUR

1946–
BAND: **PINK FLOYD**
HEIGHT OF FAME: **1970s–80s**

Some guitarists become legends thanks to their phenomenal technique, others because of their originality. Then there are those whose reputation rests heavily of the uniqueness of their tone. Names like Stevie Ray Vaughan, Eric Clapton and B.B. King might be mentioned in this context, Carlos Santana certainly, but perhaps the ultimate tone guitarist is Pink Floyd's David Gilmour. The sound of Gilmour's blues-influenced, but not exactly bluesy, Stratocaster playing on *Dark Side Of the Moon* has come to define progressive-rock guitar playing.

RIGHT: *Pink Floyd was an experimental group in nature, and David Gilmour was its ideal guitarist, someone with a superb playing skill combined with an interest in effects.*

David Gilmour was born on 6 March 1946 in Cambridge, England. He began playing acoustic guitar at age 14, before moving on to Burns Sonnet and Hofner Club 60 electrics. While still at school, Gilmour met Roger Waters and Syd Barrett. Waters and Barrett put together Pink Floyd in 1965 along with keyboardist Rick Wright and drummer Nick Mason. When Barrett's drug use began to make him unstable Gilmour was drafted into the group first as back-up and then as a replacement for Barrett.

Over the next few years the band became ever more experimental, making albums like *Ummagumma* and *Atom Heart Mother*. At first Gilmour was playing a Telecaster but, after it was stolen, he replaced it with a Strat, played through HiWatt amps, and soon a variety of effects pedals. The band took most of 1972 off to work on a new studio album. This was *Dark Side Of The Moon* and overnight it established Pink Floyd as a major league rock act. The album stayed on the charts longer than any other record in history. Follow-ups *Wish You Were Here*, *Animals*, and *The Wall* all sold in their millions and the Pink Floyd sound, with Gilmour's spacey guitar at the fore, has continued to appeal to successive generations of rock fans.

HOW TO GILMOUR-IZE YOUR STRAT

Gilmour's main stage guitar is a USA '57 Vintage Reissue Strat fitted with a shortened tremolo arm so that he can keep it in his picking hand more comfortably while playing. The other modifications are all on the electrical side.

Like all his Strats, it's loaded with low impedance EMG-SA single coil pickups, which he backs up with two more tone modules, an SPC mid booster and an EXG mid-cut/expander. The SA pickups have Alnico magnets which have a little more mid range than the ceramic S magnets. The SPC midrange boost control is used to produce more of a singing humbucker tone, while the EXG is used a great deal for rhythm, since it really helps define the notes, especially when distortion is being used. The EXG cuts the mid range right down while giving a hefty boost to both the bass and treble.

It's with the use of the SPC, though, that you really hear the Gilmour sound emerge. Turn the SPC all the way up and you get that thick bluesy sound with which he is always associated. Then there's the tremolo arm, an important part of Gilmour's sound but notoriously prone to send the guitar out of tune. Gilmour tries to minimize this by screwing down the front six screws on top of the tremolo faceplate as far as possible in order to make total contact. He feels this keeps the bar in better tune.

RIGHT: *The Fender Stratocaster has been one of the seminal instruments of the rock and pop era. It was designed by Leo Fender in 1953, and is still in production, in its modern form, today.*

Wish You Were Here

ALBUM: **WISH YOU WERE HERE**
SONGWRITERS: **DAVID GILMOUR, ROGER WATERS**
RECORDED: **ABBEY ROAD STUDIOS, LONDON**
PRODUCERS: **PINK FLOYD**

These are the acoustic guitar chords to ' Wish You Were Here'. The song starts with two acoustic guitars moving around these chords – the first plays the chords and the second guitar picks out a melody. Experiment with removing and adding a finger to these chords to vary the sound. Once you' ve mastered these chords, singing along will help you get the timing of the rhythm right.

BASIC SONG RIFF

Em⁷   G   A⁷sus⁴   G*

HERE'S HOW

1 This shows the first finger on the E note at the 2nd fret of the D string. The ring and little fingers should play the B and E strings.

2 This is simply the chord shape shown previously with the first finger removed, keep the ring and little fingers in position.

3 The ring and little fingers stay at the 3rd fret of the B and E strings; the first finger and middle finger play the D and G strings.

4 The first finger plays the A string, the middle plays the E, the ring and little fingers still on the B and E strings at the 3rd fret.

THE CORNISH BOARD

Gilmour's first Cornish board consisted of a two guitar input selector and strobe tuner feed, while the actual effects were a Dallas Arbiter Fuzz Face, an MXR Phase 100, Dynacomp and noise gate, a Uni-Vibe, Pete Cornish Custom Fuzz, and a Jim Dunlop Cry Baby. The board featured three Cry Baby sweep pedals. These were modified as tone control, volume pedal and wah-wah respectively. This new state-of-the-art board had sophisticated switching capabilities that were far ahead of most late 1970s' pedal set-ups. Each effect could be individually bypassed or configured in any sequence, and there were three outputs for various amps. This may not sound so extraordinary in today's all digital, post-Midi environment but back then, using analogue technology, it was revolutionary.

Despite the apparent complexity of Dave Gilmour's set-up, the actual contents of each track may come as something of a surprise. Essentially his sound is fairly clean, choosing different distortion units to add their characteristic sound to his signal. As an example, to reproduce the track 'Money' from *Dark Side Of The Moon* live in concert, Gilmour uses this effects combination. Main Riff: Pete Cornish Soft Sustain with Chandler Tube Driver #2. Solo: Boss CS-2 Compressor with Chandler Tube Driver #1, Sovtek Big Muff & TC Electronics digital delay. Solo (Dry Sound): Chandler Tube Driver #1 with Pro Co. Rat II Distortion.

Pete Cornish now has his own business making custom effects and boards, so, if you think your playing needs a sophisticated effects set-up that's easy to manage on stage, you'll be in good company if you look him up.

LEFT: *The bewildering array of effects pedals available to David Gilmour during live performances.*

Money

ALBUM: **DARK SIDE OF THE MOON**
SONGWRITER: **ROGER WATERS**
RECORDED: **ABBEY ROAD STUDIOS, LONDON**
PRODUCERS: **PINK FLOYD**

This song has a great walking bass-note line. The tab shows the opening notes of the song which sounds really good played on an electric guitar with no effects. It takes a little practice but once it's in your head it's a joy to play. Keep the notes thick and distinct. Keep in mind the recorded version – thinking of the sound of the cash registers crashing should keep you in time!

BASIC SONG RIFF

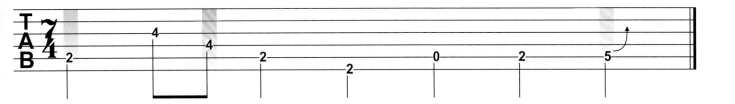

HERE'S HOW

1 Here the first finger plays the A string at the 2nd fret. Get your ring finger ready to play the 4th fret of the G string.

2 The ring finger plays the 4th fret of the G string. You can also play this phrase with your ring finger on the D string and little finger on the G.

3 You'll need your little finger to stretch to the 5th fret. Keep your other fingers in position to repeat the phrase from the start.

MULTI-EFFECT USE

In the early days of rock, guitarists tended to confine themselves to using one or two effects – generally either fuzz or wah-wah in full-on fashion. Gradually, though, as these effects became better known, and more types of effects came on to the market, guitarists started to experiment with sound, pioneering ever more complex combinations of effects. David Gilmour was in the forefront of this trend.

At the time of *Dark Side Of The Moon* he was using, amongst other things, a wah-wah, an Electro-Harmonix Big Muff, a Uni-Vibe and a Maestro Rover. The problem with using several effects at once, however, was that if they were wired up in series there tended to be a significant fall-off in the quality of the sound. Plus the simple fact of having half a dozen battery-operated pedals on stage meant there were any number of things that could go wrong. Then Gilmour heard of a man called Pete Cornish who worked for Sound City in London. Cornish had started making custom effects units, black boxes operated by foot switches, inside which Cornish would wire all the necessary electrics for each of the desired effects units. Gilmour got in touch with Cornish and began a working relationship that has gone on for more than 20 years.

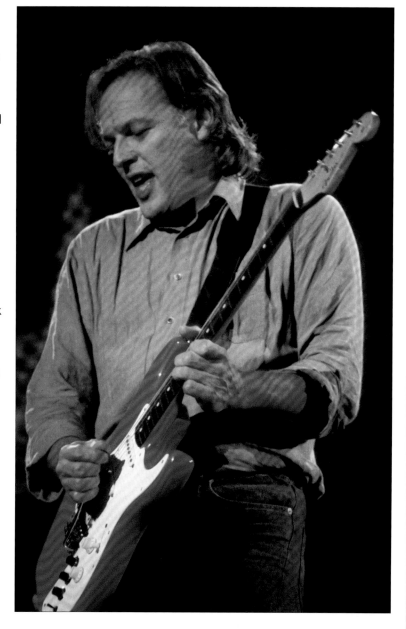

RIGHT: *Gilmour has been noted for his use of the whammy bar, using it to create a mournful, song-like tone on some of Floyd's most famous tracks.*

Time

ALBUM: **DARK SIDE OF THE MOON**

SONGWRITERS: **DAVID GILMOUR, ROGER WATERS, NICK MASON, RICK WRIGHT**

RECORDED: **ABBEY ROAD STUDIOS, LONDON**

PRODUCERS: **PINK FLOYD**

This tab shows the part of the riff after all the alarm clocks go off. It's basically two notes on the E string with long gaps before the main part of the songs kicks in. It's obviously a fairly easy riff to play but you need to get the timing spot on. To get the best effect it's best to play this riff along with the record, and this will also help with your timing.

BASIC SONG RIFF

HERE'S HOW

1 This shows the first finger on the F# note at the 2nd fret of the E string. Hit this note nice and hard after skipping up from the open E string via the first fret.

2 This picture shows the little finger at the A note on the 5th fret of the E string. Keep your first finger at the F# note.

BRIAN MAY

1947–
BAND: **QUEEN**
HEIGHT OF FAME: **1970s–90s**

Queen's Brian May has one of the most instantly recognizable guitar sounds there is.

It's a huge, almost orchestral, sound, perfectly suited to his band's own unique fusion of

pop and rock.

Brian May was born in a suburb of London, England in July 1947. He was a musical child, able to play the ukulele and piano by the time he was given his first guitar on his seventh birthday. The instrument immediately fascinated May and, while still at school, he went on to build – with his father's help – an electric guitar. Amazingly enough this instrument, known as the Red Special, and costing just £8 to make, has been the principal guitar he has played throughout his career.

May's career started with a school band called 1984. He then went on to play with the rather more successful Smile, which provided the nucleus for Queen. Queen's first album came out in 1973, and by the time of lead singer Freddie Mercury's death in 1991 they had established themselves as one of the most globally popular bands of all time. The band's twin strengths were Mercury's showmanship and May's knack for an instantly memorable riff – whether the one that comes in midway through 'Bohemian Rhapsody', or the one that underpins 'We Will Rock You'. Equally distinctive was May's deeply melodic lead work. May has released several solo albums, hosted the Guitar Legends concert alongside Steve Vai and Joe Satriani, and overseen the enormously successful Queen-tribute stage musical *We Will Rock You*. In 2005 Queen returned to touring with former Free and Bad Company vocalist Paul Rodgers on guest vocals.

RIGHT: *Brian May has created some of the most memorable guitar riffs in history. With Queen, and writing for other artists, he has composed 22 top-20 hits.*

THE RED SPECIAL

Not many guitarists have kept one main guitar with them throughout their entire career. Surely it is only May who has managed that feat using a guitar he made himself when still at school.

The guitar was made up mostly of materials May found lying around: mahogany from a fire surround for the neck of the guitar, a piece of oak for the centre block, motorbike valve springs for the tremolo springs and mother-of-pearl buttons for the neck position dots. A particularly interesting innovation was to have the three pickups wired in series, rather than in parallel as is conventional. Each pickup has an on-off switch and a phase change switch. The combination allows a huge variety of different sounds. Initially the pickups too were homemade, but May didn't care for the sound and eventually replaced them with Burns Tri-sonic single coils.

The Red Special may be a one-off, but aspiring Brian Mays will be relieved to learn they won't have to build their own copies. Ever since Queen's rise to fame there have been an abundance of imitations on the market. May himself has used an assortment of them as back-up live guitars. Copies have ranged from the frankly dodgy to the absolutely exquisite. Top of the range are the Guyton Red Special Guitars handmade by Andrew Guyton, with a price tag to match their quality; ordinary mortals might want to investigate the more workaday, but very dependable, Burns Brian May Signature Electric Guitar.

RIGHT: *Brian May's Red Special is as legendary as the guitarist himself. May created the guitar from scratch, and he has always possessed a deep understanding of the technical aspects of music production and instrumentation.*

We Will Rock You

ALBUM: **NEWS OF THE WORLD**
SONGWRITER: **BRIAN MAY**
RECORDED: **SARM WEST; WESSEX STUDIOS, LONDON**
PRODUCER: **MIKE STONE**

This is the first guitar entry into ' We Will Rock You' . Make sure you get that nice big power chord sound like Brian May on the first chord. In this riff you' ll also use your ring finger to hit that low G note on the E string. Practise using your ring finger to hit that bass note on the E string, as this will give the riff an extra punch.

BASIC SONG RIFF

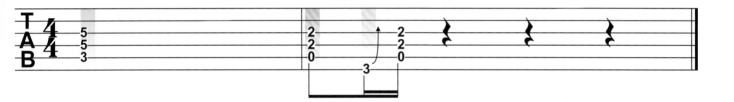

HERE'S HOW

1 This shows the first finger at the 3rd fret of the A string and the ring and little fingers at the 5th fret of the D and G strings.

2 Try using your first finger here to cover both strings at the same time at the 2nd fret on the D and G strings.

3 This is the bass note at the 3rd fret of the E string; play this with your middle finger, and try a little bend on this note.

PLAY LIKE BRIAN

So how do you get that signature Brian May guitar sound? Well first you need the right equipment. Ideally, of course you should have a decent Red Special replica, a Burns or Guild maybe. Failing that, a Les Paul will get you somewhere close. Next there's the amp. May favours using several classic 1960s Vox AC 30s all turned up to the max to produce the required overdrive, but don't try this at home unless you live several miles from the nearest neighbour. For domestic use, many classic amps – a Marshall or a Mesa Boogie say – will do a decent job with the gain kept down and the mid range EQ turned up. What you will definitely need, though, is a treble booster pedal. If you want to get every last detail right you could even use an old British sixpence coin as a guitar pick, just like Brian does.

That's the simple part, however. What is not so easy to copy is the actual playing. Having said that, Brian May's guitar parts are far from the most difficult in the business; Queen's pop/rock focus never encouraged pyrotechnics for their own sake. May's rhythm work is mostly based on using open chords with that distinctive ringing overdrive produced by the AC 30s. His soloing, meanwhile, utilizes his preferred light-gauge strings to allow a lot of string-bending and vibrato plus plenty of hammer-ons and pull-offs. The key to his style is always to focus on keeping things melodic, while giving the music a hard, strong edge.

LEFT: *In Queen, Freddie Mercury was undeniably the frontman, but May was the driving force behind the music itself.*

Bohemian Rhapsody

ALBUM: A **NIGHT AT THE OPERA**
SONGWRITER: **FREDDIE MERCURY**
RECORDED: **ROCKFIELD STUDIOS, WALES**
PRODUCER: **ROY THOMAS BAKER**

This is the guitar riff just before Freddie Mercury sings 'so you think you can stone me and spit in my eye'. Although only played over two strings it does move around a fair bit and will require some practice to perfect. Use up and down strokes with your plectrum to get extra speed. Try to make the notes distinct – it's a riff where every note counts. Experiment with different ways of playing until you feel comfortable.

BASIC SONG RIFF

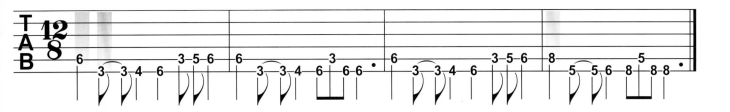

HERE'S HOW

1 You need to give yourself as much stretch as possible between the first two notes on the E and A strings – use your first and little finger here.

2 Here the middle finger plays the G note at the 3rd fret of the E string. Take your time to get it right.

3 The little finger plays the 8th fret on the A string. Note the basic shape of the fretting hand is the same throughout.

Tie Your Mother Down

ALBUM: **A DAY AT THE RACES**
SONGWRITER: **BRIAN MAY**
RECORDED: **SARM WEST; WESSEX STUDIOS, LONDON**
PRODUCER: **MIKE STONE**

For this famous Queen riff use your first finger to cover both second frets on the D and G strings at the start of the riff. You will need to keep your ring finger to hit notes on the E and A strings. Play along with the track to ensure your timing is spot on. Use down strokes with the plectrum to create a heavy rock sound. Practise down strokes between the high and low strings on the guitar.

BASIC SONG RIFF

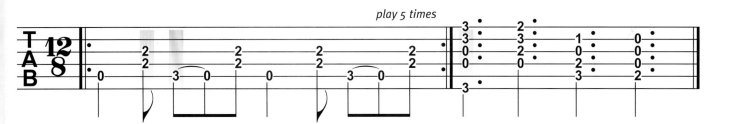

HERE'S HOW

1 The hand is ideally positioned to play all notes shown in the tab. The ring finger can move easily to the A and E strings.

2 Here the ring finger moves up to the A string to play the C note at the 3rd fret. The first finger stays in position.

3 By using your first finger for notes at the 2nd fret you are leaving your middle, ring and little fingers available for notes on the top strings.

FAR LEFT: *Brian May's career has now spanned three decades. Versions of his songs have been recorded by artistes as diverse as Def Leppard, George Michael and Macy Gray.*

NILE RODGERS

1952–
BAND: **CHIC**
HEIGHT OF FAME: **1970s**

Nile Rodgers is the godfather of funk guitar. Ask anyone for their definition of funky rhythm-guitar playing, and they'll like as not refer you to Nile Rodgers' playing on Chic's 'Le Freak' or 'Good Times'. His sinuous, choppy rhythm parts – brilliantly combined with the equally distinctive bass playing of Bernard Edwards and drumming of Tony Thompson – have come to define funk.

RIGHT: *Nile Rodgers performing at a live gig. He first joined a band when he was 16, telling the other members he could play guitar when he couldn't. He was a fast learner, however, and his natural talent soon emerged.*

Nile Rodgers was born on 19 September 1952 in New York City. He came from a musical family and his talent was evident from his early years. By the time Nile was 19, he was playing guitar as part of the house band for the world famous Apollo Theatre, accompanying a whole range of soul legends. He met Bernard Edwards in the early 1970s. At first they put together a series of rock bands, but the music industry wasn't interested in a group of black guys playing rock music. So they turned their attention to dance music and formed Chic. From their first hit, 'Dance Dance Dance (Yowsah Yowsah Yowsah)', through to 'Le Freak' and 'Good Times', their sound defined the disco era.

At first critics tended to dismiss them as commercial pap, but when musicians started to listen carefully they realized this was one of the tightest units in any kind of music. Rodgers' guitar playing in particular influenced everyone from Queen's Brian May to Prince, and his reputation spread even wider as he turned his hand to freelance writing and producing. Suddenly his unmistakably funky sound could be heard on records by acts as diverse as David Bowie, Madonna and Diana Ross. His influence, meanwhile, is still present every time a rock guitarist decides it's time to get funky and tries to imitate those deceptively simple rhythm patterns.

FUNK GUITAR

Nile Rodgers may be the best known proponent of funk guitar playing – and he certainly developed a style that is uniquely his own – but he'd be the first to acknowledge that his playing comes out of a tradition. If there's one man who actually did invent funk guitar playing, it's Jimmy Nolen. His name may be unfamiliar, but as the guitarist on practically all James Brown's classic recordings his playing most certainly isn't. Nolen developed his pervasive funk style during his 16 years with Brown. Although he was primarily a rhythm guitarist, the impact Nolen had on subsequent players was no less important or far reaching than the influence of rock and blues innovators like Chuck Berry, or B.B. King. His distinctive style of 16th-note strumming and funky, choppy chord work (relying heavily on 7th and 9th chords) provided the foundation on which virtually all modern R&B, funk and disco guitar is based.

Nile Rodgers' style has its roots in Nolen's playing and also encompasses the influence of jazz guitarists like Wes Montgomery – it's noticeable that Rodgers uses a lot of jazz chords in his playing. The other defining funk guitar sound is the use of the wah-wah pedal in rhythm playing, as typified by the theme from *Shaft*. Rodgers uses this effect from time to time, while offering the following valuable advice to would-be proponents of the style. 'Never keep time with the pedal,' he cautions. 'Use it for expression, and keep time with your hands.'

LEFT: *Nile Rodgers has emphasized the need for a good sense of rhythm to be a competent funk guitarist, and has avoided an over-reliance upon electronic gadgets.*

Le Freak

ALBUM: **C'EST CHIC**
SONGWRITERS: **NILE RODGERS, BERNARD EDWARDS**
RECORDED: **THE POWER STATION, NEW YORK**
PRODUCERS: **NILE RODGERS, BERNARD EDWARDS**

This great dance tune uses up and down strokes to create that classic Nile Rodgers clicking rhythm. The best way to achieve this is to use your thumb instead of a plectrum. Take time to practise playing rhythmically up and down whilst moving the chord between the 7th and 5th frets. The dampening technique will cut off the sound. You can do this by slightly releasing the hand holding the chord after it's played.

BASIC SONG RIFF

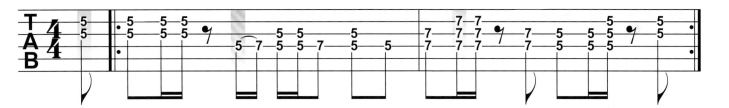

HERE'S HOW

1 Shows the start of the riff as the band sing 'Ah....' Use your first finger to cover both 5th frets on the E and B strings.

2 Practise this part in isolation. Hammer-on with your ring finger onto the 7th fret whilst your first finger holds the 5th frets.

3 You can use your ring finger across three frets at the 7th, then release leaving your ring finger to cover the 5th. Practise that rhythm with your thumb.

PRINCE

1958–2016
BAND: PRINCE AND THE REVOLUTION
HEIGHT OF FAME: **1980s**

Prince was one of the most versatile of all modern guitar players and also, as a result, one of the most underrated. He could play in classic rock style, all screaming arpeggios played high up on the neck. Live, if the mood took him, he could play like Jimi Hendrix, the full sonic freak out. Then again, if he chose to, he could play classic 1970s funk style, using the wah-wah pedal on the rhythm fills. Keep in mind that he was also an extraordinary singer-songwriter and showman, one of the real auteurs in popular music, and it's unsurprising that his guitar playing sometimes gets overlooked.

RIGHT: *Prince delivered some of the most electrifying live performances of the 1980s and 1990s, astounding audiences as much with his dancing as with his obvious musicality.*

Prince was born Prince Rogers Nelson on 7 June 1958 in Minneapolis, Minnesota. His father gave him his first guitar. Prince quickly showed a prodigious musical talent on a whole range of instruments and as a singer-songwriter, and signed a major deal with Warner Bros while in his teens. His first album, *For You*, released in 1978, saw him playing all the instruments himself. On subsequent albums he moved from the fairly straight soul of his debut to more rock- and even punk-influenced material. At this point his Hendrix-inspired guitar playing came to the fore.

His career picked up momentum and he achieved a huge breakthrough with *Purple Rain*, an album that saw him melding rock and funk influences. The album would sell over 13 million copies in the US alone, and spend 24 weeks at the top of the Billboard 200. It established Prince as a superstar. Backed by a succession of phenomenal bands, Prince seemed able to channel almost every style of rock and soul that had gone before – and every style of guitar playing too. He died at his home in Minnesota on 21 April 2016, aged 57.

PRINCE'S TELECASTER COPY

It's easy to assume that all great guitarists use top-of-the-range equipment that costs a fortune. It may be true that, as they get richer, guitar players tend to accumulate more and more expensive guitars, but it's also true that some of them have made much of their best work using less exalted instruments.

Prince is a case in point. Almost all the records that made his reputation feature a Hohner Telecaster copy. Given that many guitarists disdain the Telecaster itself in favour of the Stratocaster, to use a Telecaster copy seems the height of cheek. The guitar in question was bought in 1980 from the Knut Koupee Music store in Minneapolis. According to the store's manager, Prince probably chose the guitar because of its leopard-skin pickguard, which matched his stage outfit! But as it turned out, the budget guitar's raw tone was ideal for the clean guitar chugging and staccato rhythms of his early Punk-Funk style. He used it whilst supporting Rick James that year, on the *Dirty Mind* album, and on almost every tour to date. A Telecaster variant, the guitar differs greatly to the Fender industry standard. The Hohner is all maple and finished in blonde, as opposed to the ash and alder body of a Fender. The tonal properties of maple suit Prince well, giving the guitar a bright top end and good sustain; he chose this wood for all his later custom guitars. The cheaper construction of the guitar gave rise to problems in the studio, but Prince still insisted on using it, favouring its tone which he once described as 'raggedy'. Discontinued re-issues of the guitar can still be tracked down.

LEFT: *Prince is one of that rare breed of successful guitarists who have stuck with a cheaper model of instrument on account of what they feel is a rawness of sound.*

Purple Rain

ALBUM: **PURPLE RAIN**

SONGWRITER: **PRINCE**

RECORDED: **SUNSET SOUND STUDIO, LOS ANGELES**

PRODUCER: **PRINCE**

These chords sound absolutely great with nothing else at the start of 'Purple Rain'. To get the sound exactly the same as Prince you'll need to use a chorus pedal on an electric guitar. Practise getting the timing right just before the vocal comes in at the start of the first verse. Ensure your chords flow naturally from one another, and practise moving between these shapes to get a really smooth sound.

BASIC SONG CHORDS

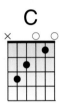
C

Am7

G

F

Fsus4

HERE'S HOW

1 This is a C chord. Use your first, middle and ring finger to hold these notes. Use single down strokes with your strumming hand.

2 By releasing your ring finger you'll form the next chord in the sequence which is Am7. Keep your rhythm regular as you change between each chord.

3 Use your first finger to play the B and E strings, your ring finger to play the D string, and your little finger for the G string.

SLASH

1965–
BAND: **GUNS N' ROSES**
HEIGHT OF FAME: **LATE 1980s**

The man behind some of the most enduringly popular guitar riffs of the past 20 years, Slash was born in London, England, in 1965 to parents who both worked in the music business. In the 1970s he relocated to his mother's home town of Los Angeles. He began playing guitar in high school and soon formed the most popular American rock band of the late 1980s, Guns N' Roses, along with singer Axl Rose, co-guitarist Izzy Stradlin, plus high-school buddy Steven Adler on drums and Duff McKagan on bass.

Their first album, *Appetite For Destruction,* came out in 1987 and still stands as one of the all-time classic hard-rock recordings. It took a year to catch on, but once MTV started playing the video for the album's power ballad 'Sweet Child O' Mine', success was assured. *Appetite For Destruction*, full of snarling twin-guitar workouts like 'Welcome To The Jungle' and 'Paradise City', revived the outlaw spirit of The Rolling Stones and Aerosmith. It went on to sell over 30 million copies. The band never quite scaled such heights again, though follow-up *Use Your Illusion* came close. As the 1990s wore on the band suffered from musical differences and drug problems, and from the mid 1990s onwards, Slash has pursued a solo career.

As a guitarist Slash's style owes most to his early heroes The Rolling Stones and, above all, to Aerosmith's Joe Perry. Over time, a blues feel has come into his playing, and Slash now cites Jeff Beck – blues-based but always experimental – as his biggest inspiration. Meanwhile, guitar shops around the world have signs forbidding novices from emulating Slash's killer guitar part 'Sweet Child O' Mine', recently voted the finest guitar riff of all time by readers of *Total Guitar* magazine.

RIGHT: *Slash gave Guns N' Roses their hard rock edge. He lists amongst his influences Jimmy Page, Mick Taylor, Eddy Van Halen and Jeff Beck.*

NO ORDINARY RIFF

'Sweet Child O' Mine' is something of an odd one out among the classic guitar riffs. For a start it powers a ballad rather than an up-tempo number. Second, instead of being made up of power chords played low down on the guitar, it uses arpeggiated chords played very high on the neck. Thirdly, where most of the great riffs are blissfully straightforward and direct, 'Sweet Child O' Mine' is positively tricksy. Maybe that's why every would-be guitar hero feels compelled to learn it: it's become something of a rite of passage.

What it does have in common with many rock classics is that it was a bit of a musical afterthought. The band already had the songs for their classic debut album when they started jamming on some chords Izzy Stradlin had come up with. Axl Rose started singing the words from a poem he'd written some time before. Meanwhile, Slash was messing round with a little guitar pattern high up on the neck. The rest, of course, is history. Without 'Sweet Child O' Mine', Guns N' Roses might never have got off the ground. It's a great Zen lesson for all guitar heroes – sometimes it's when you're not really thinking that you're actually doing your best work.

SLASH & THE GIBSON LES PAUL

One of the all-time classic rock guitars, the Gibson Les Paul had fallen somewhat out of fashion by the late 1980s before Slash brought it right back in.

He'd first played a Memphis Les Paul Copy while in school, nailing Ted Nugent's 'Cat Scratch Fever' with it. Later, he bought a real Les Paul that had once belonged to ex Alice Cooper/ Lou Reed guitar legend Steve Hunter. When the *Appetite For Destruction* sessions started, Slash was playing a Jackson. He was unhappy with the sound and increasingly desperate when his manager found him what appeared to be a '59 Les Paul. In fact it was a handmade copy made by luthier Chris Derrig. Slash fell in love with it and promptly used the new guitar to write the riff to 'Sweet Child O' Mine'.

Since then, the guitar has become his signature instrument for both live and studio work. Today, it has been retired, due to the stresses of live work, but Slash's love affair with the Les Paul has continued. Indeed the company has issued not one but two limited-edition custom Slash Les Pauls, the first a loud and proud fire burst with mother of pearl inlay and hand painted Snakepit logo, the second a rather more austere tobacco burst instrument.

ABOVE: *Slash's handling of the Gibson Les Paul is all the more remarkable when understanding that he is almost entirely self taught, learning mainly through imitating great riffs from records.*

Live and Let Die

ALBUM: **USE YOUR ILLUSION I**

SONGWRITERS: **PAUL McCARTNEY, LINDA McCARTNEY**

RECORDED: **A & M STUDIOS; RECORD PLANT; STUDIO 56; IMAGE RECORDING, HOLLYWOOD**

PRODUCERS: **MIKE CLINK, GUNS N' ROSES**

This is the part of the song where the orchestral string section plays the same riff as the band. If you want to play along with the record you'll need to tune your guitar down a semitone. The riff is played on this tab on the top three strings (E, B and G). Practise getting a distinct sound from each note in the riff. Keep in time by playing with the record.

BASIC SONG RIFF

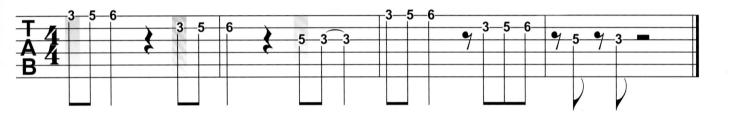

HERE'S HOW

1. Use your first, middle and ring fingers to climb up the frets on the E string. Practising this will help you play lead runs more easily.

2. This is the same riff on the B string. Try to move easily between the two. Imagining the sound of the orchestra will help keep you in time.

3. These descending notes are played with the ring and first finger on the G string. The last note is B flat – hold it and let it ring out.

KURT COBAIN

1967–1994
BAND: **NIRVANA**
HEIGHT OF FAME: **1990s**

Just as Kurt Cobain was the epitome of the anti-pop star, an idol who hated to be idolized, he was also the ultimate anti-guitar hero, a riff master who took pleasure in playing out of key on bargain-basement instruments. As with his band Nirvana as a whole, his strength wasn't in subtlety or technique, but in raw passion and the most brutal of dynamics.

If Cobain's contribution to guitar playing can be narrowed down, it's his perfection of the quiet/loud contrast. He didn't invent it – The Pixies were doing something similar years before – but Cobain took the business of alternating between quiet and loud to its ultimate, brain-shredding extreme.

Kurt Donald Cobain was born to Wendy and Donald Cobain on 20 February 1967 in Aberdeen, Washington State. His mother was a cocktail waitress and his father an auto mechanic. In high school he started listening to punk rock and on his fourteenth birthday he bought his first guitar. He dropped out of high school a few weeks before graduation to get a job, and started playing in bands. In 1986 he formed Nirvana with Krist Novaselic on bass guitar, and, eventually, Dave Grohl on drums. Their first album, *Bleach*, was released in 1989 and was only a minor hit, but they toured incessantly and signed to Geffen Records, who released their second album, *Nevermind*, which included the classic guitar riff of the 1990s, 'Smells Like Teen Spirit', alongside songs like 'Lithium' which showcased their quiet/loud dynamic. As they achieved success however, Cobain's life plunged into drug abuse and self-loathing. He married Courtney Love, recorded a new album, *In Utero*, but was evidently hell-bent on self-destruction and, in 1994, one week after a concert in Munich, was hospitalized in a coma. After waking up and leaving voluntarily, he was found three days later in his own home, dead of a gunshot wound.

RIGHT: *Kurt Cobain's raw playing was the defining quality of grunge and a direct reaction against the musical dexterity shown by many guitarists in the world of heavy rock.*

KURT'S FENDERS

Kurt Cobain generally played either Fender Mustangs or Fender Jaguars, left-handed models. These are unusual choices for a top guitarist, being fairly cheap guitars without the build quality of the Stratocaster or even the Telecaster.

BELOW: *Kurt Cobain's use of fairly cheap Fender guitars was reflected in a playing style, which often featured sloppy technique (by orthodox standards) and questionable tuning, but always a great sound.*

Kurt Cobain initially started playing them for reasons of economy – especially relevant given his penchant for destroying guitars on stage (at one time he was calculated to have destroyed over 300 guitars). However, perverse character that he was, it was also their defects that attracted Cobain to these models. Of the Fender Mustang he once commented that 'My favourite guitar in the world is the Fender Mustang. They're really small and almost impossible to keep in tune. They're designed terribly. If you want to raise the action, you have to de-tune all the strings, pull the bridge out, turn these little screws under the bridge, and hope that you've raised them the right amount. Then you put the bridge back and tune all the strings. If you screwed up, you have to do the whole process over again. But I like it, that way things sound fucked-up, and I stumble onto stuff accidentally. I guess I don't like to be that familiar with my guitar.' A more unusual approach to the guitar is hard to imagine.

Throughout his career Cobain found it hard to decide between the Mustang and its sister guitar, the Jaguar. The guitar he played on most of *Nevermind* was a 1965 sunburst (red faded out) Fender Jaguar. Eventually, unable to chose between the two, and now famous and rich enough to have what he wanted, he persuaded Fender to create a custom guitar for him, the Jag-Tang – a mutant beast that, as its name suggests, was half Jaguar and half Mustang.

Smells Like Teen Spirit

ALBUM: **NEVERMIND**

SONGWRITERS: **KURT COBAIN, KRIS NOVOSELIC, DAVE GROHL**

RECORDED: **SOUND CITY, LOS ANGELES**

PRODUCER: **BUTCH VIG**

A fantastic intro to a classic Nirvana song. It's all power chords on the bass strings so you need to ensure you hold the shapes firm as you move them around the fret board. It's best to listen to the record to get the rhythm exactly right with your strumming hand. The first part of the riff is played clean with no overdrive, then the distorted guitar comes in to really drive the riff along.

BASIC SONG RIFF

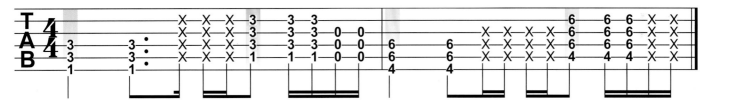

HERE'S HOW

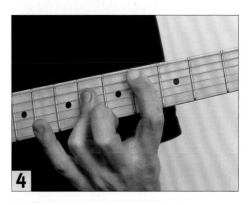

1 Here the first finger plays the first fret on the E string with the ring and little finger playing the A and D strings at the 3rd fret.

2 The shape of the chord drops down one string, the first finger plays the 1st fret of the A string, the ring finger can play all three frets of the D, G and B strings.

3 The first finger plays the 4th fret of the E string, the ring and little fingers play 6th fret of the A and D strings.

4 For the last chord, the shape again drops down one string, with the first finger playing the 4th fret of the A string and the ring finger playing the 6th fret on the D, G and B strings.

JACK WHITE

1975–
BAND: **THE WHITE STRIPES**
HEIGHT OF FAME: **EARLY 2000s**

Jack White is a man on a mission – taking rock 'n' roll back to basics. As the mainstay of The White Stripes he's emerged as a formidable songwriter, guitarist and vocalist capable of morphing between styles from folk blues through show tunes to full-on Led Zeppelin-style rock workouts. The band's third album, 2001's *White Blood Cells*, established the duo at the forefront of the new wave of rock 'n' roll bands. They also managed the remarkable feat of appealing to both MTV kids and their parents with their mix of the sophisticated and the primitive, adding up to an instinctively classic style.

RIGHT: *In The White Stripes Jack White has stripped rock music down to its absolute basics – distorted guitar and a thumping drum beat in the background.*

Jack White was born John Anthony Gillis on 9 July 1975, in Detroit, and played in assorted punk and garage bands before forming The White Stripes with his then wife Meg (using the rumour that they were brother and sister as a sales gimmick). His back to basics style is evident both in his playing, which nods to everyone from the Kinks' Dave Davies to Led Zeppelin's Jimmy Page, and in his choice of equipment. At the heart of White's sound is his main guitar – a '64 Valco Airline. On stage, White carries three guitars: the Airline, a Kay hollow body tuned to open A, and a no-name Japanese electric. He plugs into a DigiTech Whammy pedal and an Electro-Harmonix Big Muff, before running simultaneously into a Fender Twin Reverb and a rare 100-Watt Silvertone 6x10 combo.

Some find this fondness for vintage equipment, which extends also to their studio work, self-consciously retro. But whatever your preference – analogue or digital – it is undeniable that Jack White understands the primitive power of rock 'n' roll. One listen to a classic riff like 'Seven Nation Army' should convince anyone of that.

VALCO AIRLINE GUITAR

Just as punk rock rebelled against established music industry values, so punk guitarists rebelled against conventional guitar lore. Not for them the Les Pauls and Stratocasters, let alone the Paul Reed Smiths and high-end custom jobs.

The über-punk guitarist, Johnny Ramone, favoured 1960s Mosrites; Kurt Cobain went for the ugly sisters of the Fender range, the Mustang and Jaguar; and Jack White went a step further by playing a JB Hutto model 1964 Valco Airline, a guitar that most players might regard as good for having your picture taken with, but wouldn't be caught dead actually playing. It's made of fibreglass (or 'Res-O-Glas' as the manufacturers called it), which makes it difficult to keep in tune; there's no way of adjusting the pickup or the action. It's a cheap guitar, and that's something Jack White is well aware of. As he says himself 'Playing that guitar makes me feel like I have to take something that's broken and make it work. It's hollow, it's made of plastic, and it feels like it's going to fall apart. The front pickup is broken, but the treble pickup has an amazing bite. I've never had it refretted or anything. It's pretty much the way I found it, except for new tuners."

Now increasingly sought after by wannabe Jack Whites, Airline Guitars were made by the Chicago-based Valco factory, an offshoot of National-Dobro, and mostly sold by mail order giants Montgomery Ward. Their other popular model was the Silvertone and, during the 1960s, Valco produced both guitars by the truckload. These days, the guitars turn up regularly on eBay, no longer the pawn shop bargains they were before Jack White came along.

RIGHT: *The Valco Airline has won little praise for build quality or technical sophistication, but its distinctive sound has made it the choice of guitarists such as Jack White. Vintage examples can sell for several thousand dollars.*

Seven Nation Army

ALBUM: **ELEPHANT**

SONGWRITER: **JACK WHITE**

RECORDED: **TOE RAG STUDIOS, LONDON**

PRODUCER: **JACK WHITE**

These are terrific power chords that require you to turn up your amp and play loud! Once again note the two-fret interval; ensure you hit the lowest note first for maximum effect. Get used to moving the shape around the fret board. Start off slowly and build up speed. The tab shows the riff in baritone tuning, but you can play in standard tuning using the A, D and G strings.

BASIC SONG RIFF

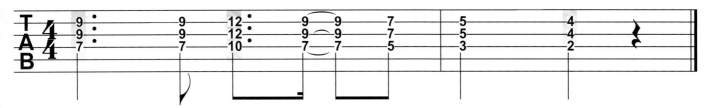

HERE'S HOW

1 Use your first finger at the 7th fret and ring and little fingers to play the 9th fret. Practise keeping these chords solid.

2 Hit the first chord twice then slide straight up to this position at the 10th and 12th frets. Concentrate on keeping your shape.

3 Let this last chord ring out, your fingers will keep the same shape throughout. Use only big down strokes with your plectrum.

BLUES GUITARISTS

Today, when we think of the blues we immediately think of the guitar. It was not always so, however. Back in the 1920s, when the first records with the word 'blues' in the title were being made, more often than not they'd be piano-led recordings, close in style to the jazz and gospel recordings of the same period. If you listen, for instance, to the recordings of the enduring icon of 1920s blues, Bessie Smith, you'll be searching in vain for a guitar part; instead you'll hear sophisticated piano and brass arrangements, played by the likes of Fletcher Henderson and Coleman Hawkins, or even Benny Goodman.

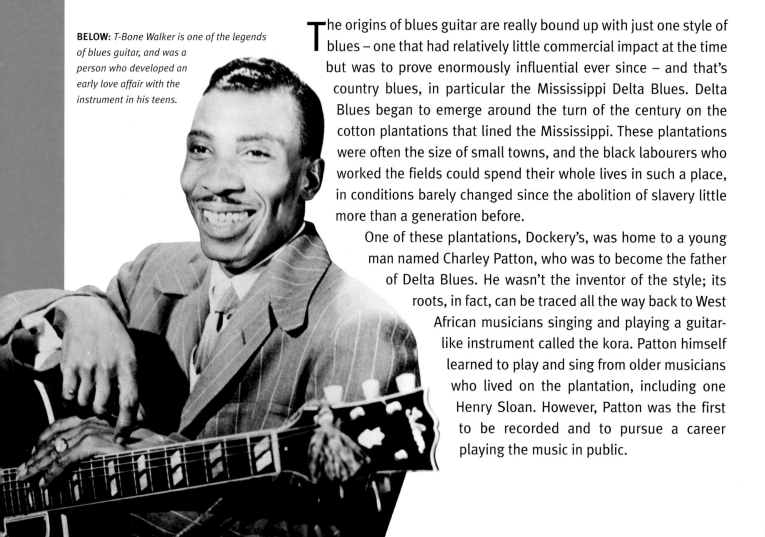

BELOW: *T-Bone Walker is one of the legends of blues guitar, and was a person who developed an early love affair with the instrument in his teens.*

The origins of blues guitar are really bound up with just one style of blues – one that had relatively little commercial impact at the time but was to prove enormously influential ever since – and that's country blues, in particular the Mississippi Delta Blues. Delta Blues began to emerge around the turn of the century on the cotton plantations that lined the Mississippi. These plantations were often the size of small towns, and the black labourers who worked the fields could spend their whole lives in such a place, in conditions barely changed since the abolition of slavery little more than a generation before.

One of these plantations, Dockery's, was home to a young man named Charley Patton, who was to become the father of Delta Blues. He wasn't the inventor of the style; its roots, in fact, can be traced all the way back to West African musicians singing and playing a guitar-like instrument called the kora. Patton himself learned to play and sing from older musicians who lived on the plantation, including one Henry Sloan. However, Patton was the first to be recorded and to pursue a career playing the music in public.

What really marked out Charlie Patton's style – and that of all the early Delta blues men – was that the guitar was no longer used as simple accompaniment, designed to underpin a vocal melody just as a piano does. Instead it provided a fierce counterpoint, even an extension, of the human voice. The singer calls out a line and the guitar answers back.

BLUES PIONEERS

Charlie Patton was to prove a huge influence on subsequent guitarists. His immediate protégé was the great Son House, responsible for records like 'Death Letter'. Son House, in turn, was to prove a great influence on a young musician named Robert Johnson, who, in part thanks to the legends that surround him, has become the one country bluesman that even casual listeners have heard of.

Robert Johnson introduced the boogie bass line, played on the bottom strings of the guitar, which now practically defines what we think of as 'blues guitar'. His slide playing was the most developed yet heard, and he added a repertoire of rundowns and turnbacks and repeats that almost defied belief – and have taken the world's finest guitar players decades to figure out. No wonder rumour had it that Johnson had sold his soul to the devil one night at the crossroads near Dockery's plantation.

The Mississippi Delta wasn't the only place to produce country blues musicians, however. Notable contemporaries of Charlie Patton included this formidable trio – all of them, by some strange coincidence, unsighted. There was Blind Lemon Jefferson from Texas, Blind Willie McTell from Georgia and Blind Blake from Jacksonville, Florida. Blind Blake had a prodigious ragtime-derived guitar style which musicians to this day have trouble deconstructing. While he was popular in his day, he disappeared without trace in the early 1930s, so he was never rediscovered and subjected to the scrutiny of blues scholars. Blind Willie MacTell was another formidable guitar

ABOVE: *Robert Johnson led a short, tough life in the early decades of the 20th century, but his superb blues playing was later to influence the likes of Eric Clapton and Keith Richards.*

ABOVE: *Gibson guitars have been a popular choice amongst the world's greatest blues guitarists, B.B. King being one of their most high profile users.*

talent who combined use of slide and fingerpicking on classic songs like 'Statesboro Blues' to make it sound as if he was playing two guitars at once.

Blind Lemon Jefferson was, in his day, the most influential of all. He was the first man to be a truly commercially successful blues performer. Unlike the blues women such as Bessie Smith who had ruled the roost before him, he didn't have a band but performed solo, accompanying himself on the guitar on genre-defining songs like 'Matchbox Blues', 'See That My Grave Is Kept Clean' and 'Black Snake Moan'.

Texas has remained a blues stronghold ever since, with artists ranging from T-Bone Walker to Albert King to Stevie Ray Vaughan. However, it was the Mississippi Delta bluesmen who were to be the dominant influence on what was to come. Gradually, in the years following Robert Johnson's death, the blues made its way north, up the river to Memphis, and then to Chicago, and along the way it became electrified. In fact the first major electric blues player was the Texan T-Bone Walker, whose jazz-inflected Gibson playing sent out shockwaves through the blues world. However, it was in the hands of Delta-born talents like B.B. King and Muddy Waters that electric blues guitar developed to the next stage.

B.B. King is almost certainly the single most important electric blues guitarist of the last half century. His style, full of vibrato and melodic invention, has been so influential that it is hard to conceive of a contemporary blues guitar solo that doesn't feature at least a couple of recognizable King-derived phrases.

If B.B. King represented an increasing sophistication in blues playing, his contemporary John Lee Hooker kept alive its anarchic primitive roots. Hooker's signature tracks, like 'Boogie Chillen', are one-chord boogies in which the guitar is turned all the way up and used to project rhythm and menace.

If there's a mid point between King and Hooker it would probably sound like Muddy Waters. Muddy Waters started out playing country blues down in the Delta, but when he came to Chicago he defined the city's aggressive, swaggering, Delta-rooted sound with his utterly confident vocals and ferocious slide-guitar attack. Technical excellence has never sounded so menacing.

Or at least not until contemporaries of Muddy's, like Bo Diddley and Howlin' Wolf guitarist Hubert Sumlin, started to kick in. Sumlin was a stunningly inventive player both on lead and rhythm duties behind the primeval roar of the Wolf, while Bo Diddley managed to cross Muddy's dynamics with John Lee Hooker's rolling one-chord boogie and African rhythms to create a sound so irresistibly catchy that it even managed to cross over to the white rock 'n' roll audience.

Up to this point in its history, the evolution of blues guitar playing – and the blues itself – had been straightforward. It was music that had originated with rural Southern blacks as an acoustic folk form, and had evolved into the electric music of urban blacks. Now, though, it was about to take a most unexpected turn.

Across the Atlantic, in the UK, a generation of young white kids had picked up on the blues and were starting to attempt to play it themselves. At first their efforts were pale imitations, but gradually some of these young Brits began to seriously come to grips with the form, and also to add in elements of their own. In the lead was a young Londoner called Eric Clapton, whose style owed plenty to both B.B. King and his fiery Texan namesake Freddie King. Whether or not Clapton was actually as skilled or as original a blues musician as his heroes is open to debate. What is certain, however, is that he became the very first 'guitar hero' and opened up a huge new white audience for the blues. Thanks to his popularity Chicago bluesmen like Muddy Waters and Buddy Guy, whose careers had been tailing off with the rise of soul music within the black communities, enjoyed new lease of life.

In America too, white bluesmen started to come to the fore. Chicago produced Michael Bloomfield, who contributed blistering guitar work to Bob Dylan's early electric period. That other great blues centre, Texas, produced first the albino Johnny Winter, a fiery player whose finest hour might just be the records he cut with Muddy Waters in the late 1970s, and then Stevie Ray Vaughan. Vaughan is arguably the most influential of all the white bluesmen – not merely a follower, he was also an innovator, and it's rare to hear a young blues guitarist today, whether black or white, who doesn't owe something to the ultimately full-on style of SRV.

HISTORY OF THE SLIDE GUITAR

There are many theories as to the origin of the slide guitar. W.C. Handy famously recalled hearing an unknown musician using a knife on the strings of his guitar. But this unknown

BELOW: *Albert King's visual trademark was his Flying V guitar, an instrument that few other contemporary musicians adopted.*

bluesman had scarcely invented the style. For centuries musicians around the world have created sounds by dragging objects across stringed instruments. One example is the West African musical bow. This is a one-stringed instrument attached to a gourd resonator, and held against the body, while the player plucks the string and uses a bone or metal to vary the pitch.

This was probably the ancestor of a bowed instrument called the Jitterbug used by African-American musicians around the Southern states of America at the turn of the century. The Jitterbug, like the bow, had one string, but this time it was attached to the floor instead of a gourd. When plucked, an object would be dragged along the string to accompany simple songs. This produced a wailing/moaning sound well suited to the early blues. The scraping technique was no doubt adapted to the guitar, once cheap models started to be available from mail-order catalogues even in the many rural backwaters.

Meanwhile a different kind of slide guitar, a forerunner of what we now know as the lap steel, was being pioneered in Hawaii. This became enormously popular after a young Hawaiian guitarist called Joseph Kekeku made some popular recordings using the steel guitar around the turn of the century. It was a flashy, eerie kind of sound that became very popular, and the Hawaiian-style lap steel started to outsell Spanish-style guitars. Soon the use of the slide began to seep into all styles of music, from the early blues to the mountain music of the Appalachians. Whatever the origins of the slide guitar, however, it is certain that it reached its apotheosis in its partnership with the blues.

TWELVE-BAR BLUES

The 12-bar blues progression is the main underpinning of the vast majority of blues tunes out there. So, in order to start playing, you'll need to know

BELOW: *Stevie Ray Vaughan had a talent comparable to the great Jimi Hendrix, but his life was cut short by a helicopter crash in 1990.*

what a 12-bar blues progression is. The basic concept of the 12-bar blues is the I-IV-V progression, where I, IV and V represent the chords that you will be using.

When you play a basic blues progression, you will only need to use three chords. The principle of I-IV-V tells you which chords to use. It's essentially a slightly oversimplified approach to figuring out which chord to use next. It's based on a numeric system, linked to the letters of the alphabet. Say you're playing in C, then the C chord will be the I; you then count three letters further up the alphabet to get to F, which will be the IV chord. Count one further letter forward and you get to the G chord and that will be the V. It's not an infallible system but it works for the keys of A, C, D, E and G, which will keep you going for a while. Thus, for the key of A, we will be using A-D-E as our I-IV-V progression. Likewise if you count out starting with E, you will find that for the key of E we will use E-A-B as our I-IV-V. Music theory terminology, by the way, calls the I the 'tonic', the IV the 'subdominant', and the V the 'dominant'.

So how to put the chord progression into use? The basic concept of the 12-bar blues is to create and resolve tension. Once you get used to the progression, you will see how the V generally creates tension in your progression and the I generally resolves tension. It may be useful to think of the 12-bar progression as divided into three mini-sections of four bars each.

Here's a simple 12-bar progression: I-I-I-I-IV-IV-I-I-V-IV-I-I/V. The first four bars (I-I-I-I) just sort of set things up, using the relaxed I chord. In the second four-bar segment (IV-IV-I-I) a little tension is introduced by switching to the IV chord for bars five–six, but resolved by switching back to the I chord in bars seven–eight. Then in the third four-bar segment (V-IV-I-I/V) the tension is increased in the ninth bar, when we switch to the V chord for the first time. The tension is gradually resolved in bars 10–11 before using a two chord 'turnaround' to set up the next 12 bars.

BELOW: *Eric Clapton, here seen in his younger days, has been one of the formative figures in modern guitar playing, not least in bringing the blues into mainstream music.*

ROBERT JOHNSON

1911–1938
BAND: **SOLO ARTIST**
HEIGHT OF FAME: **1930s**

Robert Johnson is where it all starts. His country blues style is the cornerstone of modern blues. His guitar playing still remains the gold standard as far as acolytes like Eric Clapton and Keith Richards are concerned. When his few recordings were gathered together for a double CD in 1990 they went on to sell over a million copies, helped by the legends that surround the man.

From what little we know of him, Johnson had a short life and a violent death. Chief among the many legends that surround him is the story that he acquired his extraordinary ability on the guitar thanks to a pact he made with the Devil himself, after meeting him one dark night at a Mississippi crossroads.

While it's a great story, the truth is more prosaic. Johnson actually practised. He learnt a lot from his first idol, the Delta recording star Lonnie Johnson – as well as from Skip James and Kokomo Arnold. He developed his slide style after much listening to fellow Delta bluesmen Charley Patton and Son House. The big leap forward his guitar playing took in the mid 1930s followed a year or so learning from an unrecorded bluesman named Ike Zinneman, a man who liked to practise late at night in the local graveyard. Following this tuition, Johnson seemed to have complete mastery of his instrument, and an ability to sing and play in whatever style was needed in order to make a living as an itinerant musician.

It was with his blues numbers, however, that his individuality shone through. He introduced the boogie bass line played on the bottom strings of the guitar, which now practically defines blues guitar. Add to that a repertoire of rundowns and turnbacks and repeats and Johnson had taken the guitar to the next stage.

RIGHT: *Robert Johnson lived only a short life, dying at the age of 27 after having been deliberately poisoned. He did, however, leave his mark on the world of guitar playing.*

ROBERT JOHNSON'S THUMB BASS STYLE

Back in the early 1960s, so the story goes, just when The Rolling Stones were starting out, Keith Richards played Mick Jagger a Robert Johnson record. Jagger listened to it and asked who the bass player was. Keith laughed and told him there wasn't one.

What Johnson was doing was playing a kind of bass line using his thumb on the bottom three strings of the guitar, while playing the melody on the top two strings, all at the same time. It's a style that has become basic to what we think of as blues guitar today. The bass figure, played with the thumb, provides the rolling boogie. It's not a new musical idea, it's the same basic principle as the piano player using his or her left hand to provide the bass. It's just a little trickier to enact on a guitar, because the same hand has to play both parts simultaneously, something which is every bit as hard as it sounds. Robert Johnson of course was blessed with unusually large hands and long fingers, which were a help, but essentially to master this technique you're going to have to practise very hard indeed. Once mastered, though, it's a wonderfully adaptable technique, and you don't even need to vary it all that much, Robert Johnson used very similar thumb bass patterns in almost half his recorded songs, including the likes of 'Love in Vain', 'Me and the Devil', '32-20 Blues', 'Stop Breakin' Down', 'Steady Rollin' Man' and 'Honeymoon'.

LEFT: *Robert Johnson's large hands and long fingers are evident in this photograph.*

Crossroad Blues

ALBUM: **COMPLETE RECORDINGS**
SONGWRITER: **ROBERT JOHNSON**
RECORDED: **GANTER HOTEL, TEXAS**
PRODUCER: **N/A**

This is a great blues lick starting at the top end of the guitar neck. Try to get that Robert Johnson lonesome ringing sound when you play the first few notes of 'Crossroad Blues', listen to the way it rings out high before eventually dropping down a semitone. Keep your notes clean to achieve that ringing sound. Use down strokes to get that incessant rhythm during the opening.

BASIC SONG RIFF

swing

```
      3
T 4  14  14 14 14                          4 4 4 4 4 4 4  4
A 4  16  16 16 15   16    7         7       7 7 7 6 6 5 5  4    7    —
B                   12          13      7
```

HERE'S HOW

1 This shows the first and ring fingers holding the shape on the F# and D# notes on the E and B strings.

2 Release the ring finger so that the middle finger can play the D note on the B string; this creates that descending sound.

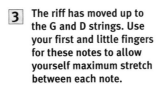

3 The riff has moved up to the G and D strings. Use your first and little fingers for these notes to allow yourself maximum stretch between each note.

SLIDE GUITAR

Robert Johnson is one of the first names most people think of when it comes to playing acoustic blues slide guitar. However, it wasn't Johnson who invented it. In fact, as far back as 1903 W.C. Handy – the man who liked to call himself 'the father of the blues' – told a story about falling asleep on a bench in a railway station in the Mississippi Delta town of Tutwiler while waiting for a train. He was awakened by the sound of a man singing and playing guitar in unorthodox fashion – rather than fretting the neck with his fingers, he was sliding a knife up and down the strings.

This was evidently slide-guitar playing in its earliest form. Essentially, slide guitar is the technique of using a smooth, hard object – usually a hollow metal or glass cylinder, for instance a bottleneck, rather than a knife – to change the pitches of the strings. The origins of the style have been traced back to African one-stringed instruments and also to Hawaiian guitar styles. Early bluesmen who used slide guitar techniques included Eddie 'Son' House, Tampa Red before Robert Johnson, and the likes of Muddy Waters and Elmore James after him. What it

offers guitar players is a whole variety of effects – glissandos, voice-like cries – and also access to the notes between the frets. Therefore it's an invaluable style for anyone interested in playing acoustic blues guitar. There are plenty of commercially available slides on offer, or if you want to be traditional you can use anything from a bottle neck to a lipstick holder. Then tune your guitar to open D and start practising.

LEFT: *A blues guitar player is here seen using a professional slide, although in the history of the great blues guitarists everything from bottles to knives have been used.*

Me and the Devil

ALBUM: **COMPLETE RECORDINGS**
SONGWRITER: **ROBERT JOHNSON**
RECORDED: **GANTER HOTEL, TEXAS**
PRODUCER: **N/A**

The tab shows a descending chord shape that stays the same as it drops from the 8th and 9th frets to the 6th and 7th frets. Experiment with similar shapes on other parts of the neck to get unusual note combinations and ringing sounds heard in lots of blues songs. Keep your strumming regular as you move down the frets. Practise accuracy when moving these shapes around the neck.

BASIC SONG RIFF

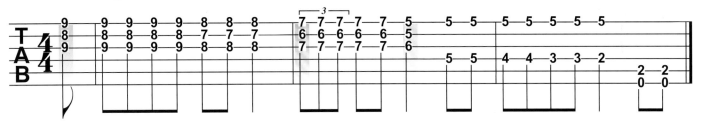

HERE'S HOW

1 Use your first finger to play the 8th fret on the B string, your middle finger on the G string and your ring finger plays the E string.

2 We have now dropped a whole tone. When you've hit this chord your ring finger will be released from the fret board to anticipate the next position.

3 Use your first finger to play the E and B strings and the 5th fret and your middle finger to play the 6th fret on the G string.

367

T-BONE WALKER

1910–1975
BAND: **SOLO ARTIST**
HEIGHT OF FAME: **1940s**

T-Bone Walker was the blues' first true lead guitarist, and undeniably one of its very best.

Modern electric blues guitar can be traced directly back to this Texas-born pioneer, who first

plugged into an amp around 1940 and completely changed the face of music in the process.

All the great blues guitarists who came after owe him a debt.

Aaron Thibeault Walker was born on 28 May 1910 in Linden, Texas. His stepfather, Marco Washington, played the bass with the Dallas String Band, and T-Bone soon learned the basics of every stringed instrument he could. One musician the band played with regularly was the legendary Blind Lemon Jefferson, and the young Walker started to assist the great bluesman as he played around the Texas bars.

Walker made his own recording debut in 1929 with a single 78 for Columbia. In 1933 he played with another guitarist named Charlie Christian who would later electrify jazz in the same way as Walker electrified the blues. Soon afterwards Walker moved to Los Angeles and played in big bands for a living, while developing a fascination with the new electric guitar in club gigs, where he would also develop an acrobatic stage act, featuring stunts like playing the guitar behind his back or with his teeth.

Walker's guitar playing on record was notably fluent and melodic. He signed to Capitol Records and had a string of hits including the immortal 'Call It Stormy Monday' in 1947. Other hits included 'T-Bone Jumps Again', which showed he could do up tempo as well as mellow, 'T-Bone Shuffle' and 'West Side Baby'.

Walker carried on recording right up till his death in 1975 but today, it is the controlled power of his work in the 1940s and early 1950s that marks him out as one of the all-time blues greats.

RIGHT: *T-Bone Walker's first musical instrument was a banjo, bought for him by his mother when he was 12. However, he longed to play the guitar so saved up his money from playing at church social events and bought his first guitar in his early teens.*

GIBSON ES 250

The guitar T-Bone Walker is generally associated with is the Gibson ES 250, an impressive hollow-bodied instrument with a wonderfully mellow tone, and only the second electric guitar ever made by Gibson.

The ES-250 first appeared in the 1940 Gibson AA catalog with the slogan: 'Gibson has created the best electric guitar possible to make.' This top-of-the-line instrument was an upgraded version of the popular ES 150. It had significant refinements which distinguished it from the earlier mid-range model. These included a larger body, a more deluxe fingerboard, headstock, tuners and tailpiece, and a bar pick-up with individual mini-blades acting as separate pole pieces for each string for 'maximum tonal reproduction'. The ES 250, complete with case, cord and the matching EH 185 amplifier, cost the enormous sum of $250 on its launch in 1940. This meant its use was for the most part confined to the successful working professional – in short, musicians like T-Bone Walker. Charlie Christian, the great jazz player, was another early adopter – unsurprisingly as he had already made his name playing Gibson's previous model the ES 150. Other notable users included 1940s big-band guitar players such as Alvino Rey and Tony Mottola.

The high price of the ES 250s meant that a relatively small number of them were ever produced and models are now very scarce indeed. A pristine example, complete with its original case and matching Gibson EH 185 amplifier, was recently sold for no less than $27,500, which makes $250 not such a bad investment after all!

BELOW: *T-Bone used his Gibson guitars to bring traditional acoustic blues riffs to the electric guitar.*

Stormy Monday Blues

ALBUM: **BORN TO BE NO GOOD; STORMY MONDAY (LIVE)**
SONGWRITER: **T-BONE WALKER**
RECORDED: **BLACK & WHITE RECORDS**
PRODUCER: **N/A**

This is a great slow blues tune by T-Bone Walker, and sounds best on an electric or semi-acoustic guitar. These are nice chords to play around with, adapt and add to your repertoire. The fingering takes a bit of getting used to, so practise moving around these shapes. This tune sounds best played slowly and mournfully.

BASIC SONG RIFF

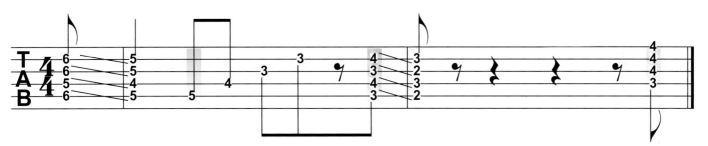

HERE'S HOW

1 The first finger covers notes at the 3rd frets of the G and B strings, middle finger on the D, ring plays 5th fret of the A string.

2 First finger on the 3rd fret A string, middle finger on the G string, ring finger on the D string and little finger plays the B string.

3 Here the first finger plays the 3rd fret of the D string and your middle finger covers the three frets of the G, B and E strings.

B.B. KING

1925–
BAND: **SOLO ARTIST**
HEIGHT OF FAME: **1950s–PRESENT**

For more than half a century, B.B. King has defined the blues for a worldwide audience. Since he started recording in the 1940s, he has released over 50 albums. A fine blues singer, he is also one of the most influential guitar players of all time. His particular contributions are his utterly distinctive use of vibrato and the use of space in his guitar solos. Where later guitarists are all about warp-fast blurs of notes, King specializes in playing a few well-chosen notes, and enhancing them with different techniques (such as vibrato and string bending) to create something remarkably close to the human voice. If there a guitarist who can truly make his instrument sing, then it is surely B.B. King.

RIGHT: *B.B. King has been one of the hardest-working blues performers in history. His love of live performance has kept him on the stage even throughout his seventies.*

He was born Riley King on 16 September 1925, on a plantation in Itta Bene, Mississippi, near Indianola. He started out playing on street corners for dimes. In 1947, he hitchhiked to Memphis, where he stayed with his cousin Bukka White, already a top blues singer. After a while he landed a gig hosting a blues radio show, and was given the B.B. (Blues Boy) nickname.

It wasn't long before King had a number one R&B hit of his own, 'Three O'Clock Blues'. He then began touring nationally, and in 1956 played an astonishing 342 one-night stands. He's kept at it ever since, playing everywhere from the juke joints and dance halls of his early days to new concert halls and amphitheatres. Along the way, he has become the most renowned blues musician of the past 40 years, and one of the most identifiable guitar stylists.

LUCILLE

BELOW: *One of B.B. King's Gibson Lucille guitars on display at 'B.B. King's Nightclub' in Universal City, California.*

In the mid 1950s, while King was performing at a dance in Twist, Arkansas, a fight broke out between some men in the audience, which led to the hall catching on fire. The story goes that King ran back in to the burning hall to save his guitar, risking death in the process, Afterwards, having discovered that the fight had been over a woman named Lucille, he decided to give the name to his guitar. Ever since that time, he has named each one of his trademark Gibson guitars Lucille.

The current Lucille is a Gibson ES 355. B.B. has been playing this model for at least 25 years. Prior to that time, he played an ES 335. The main difference between the two guitars is that the ES 355 is a solid body. B.B. likes to think of the ES 355 as the 'big brother' of Gibson's Les Paul.

Although King has a special relationship with Gibson guitars, he has played plenty of other guitars along the way. His very first guitar was a Stella acoustic and early in his career, he played and owned many different makes, such as Fender, Gretsch and Silverstone.

In his publicity, King emphasizes the notion that the guitar is a woman. He called a 1968 album Lucille and wrote in the sleeve notes that 'I'm very crazy about Lucille. She's taken me a long way, even brought me some fame ... most of all, she's kept me alive, being able to eat ... Lucille practically saved my life two or three times. Sometimes I get to a place I can't even say nothing ... sometimes when I'm blue, seems Lucille tries to help me, calls my name ... She's just like a woman, and that's the only one I've had that seemed I could really depend on. I've been married and each time separated from my wife, but Lucille never separates from me. She always stayed with me.'

Sweet Sixteen

ALBUM: **VARIOUS COMPILATIONS**
SONGWRITER: **B.B. KING, JOE BIHARI**
RECORDED: **VARIOUS RECORDINGS**
PRODUCER: **N/A**

This is an unmistakable B.B. King intro all played at the top end of the fret board. Bending strings from one note to another creates a lovely lonesome and bluesy feel. Try to get used to playing at the top end of the fret board. Always check your tuning after practising bending notes. Build up strength in your middle and ring fingers to make bending easy.

BASIC SONG RIFF

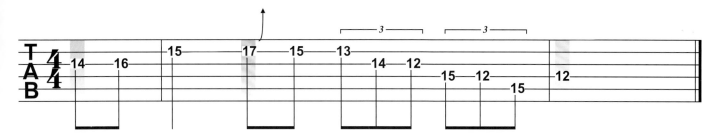

HERE'S HOW

1 You can use a hammer-on technique to play the first two notes in this intro at the 14th and 16th frets of the G string.

2 Dropping to the B string, your middle finger can play the 15th fret of the B string to allow your ring finger space to play the lovely bend.

3 By using middle and ring fingers to play the notes and bends high up the fret board you can leave your first finger to play the lower notes.

GIBSON LAB SERIES L5

B.B King generally plays Lucille through a Gibson Lab Series amp. What's unusual about that is that the L5 is a solid-state amp rather than a tube amp. Most pro guitar players turn their noses up at solid-state amps, seeing them as cheap in terms of both price and tone quality. Not sure about the difference? Put simply, tube amps have a number of tubes that contain a lot of scientific stuff like plates, grids and cathodes which end up moving energy around, resulting in sound reproduction. A solid-state amp only features integrated circuits and transistors.

Historically, tube amps are more expensive, based on the increased number and nature of the components. Tube amps may also be affected by climate, so consistency and reliability in the tubes are important. Tube amps are much heavier than solid-state amps, due to the additional output transformer. So why do so many guitarists like them?

Essentially it is the warm tone of tube amps that draws guitarists to them. On the other hand, they offer a less consistent tone that solid-state amps, and this may well be one of the factors that drew B.B. King to the Lab Series amps.

The Gibson Lab Series L5 combo guitar amplifier was a 100-Watt, 2-channel (non-switching) 2 - 12" speaker combo that was in production from roughly the late 1970s to the early 1980s. It has four inputs, a rather unusual built-in compressor, reverb, and a 'mid-frequency' knob that controls the mid range of the amplifier. It also has speaker outputs, pre-amp inputs, etc., but no effects loop. Although the amp is branded a Gibson, it was actually manufactured by a company called Norlin for Gibson.

RIGHT: *A young B.B. King is here seen practising with one of his 'Lucilles'.*

The Three O'Clock Blues

ALBUM: **VARIOUS COMPILATIONS**
SONGWRITERS: **B.B. KING, JULES BIHARI**
RECORDED: **VARIOUS RECORDINGS**
PRODUCER: **N/A**

This is a lead lick played mainly on the top strings. It also takes you high up the neck, so mastering this riff will enable you to move up and down the fret board with ease, which will help develop essential skills for good lead-guitar playing. Practise bending notes through a whole tone on high strings; to do this you'll need to bend notes two frets higher.

BASIC SONG RIFF

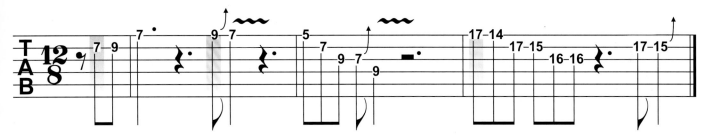

HERE'S HOW

1 The intro notes are played on the B string with the first and ring finger. Make sure you play these notes hard and with clarity.

2 You now need to take this D flat note and bend it two frets up to an E flat, all on the E string.

3 This shows the little finger playing the E string at the 17th fret whilst the 1st finger is back and ready to play the 14th fret.

FOLLOWING THE VOICE

When he was asked about the almost vocal quality of his guitar playing, B.B. King commented that, 'When I sing, I play in my mind; the minute I stop singing orally, I start to sing by playing Lucille.' It's a valuable lesson to learn that guitar playing can resemble singing – for just as a singer phrases words to invest a lyric with emotion, adding particular stresses and rhythmic content, so the guitarist can phrase runs of notes in an expressive, unique way.

King is a master at using vibrato to emphasize just the right note in such a way that the phrase jumps out at the listener. He understands that if a guitarist truly wants to communicate emotion he or she does not necessarily have to play a huge number of notes in quick succession; soulfulness, not manual dexterity, is what the listener wants. What B.B. King teaches us is that, in playing blues guitar, economy and phrasing are all important. It's something he has learned through the experience of being a singer as well as a guitarist; a singer's phrasing comes just as naturally to his guitar work as it does to his voice.

King's playing is also influenced by previous generations of blues guitarists like Blind Lemon Jefferson and T-Bone Walker. When it comes to his own playing, he used precise and complex string bends played with left-hand vibrato, to give the guitar an almost vocal tone. His phrasing always respects and enhances the sentiment of the song, producing guitar work that's as emotionally compelling – whether mournful and bluesy, or joyful and rocking – as it is technically satisfying.

LEFT: *B.B. King has expressed a certain distance from the 'purists' of the blues community, but he has done more than almost any other artist to bring blues into the mainstream.*

Sweet Little Angel

ALBUM: **VARIOUS COMPILATIONS**
SONGWRITERS: **B.B. KING, JULES BIHARI**
RECORDED: **VARIOUS RECORDINGS**
PRODUCER: **N/A**

This great B.B. King blues tune is very melodic and starts up high on the A string. It's a good tune to practise moving between your first and ring finger over a three-fret gap. It's a great riff to experiment with and adapt to your playing style. Keep it slow, steady and smokey ! Learn to move up and down fluently between the strings at the top end of the guitar neck.

BASIC SONG RIFF

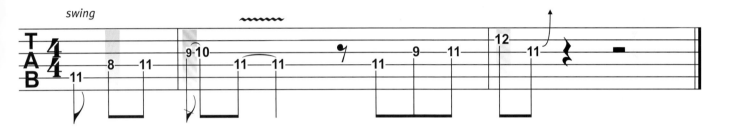

HERE'S HOW

1 Keep your first finger in position over the 8th fret on the D string whilst letting your little finger play this note at the 11th fret on the A string.

2 This is a one fret hammer-on between the 9th and 10th frets on the G string; use your first and middle fingers here.

3 Play this note at the B octave with your little finger. It sounds great if you slide into it after the notes on the G string.

ALBERT KING

1923–1992
BAND: **SOLO ARTIST**
HEIGHT OF FAME: **1960s–70s**

One of the three great blues Kings – along with B.B. and Freddie – Albert King is one of the major influences on blues and rock guitarists from Otis Rush and Robert Cray to Eric Clapton and Stevie Ray Vaughan. Yet, though his imitators have been many, few have come close to replicating Albert's own extraordinary tone.

Partly this is because he played guitar left-handed, but rather than play a left-handed guitar, or even re-stringing a right-handed guitar as Jimi Hendrix did, he simply played the guitar upside down so the bass strings are at the bottom rather than the top. As a result he pulls down on the same strings that most players push up on, thus producing a unique sound.

Albert King was born on 25 April 1923, in Indianola, MS. He taught himself to play guitar as a child, building his own instrument from a cigar box. At first, he played gospel music, but after hearing delta blues men like Lonnie Johnson and Blind Lemon Jefferson, he turned to 'the devil's music'.

He settled in St Louis in the mid 1950s. There he started playing his signature Gibson Flying V guitar and became a top local attraction, scoring his first national R&B hit. His big breakthrough came in 1967 when he signed to Stax records and released a string of singles backed by Booker T and the MGs. The combination was irresistible on numbers like 'Born Under A Bad Sign' and 'Cross Cut Saw', and the sound was an immediate hit both with the R&B audience and the new young white rock audience. Suddenly, at the age of 43, Albert King was a star, performing to packed-out audiences at the Fillmore in San Francisco and elsewhere. His recording career tailed off in the late 1970s, but as an inveterate showman he remained a major live draw until his death in 1992.

RIGHT: *Albert King has been described as the 'master of the single-string attack', and he had the ability to create perfect, clear blues phrases in the mould of Blind Lemon Jefferson and Elmore James.*

FLYING V

Back in the mid 1950s Gibson Guitars president Ted McCarty decided that his company's image needed updating. Rock 'n' roll had revolutionized the popular music scene and flamboyant characters like Bo Diddley had started playing their own customized guitars. McCarty, a trained engineer, decided to respond to this challenge by designing commercially produced guitars that completely dispensed with the old rounded acoustic-style shape of most electric guitars. In 1958, Gibson unveiled three radical new models: the Flying V, the Explorer and the Moderne.

The industry was shocked and uncertain. The Moderne never made it into commercial production while the Explorer and Flying V – so called for its revolutionary v-shape – were produced only in very limited quantities. Those guitar shops that did order them generally used them as novelty display items rather than promoting them as playable instruments. Albert King was one of the few brave souls actually attracted by the radical-looking Flying V, but too few others followed suit. Less than a hundred Flying V guitars were sold, and Gibson moved on to other new models, shelving the Flying V for a decade. It was only revived in the 1960s as the musical climate became more experimental, and again in the 1970s when the Flying V suddenly became the guitar of choice for heavy-rock groups like Wishbone Ash and The Scorpions. Original Flying Vs now have a considerable rarity value, selling for tens of thousands of dollars. Subsequent Flying Vs have had significantly different specifications to the originals, but in the 1990s Gibson manufactured a small number of custom copies of the 1958 originals. However, these have a list price of over $13,000, so hardly constitute a viable way for most guitarists to reproduce the exact sound of Albert King.

BELOW: *The Flying V guitar had little commercial success, Albert King being one of its few high-profile patrons.*

A typical Albert King lead lick

Here's the start of the kind of lead lick that Albert King incorporated into many of his blues tunes. It's played around the top B and E strings and features four climbing notes before sliding up to a screeching A note at the 10th fret of the B string.

Try to change the speed during the riff – speed up when you ascend the scale, then slow down to play that mournful slide up at the end.

BASIC RIFF

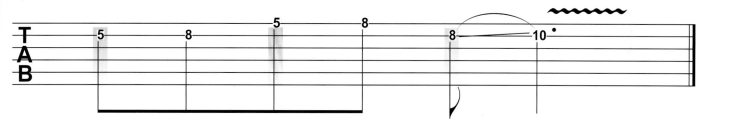

HERE'S HOW

1 Use your index finger to start the run at the 5th fret of the B string. Use your little finger to play the next note at the 8th fret of the B string.

2 Next bring your index finger up to the 5th fret on the top E, again using your little finger to play the 8th fret, this time on the top E.

3 Now use your little finger to slide from the 8th fret of the B string up to that A note at the 10th fret of the B string.

ERIC CLAPTON

1945–
BANDS: **YARDBIRDS, JOHN MAYALL'S BLUESBREAKERS, CREAM, DEREK AND THE DOMINOES**
HEIGHT OF FAME: **1970s–PRESENT**

Eric Clapton was the original guitar hero. Before Clapton, the guitarist was seen as just another musician in the band, standing behind the singer. A few aficionados might know who was hot, but the general public had no idea. Then came Clapton. His playing, first with the Yardbirds and then with John Mayall's Bluesbreakers was so startling, so incendiary, that an amazed audience started to spray paint the slogan 'Clapton is God' around London. Not that Clapton himself was too impressed by this. He was an unwilling hero, a quiet man who just wanted to get on with making music.

Clapton was born in Surrey in southern England in 1945. He started playing the blues while at art school in the early 1960s and acquired a Kay guitar. Soon afterwards he joined the Yardbirds, then left (to be replaced by Jeff Beck) when he decided they were becoming too commercial. His brief stay with John Mayall's Bluesbreakers was pivotal. In this band he was allowed to give his blues playing free rein.

Clapton's guitar hero period peaked with his next band, Cream, a hard-rock trio in which he could solo for as long as he liked. After the band split up he made one classic album with Derek And The Dominoes, featuring his masterpiece 'Layla', before succumbing to heroin addiction for several years. Once recovered, his comeback record, *461 Ocean Boulevard*, saw him playing acoustic guitar and dobro much of the time, the mood downbeat and song-based. Through the 1970s and 1980s his work headed into commercial pop-rock, before coming back to basics in the 1990s with a series of traditional blues albums.

RIGHT: *Eric Clapton, pictured here at a 1988 concert in New York, has done more than almost any other artist to bring blues into the mainstream, although he is equally known for his talents in rock and pop.*

CLAPTON'S ELECTRIC GUITARS

Clapton has had two major loves as far as electric guitars go. Through his early years, up till the demise of Cream, he was a Gibson Les Paul man. Since then – and following the influence of Jimi Hendrix who persuaded so many British guitarists to make the same switch – it's been Fender Stratocasters all the way (most famously the cannibalized instrument known as 'Blackie' which he auctioned for $450,000 for his Crossroads charity).

ABOVE: *Clapton's 'Blackie' guitar became one of rock's most expensive instruments.*

The signature instrument of Clapton's early guitar hero days was a rather more flamboyant instrument. The guitar started life as a 1961 Les Paul SG. In advance of the band's first US tour in 1967 he asked the Dutch artist collective, 'The Fool' (responsible for several other pop-art projects, mostly for The Beatles), to give the instrument a custom psychedelic paint job. The result was an impressively psychedelic instrument entirely in keeping with the times. Times change though, and following the break-up of Cream Clapton switched guitars and gave the Fool Guitar to a singer songwriter called Jackie Lomax who was making a record for Apple. Two years later a new American guitar hero about town, Todd Rundgren, happened to meet up with Lomax and was horrified to find the Fool Guitar in beat-up condition. He gave the hard-up Lomax $50 and had the guitar restored to its former glory, using it both on stage and in the studio until the guitar became too fragile to risk doing further damage.

BLACKIE

During the early part of his career Clapton was always associated with Gibsons – his championing of the Les Paul led Gibson to put it back into production in 1968, eight years after it had been discontinued. Following the emergence of Jimi Hendrix, though, Clapton switched to Fender Stratocasters, and these have been his main stage and studio electric guitars ever since. There's one nicknamed 'Brownie' that he used to play 'Layla', and was recently auctioned for $450,000 by Clapton to support his Crossroads drug rehabilitation charity. The most famous of his Strats, however, is the one Clapton nicknamed 'Blackie'. Blackie was put together by Clapton from three different Stratocasters. These came from a lot of six he bought in at the Sho-Bud music store in Nashville, Tennessee in 1970. Three of the six he gave away as presents to George Harrison, Steve Winwood and Pete Townshend. From the remaining three, he took the best parts and assembled Blackie. He played the guitar on stage and in the studio right up until 1987 when it was finally retired. Eager not to lose the sound of such a well-loved instrument, Clapton worked with Fender to produce The Eric Clapton Signature Stratocaster, a guitar designed to recreate Blackie, but with modern electronics. Particular enhancements have been made to the compression sound. A dedicated tone button allows the compression to fatten the sound considerably. At first the guitar was only available commercially in Ferrari Red, 7-Up Green and Charcoal Grey, but by 1991 Clapton relented and allowed the guitar to be commercially produced in black as well, much to the delight of Clapton wannabes.

Sunshine of Your Love

ALBUM: **DISRAELI GEARS (CREAM)**

SONGWRITERS: **ERIC CLAPTON, JACK BRUCE, PETE BROWN**

RECORDED: **ATLANTIC STUDIOS, NEW YORK**

PRODUCER: **FELIX PAPPALARDI**

This great opening riff is all played at the top end of the guitar neck on the bass strings. Play this riff on an electric guitar and turn the tone control right down to achieve that warm Clapton tone. Use down strokes with the plectrum, keep the notes evenly paced and practise moving between the three bass strings.

BASIC SONG RIFF

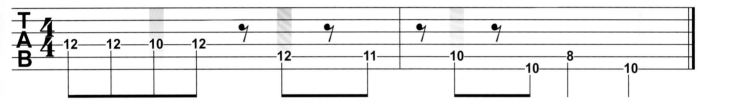

HERE'S HOW

1 This shows the ring finger at the D octave 12th fret, leaving your other fingers free to play notes on the lower frets.

2 Here the finger comes up to the A octave 12th fret of the A string. Use your middle and first finger on the next two notes.

3 Bring your ring finger up to the 10th fret of the E string whilst your first finger gets ready to play the 8th fret of the A string.

IT'S ALL ABOUT THE TONE

During the 1960s Eric Clapton not once but twice revolutionized the sound of the electric guitar, at least in Britain. It began with the album he made with John Mayall's Bluesbreakers. The unaccompanied guitar intro to 'All Your Love' made people jump out of their seats, it sounded so ferocious. The tone was reminiscent of Chicago blues players like Freddie King, but even more muscular. It was a tone Clapton achieved by plugging his Gibson Les Paul into an early Marshall Amp, a 1962 model 2x l2 Marshall combo fitted with a pair of KT66 power tubes, rather than the normal EL34s. Clapton played the combo full out and had the microphones placed across the room to pick up on the full force of this overdriven distorted sound.

The 1960s was a decade when technology was changing fast and by the time Clapton recorded with his next band Cream, his tone had changed too. He was playing a new Les Paul, after his previous one had been stolen; more significantly he was now playing through the classic Marshall 100-Watt amps with the new 4x12 Cabinets, stacked up in the studio. The result was louder than ever, but the better quality of the amplification meant that it was clearer too, offering a more melodic sound that aficionados soon dubbed 'woman tone'.

RIGHT: *Clapton's sound was influenced by the blues masters he listened to as a child, such as Robert Johnson and B.B. King. This picture was taken in 1967 during the recording of Cream's Disraeli Gears album in New York.*

Crossroads

ALBUM: **WHEELS OF FIRE**

WRITTEN BY: **ROBERT JOHNSON**

RECORDED AT: **THE FILLMORE WEST, SAN FRANCISCO**

PRODUCED BY: **FELIX PAPPALARDI**

A great rock blues riff that's really good fun to play. On the recorded version by Cream it's actually played quite fast, but you can slow it right down to practise getting the notes right. Set your amp to a dirty overdriven sound to achieve authenticity. Use your strumming hand to achieve a good bluesy boogie feel. Keep repeating the riff until you feel comfortable playing it at speed.

BASIC SONG RIFF

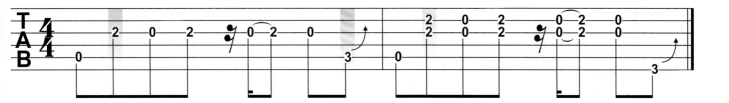

HERE'S HOW

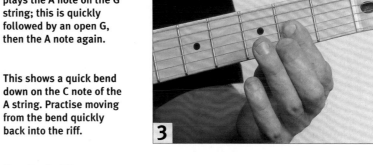

1 Following the open A string the first finger plays the A note on the G string; this is quickly followed by an open G, then the A note again.

2 This shows a quick bend down on the C note of the A string. Practise moving from the bend quickly back into the riff.

3 Here the first finger covers the 2nd frets of the B and E strings. Strum these notes together in quick succession.

DOBRO

When Clapton came back from heroin addiction with 1974's *461 Ocean Boulevard* album, many long–time fans were aghast. For this was an album of laid-back songs with hardly a guitar solo to be heard. The dominant influence on his guitar playing was no longer Albert or Freddie King but Oklahoma singer-songwriter J.J. Cale. And much of the time Clapton was playing a Dobro!

A Dobro was about the least likely guitar-hero instrument you could imagine. It was invented in the 1920s by the Dopyera brothers at a time when guitarists were looking at ways of making their instruments louder so they could be heard in a swing band. The Dobro achieved this by incorporating a resonant aluminium cone and a steel body. The guitar is played horizontally and fretted with a steel bar ('a steel'), The result is a sound midway between blues bottleneck slide guitar and a pedal steel guitar. In fact, the introduction of first the electric guitar and then the pedal steel drove the Dobro almost out of existence by the 1940s; only the devotion of a handful of country and bluegrass musicians kept it alive. By the early 1970s, however, rock guitarists like Clapton and Ry Cooder were taking an interest in traditional country music, and found the unique sound of the Dobro fascinating. It's an indication of the instrument's growing popularity that, since 1993, Dobros have been manufactured by Gibson, who also produce signature editions endorsed by the virtuoso likes of Jerry Douglas.

RIGHT: *Eric Clapton's use of a particular guitar has an enormous commercial value for a company. Both Fender and C.F. Martin & Co. have honoured Clapton with signature models.*

Layla

ALBUM: **LAYLA AND OTHER ASSORTED LOVE SONGS**
WRITTEN BY: **ERIC CLAPTON, JIM GORDON**
RECORDED AT: **CRITERIA STUDIOS, MIAMI**
PRODUCED BY: **TOM DOWD**

Another very famous Eric Clapton riff, all played at the top end of the guitar neck. On the recorded version there are lots of multi-tracked guitars, but this tab will at least enable you to play the basic riff. You will need to practise to get the riff up to speed. Listen to the record to get the exact phrasing, and practise the fast phrases between the 10th and 13th frets.

BASIC SONG RIFF

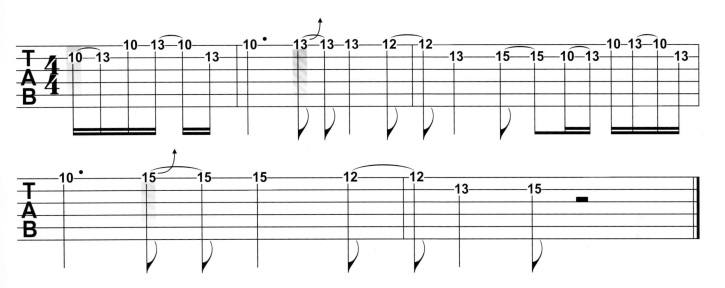

HERE'S HOW

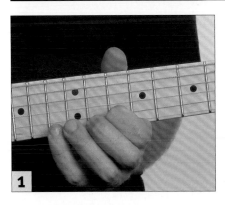

1 This shows the first finger at the 10th fret of the B string. Play this very fast hammer-on to the 13th fret with your little finger.

2 Here the riff goes up to the top E string. Play these notes at the 10th and 13th fret with your first and little fingers. Bend the highest note up.

3 This is the highest point of the riff at the 15th fret of the E string. Play this note with your little finger.

STEVIE RAY VAUGHAN

1954–1990
BANDS: **THE NIGHTCRAWLERS; DOUBLE TROUBLE**
HEIGHT OF FAME: **1970s**

In his short life Texas bluesman Stevie Ray Vaughan made a hell of a splash. He played guitar with David Bowie before becoming the first white musician to win a W.C. Handy Blues Instrumentalist of the Year award. Following his death in a helicopter crash, he has become a legend – a guitar player who married extraordinary technique with unbridled passion. At a time when the blues was slipping out of the consciousness of the average rock fan, Stevie Ray Vaughan kept the flame alive and in turn inspired a whole new generation of players.

Vaughan was born in Texas on 3 October 1954 at the Methodist Hospital. He was inspired to play guitar by his older brother, Jimmie. Leaving school at the age of 17, Stevie played in a series of rock bands before joining blues band The Nightcrawlers. At around this time, Stevie bought a battered '63 Stratocaster in Ray's Music Exchange in Austin. He named it 'Number One' (or sometimes 'First Wife') and this became his favourite guitar for the rest of his life.

The Nightcrawlers never quite made it, but Stevie persevered, playing a series of locally successful blues bands before forming his own group Double Trouble. A tape of the band playing live ended up in the hands of Mick Jagger, who invited them to play at a party for The Rolling Stones. This break led to Ray being hired by Bowie.

The Bowie connection raised Stevie's profile but what was even more pleasing was the success of *Texas Flood*, which was nominated for two Grammys. A string of hit albums followed. Unfortunately, along with the success came alcohol and drug problems which led to Vaughan going into rehab after collapsing on stage. Emerging sober, he recorded two more hit albums before his tragic death in a helicopter crash following a gig with Eric Clapton on 26 August 1990.

RIGHT: *Stevie Ray Vaughan's dexterity with the electric guitar led some critics to make a comparison with Jimi Hendrix, such was his level of talent.*

NUMBER ONE STRATOCASTER

Stevie Ray's favourite Stratocaster was one he bought in Ray's Music Exchange in Austin, Texas in his early years and nicknamed 'Number One'. This guitar was a battered 1963 model with a 1962 neck. Stevie Ray often said in interviews that he knew straight away that there was something special about it. 'I didn't even have to play it – I just knew by the way it looked that it would sound great. I was carrying another Strat and asked if Ray would like to trade. Thank God he did.'

Number One originally had a white pickguard and a right-handed tremelo bar. Stevie replaced the white pickguard with a black one and added 'SRV' lettering. In 1977 he added a gold left-handed tremelo – left handed to give him an upside-down guitar feel a la Jimi Hendrix. Eventually Stevie replaced the frets with Dunlop 6100 bass-style frets. These huge frets gave Stevie Ray the sustain he needed and helped during string bending. They were also helpful as he always used the thickest string sizes, ranging from .013 right up to .018.

Such strings are very hard on the fingers but if Stevie demanded a lot of his hands, he demanded even more of his guitar. Number One was severely abused during its lifetime with Stevie. On stage, Stevie Ray would kick it, pound it, rattle it, and hold it by the tremelo bar. Sometimes he would even bounce his guitar off a wall, catch it, and keep playing. The guitar finally had to be retired in 1989. Rumours suggested that it was buried with Stevie but in fact it's now in the possession of his brother Jimmie.

RIGHT *Stevie Ray's infamous 'Number One' guitar. It was much abused throughout its lifetime, but yielded the superb Stevie Ray sound.*

Pride and Joy

ALBUM: **TEXAS FLOOD**

SONGWRITER: **STEVIE RAY VAUGHAN**

RECORDED: **DOWN TOWN STUDIO, LOS ANGELES; RIVERSIDE SOUND, TEXAS**

PRODUCER: **DOUBLE TROUBLE, JOHN HAMMOND, SR.**

For this Stevie Ray Vaughan riff you'll need to tune down a semitone to get it to sound like the recorded version. It's a great blues intro which you can try and adapt and experiment with. Make that slide up from the 3rd fret to the 5th fret on the B string really ring out. It's a superb riff for practising your slides and bending note, and it also sounds good played slow or fast.

BASIC SONG RIFF

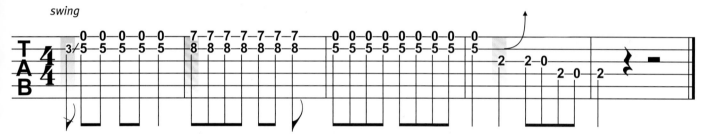

HERE'S HOW

1 This shows the slide up from the 3rd to the 5th fret on the B string. Make sure you play the open E and let the notes ring out.

2 Here the picture shows the first finger at the 7th fret of the E string and the middle finger at the 8th fret of the B string.

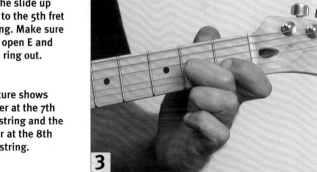

3 The middle finger pulls this bend on the A note at the 2nd fret of the G string. Your middle finger can also play the following notes on the D string.

IBANEZ TUBE SCREAMER

An Ibanez Tube Screamer is an overdrive/distortion pedal, one which fattens and dirties up the sound of the guitar, making it ideal for blues playing. Its effect isn't as extreme as some: it allows the true sound of the guitar to come through. Most players use the device in conjunction with a tube amp to give it some extra power. The first Ibanez Tube Screamer to be manufactured was the green TS-808 overdrive pro in the late 1970s which followed on from the same company's regular overdrive pedals.

Stevie Ray Vaughan used both the early TS-808 and the later TS-9 Ibanez Tube Screamer stomp boxes in his career. The TS-808 is easily distinguished from the TS-9 by its small black knobs, smaller stomp button, white script on the housing, and darker green colour.

Stevie used the Tube Screamer as his primary distortion device. He employed it to add overdrive at the front end of his tube amps, and also to add a natural tube-like saturation and sustain to his lead. He believed that it particularly suited the tone of the Stratocaster, but would adjust his settings depending on which amp he was using. When he used smaller Fender amps that had natural overdrive, he used the TS set clean with the level up high to push the amp for more distortion. When he played through big clean amps he turned the drive up further in order to get the distortion from the Tube Screamer.

Today, the Ibanez Tube Screamer has become a coveted pedal and commands high prices, largely thanks to its association with Vaughan.

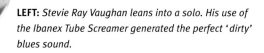

LEFT: *Stevie Ray Vaughan leans into a solo. His use of the Ibanex Tube Screamer generated the perfect 'dirty' blues sound.*

Scuttle Buttin'

ALBUM: **COULDN'T STAND THE WEATHER**
SONGWRITER: **STEVIE RAY VAUGHAN**
RECORDED: **THE POWER STATION, NEW YORK**
PRODUCER: **STEVIE RAY VAUGHAN**

This tab shows the three chords used at the start of ' Scuttle Buttin' '. The lead part is fairly difficult to master but these fast-flowing bluesy chords are great fun to play. You can also experiment with these chords and use them with other blues-based tunes, so try to incorporate them into your repertoire. Practise switching between these chords until you get the change smooth, then when you feel ready try using them to jam along with other musicians.

BASIC SONG CHORDS

E7♯9

A7

Bm7

HERE'S HOW

1. The first finger plays the D string, the ring finger plays the D and the little finger plays both 3rd frets on the B and E strings.

2. Here the middle finger plays the D string, the ring finger plays the B and the little finger plays the G note on the E string.

3. Start with the first finger on the A string, middle finger on the G, ring finger on the E and little finger on the B string.

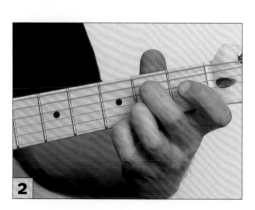

JAZZ GUITARISTS

Jazz is one area of popular music where the guitar is less than all powerful. If you ask an average listener what the key rock'n' roll instrument is, they'll tell you it's the electric guitar. Ask what the key jazz instrument is, though, and they'll more than likely tell you it's the saxophone. However, the guitar is a versatile instrument and one that has a way of forcing itself to the fore. In the early days of jazz, if it was used at all, it was only to provide a basic rhythmic accompaniment, while these days, in the hands of musicians like Pat Metheny or Bill Frisell, it's a well-respected lead instrument. So, ask the question again in another 50 years or so, and maybe you'll get a different answer.

The absence of guitar from the beginnings of jazz is easy to explain. Jazz has its roots in the marching bands of New Orleans, which produced such founding figures as the legendary Buddy Bolden and the immortal Louis Armstrong, and which were dominated by brass instruments. Thus early jazz combos featured horns, which are loud instruments, plus bass and drums. An unamplified acoustic guitar simply couldn't make itself heard over such a line-up. Banjos, which have a slightly more ringing tone, were used occasionally, but were still hard for primitive recording devices to pick up on. It was only with the development of the microphone in the 1920s that the acoustic guitar – till then generally associated with classical or folk music – made its way into jazz.

The man largely responsible for its introduction was Eddie Lang, an Italian-American whose real name was Salvatore Massaro (and would hide behind the alias 'Blind Willie Dunn' when he recorded blues records, in a rare instance of a white musician having to pretend to be black rather than vice versa). Single-handedly Lang demonstrated that the guitar could be used in jazz not only as a rhythm instrument – the way banjos had been used in the past – but, given a well placed microphone, as a lead instrument too. Lang played the first single string guitar solos on record and worked with all the great names of early jazz – Louis Armstrong, Kid Oliver, Joe Venuti, Bix Beiderdecke and others. In 1932 he teamed up with the vocalist Bing Crosby, who was the first in his field to understand the technical implications of microphone recording for a singer. Sadly, a year into their partnership, in 1933, Lang died following a botched tonsillectomy.

JAZZ GUITAR GIANTS

A year later the next great jazz guitar virtuoso emerged, and, to general amazement, he was not an American but a French gypsy named Django Reinhardt. His 1934 recordings with the Hot Club of France were revelatory. Django brought in the influences of European classical and gypsy folk music and suggested new possibilities not just for jazz guitar but for jazz itself. Despite having only two functioning fingers on one hand, Django was a prodigious virtuoso and also a notable composer whose 'Nuages' remains a staple for any aspiring jazz guitarist.

Not all jazz guitarists were as flamboyant as Lang and Reinhardt, however. Freddie Green, for example, stayed with Count Basie for nearly 50 years and throughout that time he was content to be the mainstay of the band. Nicknamed Mr Rhythm, Freddie Green stuck valiantly to his task. Where other guitarists took to single-string soloing and then to the new electric guitars, Freddie Green stuck to the often unnoticed but invaluable job of keeping a beat as regular and as organic as a heartbeat. There are plenty of contenders for the greatest jazz lead player of all time, but there's only one for the title of the greatest rhythm player.

FAR LEFT: *Charlie Christian – one of the formative jazz guitarists. Guitars were not central to the origins of jazz music, but have steadily become more influential.*

ELECTRIC REVOLUTION

If Freddie Green is one of the great unsung heroes of jazz guitar, the next great innovator is one of the great what-ifs. Like Eddie Lang before him, Charlie Christian revolutionized jazz guitar. Christian's great innovation was again linked to technology. In this case that innovation was the advent of the electric guitar.

Christian wasn't the first jazzman to go electric; another jazzman, Eddie Durham, had done that, playing first with Jimmie Lunceford, and then alongside Freddie Green in the Count Basie Band, which was where Christian first encountered his playing. After seeing Durham play, Christian went out and bought himself an electric guitar, and within two years he was playing with Benny Goodman, and almost single-handedly writing a new vocabulary for his instrument. With the power of the electric guitar he was able to make the instrument swing like a horn; indeed many of the innovations Charlie Parker would come up with on the saxophone were at least partially anticipated by Christian's work with Goodman. Sadly, after just three years as a recording artist, Charlie Christian contracted TB and died in 1942. His small stack of recorded works are a jazz guitar treasure trove to rank alongside Robert Johnson's blues recordings.

PUSHING THE BOUNDARIES

Christian's innovations were immediately followed up by other guitarists. Another key player of the 1940s and 1950s was George Barnes, whose 1946 recording of 'Lover Come Back To Me', on which the guitar was the only solo instrument, backed by bass, drums and rhythm guitar, really pushed the boundaries forward and anticipated the work of the next great pioneer in the field, Tal Farlow.

Farlow was working as a sign painter when he heard Charlie Christian on the radio and promptly decided to take up the guitar. He taught himself how to play all of Charlie Christian's solos by listening to Benny Goodman records. He then moved to New York and played with the likes of Buddy deFranco, Artie Shaw and Red Norvo, before making a series of recordings under his own name in the 1950s that established him as one of the greatest jazz guitarists of all time. His innovations included a willingness to use the whole range of the guitar to play solo lines, and a fondness for chromatic chords, all coupled with extraordinary speed, a distinctly unorthodox technique and, of course, a continued adherence to the central jazz tenet that it don't mean a thing if it ain't got that swing.

The other great name of 1950s jazz guitar was Barney Kessel from Muskogee, Oklahoma. Another Charlie Christian disciple, he picked

ABOVE: *Virtuoso jazz guitarist Django Reinhardt is pictured here jamming with Duke Ellington and his band in 1939.*

the opposite coast to Farlow and moved to Los Angeles, where he worked on the Marx Brothers live show as well as recording with Charlie Ventura, Roy Eldridge and Artie Shaw. From the mid 1950s on he concentrated on recording rather than touring and, while he was an avowed disciple of Christian, his career could hardly have panned out more differently. Christian's playing survives on only a handful of discs and was, initially at least, mostly an influence on fellow guitarists. Barney Kessel, by contrast, played on literally thousands of recordings and is probably more than any other individual, responsible for instilling the notion of the jazz guitar in the popular consciousness. In fact, he may be one of the most recorded musicians in the history of recorded music.

Not all jazz guitarists followed Christian's electric lead however. Charlie Byrd, a jazz guitarist who'd studied with the classical guitar legend Andres Segovia in the mid 1950s, began to play the concert (acoustic) guitar in a jazz setting. Byrd's first successes saw him incorporating classical influences into his playing, but the record that made him an international star brought in a more exotic influence, that of the Brazilian samba. In 1962 Charlie Byrd had travelled to South America, and on his return to the US he recorded the classic *Jazz Samba* with Stan Getz, which became a huge hit with the wider public.

Popular though it was, the jazz samba movement was something of a passing craze. The next major innovator in jazz guitar was yet another Christian disciple, Wes Montgomery. After an apprenticeship spent playing rhythm guitar with the Lionel Hampton band, he formed The Wes Montgomery Trio and made a string of classic recordings between 1959 and 1963. Wes Montgomery's particular gift was for melodic improvization. He could make the most hackneyed jazz standard sound fresh. What marked him out to the casual listener, however, was the warmth of his sound, achieved by using his thumb rather than a pick, like almost all his predecessors.

So popular was this warm sound that from 1963 his records became increasingly oriented toward a mass market, full of orchestration and contemporary pop tunes. These recordings were more significant for their commercial success than for the musical qualities, and hardly go down well with jazz-guitar purists. However, they made Wes Montgomery a household name and helped elevate the guitar to a whole new level in American popular music. Wes Montgomery died suddenly of a heart attack in 1968. He left behind a legacy that included changing the guitar's place in popular culture. For the jazz guitarist who concentrates on his earlier work with the trio, he left an unsurpassed musical legacy. He also had an enormous influence on his contemporaries,

BELOW: *Pat Metheny is a leading modern Jazz guitarist, a musician with an accessible style who is not afraid of experimentation.*

including great melodic jazzers like Grant Green and Jimmy Raney.

By the time Wes Montgomery died in 1969 the electric guitar had been well and truly claimed by rock'n'roll, and for jazz guitarists that came after Wes the influence of Jimi Hendrix is often just as potent as that of Charlie Christian.

ROCK INFLUENCES

The first major jazz figure to take on board the influence of rock music was the great Miles Davis. From the late 1960s onwards his bands almost always included fiery lead guitarists, from John McLaughlin, who played with him on the epochal *Bitches Brew*, to Mike Stern and John Scofield, who accompanied him in his latter years.

Bitches Brew ushered in an era of jazz rock, which saw players crossing over from both sides of the musical divide. Rock guitarists like Frank Zappa and the Soft Machine's Allan Holdsworth became increasingly influenced by jazz, while jazz-schooled players from Larry Coryell to Sonny Sharrock found themselves incorporating rock dynamics into their technically complex playing. At its worst jazz rock would see technique being prized a long way ahead of creativity – as if all guitarists were locked in a battle to see who could play the most notes in the shortest period of time. At its best, though, if you return to Miles Davis' records like the aforementioned *Bitches Brew* and *In A Silent Way*, this was a period that opened up new possibilities for jazz guitarists, allowing them to step out of the overly polite formula that the success of Wes Montgomery and others had ushered in.

Not of course that the We Montgomery tradition simply died out. Instead it developed into what became known as jazz funk – essentially mellow dance music with a jazz feel. Notable players in this area were Earl Klugh, Robben Ford (another Miles Davis alumnus) Eric Gale and above all George Benson. A fine underrated guitarist in the Montgomery mould, and a smooth soulful singer, George Benson hit the big time with the multimillion selling *Breezin'* and never looked back.

In complete contrast to the smooth sound of Benson are those guitarists intent on pushing jazz to its sonic limits. These include the likes of Ornette Coleman's sideman James Blood Ulmer and the subtle experimentalist Bill Frisell.

Undoubtedly the most popular out and out guitarist in the jazz world today is Pat Metheny, a musician who takes his inspiration from jazz, classical and rock music, but has fused them all into a sound that can only be classified as Pat Metheny jazz guitar.

CHARLIE CHRISTIAN

1916–1942
BAND: **SESSION MUSICIAN**
HEIGHT OF FAME: **1930s**

Charlie Christian was the founding father and primary architect of the modern jazz-guitar style. He was the first major soloist on the electric guitar. Before Christian guitarists were predominately un-amplified acoustic musicians who were relegated to strict rhythm-guitar roles in an ensemble. With Christian the electric guitar became a distinct solo voice, equivalent to a saxophone, trumpet or clarinet, and capable of the same levels of expressiveness and intensity. Following Christian's initial appearance and short career, a school of disciples emerged – not only jazz players like Barney Kessel and Tal Farlow, but also blues and rock guitarists from T-Bone Walker to Scotty Moore, all of whom spread his influence far and wide.

RIGHT: *Charlie Christian was a pioneer in the field of electric jazz guitar in the blues, and as such cast an influence that reached up to the likes of Hendrix and Clapton.*

Charles Henry Christian was born in Bonham, Texas, on 29 July 1916. The young Charles took informal guitar lessons from his father and became serious about the instrument in 1933, when, along with his friend, T-Bone Walker, he took lessons from Ralph 'Big-Foot Chuck' Hamilton. Then in 1937 Christian bought his first electric guitar, probably a Gibson ES 150, and began to assemble the components of his horn-like approach. His distinctive sound soon made him a regional star and in July 1939, jazz producer John Hammond set up an audition with Benny Goodman. Christian was hired and relocated to New York City.

Charlie Christian's playing on tunes like 'Air Mail Special', 'Honeysuckle Rose', and 'Solo Flight' soon made him one of the biggest names of the swing era. By 1940 he was pushing the boundaries further, mixing with the new bebop musicians like Dizzy Gillespie and Thelonious Monk. Sadly he had always been troubled

by respiratory problems and on 2 March 1942 he died from tuberculosis. In a period of less than three years, Charlie Christian had emerged from total obscurity to produce a copious body of material which forever altered the course of guitar playing in jazz.

THE CHARLIE CHRISTIAN GUITAR SOUND

Charlie Christian is the man responsible for what we all now think of as the classic jazz guitar sound. Christian favoured Gibson arch-top hollow-body guitars, generally with f-holes, equipped with built-in electromagnetic pick-ups. The second important element was the amplification. Christian used Gibson EH (Electric Hawaiian) amplifiers, the EH 150 and the EH 185. Using this equipment with its combination of a pick-up in the neck position, a resonant hollow body and relatively small, not particularly powerful, amps, Christian achieved a thick, but clean, tone which was well suited to the single note lines of his impeccable solos.

CHARLIE CHRISTIAN'S GIBSONS

Charlie Christian's favourite guitar was the Gibson ES 150. Gibson announced the production of the first Electric Spanish guitar, the ES 150 in mid-1936 as 'Another miracle by Gibson – a true, undistorted tone amplified by electricity.'

One of its earliest fans was Count Basie's guitarist Eddie Durham who persuaded Charlie Christian to try one out. The rest, of course, is history and it wasn't long before the ES 150 became known to one and all as the 'Charlie Christian model'. Christian is known to have played at least three different ES 150s during his short career. The ES 150 was a non-cutaway acoustic with a carved spruce arch top and maple back and sides. It had a mahogany neck, a rosewood fingerboard and an ebony bridge.

The ES 150 was fitted with a single bar pickup, also now known as a 'Charlie Christian pickup', which was adjustable for height and could be tilted slightly. The pickup itself was close to the fingerboard, which gave the guitar

a deep bass-heavy tone. Christian adjusted the pickup closer to the body, away from the strings. This resulted in a warmer, mellow tone quality, with less output.

Christian also played the Gibson ES 250 guitar. Introduced in late 1939, this was basically an L-7 type with a larger, superior-grade 17in (43cm) body, inlays on the fingerboard, and a modified Charlie Christian pickup with a deeply notched blade to better balance the string response. Christian is thought to have played at least four of these models between 1939 and 1942.

LEFT: *Charlie Christian's Gibson guitars provided a clarity of sound essential for the basic early recording techniques.*

I Found a New Baby

ALBUM: **THE GENIUS OF THE ELECTRIC GUITAR**
SONGWRITERS: **SPENCER WILLIAMS, JACK PALMER**
RECORDED: **COLOMBIA STUDIOS, NEW YORK**
PRODUCER: **N/A**

All great jazz players can slip easily between complex chords and playing lead runs and scales. You can use this passage to practise this technique. Movement between the notes needs to be smooth and sound easy. Holding a 'chord shape' means you can play individual notes much more quickly. Make the shapes shown and practise moving between them. Try to make the pattern flow and sound easy so that your fingers begin to move naturally to the frets.

BASIC SONG RIFF

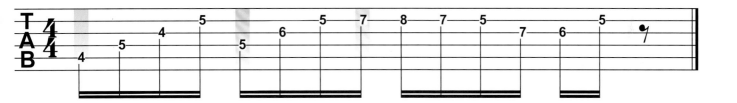

HERE'S HOW

1 Use your first finger on the A string and second finger on the G string. Use your ring and little finger on the D and B strings.

2 Slide up one fret to make this shape and practise forming the shape using first, middle and ring fingers – practise moving between these shapes.

3 Slip between the chord shape and single note section by using your little finger at the 7th fret of the B string on this part.

DJANGO REINHARDT

1910–1953
BAND: **QUINTET OF THE HOT CLUB OF FRANCE**
HEIGHT OF FAME: **1930s**

If the word 'genius' means anything perhaps it should refer to those whose talents are impossible to classify. Such a person was the gypsy guitarist, Django Reinhardt. Reinhardt was not a trained musician in the ordinary sense. He never learned to read and write – words or music. However, his instrumental technique was so unorthodox and his music so brilliant that it amazed fellow guitar players the world over. Almost all the great jazz guitarists of the second half of the twentieth century have acknowledged their debt to him. Some, like Joe Pass and Herb Ellis, have even recorded tributes to him.

RIGHT: *Django Reinhardt was actually one of a number of gypsy jazz guitarists making their presence felt in Europe during the 1930s, but he achieved fame through playing alongside the likes of Stephane Grapelli.*

Jean Baptiste 'Django' Reinhardt was born on 23 January 1910, in Liverchies, Belgium, but grew up in a gypsy camp outside Paris. He first studied violin, then proceeded to a banjo-guitar. By the time he was 13 he was good enough to play in Parisian dance halls, and in 1922 he began professional work. In 1928, however, he was the victim of a caravan fire, resulting in major damage to the first two fingers of his left hand. Despite this setback, Reinhardt managed to develop a revolutionary two-finger technique.

By 1930 Reinhardt was playing in public in Paris again and taking in the influence of American jazz musicians like Louis Armstrong, Duke Ellington and guitarist Eddie Lang. In 1934 he met violinist Stephane Grappelli, with whom he founded the Quintet of the Hot Club of France. The group achieved international acclaim within a year and recorded some 200 sides including such classic original compositions as 'Djangology', 'Minor Swing' and the international hit, 'Nuages' before World War II put their career on hold. After the war, Reinhardt toured the United States with

Ellington in 1946, where he played an amplified guitar for the first time, but the critics were dismissive of his work. Reinhardt returned to Europe, thoroughly disillusioned with the United States. Back in France he turned his musical interest to bebop, continuing to play an electric guitar. He died from a stroke at the age of 43 on 16 May 1953 in Fontainebleau, France.

DJANGO'S FINGERS

On the morning of 2 November 1928, Django was engulfed in a fire in the caravan in which he was living. He was taken to hospital where it was found that, amongst other terrible injuries, the two middle fingers of his left hand were welded together. After six months of constant treatment, the burnt flesh was moulded back into the shape of two fingers, but they were paralyzed and useless. Nevertheless, a doctor suggested to his relatives that they bring Django a guitar.

Overcoming terrible pain Django worked furiously with his left hand and finally managed to devise a new chording technique to compensate for the loss of the use of the fingers. He used his damaged third and fourth fingers to a limited extent on the first two strings and used the first and second left-hand fingers most of the time in single-note work. Most innovative, though, was the way in which he would play his octave passages on any two strings, with a 'damped' string in between, i.e., on first and third; second and fourth; third and fifth; etc., so as to avoid rushing up and down the fingerboard. His chromatic runs, meanwhile, if played in the first position, were fingered; or if played up the fingerboard, he would gliss them with one finger.

Inevitably, Reinhardt sought out unusual chord shapes using his damaged fingers. He also made extraordinary use of his good right hand. If you are lucky enough to see archive footage of Django, just watch and wonder: this is one guitarist whose style it could take a lifetime to emulate.

LEFT: *Reinhardt's hand injury led to his playing some unique chord progressions and distinctive melodies.*

Nuages

ALBUM: **VARIOUS COMPILATIONS**
WRITTEN BY: **DJANGO REINHARDT, JACQUES LARUE**
RECORDED: **VARIOUS RECORDINGS**
PRODUCER: **N/A**

This is a gorgeous tune played by the master of jazz guitar. Although you may not be able to accomplish some of Django's more dazzling runs, the tab shown here gives you the basic theme of 'Nuages' which you should be able to master with a little practice. To exercise fingers, practise ascending and descending runs on the B string as shown. Get used to moving between lead runs and chords with ease.

BASIC SONG RIFF

swing

HERE'S HOW

1 Starting at the 8th fret on the B string with your little finger, start the descending run using your ring, middle and first fingers.

2 Move from the descending run on the B string to this chord using all four fingers. Practise the run then form the chord straight after.

3 Play the B string with your first finger; your middle finger plays the G string, and your ring and little fingers play the A and D strings.

PAT METHENY

1954–

BAND: **PAT METHENY GROUP**

HEIGHT OF FAME: **1980s–90s**

Pat Metheny is the most influential jazz guitarist of modern times. His style looks backwards and forwards at the same time. On the one hand he comes out of the jazz tradition – he plays guitar almost like a horn player, with an extraordinarily loose, fluid style. On the other hand, he has constantly embraced new technology to become one of the great pioneers in using guitar synthesizers, from the 1980s onwards.

Pat Metheny was born into a musical family in Kansas City on 12 August 1954. Starting on trumpet at the age of eight, Metheny switched to guitar at age 12. By 15, he was working regularly with the best jazz musicians in Kansas City. He burst onto the international jazz scene in 1974, playing with vibraphone great Gary Burton, before releasing his first album, *Bright Size Life*, in 1975. Over the years, he has performed with artists as diverse as Steve Reich, Ornette Coleman, Joni Mitchell and David Bowie. He has been part of a writing team with keyboardist Lyle Mays for more than 20 years. His body of work includes compositions for solo guitar, small ensembles and large orchestras.

Metheny was one of the very first jazz musicians to treat the synthesizer as a serious musical instrument. He was also instrumental in the development of several new kinds of guitar, such as the soprano acoustic guitar, the 42-string Pikasso guitar, Ibanez's PM-100 jazz guitar, and a variety of other custom instruments.

He has won 15 Grammy Awards including an unprecedented seven consecutive Grammys for seven consecutive albums. His extraordinary popularity for a jazz artist has been cemented by his non-stop touring – Metheny has actually spent most of his life on tour, averaging between 120–240 shows a year since 1974.

RIGHT: *Pat Metheny is a major tour artist. He does not have just one single musical identity, but shifts styles according to the demands of his audience and musical genre.*

ROLAND GR300

Synthesizers appeared on the music scene during the late 1960s and early 1970s. These early models invariably used keyboards to control them, and thus it was only keyboard players who used them at first.

Soon the synthesizer manufacturers started work on designing a synthesizer that could be triggered by a guitar rather than a keyboard. Early models included the Arp Avatar and the Korg X911 but most of these units were severely flawed. Some did not allow string bending and others mis-triggered if you held a note too long, or in some cases if you didn't hold it long enough. This forced the guitarist to play very slowly and deliberately. Forget slides, harmonics, and even sloppy but spirited playing: if you couldn't play every single note clearly and directly, you might as well have turned the unit off.

Then came the Roland GR300. This was the first guitar synth that had the speed and accuracy of response to allow a guitarist to play like a guitarist rather than simply concentrating on cleanly triggering the module. It offered a range of processing options and the accompanying floor unit could be set to play root and harmonic duets. Pat Metheny was an early adopter. 'I just picked the GR300 up and I couldn't believe it, because it worked,' he told *Guitar Player* magazine, 'I could play all my kind of weird phrasings and it translated.'

Remarkably enough, after two decades of further technical innovation, Metheny still plays the GR300, and it remains one of the greatest guitar synths ever manufactured.

BELOW: *Pat Metheny's studio collaborations have included the likes of jazz players such as Charlie Haden, Dave Holland, Roy Haynes and Ornette Coleman.*

Travels

ALBUM: **TRAVELS**
SONGWRITERS: **PAT METHENY, LYLE MAYS**
RECORDED: **RECORDED LIVE IN DALLAS, TEXAS**
PRODUCERS: **PAT METHENY, MANFRED EICHER**

This is a lovely melody by Pat Metheny from the album Travels. *The individual notes should be picked with a nice clear tone; listen to the theme of the piece a few times to get the melody in your head. The melody is shown over two strings, so practise moving with ease between both. If you play along with the record try to improvise a few of your own notes within the theme.*

BASIC SONG RIFF

HERE'S HOW

1 Your little finger will play this 6th fret on the B string. Practice getting the phrasing exactly right with your picking hand.

2 Here your first finger plays the A note on the G string. Experiment with phrasing and your own notes when you play around this lovely theme.

ABOVE: *Pat Metheny's guitar style with the Pat Metheny Group is difficult to locate. While sitting recognizably in the category of jazz, it also makes incursions into the territories of funk, pop and easy listening.*

Phase Dance

ALBUM: **PAT METHENY GROUP**
SONGWRITERS: **PAT METHENY, LYLE MAYS**
RECORDED AT: **TALENT STUDIOS, OSLO**
PRODUCED BY: **MANFRED EICHER**

The tab for this riff calls for smooth interaction between the three highest strings (E, B and G). By playing two notes together on the B and G strings it gives the tune a lovely ringing quality. You can let your first finger do the work by covering all the notes at the 5th fret across all three strings. Practise your picking technique, switching between two notes on the B and G strings and single notes on the E string.

BASIC SONG RIFF

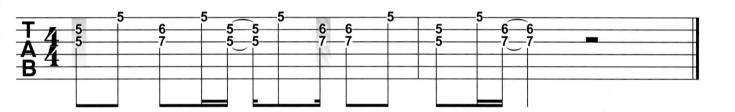

HERE'S HOW

1 Notice how the first finger covers all the notes at the 5th fret on all three strings. Get used to moving between double and single notes.

2 Use your middle and ring fingers for these notes on the B and G strings. This keeps the first finger free to cover single notes on the E string.

The whole riff is based around this pattern. Learn to play it fluently, speeding up as you get more comfortable and confident.

COUNTRY GUITARISTS

Country music in its earliest form is essentially the rural folk music of America, as brought over by settlers from Europe in general, and the British Isles in particular. There's no magical moment of beginning. Whether one considers an act like the Carter Family, recording in the 1920s, to be 'country' or 'folk', it's hardly a scientific distinction. Broadly speaking, one might say that the transition from rural singers entertaining their communities with renditions of folk songs to professional artists recording original material with its roots in the folk style is the transition from folk to country. By the 1930s, the success of acts like the Carter Family had put country music firmly on the musical map.

Just as the precise origins of country music are difficult to pinpoint, so too is the moment at which the guitar became a major instrument within it. The guitar had arrived in America with early European settlers, and gradually European guitar makers came to America and began building instruments there. They were still fairly rarefied instruments, however, until the Industrial Revolution of the late 1800s came along, and with it the technology to mass produce musical instruments, amongst them the guitar. Even then, however, the guitar was originally still seen as more suitable for classical music, as it didn't produce enough volume to compete with the fiddles and banjos popular with the folk-based string bands of the day. The appearance of the louder steel string guitars changed that a bit, but it was only the adoption of the guitar by black Southern blues players that really started to spark the instrument's popularity.

Gradually white musicians started trying the new instruments out and, by the early 1900s, quite a few white rural string bands featured guitars. Typical in this respect was one of the first significant country guitar players, Sam McGee, later to play in the band at the Grand Ole Opry. He learned about guitar picking from black railroad workers who played during their lunch breaks near his Tennessee home.

As folk musicians and string bands started developing the rudiments of what we would now recognize as country music, so the popularity of the guitar spread, helped hugely by the fact that cheaply produced models were appearing in the new mail order catalogues. The first major country music star was Jimmie Rodgers, 'the singing brakeman'. He played a guitar and provided a huge further boost to the instrument's popularity. Jimmie Rodgers helped sell many guitars in the late 1920s and early 1930s through his use of the instrument.

Gradually the first country guitar stylists began to emerge. First there was the Carter Family's Maybelle Carter. She developed her famous drop-thumb guitar style, as typified by her solo work on 'Wildwood Flower', providing the inspiration for generations of country pickers. Then came Karl Farr of The Sons of the Pioneers. His acoustic guitar playing began to show a distinct jazz influence, derived from players like Django Reinhardt. Soon country guitarists like California's Porky Freeman started to show levels of virtuosity only previously seen in the jazz field – as illustrated by Freeman's hit recording of 'Boogie Woogie on the Strings' or Zeb Turner's 'Zeb's Mountain Boogie'.

PICKING PIONEERS

Perhaps the definitive country music guitar style is the fingerpicking style, more particularly the syncopated Western Kentucky thumb and index finger picking style pioneered by Kennedy Jones. Jones himself used a thumb pick, but his style formed the basis for the picking of Ike Everly and Mose Rager, who in turn taught the style to the man who would bring it to a much wider audience, the great Merle Travis.

Travis was born in Rosewood, Kentucky, on 29 November 1917. He became fascinated with the playing of Everly and Rager and made a point of showing up whenever they performed in the area. Later he formed a group called the Drifting Pioneers who, in 1939, joined the musical staff at 50,000-Watt WLW Radio in Cincinnati. His abilities as a guitar soloist were obvious to the management, and he began playing on the station regularly, helping to spread the gospel of fingerpicking.

One such listener to WLW was the then 16-year-old Chet Atkins. Travis's playing immediately inspired him. In March 1944 Travis moved to Los Angeles, where he quickly found work as a sideman

FAR LEFT: *Scotty Moore was the guitar sound behind Elvis Presley, his talent immortalized in records such as 'That's All Right' and 'Jailhouse Rock'.*

with the western swing bands of Porky Freeman and Ray Whitley. In 1945 he recorded his first disc under his own name. The following year his disciple Chet Atkins made his own debut with a recording of *Guitar Blues*, a laid-back, late night blues recorded on electric guitar.

By 1946, Travis' reputation was such that he'd begun doing session work for Capitol Records, the major independent label on the West Coast. In March, Travis was signed to Capitol as a solo artist. He soon began taking guitar breaks on his records, which became extremely influential. By the late 1940s Travis was established as the nation's top country guitarist. Chet Atkins' popularity was, meanwhile, only just beginning to build after his 1947 signing to RCA Victor.

POSTWAR DEVELOPMENTS

A number of other fine guitarists developed in the wake of Travis, among them the Texas-based singer and band-leader Hank Thompson, who had a string of hits in the 1940s and 1950s. He became an excellent fingerpicker, following Merle Travis's example to the point of having Gibson custom-build him a Super 400 electric.

By 1950 Chet Atkins had started to come out from Travis's shadow. He'd had a solo spot on the Opry as Red Foley's guitarist around 1946, and then worked as a sideman until Steve Sholes signed him to RCA in 1947. It soon became apparent, however, that Chet's direction was more oriented towards instrumentals, and RCA began to release instrumental sides by him which quickly became popular.

It's no doubt largely because he recorded as an instrumentalist that Chet Atkins is a better known as a guitarist than Merle Travis. While Travis was concentrating on a career as a singer, songwriter and guitarist, Chet was almost exclusively recording instrumentals. While Merle was recording vocals for Capitol, Chet was racking up numerous instrumental hits and gaining a strong reputation for his work in the fledgling Nashville recording scene. Chet also developed a style that differed significantly from Travis as he started to incorporate the influences of non-country instrumentalists like Les Paul and Django Reinhardt.

Many other guitarists began to be influenced by Atkins, not just in the US but also in the UK, where he was a big influence on the likes of George Harrison and even Ritchie Blackmore. Many of them were unaware how much actually came from Merle Travis. One American guitarist who learned from both Chet and Merle was Scotty Moore. When, in the summer of 1954, Scotty started working with Elvis Presley on his epochal Sun sessions, and Presley recorded his version of 'That's All Right', Moore's accompaniment was straight out of Travis and Atkins' style book.

Other legendary early rock stylists heavily influenced by the Atkins/Travis style included Eddie Cochran, Duane Eddy, and, above all, Jerry Reed, who took the Atkins/Travis styles a quantum leap ahead. Reed began as a rocker, recording for Capitol, but by the 1960s he was a Nashville studio musician with his own style of fingerpicking. Where Travis used the thumb and index finger almost exclusively, and Atkins used his thumb and at least two other fingers, Reed used them all.

Chet Atkins and his followers are all, of course, associated with the electric guitar, typically the big bodied Gretsches. However, acoustic stylists, generally working in the acoustic style that was starting to became known as bluegrass, were making their own innovations. Lester Flatt developed a dynamic guitar style full of bass runs while playing first with Bill Monroe's Blue Grass Boys and then with Earl Scruggs. Other fine bluegrass guitarists included The Stanley Brothers' George Shuffler, who crosspicked his instrument, and guitarist Doc Watson who came up with the idea of fingerpicking fiddle tunes.

In the mainstream of country music, however, it was electric guitars that ruled the roost by the 1960s. Scotty Moore's innovations were developed by the Telecaster-playing James Burton working successively with Ricky Nelson, Elvis Presley and Emmylou Harris. Bakersfield country star Buck Owens was another fine electric stylist, as was his regular lead player Don Rich, and fellow Bakersfield legend Merle Haggard's guitarist Roy Nichols. Glen Campbell was another artist best known as a singer, but actually a formidable guitarist as well, who played on a huge number of 1960s country and pop hits, even working with Phil Spector.

ABOVE: *Chet Atkins – aka 'Mister Guitar' – was a pioneer of what is today known as the Nashville sound, and he helped the spread of popular country music.*

In the 1970s country got a shot in the arm as the outlaw movement rejected the 'countrypolitan' blandness of much Nashville fare. The outlaws – Waylon Jennings, Willie Nelson and others – wanted to give the music some rock 'n' roll attitude and, of course, that meant turning up their guitars. Waylon Jennings' aggressive Telecaster came to the forefront, as did that of the British guitar hero Albert Lee, when he was drafted in to take over James Burton's role with Emmylou Harris's Hot Band. The Telecaster remained the country guitar of choice well into the 1980s, thanks to the likes of Dwight Yoakam's guitarist Pete Anderson and the session ace Jerry Donohue. By the turn of the decade, acts like the internationally massive Garth Brooks, with his lead-guitar player James Garver, were leading county music and country guitar playing right into the mainstream.

During the 1990s, perhaps as a reaction to the new popular country, acoustic country had something of a revival, considerably inspired by Willie Nelson's distinctively jazzy approach on the one hand and the technical bluegrass flash of players like Tony Rice and Ricky Skaggs on the other. These days, country music finds itself at a point where it's looking backwards and forwards at the same time, with guitar players studying the approach of Merle Travis and Maybelle Carter, then figuring out how to take it to the next stage.

SIGNATURE GUITARS

Jimmie Rodgers appears to have been the first country singer to have a guitar model named for him, when Weymann created their 'Jimmie Rodgers Special' model in 1930. This started a trend. As country music began to develop stars, so the manufacturers used their success to sell more guitars. In 1932 a WLS National Barn Dance singer, 'Arkie the Arkansas Woodchopper', had Martin guitars build him one of their large D-2 'dreadnought' guitars with a herringbone wood trim. It became the classic Martin D-28. The following year his fellow Barn Dance star, Gene Autry, had Martin build him an elaborate pearl inlaid version that became the D-45. And while these were top-of-the-range instruments, there was also an obvious market for cheap instruments that bore a star's endorsement. So Sears Roebuck began marketing its inexpensive 'Gene Autry' guitars in the 1930s, and these were the first guitars many young future guitar stars owned. The practice has continued to flourish ever since and today Martin Guitars manufacture signature models endorsed by a whole range of country stars from Johnny Cash to Willie Nelson, as well as historical models replicating guitars used by the likes of Hank Williams and even Gene Autry.

FINGERPICKING

The basic fingerpicking style (known as the 'choke' style) consists of the right-hand index finger picking out the melody while the thumb, usually equipped with a pick, plucks out a constant alternating bass accompaniment. The net result is a self-contained, rich, varied sound that gives the illusion of a lead and rhythm guitar being played simultaneously. Talented players have introduced their own individual variations of the basic style to create a personal sound. Merle Travis, for instance, would also brush the fourth, third, and second strings with the thumb on the upstroke while muting the strings with the right hand so as to create a percussive accompaniment. On occasion, Travis would add even more variety by interjecting a single-string melody.

The earliest fingerpicking styles evolved slowly, handed down from guitarist to guitarist in the Appalachian regions. One of the first influential guitarists from this area was a black bluesman from Louisville, Kentucky, named Sylvester Weaver, allegedly the first blues guitarist to ever record. His 1924 recording of 'Smoketown Strut' demonstrates the basic elements of what we have since come to think of as country fingerpicking. His intricate style led his label to dub him 'the man with the talking guitar'. The same tag would be given to Merle Travis in later years.

Another black guitarist, Arnold Schultz, may have had an even greater impact on the development of Kentucky fingerstyle. Though segregation was the norm back then, Western Kentucky seemed surprisingly open-minded to musical integration, and Schultz was a favourite at white square dances where he met and influenced, among others, a young Bill Monroe. Kennedy Jones was another guitarist influenced by Arnold Schulz. He in turn influenced Mose Rager and his long-time friend Ike Everly (father of Don and Phil), two former coalminers who started playing together in the early 1930s, and influenced many budding guitarists, among them the great Merle Travis.

MAYBELLE CARTER

1909–1978
BAND: **THE CARTER FAMILY**
HEIGHT OF FAME: **1930S–40S**

'If it hadn't been for Mother Maybelle,' said music writer Hazel Smith, 'Jimi Hendrix might have been a banjo player.' This may be overstating the case a little, but there is no doubt that Maybelle Carter is one of the absolute pioneers in modern guitar playing. Every folk and country guitarist owes something to Maybelle Carter and most realize as much. Most blues and rock guitarists also owe her something as well, but hardly any of them appreciate it.

Maybelle Carter, playing with the Carter Family, single-handedly introduced the guitar as a lead instrument in country music. She took an instrument solely used for rhythm and basic chord accompaniment, and by devising her own technique for playing a bass-string melody accompanied by brushed chords on the treble strings, brought it to the forefront of popular music, a position it has held ever since.

Born Maybelle Addington in Nickelsville, Virginia, in 1909, Maybelle Carter grew up in a rural, mountain-dwelling family that spent much of their time playing music for social reasons. By the age of 12 she was known as a fine instrumentalist. In due course she formed a group, The Carter Family, along with her cousin Sara and her husband A.P. Carter, eventually coming to the attention of the Victor Talking Machine Company.

The recordings made by the Carter Family were an immediate hit and Maybelle used her first royalty check to purchase a Gibson L-5 archtop, the best model available from Gibson at the time, costing the then astronomical sum of $250. Armed with this new guitar, Maybelle helped the Carters to record a repertoire of folk and country songs that became the bedrock of American folk music – including the likes of 'Little Darling Pal of Mine', 'Keep on the Sunny

RIGHT: *Maybelle Carter (centre) with The Carter Family. Armed with Gibson guitars, Carter helped lay the foundations of modern bluegrass and country.*

Side', 'Wildwood Flower' and 'Will the Circle Be Unbroken?'

After the Carter Family dissolved as a group, Maybelle eventually formed a band with her daughters, Helen, Anita and June, which revived the original Carter Family's music in the late 1960s. Mother Maybelle, as she was known to the world, died in 1978.

GIBSON L-5

When Maybelle Carter bought her Gibson L-5 archtop in 1929, it cost proportionally as much as a new car today. However, it was an extremely sound investment, as she used the Gibson L-5 for nearly every recording and personal appearance for the next ten years. While on tour with The Carter Family in the 1950s, Elvis Presley would often borrow the Gibson from Carter when he broke a string on his own guitar.

The Gibson has a l6in (40.6cm) wide body, narrow snakehead peghead, maple neck and ebony fingerboard with white binding and dot inlay. It was originally set with banjo pegs, but Maybelle customized the guitar over the years with replacement tuners, pickguard and tailpiece.

Following Maybelle's death the guitar remained in the care of her family. It was loaned to the Country Music Hall of Fame in 1998 but was reclaimed in 2004 and put up for sale. Billed as the most important guitar in the history of popular music it was put on the market by Gruhn Guitars of Nashville with the extraordinary price-tag of $575,000. The uncertain fate of the guitar made national headlines and a local philanthropist eventually stepped forward making a $1,000,000 donation to the Hall of Fame in order to keep the guitar on public display.

LEFT: *Maybelle Carter's Gibson L-5 archtop has become almost an icon in the country music community.*

Wildwood Flower

ALBUM: **WILDWOOD PICKIN'**
SONGWRITERS: **A.P. CARTER**
RECORDED : **RCA VICTOR STUDIOS, CAMDEN, NJ**
PRODUCER: **JEFF ZARAYA**

This intro sounds best played on an acoustic guitar. It is played on the bass strings, which establishes the rhythm before the chords come in. Although in the same key on the recorded version the tune is actually played on the high strings, but either way it sounds great. Maybelle Carter also used the hammer-on technique on the D string. Practise mixing hammer-ons with straight picked notes on the bass strings.

BASIC SONG RIFF

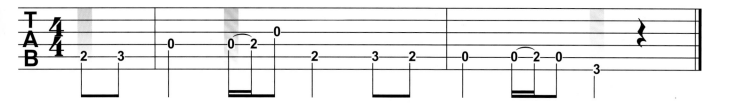

HERE'S HOW

1 Use your middle and ring finger for the move from B note on the A string to C note. Make those intro notes punchy and solid.

2 This is the hammer-on played with the middle finger on the D string, make sure you play the open G string straight after the hammer on.

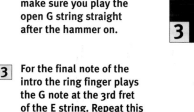

3 For the final note of the intro the ring finger plays the G note at the 3rd fret of the E string. Repeat this until you feel comfortable.

CHET ATKINS

1924–2001
BAND: **SOLO ARTIST**
HEIGHT OF FAME: **1950s–60s**

Unusually for an instrumental virtuoso, Chet Atkins was also an enormously influential producer. In fact it's fair to say that without Chet Atkins' production skills and musical vision, country music may never have crossed over into the pop charts in the 1950s and 1960s. During those decades, he helped create the Nashville sound, a style of country music that owed nearly as much to pop as it did to honky tonks. At the same time he was a consistently sensational guitar player, a musician who combined the complexity and technique of jazz with a country-pop sensitivity. Simply put, he was as classy as popular guitar playing gets.

RIGHT: *Chet Atkins earned the label 'Mister Guitar' on account of his exceptional talent with a country tune, and he is one of history's most recorded instrumental artists.*

He was born on 20 June 1924 in Lutrell, Tennessee. He didn't begin his musical career by playing guitar. Instead, on the recommendation of his older brother, Lowell, he began playing the fiddle. However, Chet soon became attracted to the guitar, and at the age of nine he traded a pistol for a guitar. Atkins learned his instrument rapidly, inspired by Merle Travis, becoming an accomplished player by the time he left high school in 1941.

After years playing live as a backing musician, word of his prowess reached Nashville, where RCA boss Steve Sholes made Atkins the studio guitarist for all of the RCA studio's Nashville sessions in 1949. The following year, Mother Maybelle and the Carter Sisters hired him as a regular on the Grand Ole Opry. While he worked for RCA, he played on many hit records and helped fashion the Nashville sound. In 1953 the label began to issue a number of instrumental albums that showcased Atkins' considerable talents. Not only did his records sell well, he designed guitars for Gibson and Gretsch; the popularity of these models continues to the present day. Atkins' career continued

to prosper. He became manager of RCA's Nashville division and, while his own recordings dwindled in popularity in the 1970s, his reputation revived again in the 1990s following duet albums with the likes of Jerry Reed and Mark Knopfler. During his career he received 11 Grammy awards and nine CMA Instrumentalist of the Year honours. He died of cancer in 2001.

CHET ATKINS' COUNTRY GENTLEMAN

Given that he was not only a musician but also a business-savvy Music Row executive, it's hardly surprising that Chet Atkins was one of the first guitarists to have his own signature model guitar put into production. The guitar in question was the 1958 Gretsch Country Gentleman. The Country Gentleman is considered by many to be one of the holy trinity of 1950s Gretsch guitars, along with the 6120 and White Falcon. The other two may be more eye-catching but the Country Gentleman, as its name suggests, has an elegance (and some would say playability) the others lack. The fact that George Harrison often played one doesn't hurt, either.

The Gentleman was released in 1958, after considerable input from Atkins, and it was placed between the 6120 and Falcon in price. Originally it had a 43cm (17in) single cutaway body with fake f-holes inlaid into the mahogany-finished maple top. The closed body was a concession to Atkins, who was constantly hounding Gretsch to produce a semi-hollow guitar with a solid block through the centre, like Gibson's ES 335, in order to get more sustain and less feedback. Some early 1960s Gentlemen also appear with real f-holes, though.

Gretsch kept on making the guitars, albeit with regular modifications, until 1978 when Atkins jumped ship to Gibson, taking the name with him. Gretsch renamed the guitar the Country Squire and kept on producing them, while Gibson now make a considerably different guitar under the Country Gentleman name. Atkins' own Gentleman recently came onto the market at a very reasonable $50,000.

LEFT: *The Gretsch Country Gentleman was Atkins' formative instrument until he moved to Gibson in 1978.*

Mr Bojangles

ALBUM: **ALMOST ALONE**
SONGWRITER: **JERRY JEFF WALKER**
RECORDED: **CA WORKSHOP; CREATIVE RECORDING, NASHVILLE**
PRODUCER: **CHET ATKINS**

The best way to play this lovely tune is to form a chord shape like a C; this will enable you to pick out the notes fluently with your picking hand. The tune is based around the chords C, Am and G7. Keep your fingers clear of the stings not being played. Keep notes clean and separate. Use up and down strokes with your plectrum, as this will help to increase speed.

BASIC SONG RIFF

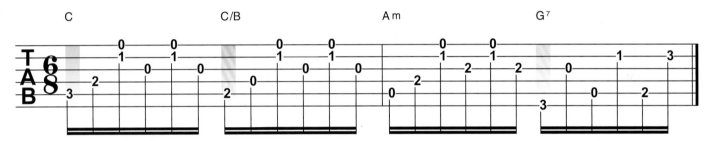

HERE'S HOW

1 This is the C chord minus the use of the E (6th) string. Pick out the notes shown in the tab from this shape.

2 Let the middle finger come up from the 2nd fret D string to play the B note on the 2nd fret of the A string.

3 For the third chord (A minor) use your middle finger at the second fret of the D string, ring finger at the second fret of the G string and first finger at the first fret of the B string.

SCOTTY MOORE

1931–2016
BAND: **ELVIS PRESLEY; SESSION MUSICIAN**
HEIGHT OF FAME: **1950s–60s**

Scotty Moore was one of the great pioneers of guitar. As Elvis' original guitarist he was at the heart of the fusion of country and R&B that came to be known as rockabilly. His sharp, memorable licks and keen sense of when to play hard and when to pull back complemented Presley's vocals perfectly. Also, while Moore is generally associated with Elvis' early material – particularly the groundbreaking recordings made at Sun Studios – he actually continued to play on the records until the late 1960s, with much of his finest work appearing on early RCA classics like 'Hound Dog' and 'Jailhouse Rock'.

RIGHT: *Scotty Moore is pictured here with the king of rock 'n' roll himself, Elvis Presley. Many critics believe that his recording of 'That's All Right' with Elvis in 1954 inaugurated the era of rock and pop.*

Scotty Moore was born Winfield Scott Moore III on 27 December 1931 on a farm near Gadsden, Tennessee. He began playing guitar at the age of eight, learning from family and friends. He enlisted in the US Navy in 1948, serving in Korea and China. Discharged in January 1952, Moore settled in Memphis. He formed a country band, recording a single for Sun Records in the spring of 1954. Soon afterwards the band met up with another hopeful, one Elvis Presley, and on 5 July 1954 the team recorded 'That's All Right', the first great rockabilly record.

At first, Moore and Black were almost equal partners with Presley, and Moore also became Presley's first manager. Soon, however, it became clear who the star was, but Scotty remained Elvis' favourite guitarist, integral to his sound. Moore's ongoing work with Elvis finally came to an end in the late 1960s, although he did make an appearance on stage with the King on his heralded 1968 television comeback special. Moore returned to the stage in the 1990s, performing with Carl Perkins and on Elvis tribute shows. He died on 28th June 2016, aged 84.

THE GUITAR THAT CHANGED THE WORLD

The Gibson L5 has been one of the great success stories of guitar history. Originally manufactured in the early years of prohibition, it is still in production – albeit in an updated version – over 80 years later. Along the way it has helped revolutionize folk and country (thanks to Maybelle Carter), jazz (courtesy of Wes Montgomery) and rock 'n' roll (pioneered by Scotty Moore).

Originally manufactured in 1922, the Gibson L5 is the precursor of the modern archtop guitar. It was the first archtop to feature f-holes, which allowed it to project through the horn-dominated bands of the day. Its strong, full, warm sound was an immediate and overwhelming success. As electrification was introduced, Gibson began to manufacture electric – or semi-acoustic – versions. Scotty Moore traded his previous guitar, a Gibson ES 295, for one of these on 7 July 1955 at Memphis' legendary music store, the O.K. Houck Piano Co.

Why the change? Scotty said it was simply 'because the workmanship was just so much better in the L5 – and,

of course, it cost more too.' It was first used to record 'Mystery Train' and featured on most of the subsequent RCA recordings until January 1957 – that's to say it was used to create the absolute, original classics of rock 'n' roll. Moore played it live as well, using a custom-built Echosonic amplifier by Ray Butts, which he acquired around April 1955, and which gave him the ability to perform live with his signature slap-back echo sound.

LEFT: *Scotty Moore was an ideal guitarist for Presley. His openly expressed philosophy of 'keep it simple' meant his guitar did not compete with the singer but still provided the driving force of rhythm and melody.*

Mystery Train

ALBUM: **VARIOUS COMPILATIONS**
SONGWRITERS: **HERMAN PARKER JR, SAM C. PHILLIPS**
RECORDED: **SUN STUDIO, MEMPHIS**
PRODUCER: **SAM C. PHILLIPS**

This riff makes use of the bass strings to create a lovely driving country rock sound. The riff starts with a hammer-on and is based around the chords E and A. The way Scotty Moore and the rhythm section play this tune actually makes it sound like a train. Try to achieve a rhythm like a train moving along. Practise picking bass notes before hitting chords. Use this technique on other intros.

BASIC SONG RIFF

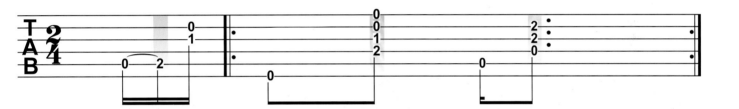

HERE'S HOW

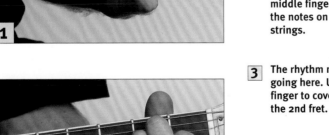

1 The middle finger is used for the hammer-on intro; this leaves the first finger ready to play the A flat note on the G string.

2 For this section play the open strings to form a chord. The first and middle fingers are holding the notes on the G and D strings.

3 The rhythm really gets going here. Use the first finger to cover all notes at the 2nd fret.

ECHOSONIC AMPLIFIER

The key to Scotty Moore's revolutionary guitar sound was his use of echo. And that echo was down to a remarkable amplifier, the Echosonic. Scotty first heard Chet Atkins using one. 'I don't remember the name of the record,' he recalled years later, 'but I heard one of Chet's instrumentals on the radio. His guitar had the same slap, but it was a little bit different to what I was used to hearing Sam Phillips do with us. I said, "Damn. How is he doing that?"'

After some investigation, Scotty located the man who made the amplifer, an accordion player and electronics whiz named Ray Butts, and bought one. It was only the third one ever to be made. The 25-Watt amp featured a built-in tape delay system that gave Scotty his slapback echo sound. Unlike studio echo, he was able to use this

live as well. Legend has it that in his early days of performing with Elvis the PAs that venues supplied were often so inadequate that sometimes Elvis himself would plug his mic into the Echosonic as well.

The first recording Moore used his new purchase on was 'Mystery Train' in July 1955. Thereafter, he employed it on every subsequent recording and performance throughout his career with Elvis, right up until their last appearance together, the 1968 NBC-TV special. Moore used it again when he returned to performing, but has since retired it for fear of damage in transit.

Only 68 Echosonics were ever produced, all handmade one at a time. Apart from Scotty and Chet Atkins, other owners included Carl Perkins and Roy Orbison. Scotty still has his to this day.

LEFT: *Scotty Moore on stage with Elvis during a 1950s TV show performance. Moore worked with Elvis through to the late 1960s.*

Heartbreak Hotel

ALBUM: **VARIOUS COMPILATIONS**
SONGWRITERS: **TOMMY DURDEN, MAE BOREN AXTON, ELVIS PRESLEY**
RECORDED: **RCA STUDIOS, NASHVILLE**
PRODUCER: **STEVE SHOLES**

This is a great tune to practise your rock 'n' roll licks on. The slower pace means you'll be able to use this tune to build up speed for faster songs. The solo shown on the tab is at the top of the neck and sounds great against a rock 'n' roll rhythm section. Use your ring and little fingers to slide up to the 12th fret to create a nice rock 'n' roll sound.

BASIC SONG RIFF

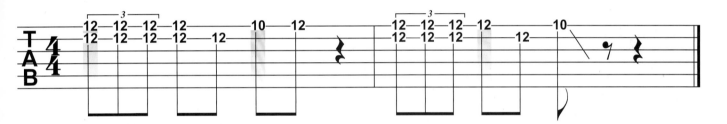

HERE'S HOW

1 Slide into the riff playing both E and B strings at the 12th fret. Practise this slide, as it's used a lot in rock 'n' roll.

2 Hold your first finger back ready to play the 10th fret on the E string. Keep in mind the rhythm to help you with your timing.

3 Accentuate the last two notes on the E string. All great guitar solos are tunes in their own right, so listen for the melody.

FOLK GUITARISTS

Folk music is notoriously hard to define, partly because different people use the term to refer to wildly different types of sound. Perhaps the most generally accepted definition is that folk music is the music of the people, passed down through the generations and performed as part of the life of a community, rather than as a commercial undertaking. However, even if you take this definition as a starting point, it can still include a huge variety of music – delta blues, Appalachian mountain music, bluegrass, Celtic or English traditional music, gospel music, union songs, traditional music from Africa, Asia, and other parts of the world.

On the other hand, there are plenty of people who use the term 'folk music' to mean 'anything that's played on the acoustic guitar'. It's a definition that allows all sorts of artists to be bracketed as 'folk'. The result of all this is that anyone from an earnest singer-songwriter through a 1960s protest singer to a 1920s sharecropper might be described as a folk musician. Believe it or not, they don't all play the guitar the same way!

Well, this is isn't the place to debate the rights or wrongs of such definitions. Instead we'll endeavour to give you a brief outline of some of the principal guitar styles that might be described as 'folk'.

THE AMERICAN TRADITION

First off, we'll look at the guitar styles that have developed out of American traditional music, particularly country and blues. Two of the key influences on folk guitar playing both came up in the same area at the same time. Both Elizabeth Cotten and Rev. Gary Davis were born in the last decade of the 19th century in the Carolinas, and both played in the ragtimey, two-finger Piedmont style, but with strikingly different results. Cotten's playing combined elements of all the different music that was in her family – rags, dance tunes, hymns and parlour songs.

Her simple fingerpicked style provided the model for 1950s folk-boomers to learn from.

Cotten's influence was largely felt at second hand thanks to the adaptation of her style by commercial folk singers like Peter Paul and Mary. The Rev. Gary Davis was rather more of a star in his own right. His complex style, with its mix of ragtime and gospel influences derived from Blind Blake, had a more direct influence on the folk-boomers, with songs like 'Candy Man' and 'Cocaine Blues' becoming coffeehouse standards.

Another blues-based guitarist who had a powerful influence on folk music was Leadbelly. Leadbelly's trademark 12-string acoustic playing had a rhythmic drive that was to prove a huge influence on folk musicians to come. In particular, it influenced Leadbelly's regular associate, the pivotal figure in pre-1960s American folk, Woody Guthrie. Guthrie in turn would influence all the guitar-playing folk protest singers to come, from Pete Seeger and Ramblin' Jack Elliott to Bob Dylan and his whole legion of imitators. Woody Guthrie adapted old folk tunes as the settings for new lyrics which protested against poverty, injustice and bigotry, and he constructed simple, durable guitar parts to go with them. His goal was not to impress listeners with guitar wizardry, but to encourage them to pick up their own guitars, sing their own songs or pass his own songs along.

During the 1940s and 1950s this style made its way into the pop charts, with the gentle folk recordings of The Weavers and The Kingston Trio. In the 1960s, though, a huge boom in interest in folk music amongst college kids led to a whole range of more experimental new talents emerging. There was Ramblin' Jack Elliott who could swing from the Woody Guthrie style 'Roll in My Sweet Baby's Arms' to the Rev. Gary Davis-like 'Railroad Bill'. Or there was the expert fingerpicking of Dave Van Ronk, adding new sophistication to his interpretations of Leadbelly classics. Joan Baez, meanwhile, inspired a generation of young women to try their hand at folk guitar.

ABOVE: *Woody Guthrie was a key figure in the development of American folk music, pre-dating and inspiring the 1960s generation of singer-songwriters which included Bob Dylan and Joan Baez.*

BRITISH ARTISTS

On the other side of the Atlantic the guitar took a little longer to be accepted as an appropriate instrument for folk music. The traditional instruments for British folk music were more likely to be concertinas or fiddles, or even banjos, than guitars. All that changed with the skiffle boom of the 1950s. In a rough counterpart to the American folk boom, skiffle consisted of white teenagers dong their best to impersonate Leadbelly.

One of these young skiffle guitarists was Martin Carthy, and as his interest turned to British folk music, so his immersion in the possibilities of the guitar as a folk instrument developed. Over the succeeding 50 years Carthy managed to more or less invent what is now seen as English folk guitar playing, characterized by spare fingerpicking and rock-solid thumb attack. It's a style of accompaniment that's both remarkably propulsive and sensitive to the demands of the song.

Other notable guitarists who appeared in Carthy's wake include Nic Jones, a gifted artist whose career was sadly cut short by a car accident that left him unable to play or sing, and the Scottish legend Dick Gaughan. Gaughan favours a flatpick and his best work is heard on his interpretation of classic folk ballads like 'Willie O'Winsbury' or 'Craigie Hill', involving a stunning integration of chordal accompaniment and fiery melodic work. He's also one of the finest interpreters of Celtic dance tunes, using the flatpick technique. His guitar ornaments can mimic fiddle bow skips or even bagpipe squawks. Like Carthy he regularly experiments with alternate tunings, for instance using EADEAE or EAAEAE to imply pipe drones under the melody.

Fine Irish folk guitarists include Paul Brady, whose 1970s recordings show him incorporating double-course technique into his flatpicking style, adding a rawness and urgency, and the Bothy Band's Mícheál Ó Domhnaill. Ó Domhnaill is probably the most widely imitated Irish guitarist. He built a unique style around DADGAD and establishes wonderfully interlocking rhythms and counter-rhythms.

INSTRUMENTAL FOLK

All the folk guitar players mentioned so far essentially use the guitar as an accompaniment, albeit often a very elaborate one. During the 1960s, however, a new school of folk guitarist emerged who concentrated on purely instrumental work. These players, unsurprisingly enough, tend to be the ones who have lifted the style into new levels of technical virtuosity.

The pioneer in this direction was John Fahey, who started recording in 1959. Fahey took traditional blues and country acoustic guitar licks and used them to create a kind of American

BELOW: *Folk music is not necessarily about traditionalism. John Fahey was known for his acoustic experimentation, and his popularity underwent a resurgence with the musical avante garde during the 1990s.*

primitive classical music. Being a composer became the defining aspect of his music, as for many of his successors, who describe themselves as guitarist-composers. Among the first of these was Robbie Basho, who began his recording career on Fahey's own label. He was in some ways even more influential on the current crop of New Age guitarist-composers, with his love of Eastern music.

Another guitarist to debut on Fahey's label was Leo Kottke, who took the Fahey/Basho idea, and succeeded in bringing it to a mass audience. His 1969 album *Six- and 12-String Guitar* is arguably the most influential guitarist-composer record ever made. Increasingly, since the 1970s the development of instrumental guitar music in the US has inclined towards New Age. This shift began to pick up momentum in the 1980s with the success of Windham Hill Records with guitarists like Alex de Grassi, whose effortless flowing arpeggios and relaxed style really came to define New Age guitar, as did that of label mate Michael Hedges, with his prodigious two-hand tapping techniques.

BLUES EXPERIMENTATION

While the Windham Hill and Takoma artists were redefining fingerstyle guitar in the States, something similar was happening on the other side of the Atlantic. The British counterpart to John Fahey was another experimentalist named Davey Graham. Graham's album *Folk, Blues And Beyond* mixed traditional English folk with blues and North African influences to stunning effect. He was also one of the first British guitarists to experiment with alternate tunings, especially the enormously influential DADGAD.

Graham's disciples included John Renbourn and Bert Jansch, two fine guitar players who briefly teamed up in the group Pentangle. Renbourn's style is ornate, bringing influences from pre-Baroque English styles. Bert Jansch is a spikier guitarist. Heavily influenced by Graham's discovery of DADGAD, Jansch is a brilliant finger-stylist whose influence is not merely apparent in the likes of Donovan, but on the acoustic work of Jimmy Page as well.

All of these schools of folk guitar playing have their adherents, but perhaps the most influential of all are the ones we don't even think of as guitarists, or at least not as guitarists first and foremost. These are the 'folk' singer-songwriters who began to appear during the late 1960s, spearheaded by Paul Simon, Joni Mitchell and James Taylor. They may not have inspired people to become guitar virtuosos, but to do something arguably more important: to pick up the guitar in the first place.

ALTERNATE TUNINGS

So why do so many folk guitarists, from Joni Mitchell to Davey Graham, delight in using alternate tunings? Well perhaps the real question is why on earth standard guitar tuning is standard? After all the standard EADGBE tuning is actually based on a pretty strange combination of a major 3rd and four perfect 4ths, which makes some chords pretty difficult to play. The reasons for its adoption are partly historical, to do with the development of the instrument out of the lute, partly mechanical, as it doesn't place too much stress on any of the strings, and partly just luck, that this particular tuning happens to be the one that has stuck. Once a standard has been established, it makes everyone's life easier to stick with it. Plus once you've got a guitar tuned one way it's a considerable hassle to keep retuning it for different songs, particularly when playing live (assuming you don't have a guitar roadie waiting to supply you with any one of a dozen guitars kept in different tunings).

However, it's a mistake to let that put you off, as experimenting with tunings opens up a whole world of options, and they're not just for experts either. In fact it's a lot easier to play the basic chords in some alternate tunings.

The most common alternate tunings are what are known as open tunings, in which the open strings of the guitar are tuned to form a simple chord: thus the strings of the open C tuning form a C major chord, the strings of the open G tuning form a G major chord, etc. Invariably, this makes it easy to play in the 'natural' key of the tuning.

Another common use of open tunings is to play the open strings as drones. This is an easy way to create unusual chordal combinations and interesting sustained tonal clusters. They are also a big help when you are playing bottleneck or slide guitar, since you can place the slide at any fret and play a full six-string chord. Similarly, harmonics have extra possibilities in open tunings. You can play a full six strings of harmonics at the 12th, 7th and 5th frets.

Other options include tunings based on those of other instruments such as the mandolin, the cittern and the oud, which can produce some truly innovative sounds. Another option is to try out regular tunings, in which the strings are tuned uniformly up the fretboard. This allows chord forms to be moved up and down the fretboard like a normal bar chord, and also sideways across the fretboard, allowing even a novice guitarist access to a whole range of chords with minimal variation in fingering.

If the idea of retuning still intimidates you, maybe you should consider a MIDI guitar controller. With the flick of a button you can change the tuning of all six strings; and suddenly the possibility for experimentation is endless.

FLATPICKING

The two main styles of picking in folk guitar are known as fingerpicking (which is discussed in the country chapter) and flatpicking. Basically flatpicking is the technique of playing a guitar with a flat pick (or flat plectrum) rather than with fingers, finger picks, or a thumb pick. The plectrum is a thin sliver, generally made of plastic, nylon or tortoiseshell, and using it brings significantly different tones out of a steel-string guitar.

Both fingerstyle and flatpicking styles emerged in the early part of the century when musicians realized the guitar was capable of being more than simply a rhythm instrument. The term 'flatpicking' originated with early lead acoustic guitar players in traditional country and bluegrass music who started using plectrums. Some of the flatpicking pioneers included Don Reno and Bill Napier in bluegrass music, Django Reinhardt and Eddie Lang in jazz music, and the Delmore Brothers, the Blue Sky Boys, Jimmie Rodgers and Hank Snow in country music.

During the 1960s and 1970s the flatpicking technique became more widespread as the lead guitar became more prominent in bluegrass, folk and traditional music. Major exponents of the style include the likes of Doc Watson, Clarence White, Tony Rice and Norman Blake. The basic technique involves holding the plectrum with only your thumb and index finger to play the lower notes, while picking the upper notes with your middle and/or ring fingers. The most popular style of guitar for flatpicking is definitely the dreadnought, the larger style acoustic as manufactured by Martin. This is partly down to tradition and partly due to their bass response, making them the ideal guitars for bluegrass, which involves plenty of rhythm playing behind a string band.

BELOW: *Nick Drake was a quintessentially British folk guitarist, and is known for his highly unusual tunings.*

JOHN FAHEY

1939–2001
BAND: **SOLO ARTIST**
HEIGHT OF FAME: **1960s**

John Fahey is a guitarist who spent 40 years treading his own path. Like many of his contemporaries growing up in America in the 1950s, he was entranced by rediscovering the pre-war country and blues pickers. Few others, however, dipped into their work in such detail or succeeded in turning those influences into something equally mysterious and profound.

Some aspects of his guitar playing are almost self-consciously 'traditional', but Fahey's playing showed that fingerpicking techniques derived from country and blues could also be used to incorporate elements from Indian music and even touches from modern classical composers like Bela Bartok. It's a combination that the rest of the world is still catching up with.

Fahey was born on 28 February 1939, in Washington, D.C. The young Fahey developed a diverse musical taste embracing, pop, modern classical, and Episcopalian hymns. In his early teens Fahey bought his first guitar, a Silvertone, for $17, and began to try to play all the different kinds of music he loved. Increasingly he became drawn to American folk music.

He made his first album in 1959, giving himself the jokey pseudonym 'Blind Joe Death'. Through the early 1960s his albums steadily became more ambitious, taking in Eastern influences and stretching out to 20-minute improvisations, thus anticipating the experimentation of groups like The Grateful Dead. He also employed a whole range of unusual guitar tunings. He ran his own label, Takoma, until the 1970s, releasing records by protégés like Leo Kottke. In 1986 he contracted Epstein-Barr syndrome, a long-lasting viral infection, and the illness led to a downturn in his career. However, his work enjoyed a revival in the 1990s, and Fahey returned to recording and performing to considerable acclaim before his death in 2001.

RIGHT: *John Fahey returned to the live music scene in the 1990s, and is pictured here at a New York City gig in 1997.* City of Refuge, *his current album at the time, demonstrated his ongoing experimental fusion of folk and blues.*

AMERICAN PRIMITIVE

John Fahey's own name for his singular guitar technique was American Primitive. It's an atmospheric phrase that does indeed get to the heart of the Fahey project. Essentially, Fahey began by deconstructing the unschooled but remarkably complex playing of men like Robert Johnson or Charlie Patton and applying it to very different musical styles. He achieved this through the use of what is more commonly known as fingerstyle guitar. This is based on the strong right-hand techniques used by pioneering delta blues players coupled with alternate tunings.

Taking the picking first, the key is the syncopation, and in Fahey's playing this was often applied to unusually slow tempos. Thus Fahey might have played a three-note chord on the treble strings and moved in half steps up and down the neck of the guitar while the thumb kept alternating on open strings. However, while in jazz playing a chromatic move like this would be done at lightning pace, Fahey might dwell on each half step for a measure or two before moving on. Meanwhile the right hand would be offering a ragtime-like syncopation. The result of this, in Fahey's playing, would be to add the kind of dissonance you might find in Bartok to traditional American fingerpicking: American primitivism in action.

As for the tunings, Fahey would employ a whole range from the relatively familiar open G (DGDGBD) and open D (DAD#FAD) to the distinctly unusual open C (CGCGCE), open D minor (DADFAD), open G minor (DGDGBflatD) and C drone (CCCGCE).

LEFT: *Alongside being a musical eccentric – factory noises and trains featured in some of his recordings – Fahey was known to be a difficult and reclusive character, as unique as his music.*

The Yellow Princess

ALBUM: **THE YELLOW PRINCESS**
SONGWRITER: **JOHN FAHEY**
RECORDED: **SIERRA SOUND LABORATORIES, BERKELEY**
PRODUCERS: **SAMUEL CHARTERS, BARRET HANSEN**

This intro uses a fingerstyle technique to pick out notes on bass and high strings. Practise playing fingerstyle to improve your sound; there is a vast repertoire of folk tunes and instrumentals like this lovely John Fahey piece that you will be able to play once you have fully mastered this style of playing. Use your thumb to pick out notes on the bass strings. Learn to keep in time whilst playing in this style.

BASIC SONG RIFF

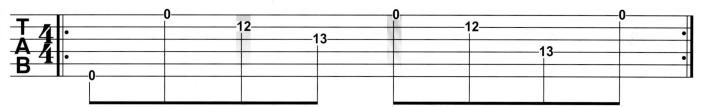

HERE'S HOW

1 Shows the B and A flat notes on the B and G strings, hold down both notes together ready for your picking hand to play them.

2 Note the thumb ready to play the E open string and the first and middle fingers ready to play the other notes in the tune.

NICK DRAKE

1948–1974
BAND: **SOLO ARTIST**
RECORDED: **LATE 1960s–EARLY 1970s**; HEIGHT OF FAME: **1990s–PRESENT**

As a person, the increasingly legendary British singer-songwriter Nick Drake was elusive, almost impossible to pin down. The same goes for his guitar playing. His friend and string arranger Robert Kirby once commented that while most distinctive guitarists have plenty of imitators, Nick Drake hardly has any.

The reason why? 'Perhaps because it's so damn difficult.' Not only was Nick Drake fond of unusual tunings (which he never wrote down), he was also given to fantastically intricate fingerpicking patterns. It's this maverick originality that made Nick Drake one of the most brilliantly individual of all British guitar players.

Nick Drake was born in what was then Burma on 19 June 1948. His family returned to England when he was two and he went to Marlborough public (private) school when he was 13. While he was there he started playing the guitar and writing songs. From school he went on to Cambridge University and while still a student landed a recording deal with Island Records and top producer Joe Boyd. This team would put out two albums, both now regarded as classics. The first album, *Five Leaves Left*, was full of delicate guitar work and wonderfully complementary, very English string arrangements. The second, *Bryter Layter*, continued in the same vein, and when it failed to sell Drake was crushed. His final album, *Pink Moon*, produced by Drake and John Wood, was a sparse, dark record performed almost entirely solo. It was released in 1972 but, like its predecessors, failed to be a commercial success. Drake relapsed into a depression which was to last on and off till his tragic death in November 1974 following an overdose of sleeping pills. Since that time, his popularity has steadily grown, as subsequent generations have discovered the singular talents of a man sadly ignored by his own generation.

RIGHT: *Nick Drake was a talented, if vulnerable, folk guitarist. His first guitar was purchased for £13, and many of the songs he wrote while at Cambridge University would be heard on* Five Leaves Left.

449

River Man

ALBUM: **FIVE LEAVES LEFT**
SONGWRITER: **NICK DRAKE**
RECORDED: **LONDON, UK**
PRODUCER: **JOE BOYD**

This is a gorgeous tune which sounds lovely strummed or picked. It requires a change of tuning to CGCFCE. Be careful to avoid breaking strings when you change the tuning. The diagram shows the first two chords in the song. Another chord used in the song is A flat. Try singing the vocal melody as you practise moving between these chords and add the A flat chord.

BASIC SONG CHORDS

HERE'S HOW

1. The first finger is on the 2nd fret of the G string, ring finger on the 4th fret of the B string and the middle finger plays the E string.

2. Try your first finger on the 2nd fret of the G string, your middle finger and ring fingers on the 3rd frets of the B and E strings.

LEFT: *Nick Drake was a remarkable musician who saw little commercial success during his short life. These photographs were taken by Keith Morris, the only professional lensman known to have photographed Drake during just three sessions, one for each of his albums.*

CHORD CHARTS

From the simple to the advanced, this section contains all the chords featured in each of the 39 practice sessions. An at-a-glance reference guide, it explains how each chord is composed, what fingering to use, and how to play it.

This section also takes you through chord-playing exercises, alternative fingering and how to move between chords. Here you'll learn when to use a capo, how to play barre chords, what a 'broken chord' is, why there are such things as two-string chords, why Johnny Cash's 'Folsom Prison Blues' is a country song with a blues chord progression, and why you might want to tune your guitar differently.

With helpful chord diagrams, clear text and examples from Buddy Holly, Radiohead, Oasis, Eric Clapton, Elvis Presley, The Beatles, The Rolling Stones, Free, Sheryl Crow, The Police, Joni Mitchell, Blur, Blondie and Queen, this section is an easy-to-use guide to mastering a wealth of guitar chords.

CHORD CHART

This is a recap of the chords introduced in the second section of *The Guitar Book*: the chords E minor, A minor and D minor. Whenever you have time to spare, reach for your guitar and indulge in a little practice. Even if you don't have the time to play all the exercises, you should at least try to spend a few minutes going through these chords every day.

Get used to the shapes your fingers make while playing, and with practice, they'll soon become second nature.

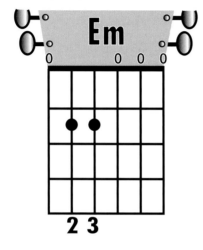

Above: E minor is one of the first chord you need to learn. Place your 2nd finger at the 2nd fret of the 5th string. Your 3rd finger goes at the 2nd fret on the 4th string. Finally, strum all of the strings together.

Above: A minor. As in the Em chord, place your 2nd and 3rd fingers at the 2nd fret, but this time on the 3rd and 4th strings. Add your 1st finger at the 1st fret on the 2nd string, strum five strings, and you're playing Am.

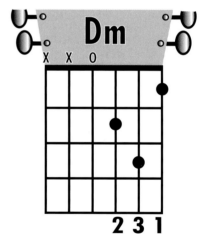

Above: Finger positions for the Am chord.

Above: For the D minor chord, place your 1st finger at the 1st fret of the 1st string, your 3rd finger at the 3rd fret on the 2nd string, and your 2nd finger at the 2nd fret of the 3rd string.

There's an alternative method of playing Dm: putting your 4th finger on the 2nd string instead of your 3rd. Play whichever is most comfortable, and avoid playing the 5th and 6th strings.

CHORD CHART – 2

As well as the chords that you were introduced to in the first session – Em, Dm and Am – we have used three new power chords in The Beatles' *I Saw Her Standing There*. Power chords are a quick and simple way of forming chords with only two or three strings. Here's a visual recap of the A, D, E and B power chords; take care to play only the strings shown, remembering not to play the strings marked with an X. Apart from the B shape, these chords all use the 2nd finger at the 2nd fret, but on a different string each time, so you should be able to change between chords smoothly and quickly.

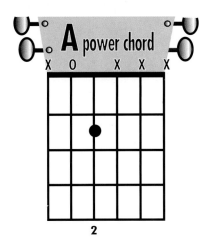

1. The A power chord is the first of the four power chords featured in the second chapter. Place your 2nd finger at the 2nd fret on the 4th string. Now play the 5th string open (A), striking the fretted 4th string at the same time.

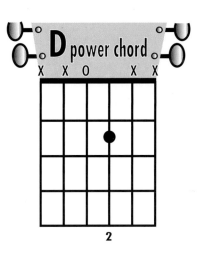

2. Change to the D power chord finger position. Move your 2nd finger across from the 4th string, placing it at the 2nd fret on the 3rd string. Play the open 4th string (D), striking the fretted 3rd string at the same time.

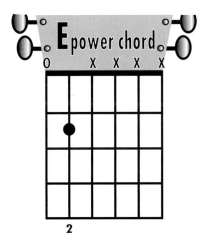

3. Now form the E power chord. As with the previous two power chords, the 2nd finger is positioned at the 2nd fret – but this time on the 5th string. Play the open 6th string (E) and this fretted string together.

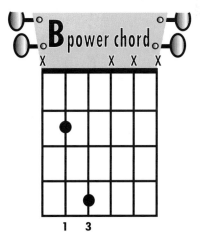

4. The B power chord as you played it in this finger positon before. It's the A power chord moved up two frets, with the 1st finger at the 2nd fret on the 5th string and the 3rd finger at the 4th fret on the 4th string.

CHORD CHART – 3

Here, we've introduced more power chords, with a simple two-note chord shape that uses your 1st and 3rd fingers. Below, we've shown this shape and the names of the chords it makes at different fret positions. You'll notice that some have the same names as the power chords featured in the second feature, but this time they're in different positions.

Even though your hand is in a different place on different strings, the chords are actually made up of the same notes.

Also shown here are the chords from the first chapter, which you should be familiar with by now, and which are, hopefully, becoming more comfortable to play.

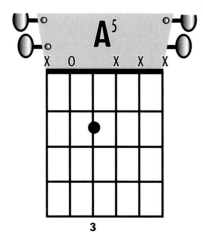

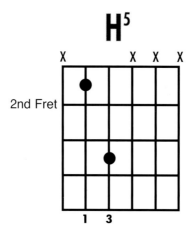

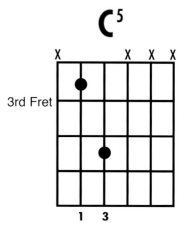

1. Using the 3rd finger to fret string 4 will make changing to the following power chords much easier.

2. Moving the A5 shape up two frets, and adding finger 1 at fret 2 of string 5 makes this B power chord – B5. This shape forms the basis for the power chords that follow.

3. Moving up one fret, the B5 power chord becomes a C power chord – C5.

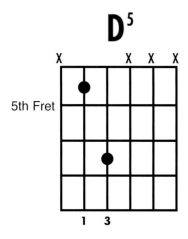

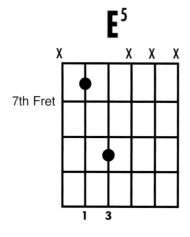

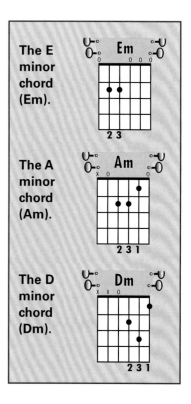

The E minor chord (Em).

The A minor chord (Am).

The D minor chord (Dm).

4. Moving up another two frets, the C5 shape becomes a D power chord – D5.

5. Moving up another two frets, the D5 chord becomes an E power chord – E5.

CHORD CHART - 4

This session's song, *Wonderwall*, introduces five rich-sounding chords – Em7, G major, Dsus4, A7sus4 and Cadd9. The chord names are complicated because of the additional notes that give the chords their particular qualities. Try comparing the shape of an E minor (Em) from the very first session with the E minor7 (Em7) of this one. Compare, too, the Dsus4 and A7sus4 chords with the D and A power chords – D5 and A5 – from the third session. (See below for a recap on earlier chord shapes.) You're now well on the way to building up a useful vocabulary of chords. Practise them whenever you can and, above all, practise changing between them.

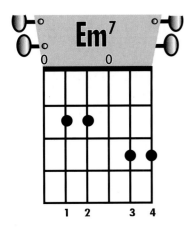

Above: Place fingers 3 and 4 behind fret 3 on strings 2 and 1. Place fingers 1 and 2 behind the 2nd fret on strings 5 and 4. Strings 6 and 3 are played open.

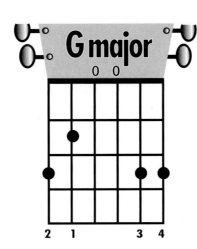

Above: Retain the E minor7 shape, but shift finger 2 over to fret 3 on string 6 to form the very useful G major chord.

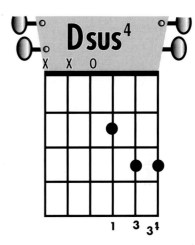

Above: The same shape on the top two strings, plus the addition of finger 1 behind fret 2 on string 3, and string 4 (D) played open, produces Dsus4.

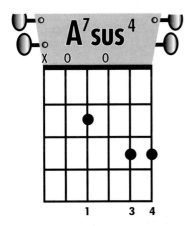

Above: The same shape on the top two strings, plus finger 1 behind fret 2 on string 4, with string 5 and string 3 played open, gives you A7sus4.

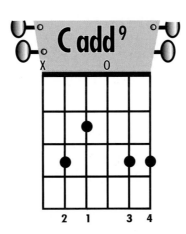

Above: The chord Cadd9 is essentially the same chord shape as A7sus4 (left), but with the addition of finger 2 placed at fret 3 on string 5.

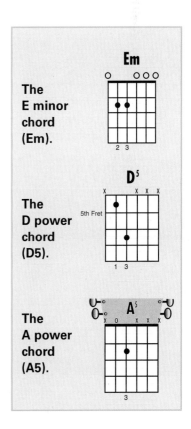

The E minor chord (Em).

The D power chord (D5).

The A power chord (A5).

CHORD CHART – 5

Here are four of the most commonly used chords in a guitarist's repertoire: G, D, C and E minor. These will crop up time and again, so use this page to help commit them to memory. The G and E minor patterns should be quite familiar by now, so concentrate on D and C. In a spare moment, you could practise strumming the C chord rather than picking out the arpeggio, and maybe even have

a go at shifting between it and any of the other three chords.

There is also a reminder of the Em7, Cadd9 and Dsus4 chords. It's worth comparing the sound of a Cadd9 to a straightforward C chord, or the effect the sus4 has on a D chord.

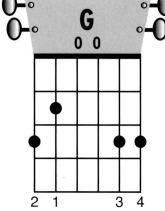

Above: Place fingers 3 and 4 at the 3rd fret on strings 2 and 1, respectively. With the thumb low, reach over to the 3rd fret on string 6 with finger 2. Finger 1 drops on to string 5 at fret 2.

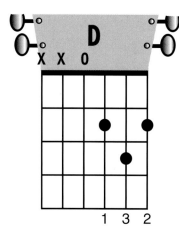

Above: From the G chord, leave finger 3 in place, release finger 4 and pull fingers 1 and 2 towards strings 3 and 1. Keep your thumb still and your fingers close to the strings as you make the shift.

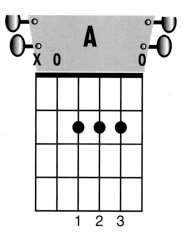

Above: The last new chord, an A major from the song *Pretty Vacant*. Place fingers 1, 2 and 3 at fret 2 on strings 4, 3 and 2, respectively. Strings 5 and 1 are played open.

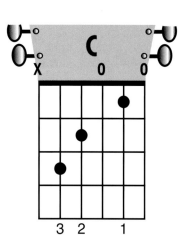

Above: Keep your thumb low and straight and arch your fingers. From the bass, strike the chord's five strings one by one, until the notes all sound at the same time.

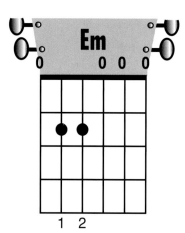

Above: Here, finger 1 plays string 5 at fret 2, and finger 2 plays string 4 at fret 2. This fingering links up best with the other chord shapes in Clapton's *Wonderful Tonight*.

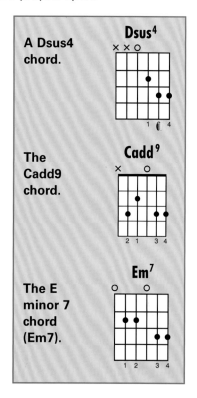

A Dsus4 chord.

The Cadd9 chord.

The E minor 7 chord (Em7).

CHORD CHART - 6

Here's an at-a-glance reminder of every chord covered in session 6: chords of C major 7, G6 and Em11/F# as well as a recap of E minor. Power chords of E5, C5 and G5, plus the D/F# shape are also featured. C major and Cadd9 add to an already substantial list. Try memorizing them if you can and even if you're short of time, you'll probably manage to practise a few shapes on a daily basis.

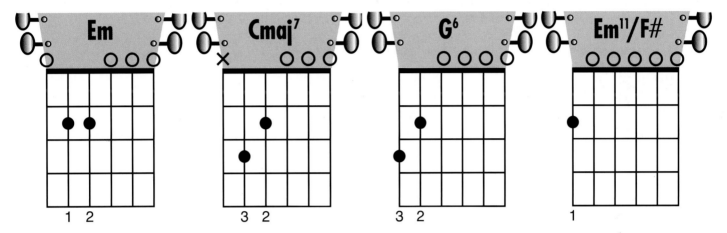

Above: Only C shapes follow E minor in session 6, so using fingers 1 and 2 makes the changes a lot easier. Check that the underside of finger 2 is not damping the open 3rd string.

Above: C major from session 5, with finger 1 off to give an open string 2. The two similar chords create different effects. From E minor, replace finger 1 from string 5 with finger 3 at fret 3.

Above: This is effective following C major 7, as in *Zombie*. Shift fingers 2 and 3 together across to the bottom two strings. Curve the fingers well so that the four open strings can ring clearly.

Above: In isolation, the five open strings clash with the F# in the bass and do not make easy listening. However, following on from the other *Zombie* chords it seems to fit perfectly.

TWO-STRING CHORDS

A 5 after a letter implies a power chord shape. For E5, use the two bass strings of the full E minor chord. For C5, slip finger 1 up to fret 3, then use the 3rd finger to place fret 5 on the 4th string. Keep the 1st and 3rd fingers stretched as you change from C5. You then have the shape ready to drop onto strings 6 and 5 for the G5 chord. D/F# has an important linking role in the *Zombie* verse. If you have a good stretch, then finger 1 can reach back to fret 2 from the G5 shape. If not, try using the 4th finger at fret 5 instead of the 3rd. To show higher fret positions, the starting frets for C5, G5 and D/F# are labelled.

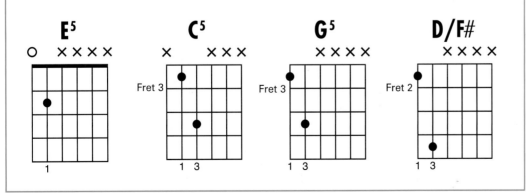

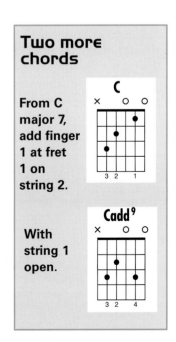

Two more chords

From C major 7, add finger 1 at fret 1 on string 2.

With string 1 open.

459

CHORD CHART – 7

Five chord shapes feature strongly here. Of these, A major made an appearance in the fifth session, but the other four chords are new. These all have curious sounding names based upon the selection of notes contained within each chord. See if you can memorize these new chords to help you play

Fake Plastic Trees and also for future reference. After

all, you never know when that Bm11 chord might come in handy! When you have a few moments to spare, go back over the G, D and C major chords learnt earlier. These are frequently used, so practise shifting quickly and precisely from one to another.

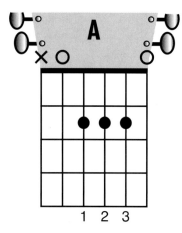

Above: Place fingers 1, 2 and 3 at fret 2 on strings 4, 3 and 2. Play strings 5 and 1 open but don't play string 6. Press firmly with finger 1 to avoid any buzzing of the string against the fret.

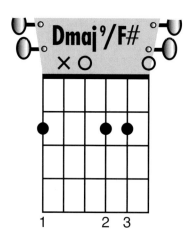

Above: From the A chord position, shift your 1st finger from the 4th string over to the 6th string. Strum all six strings but block string 5 with the underside of finger 1.

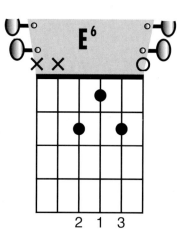

Above: This contains only four strings, including an open 1st string. Finger 2 goes on string 4 at the 2nd fret, finger 1 on string 3 at fret 1, and finger 3 remains in its Dmaj9/F# position.

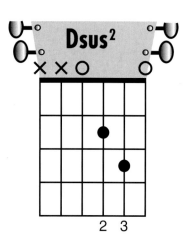

Above: This is D major with an open 1st string. The stretch between fingers 2 and 3 can be awkward, so try twisting the wrist slightly to the right to improve the 3rd finger location.

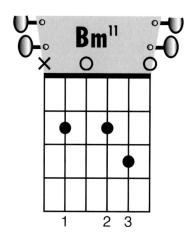

Above: Add finger 1 to string 5 at fret 2 to change Dsus2 to Bm11. It can be hard making the open strings sound, so drop the thumb lower and roll the wrist a little to give your fingers more arch.

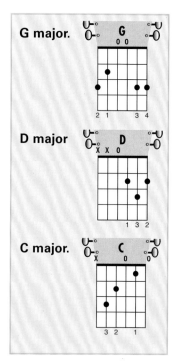

G major.

D major.

C major.

CHORD CHART - 8

In this session, E major, one of the most used chords in a guitarist's repertoire, appears for the first time. G major makes yet another important contribution to the practice pieces, as does A major. Power chords feature heavily, as you combine the E5, G5 and A5 chord shapes, all of which are formed on the two bass strings. The chord riff in the solo exercise adds D major and the G/D shape to our list.

Try to work on all of these shapes regularly, and don't forget to keep running through the pages of earlier sessions so that all of these chords stay at your fingertips.

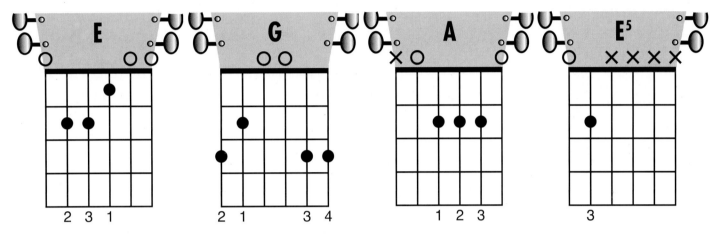

Above: Place finger 2 on string 5 at fret 2, finger 3 on string 4 at fret 2, and finger 1 on string 3 at fret 1. The other three strings are played open.

Above: From E major, move fingers 1 and 2 diagonally over to the 5th and 6th strings. Close the distance between them as you make the shift.

Above: From G major, pull fingers 1, 2 and 3 into line, dropping them onto strings 4, 3 and 2 at fret 2. Play open strings 1 and 5, but not string 6.

Above: Form E5 using finger 3 to make shifting to G5 easier for the practice pieces. Use an open 6th string as well as fret 2 on string 5 with finger 3.

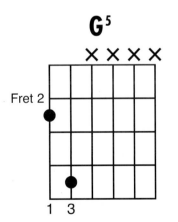

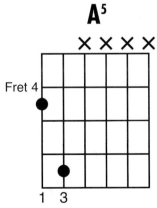

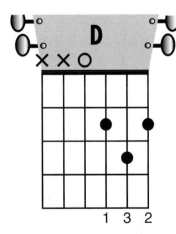

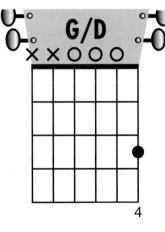

Above: G5 has finger 1 at fret 3 on string 6 and finger 3 on string 5 at fret 5.

Above: For A5, use the same strings as G5, but two frets higher at frets 5 and 7.

Above: The triangular D major finger pattern was studied in one of the previous sessions.

Above: This is a form of G major but with the open 4th string, D, as its bass note.

CHORD CHART – 9

This session's exercises make use of only four power chord shapes: F#5, A5, B5 and D5. There are fewer chords than in previous sessions because a higher proportion of your time is spent on lead guitar work, which includes playing a riff as well as a substantial solo. The chords all use fingers 1 and 3 spread across strings 6 and 5. You will discover countless rock songs that shift a single power chord shape up and down the frets in this manner.

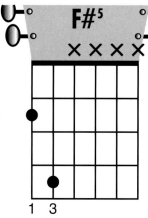

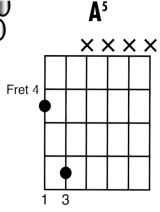

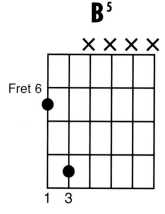

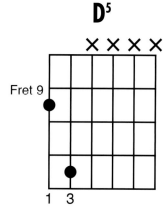

Above: This two-string chord has finger 1 at fret 2 on string 6, together with finger 3 at fret 4 on string 5. A low, vertical thumb behind the middle finger helps with the stretch over to the bass strings.

Above: From the previous chord, release the finger pressure slightly and shift the F#5 shape three frets up the guitar neck. Lock fingers 1 and 3 just behind frets 5 and 7, then strike strings 6 and 5 together.

Above: Move the A5 chord shape up two frets for this power chord. You can lean the 3rd finger slightly against string 4. This will stop the string from sounding, should you accidentally strike it as you strum the chord.

Above: The same finger shape again, only this time squeezed into the much narrower 10th and 12th frets. Because finger 1 is at fret 10, this power chord can be described as being in 10th position.

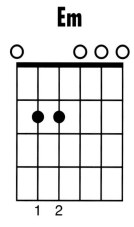

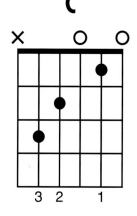

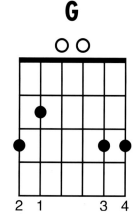

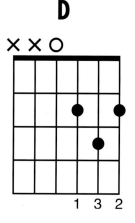

Revised chord shapes, using the capo at the 2nd fret

You worked through a sequence of four other chords in some exercises: E minor, C major, G major and D major. These are all chords which you're already quite familiar with, though not with a capo across the 2nd fret. The capo is not an intrinsic part of these chords – it simply raises their overall pitch to give a special tonal effect, avoid difficult chord changes or, most commonly, suit the range of a singer's voice. These are among the most frequently used chords, so give them plenty of practice, with and without the capo.

CHORD CHART - 10

More chord shapes! You are familiar with five of the six chords already and have practised them regularly. The new chord, F major, is almost certainly the hardest shape because it involves barring the 1st and 2nd strings. For now, always place finger 1 of this chord last, as this will give the best chance of a relaxed and accurate hand position. Bar chords will be essential later on, so practise this shape as often as possible to achieve a comfortable finger placement.

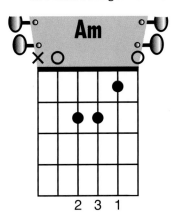

Above: This is the most used chord in *The House Of The Rising Sun*. Place finger 2 on string 4, with finger 3 directly beneath it and finger 1 on the 2nd string. Strings 5 and 1 are open.

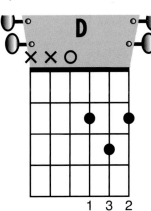

Above: The change from A minor to C major is relatively easy to achieve. Remove finger 3 and stretch it over to fret 3 on string 5. Keep the fingers arched to allow open strings 1 and 3 to sound clearly.

Above: This is a four-string chord, so avoid any contact with strings 5 and 6. Hold the fingers close over the strings as you move from C major, and try to form the triangular shape of the D chord during the shift.

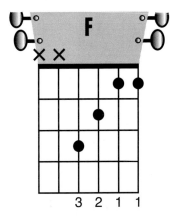

Above: When moving from the D shape, lift fingers 3 and 2 as a unit up to strings 4 and 3, respectively. Then lower finger 1 firmly onto strings 1 and 2 at fret 1, while taking care not to collapse fingers 2 and 3.

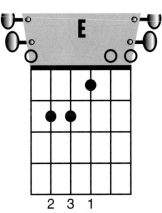

Above: From A minor, lift all three fingers up one string, then strike all six strings. From C major, lift fingers 1 and 2 up a string onto the same frets and slot finger 3 in beneath finger 2 on string 4.

Above: Following on from A minor, shift fingers 1 and 2 down onto strings 1 and 3 at frets 1 and 2, respectively. Add finger 3 at fret 3 on string 2 and play an open 4th string as the bass note.

Revised chord shapes

This is an ideal chance to bring together the other shapes you know that regularly appear in songs. You should be familiar with E minor and G major as both have featured in earlier exercises. Try combining these with A major, then you could even add one of the strum patterns you have learned.

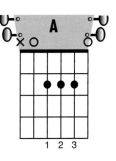

CHORD CHART – 11

Some of this session's exercises feature the new, three-string power chord shape. The addition of a third string to the power chord pattern used previously gives these chords an even stronger sound. This does not mean that the two-string power chord is now obsolete; it will crop up regularly in other songs. In the course of the session, your power chords shifted through many fret positions. Here are all the different shapes, with reference to any patterns used again at other frets.

G⁵
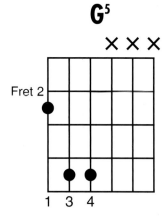
Fret 2

1 3 4

Above: This power chord is played on strings 6, 5 and 4. This particular shape uses fingers 1, 3 and 4 and is also used for A5 in 5th position, B5 in 7th position and C5 in 8th position.

D⁵
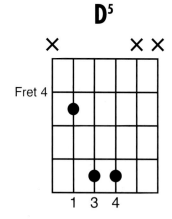
Fret 4

1 3 4

Above: To form D5, release and move the G5 chord up to 5th position and onto strings 5, 4 and 3. Keep your thumb low and fingers curved and avoid plectrum contact with strings 6, 2 or 1.

Em
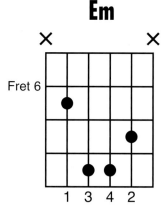
Fret 6

1 3 4 2

Above: The only non-power chord here, this form of E minor is essentially D5 moved up two frets to 7th position, with finger 2 added to string 2 at fret 8 to give the chord its minor identity.

C⁵
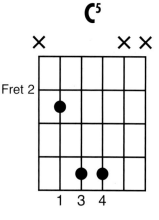
Fret 2

1 3 4

Above: C5 is the same as D5 played in 3rd position. It can be approached from both A5 and E minor. Played in 1st position it is B♭5, in 2nd position it is the B5 chord and in 7th position it is E5.

A⁵
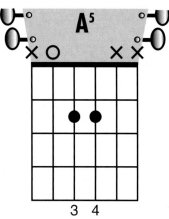

3 4

Above: Play an open A (5th) string and use fingers 3 and 4 for the fretted notes (to make the change to C5 easier). This is the only chord box to include the nut.

Additional solo chord shapes

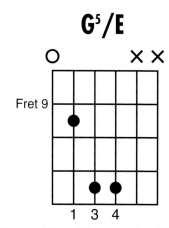

G⁵/E
Fret 9

1 3 4

Above: G5 in 10th position. The E refers to the open E string played under the G5 shape. F#5/E uses this shape in 9th position, and E5 can be played like this in 7th position.

E⁵
Fret 6

1 3 4

Above: This form of the E5 chord is unusual in that it fills out the fretted E5 shape used in the exercises by also including the remaining three open strings.

CHORD CHART – 12

Your chord work is divided between power chords and full strummed chords. The B♭5, C5, F5 and G5 chords return to the two-string power chord shape used in the very first sessions. A new study point is the F5 shape played on the D (4th) and G (3rd) strings. The E, A and D major chords have all featured previously. However, this is the first time they have been used together, so the changes between these shapes present new challenges for you. In this and future Chord Charts, the headstock is not shown, instead the top nut is represented by a thick top line.

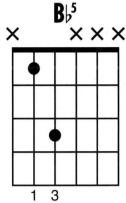

Above: Played in 1st position, this is the only one of these power chords to show the nut of the guitar in its chord box. Place finger 1 on the A (5th) string at fret 1, with finger 3 on the D (4th) string at fret 3.

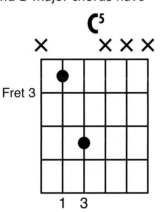

Above: The four frets shown in a chord box cannot accommodate the 5th fret needed here, so the chord box starts at fret 3. From B♭5, shift the same finger shape up to frets 3 and 5 on the same strings.

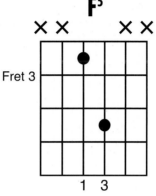

Above: Also played in 3rd position, meaning that finger 1 is based at fret 3. Move the C5 shape onto the D (4th) and G (3rd) strings. F5 is more commonly found in 1st position on the E (6th) and A (5th) strings.

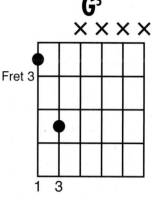

Above: Another 3rd position power chord using two strings only – the root note and the 5th from the G scale. Keep practising this power chord as shown, then try to experiment as you go along.

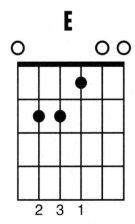

Above: Any major chord can be referred to by its letter only (i.e. E). The main problem with this shape is blocking the open B (2nd) string, so be sure to keep your fingers curved.

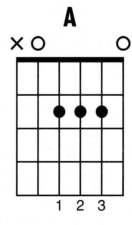

Above: An easy shape to remember, since all three fingers are placed at fret 2. Do not play the bottom E (6th) string, and play the A (5th) and E (1st) strings open.

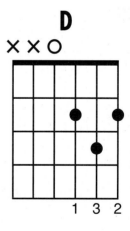

Above: From A major, lead with finger 3 by shifting one fret along string 2. Keep fingers 1 and 2 at fret 2, but move them onto strings 3 and 1. Play string 4 open, but not strings 5 and 6.

CHORD CHART - 13

This session's chords are mainly power chords, although their left hand shapes are more diverse than usual due to the use of open strings down in 2nd position. Only the principal chord shapes from the exercises are shown here, and none of them have any of the added fingers that appear frequently in numerous rock songs to create an interesting shuffle riff effect.

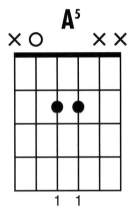

Above: This is the fullest of the A5 chords played in this session, with finger 1 barring the D and G strings at fret 2 and an open A string as the bass note. Other forms drop the use of either the open A or the fretted 3rd string.

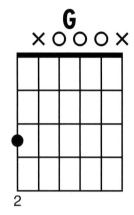

Above: The G major chord shape is played with finger 2 on the bottom E at fret 3 and is the only fretted note. The chord is major because the open B string is the 3rd step of the G scale.

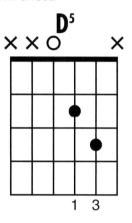

Above: Using fingers 1 and 3 eases the change from G5 to D5. The D5 chord shape is also played without the B string note – this omits the higher octave, leaving the basic power chord form of the root and 5th.

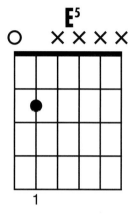

Above: To recap, here is a simple, two-string power chord from the very early exercises. Using finger 1 on the A string allows you to play alternately the fret 4 note on the same string with the 3rd finger.

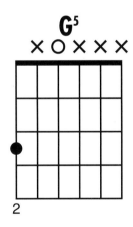

Above: This version of G5 occurs frequently throughout the exercises. Use the underside of finger 2 to mute string 5, making it possible to strum through strings 6 and 4 together.

Useful solo chords

Four different power chords as used for example in The Beach Boys' in *I Get Around*. The patterns are familiar, using fingers 1 and 3 on neighbouring strings for each of the four shapes.

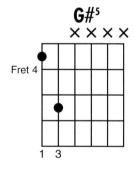

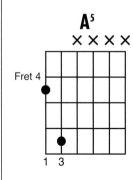

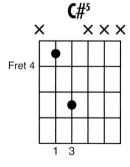

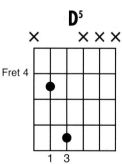

CHORD CHART – 14

Full chords play an important part in this sessions's exercises. The lengthy verses are constructed over a constantly repeated sequence of two bars of D major 7 followed by two bars of G major. The chorus is darkened a little by the addition of an old favourite, the E minor chord, and a fleeting appearance from the A6 chord lends a dash of harmonic colour to the song's closing stages. It's an enjoyable diversion to play chords throughout instead of mixing in the lead lines.

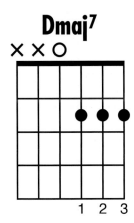

Dmaj⁷

Above: D major 7 with fingers 1, 2 and 3 placing the fret 2 notes. Barring finger 1 across the three top strings is a commonly used alternative fingering. An open D string completes the chord.

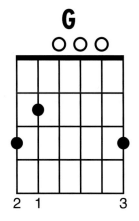

G

Above: The B string remains open in this new form of G major. The difference in sound between this and the four-finger version is subtle and the two forms are generally considered interchangeable.

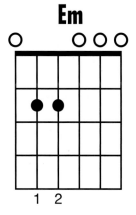

Em

Above: A familiar chord requiring no further introduction. The use of fingers 1 and 2 allows finger 1 to remain in the same place as you shift to G major for the chorus section of the *Babies'* song.

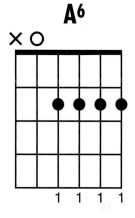

A⁶

Above: A rich-sounding chord, the top three notes of which are identical to D major 7. The row of number 1s below the chord box shows that finger 1 bars the top four strings. The A string is played open.

Power chord shapes

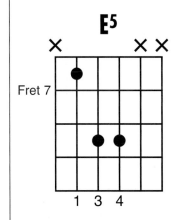

E⁵

Fret 7

Above: A three-string shape in 7th position, it provides the template for F#5, D#5, D5, C#5 and B5.

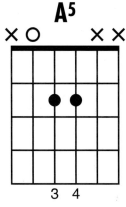

A⁵

Above: Using fingers 3 and 4 for A5 makes it easier to shift down from 7th position.

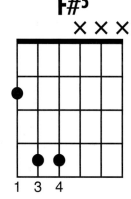

F#⁵

Above: The final chord of the riff. The sound is one octave lower than the 9th position F#5.

CHORD CHART - 15

The three-string power chords featured here are fretted at various locations on the bottom three strings, as well as on the A, D and G strings. A new development is their 'broken chord' treatment alongside the waves of downstrummed chords. The solitary exception to the power chord rule is the A♭ major shape, which gains its major status by the inclusion of the all-important major 3rd in its sound.

A♭

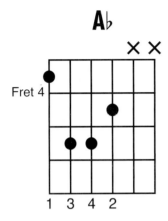

Fret 4

1 3 4 2

Above: From the A♭5 chord base, adding finger 2 to string 3 turns this into a major shape. For now, do not play the top two strings, but later on you will have to bar finger 1 across all six strings to form the major bar chord shape.

A♭5

Fret 4

1 3 4

Above: The similarity between this chord and A♭ major is clear to see. Removing finger 2 from the A♭ shape leaves the root note in the bass, the 5th step of the scale on the A string and the upper octave on the D string.

D♭5^(1)

Fret 4

1 3 4

Above: The bracketed number 1 shows that there is more than one version of this chord used. The three-string shape shown here uses the same finger pattern as A♭5, only this time on the A, D and G strings.

D♭5^(2)

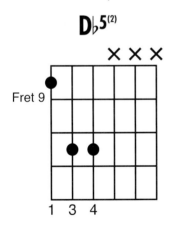

Fret 9

1 3 4

Above: If you play this after version 1, you will notice that there is no difference between the two. This version contains exactly the same notes, played further up the frets on lower strings.

F5

Fret 8

1 3 4

Above: This power chord gives a lighter effect as it contains high notes in 8th position on the A, D and G strings. It shares the shape and strings with D♭5, but is played four frets higher.

C5

Fret 8

1 3 4

Above: Another 8th position chord, but with a stronger sound because of its location on the bottom strings. A♭5, the 9th position D♭5 and B♭5 all use the same pattern on the same strings.

CHORD CHART - 16

These exercises arranged with *Freak Scene* by Dinosaur Jr in mind contain several familiar chords as well as some new shapes. D major, E minor and A major combine to form an accompaniment and a guitar solo, and have all appeared previously. The other commonly used full chord to feature is E major. Power chords are represented by E5 and F#5, although the latter is distinguished by its use of the left thumb to place the fretted note on the bottom E string.

D
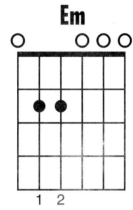

Above: The pivotal chord, D major uses the triangular pattern of fingers studied in other issues. The root note is the open D string. Do not play the bottom two strings, which are crossed on the chart.

Em
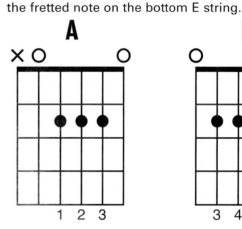

Above: The very first chord you studied, but here you are using fingers 1 and 2 for the fret 2 notes. Play the four remaining strings open, as indicated by the circles above the relevant strings.

A
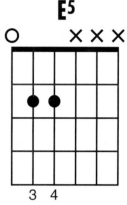

Above: The A major chord occurring after E minor. This is a straightforward shift which requires only a small movement up one string and the addition of finger 3.

E⁵

Above: This three-string power chord alternates with Aadd9. The shift is simplified by the use of fingers 3 and 4 for the fret 2 notes. A wristy plectrum action minimizes the risk of contact with the G string.

Aadd⁹
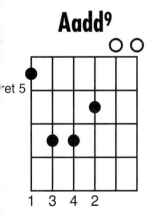
ret 5

Above: Identical in shape to the A♭ major chord featured in the previous session, but this time in 5th position with added colour from the open B and top E strings. The open B is the 'add9'.

E
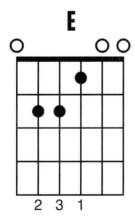

Above: By adding finger 1 to the G string, this chord is transformed from minor into major. The other five strings are either notes 1 or 5 of the E scale at various octaves.

F#¹¹
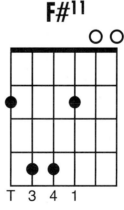

Above: A suitably extravagant name for an intricately fingered chord. The 'T' denotes the left thumb, which places the fret 2 note on the bottom E string, enabling you to place the other fretted notes.

F#⁵
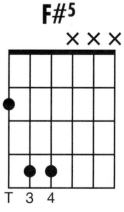

Above: This power chord consists of the bottom three strings of the previous F#m11 chord. For this reason, Make sure to keep the thumb in position ready to play the lowest note.

CHORD CHART – 17

Again, chord playing is very much centre-stage here. In fact, there are so many chord shapes in these exercises that familiar chords such as D major, G major and E minor have been omitted from this page. The full barre chord is featured for the first time. The bold line across the top of all but the D6add4 chord box represents the capo at fret 4, instead of the nut as is customary.

Cmaj⁷

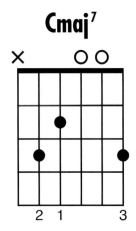

Above: The C major 7 chord has been used before. Here however, finger 3 is at fret 3 on the top E string, leaving fingers 1 and 2 to fret the lower string notes.

D⁶add⁴

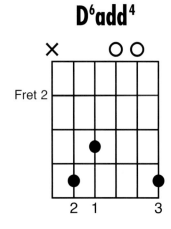

Above: D6add4 has the same shape and fingering as C major 7, but is located two frets further up, at 4th position. The 'Fret 2' marking refers to the 2nd fret above the capo.

Gadd⁹

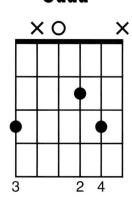

Above: The Gadd9 chord. Apart from this version, an open A string can replace the open D string for an unusually bass-heavy effect.

D/F#

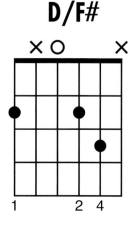

Above: Substitute finger 3 for finger 4 for an easier change to G major. Another version of this chord consists of the 1st and 2nd finger notes only.

F

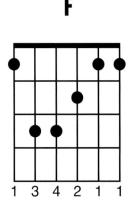

Above: Notable as the first full barre chord in this book so far. The 1st finger bars all six strings at fret 1, while the other fingers form an E major shape.

C

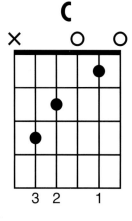

Above: C major was prominent in an earlier session. Here, a change from F major allows finger 3 to stay in the same place on the A string at fret 3.

Em⁷

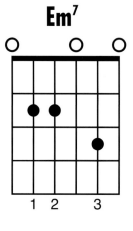

Above: A different version of the chord used earlier. On this occasion, the top E string is open, with the same Em7 symbol marking the open string chord.

CHORD CHART – 18

These exercises concentrate mainly on chord playing. However, the rhythm guitar approach is different from anything you have played so far. The reggae style gives rise to bright, punchy chords on the top three strings, leaving the lead guitar to riff on the lower strings and the bass guitar to add distinctively strident lines beneath. Remember to form a half-barre with finger 1 for each chord, apart from the six-string A major shape, which requires a full finger barre.

A⁽¹⁾

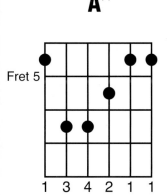

Above: The full A major barre chord has the same finger pattern as F major, but is placed in 5th position instead of 1st. Keep the thumb low for the straight, flat placement of finger 1.

A⁽²⁾

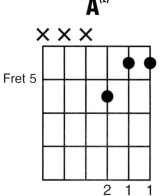

Above: This shape is identical to the top half of the A barre chord. Although finger 2 is on the G string, a better hand shape is gained by barring all three top strings with finger 1.

F#⁽¹⁾

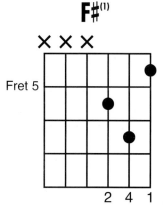

Above: F# minor is another chord played in 5th position. You might notice that the root note, F#, is not the lowest in the chord, but this is not unusual with high-string chords.

F#⁽²⁾

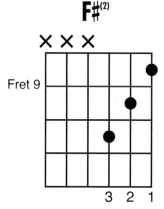

Above: This 9th position version of F# minor uses the same notes as the 5th position form, but in a different order. The result is a higher top note and a subtly different sound.

D

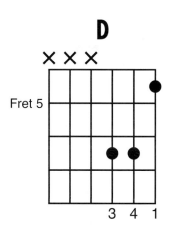

Above: By playing this chord shape instead of your usual D major, the highest note stays the same as for the A and F# minor chords. This close relationship is common in jazz guitar playing.

C#m

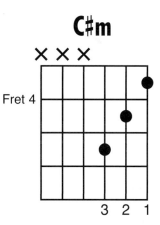

Above: This 4th position chord uses the same finger pattern as F# minor in 9th position. These flexible three-string shapes allow you to move from chord to chord with ease.

E

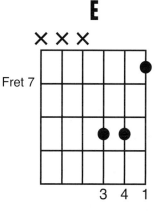

Above: Another shape that results in a new major chord when moved to a different fret position. D major at 5th position becomes E major when shifted to 7th position.

CHORD CHART – 19

This session has an equal share of riffing and chord work, and even contains a 'chord solo' using three chord favourites – G major, E major and D major. Two new chords are also featured, most notably B major, which introduces the concept of the A shape barre chord, leading on from the six-string barre chords in previous sessions. If you are applying these chord boxes to the exercises, remember that the bold line at the top of each box represents the capo at fret 1.

E

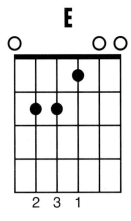

Above: The E major 'key chord' has a principal role to play as the one around which the other chords revolve.

Dsus²

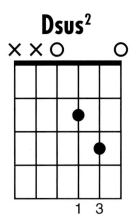

Above: An altered form of the D major chord also featured. The open top E string is the 2nd degree of the D scale referred to in its title.

B

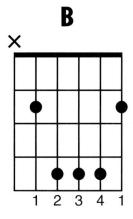

Above: Your first barre chord to use the A major shape. Use the finger barre to place the notes on the 1st and 5th strings.

A

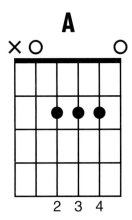

Above: The usual shape but with a less common fingering. The use of fingers 2, 3 and 4 results in a much smoother and easier shift from the B major chord.

G

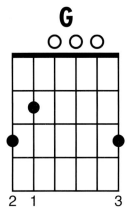

Above: A familiar shape in *The Guitar Book*, though less frequently used so far than the four-fingered G major chord. A low thumb helps the six-string stretch between fingers 2 and 3.

D

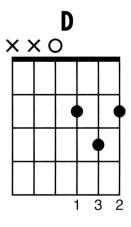

Above: The instantly recognizable triangular finger pattern of this four-string chord. The root note, D, is doubled one octave higher at fret 3 on the B string.

CHORD CHART - 20

The A, G and D major chords, which have all featured regularly in previous sessions, lie at the heart of the exercises based on the song by Cast. The Dsus4 chord, which returns after a long absence, is joined by the new Asus4 chord. Both are used to add some colour to their parent chords of D major and A major, respectively. Even though your recently rehearsed barre chords are not involved here, keep practising these crucial shapes in readiness for their return in future exercises.

A⁽¹⁾

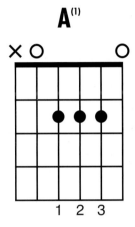

Above: This is the most commonly used form of the A major chord, with fingers 1, 2 and 3 squeezed into the 2nd fret. Make sure that finger 3 is clear of the open top E string.

A⁽²⁾

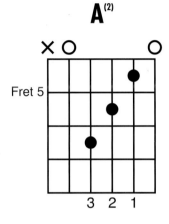

Above: This is an effective 5th position alternative to the conventional A major shape, from which the open A and top E strings are retained. The bottom E string is not played.

Gmaj⁹/A

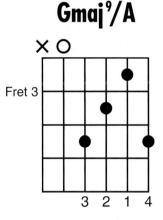

Above: The B, G and D string notes form a G major chord in 3rd position, with A (the 9th note above) added on top. An open A string at the bottom transforms the chord's sound.

G

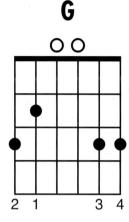

Above: G major is a frequently used shape played in 2nd position. The regular exchanges with D major make this shape preferable to the three-finger version of the chord.

D

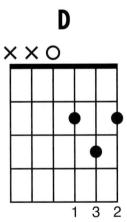

Above: This chord is of great importance as it this session's key chord. Curve the fingers to prevent the collapse of finger 3 onto the 1st string.

Dsus⁴

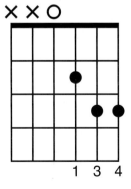

Above: The 4th finger 'suspends' from the D major chord, and often resolves as the top string note falls a fret back to form D major.

Asus⁴

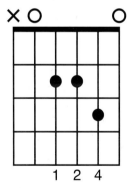

Above: The major 3rd from the A chord is replaced by note 4 of the A scale, making the B string note fret 3 instead of fret 2.

Gmaj⁷

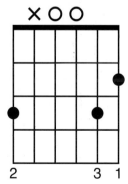

Above: Though lacking a major 3rd, the effect of the major 7th on the top E string justifies the chord's name. Mute the A string with the underside of finger 2.

CHORD CHART – 21

Chords galore! Many of these chords contain idiosyncrasies that set them apart from conventional chord shapes. The D#, E and C major chords don't contain a top E string note. Therefore, the full A shape barre chord has to be modified to mute the top string. The 1st position E major chord in the solo does not include the top two strings. The Cadd9♭5 chord is not one you come across every day, and the F5 shape is noteworthy for its unusual location.

D#

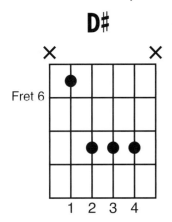

Above: Played in 6th position, this shape is closely related to the A shape barre chord featured earlier. The difference lies in the absence of a top string note.

E⁽¹⁾

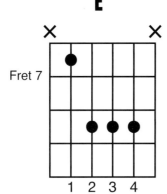

Above: This is the same as the D# chord shifted up one fret to 7th position. The 1st finger places the A string note and also mutes the top and bottom strings.

B

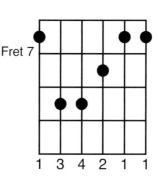

Above: B major is the full E major barre chord shape played in 7th position. This is known as the 'dominant', or 5th, chord in the key of E major.

E⁽²⁾

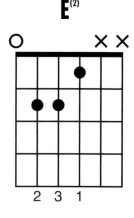

Above: Unusually, the top two strings of this version of E major are not used during their brief appearance, hence the crosses above these strings.

Three solo chords

Cadd9♭5

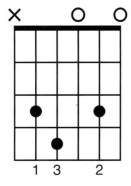

Above: A chord to be used sparingly, though it's perfect within some songs' context. The fret 4 note on the D string is the flat (♭) 5 note and cause of the discordance.

C

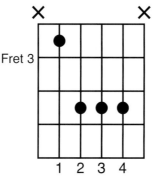

Above: This C chord is played in 3rd position, but otherwise is identical to the D# and E major chords introduced in an earlier session.

F5

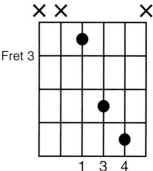

Above: This unusual power chord shape shares its 3rd finger location with C major. This presents a short cut as you switch between the two chords.

CHORD CHART - 22

Here's a valuable chance to perfect some important shapes that will keep turning up in your playing. Of course, every song brings these well-known chords together in a different order, which raises interesting questions about how best to change from one shape to the next.

Make a habit of practising these chord shapes as often as possible.

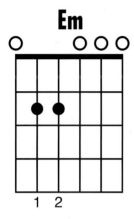

Above: E minor is a regular visitor in *The Guitar Book*. On this occasion, fingers 1 and 2 place the fretted notes in order to ease the shift to C major.

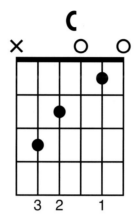

Above: C major is an essential chord to have in your repertoire. The identical 2nd finger location is the key to a smooth change to or from E minor.

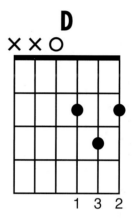

Above: D major is another favourite. Aim to place the triangular finger pattern as a single unit rather than one finger at a time.

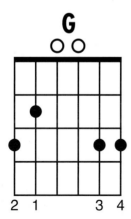

Above: G major is the key chord for *There She Goes*. This particular shape dates back to *Wonderwall* and shares its 3rd finger location with the D major chord.

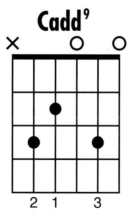

Above: Cadd9 consists of the C major chord with an added 9th step above C – which is the note D. The 9th occurs at fret 3 on the B string and replaces the octave C.

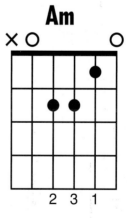

Above: Although a minor appears only fleetingly in the exercises, it's quite a commonly used chord and is sure to crop up more or less regularly in your playing.

CHORD CHART – 23

Open G tuning leads to some unorthodox chord shapes and explains the curious finger pattern for C major. This tuning system has its roots in the Blues and is ideal for playing chords with a slide or bottleneck, as well as for playing rock'n'roll in the style of Keith Richards. Before attempting these chords, tune your open strings, from bottom to top, to D, G, D, G, B and D. For the dropped D power chord, keep the bottom string tuned to D, but re-tune the 5th string up to A.

①= D   ②= H   ③= G   ④= D   ⑤= G   ⑥= D

C

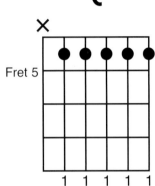

Above: With open G tuning you can create C major using just a 1st finger barre across the top five strings at fret 5. Avoid the bottom string, as this would put a G at the root of the chord.

Fadd2/C

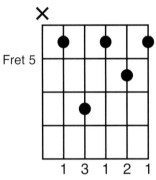

Above: This chord shape gives rise to a shuffling harmony, as displayed in the song's verse. The top-string note is the add2 and is understated in the original Stones' recording.

B♭

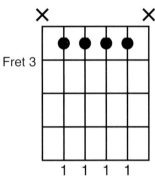

Above: The finger barre at fret 3 gives you B♭ major. The top string isn't played here, hence the cross, but usually the note is a perfectly valid part of a B♭ major chord.

E♭/B♭

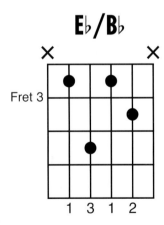

Above: E♭/B♭ is virtually the 3rd position equivalent of the Fadd2/C chord, but made easier to label by the absence of a top-string note. Literally, it is an E♭ major chord with a B♭ as the lowest note.

F5

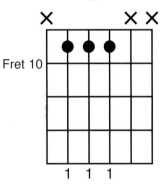

Above: The finger barre is now at fret 10. The 2nd string is not played, resulting in a power chord rather than a full-blown major chord. As with all these shapes, the bottom string is not included.

A5

⑥= D

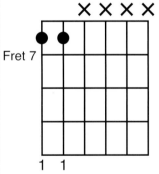

Above: With string 5 at standard A pitch and string 6 tuned down to D, power chords can be played with finger 1 lying across both strings. In this instance, lay the finger barre across fret 7 for A5.

CHORD CHART – 24

There's no shortage of chords in this session! Many of the most common 1st position chords are featured, making *On And On* an invaluable revision aid. On another level, this and many other modern ballads make great use of the open strings and static fingerings to create fresh and interesting-sounding chords, such as Cadd9 and A7sus4. A more unusual feature is the alternation of G major with D minor, resulting in an ambiguous mood in the intro and verses.

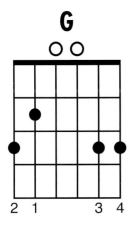

G

2 1   3 4

Above: As G major is a key chord here, it repeats frequently. The four-fingered shape works well with D minor, allowing finger 3 to stay in the same place.

Dm

2 3 1

Above: D minor was one of the first chords to feature in this book. Here, it is unusually paired up with G major. A low thumb improves the stretch of the fingers.

C

3 2   1

Above: The five-string chord of C major, chord IV in the key of G major and thus a primary chord. As C and G crop up together, spend some time shifting between them.

F

3 2 1 1

Above: The shorter form of F major, as played in *The House Of The Rising Sun*, makes a quick appearance. Barring only strings 1 and 2 makes the change to A minor easier.

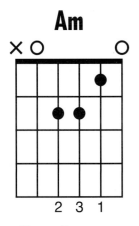

Am

2 3 1

Above: Due to an unusual change of chord sequence, A minor is another chord to appear only momentarily in this session.

G^6/H

1   3

Above: G6/B is a 'passing' chord used to smooth the shift from G major to Cadd9. The open top E string provides the 6th note referred to in the name.

Cadd^9

2 1 3

Above: Cadd9 appears in this form, as well as with the 4th finger at fret 3 on the top E string. It works well with G major, since it retains much of the G chord shape.

A^{7}sus^4

1   3 4

Above: A7sus4 shares the same finger 3 and 4 locations as G major, Cadd9 and Dsus4. This gives the chord sequence a unifying effect.

CHORD CHART – 25

Dropped D tuning and some spicy-sounding chords contribute to the interesting look of this chord chart. The rows of finger 1 symbols beneath the boxes show that the finger barre is an integral part of all the shapes, apart from D5. The barre should lie across the top strings as well, despite the crosses, which are there to show that these strings are not played. The D barre chord needs a conventionally tuned bottom E string. The chord includes only the lower four strings but is more often played across all six strings, hence the bracketed fingerings.

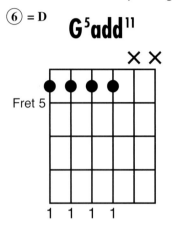

Above: With string 6 tuned down to D, the G5 part is covered by barring the bottom three strings at fret 5. The added 11 also requires you to barre string 3.

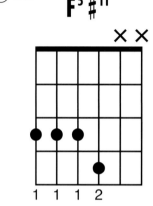

Above: F5#11 is not a chord you are likely to need very often. The addition of finger 2 on the G string gives this chord a distinctly sinister edge.

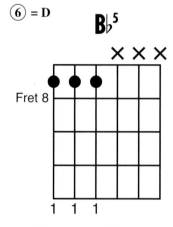

Above: As with standard tuned power chords, extending the shape to include the 4th string adds the octave to beef up the chord's sound.

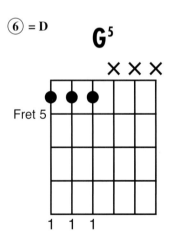

Above: The same shape as Bb5, only this time in 5th position. Mute the upper three strings by making a light contact with this part of the finger barre.

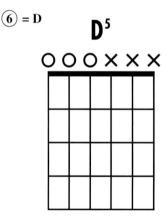

Above: A curious-looking chord because of the lack of any left hand fingering. With dropped D tuning, the open bottom three strings are D, A and D.

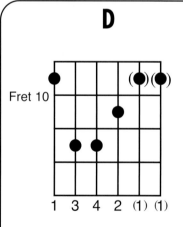

Above: This D barre chord is played in 10th position. The identical shape is used to create five other major chords by shifting to different fret positions.

CHORD CHART – 26

A lengthy guitar solo and large chunks of two-string chord shuffle mean that Buddy Holly's *That'll Be The Day* is thin on full-blown chord shapes. However, the key chord of E major appears in a few different guises and the B7 shape is a useful new pattern to add to your ever-growing repertoire. F# major is the only barre chord, and then there's some handy practice of the barred D7 and C7 chords. Remember that you need a capo at fret 5 to play all the chords in the exercises.

(capo at fret 5)

E⁽¹⁾
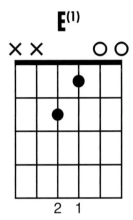

Above: This form of the E major chord uses only the top four strings of the six-string shape you've used in earlier exercises.

B⁷
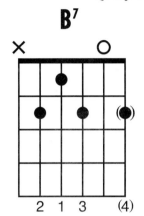

Above: This form of B7 is often used when playing in the key of E in 1st position. The shape more commonly also includes the 4th finger at fret 2 on the top E string.

A⁵
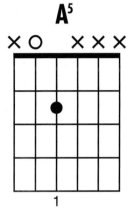

Above: A5 acts as the basic shape for the boogie-woogie shuffle. Finger 1 stays in place on the D string, while finger 3 rocks on and off the same string at fret 4.

E⁽²⁾
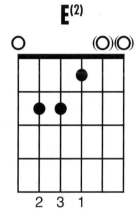

Above: This is the conventional E major shape, with fingers 1, 2 and 3 in action. All six strings are played only at the very end, hence the bracketed noughts.

Solo chords (no capo)

F#
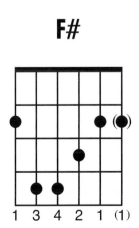

Above: F# major is a six-string barre chord based on the E shape. The barre extends across the top string, but Holly's light strums make no contact with it, which explains the brackets.

Cmaj⁷
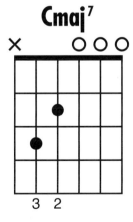

Above: C major 7 is often used for its warm, mellow sound and because of its simple fingering. Removing finger 1 from a standard C shape gives you an open B, which is the major 7.

D⁷
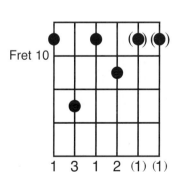

Above: The D7 barre chord is closely related to the F# chord. Swiftly moving the D7 shape to 8th position gives you C7, which occurs in quite a few rock 'n' roll riffs.

CHORD CHART - 27

Strummed chords play an important role in Sheryl Crow's song – they feature in the chorus in a fairly straightforward manner and form the basis of the verse riff. The majority of the chord work favours shapes without a top E string note, while the G shapes are noteworthy in that you have to mute the A string. *There Goes The Neighborhood* is played with a capo at fret 1, but for practice purposes, these chords can be studied with or without one.

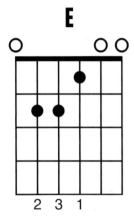

E

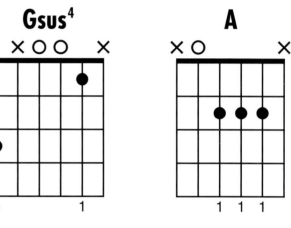

G   **Gsus⁴**   **A**

Above: E major crops up on a regular basis. It appears in a number of shortened forms, including one that uses only the four lower strings.

Above: This is still a G major chord, although it's not one of the full shapes. Use finger 3 both to fret the lowest string and to damp out the sound of the A string.

Above: Gsus4, related to the G shape, features a fret 1 note on the B string. Drop finger 1 lightly against the top string to ensure that the top E is not heard if accidentally struck.

Above: This is a conventional-looking A major shape, but it's played with a barre across the fret 2 notes. Once again, you should avoid playing the top E string.

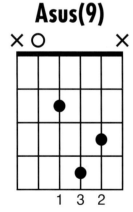

Asus(9)

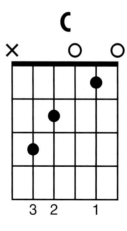

C

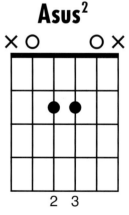

Asus²

Above: Asus(9) is in fact an Asus4 chord with an added 9th. Use finger 1 to barre the top four strings. A light contact with string 1 ensures that it doesn't ring if accidentally struck.

Above: This conventional C chord shape should be very familiar to you by now. Try using a high left thumb to damp out the bottom E string so that you can go for your strums with confidence.

Above: A new shape, the Asus2 chord is closely related to A major and is commonly found shifting to or from a full A major shape. Try practising this chord a few times to get used to it.

CHORD CHART - 28

Despite plenty of lead playing in *Staying Out For The Summer*, there's still room for a few useful chord shapes. You've played most of these chords before, but as you know, there's no substitute for regular practice in different combinations with new and varied strum patterns. Although the B minor 7 chord is not featured in the practice pieces, you will find it included here so that it's possible to replace the lead parts with a strummed accompaniment throughout.

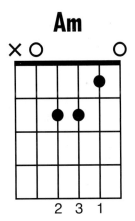

Am

Above: Considering the upbeat feel of the Dodgy song, it's surprising to find that the key of the song is the traditionally melancholy A minor. A high thumb helps to mute the bottom E string.

C

Above: C major is the chord most associated with A minor – it's what is known as A minor's 'relative major'. A simple transfer of finger 3 to the 5th string transforms A minor into C major.

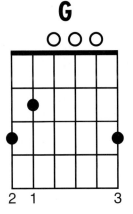

G

Above: G major crops up regularly in the practice pieces. However, this three-fingered version of the chord, which uses an open B rather than a D on the 3rd fret, is less common.

Dm⁷

Above: D minor 7 is familiar from an earlier session's riff exercise. The addition of the 7th on the B string at fret 1 warms the somewhat gloomy sound of the D minor chord.

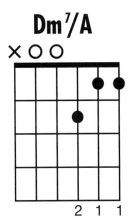

Dm⁷/A

Above: Dm7/A is a subtle adaptation of D minor 7, quite easily achieved by adding an open A string beneath the existing four-string shape. You can use finger 3 instead of finger 2 on the G string.

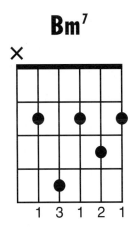

Bm⁷

Above: Although B minor 7 doesn't feature in a specific practice piece in this session, this barre chord shape is still worth memorizing and a useful addition to the shapes you already know.

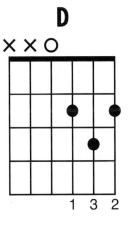

D

Above: D major is another chord featured here. This four-string shape should be familiar to you from several different sessions' exercises. Remember that practice makes perfect – so keep playing!

CHORD CHART – 29

When taken out of context, this selection of chord shapes from *All Right Now* by Free looks unusual. A major is the closest to a conventional full chord shape, although even this contains no open top-string note and is played with a finger barre. The two versions of the D chord avoid the regular triangular shape, and the A5 and G5 chords are located an octave higher than usual.

A

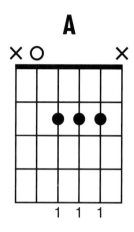

Above: This is the exact same form of A major that you played in the Sheryl Crow song. It features a barred 2nd fret fingering and has no open top E string note.

D(1)

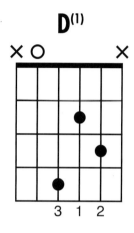

Above: Strictly speaking, this is a D/A chord because open A is its lowest note. In the exercises, however, the 5th string is always played before the rest of the chord, which keeps the D chord identity strong.

A5

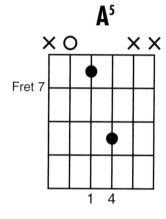

Above: This is one of three A5 shapes. Using fingers 1 and 4 makes the shifts easier, and the open A string gives more weight to the chord's sound.

D(2)

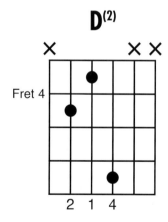

Above: This D major pattern is governed by the melodic shape of the chorus accompaniment. It follows on nicely from the 5th position G5 chord.

G5

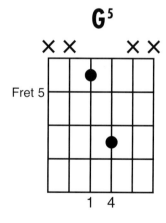

Above: On this occasion, G5 is played in 5th position on the D and G strings. As with the A5 shape, finger 4 replaces the more common 3rd finger for the upper note.

A5/E

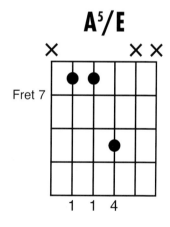

Above: The chorus also features this variant of the A5 chord. The addition of fret 7 on the 5th string means that you should use a 1st finger barre.

CHORD CHART - 30

Although these exercises are as challenging as always, the chord shapes are very simple to understand. Most are three-string power chords that can be played with a barre because of the dropped D tuning of the bottom string. More unusual is the use of fingers 2 and 3 to form a barre for some of these power chords, which has the benefit of cutting down the amount of left hand shifts. Note that the solo chords require you to re-tune your guitar to the standard E, A, D, G, B and E pitch.

① = Es   ② = B   ③ = Ges   ④ = Des   ⑤ = As   ⑥ = Des

C⁵

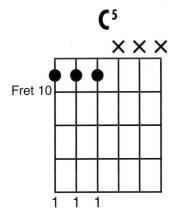

Fret 10

Above: The 6th string is tuned a tone lower than the others, making this C5 chord playable by barring the three strings with finger 1. Aim to mute the other strings.

D⁵⁽¹⁾

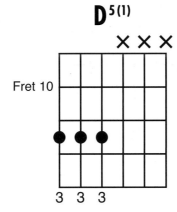

Fret 10

Above: This form of D5 uses the same shape as C5 but is played at fret 12. The quick alternation with C5 makes sense of using the unorthodox 3rd finger barre.

D

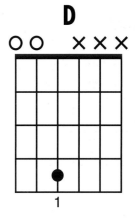

Above: This is the only major chord used here. A light contact of finger 1 with the 3rd string provides a safety net in case you strum too far.

D⁵⁽²⁾

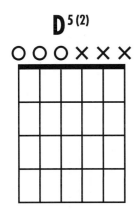

Above: This D5 shape couldn't be simpler. It's one octave lower than 12th position D5, which means you need only the bottom three open strings.

E

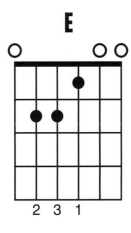

Above: To recap, the chord of E major. This is the standard 1st position shape involving all six strings.

A⁵

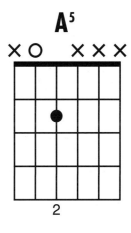

Above: The A power chord. Using finger 2 works best in the context of a riff, although finger 1 is more common.

CHORD CHART - 31

With an emphasis on rhythm guitar, this session focuses strongly on chord shapes, many of which you have come across before in this book. The likes of D, A minor, G and A are essential chords that you should always have at your fingertips, while even the G/F# and Asus4 shapes are common enough to warrant committing to memory.

Remember to capo the 2nd fret if you want to try out these chords with any of the session's practice pieces.

D
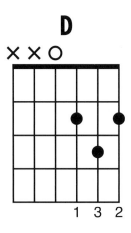

Am

G
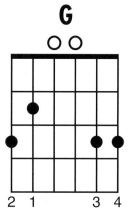

G/F#
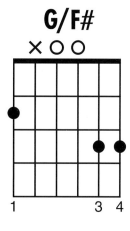

Above: D major is the song's key chord. It also appears with an open A string at the bottom, making it D/A. With D/A, using a half-barre makes the shifts to and from B minor easier.

Above: A minor is a five-string chord played in 1st position. Remember that minor chord symbols are differentiated from their major equivalents by the use of a small 'm' after the note name.

Above: G major is another shape you have used many times before. For the best sound, keep your fingers arched and positioned as far to the right as possible in each fret.

Above: This G chord with an F# bass note sounds strange when played out of context. Its rightful place is as a linking chord between G and E minor 7.

Em⁷
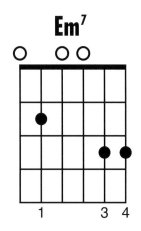

A

Bm
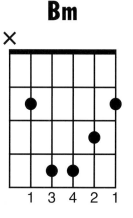

Asus⁴

Above: E minor 7 is a common variation of E minor. On this occasion, the 7th referred to in its name appears twice – once on the B string at fret 3 and also as an open D string.

Above: Here, the A major chord features the traditional 1st, 2nd and 3rd fingers squeezed neatly into fret 2, rather than the 1st finger barre that has been used previously.

Above: The B minor barre chord shape is very useful. By moving it to different fret positions you can create a host of minor chords. Try to mute string 6 with the tip of the 1st finger barre.

Above: Asus4 is almost identical to A major, but replaces the major 3rd with the 4th degree of the A scale. This requires the use of finger 4 at fret 3 on the B string instead of finger 3 at fret 2.

CHORD CHART - 32

A traditional Blues chord sequence features only three chords – the tonic (I), the subdominant (IV) and the dominant (V). Although *Folsom Prison Blues* by Johnny Cash is a country song, the Blues chord progression is central to its structure. This is why just three chords feature in the session – E, A and B7.

However, as the following six shapes show, there's more to it than this, since you'll find three different forms of A chord and two versions of B7 in the original. Each is played with a capo at fret 1, but the capo is optional if you are practising the shapes without the recording.

B⁷⁽¹⁾

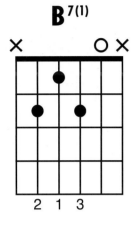

2 1 3

Above: B7 is the original song's dominant 7th chord in the key of E major. It is also often played with finger 4 on the top E string at fret 2.

E

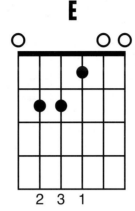

2 3 1

Above: The key chord of E major is played in its full six-string form in the practice pieces. In the original, the strings are split in flatpicking style.

A⁵

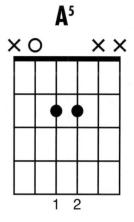

1 2

Above: This three-string A chord features in song's verses. The lack of a fret 2 note on the B string makes this a power chord rather than a major shape.

A⁽¹⁾

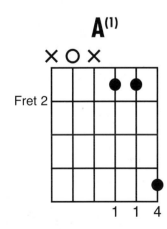

Fret 2

1 1 4

Above: This form of A major cannot be strummed, due to the absence of a 4th string note. However, when flatpicking, the bass note is separated and the top three strings are strummed together.

A⁽²⁾

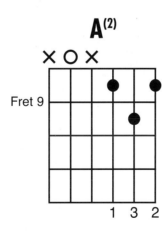

Fret 9

1 3 2

Above: The fretted notes for this version of A major use the pattern you would normally associate with D major, but in 9th position. An open 5th string completes the shape.

B⁷⁽²⁾

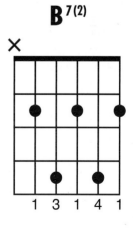

1 3 1 4 1

Above: B7 as a barre-chord shape is very useful. It's slightly more comfortable to place than the full B major barre-chord, since there are two and not three notes played at fret 4.

CHORD CHART – 33

The lack of any chord work in *Hanging On The Telephone* by Blondie forces a break with *The Guitar Book's* tradition of listing a session's principal shapes here on the chord chart page. However, the song does have a rhythm guitar part, so listen to the original song and then try out these chord shapes if you fancy strumming along instead of playing lead.

E♭

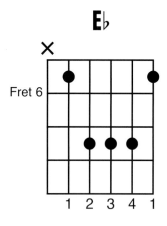

Above: E♭ is an A shape barre chord, meaning that it is based on the 1st position A major finger pattern. The same shape in 1st position can be used for B♭ major.

Gm

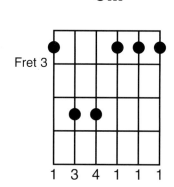

Above: G minor is an unusual key for a pop song, but the associated bunch of unfriendly guitar chord shapes are less relevant to Blondie's lead guitar-dominated approach.

Fsus⁴

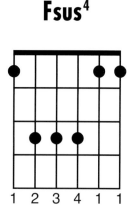

Above: Fsus4 is not a chord you come across every day. Practise this chord regularly as it is a useful addition to your list of chord shapes.

Cm

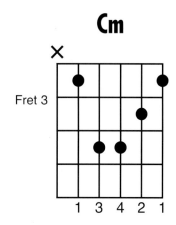

Above: The five-string C minor barre chord shape is another very useful one to have at your fingertips as it gives access to lots of chords that don't include any open strings.

Dm

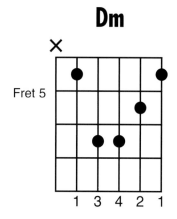

Above: D minor uses the same five-string barre chord shape as C minor, only this time in 5th position. In the context of the Blondie song, this is a better option than the first session's D minor shape.

F

Above: Together with E♭, Cm and Gm, F major completes a set of four essential barre chord shapes. These patterns allow you to play any major or minor chord by transferring their shapes to different fret positions.

CHORD CHART - 34

There are more chord shapes in *Marblehead Johnson* than we can document in the limited space available on this page. Not only does the song feature strummed chords, such as the ones shown here, but other shapes are placed that never sound as a full chord, such as the C major notes. Because there are so many, some only feature briefly, such as Am and Dsus4.

Asus2

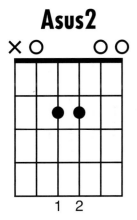

Above: Asus2 is a rich-sounding chord given added bite by the slight clash of the open B string (the suspended 2nd) against the neighbouring A note played on string 3.

Dsus2

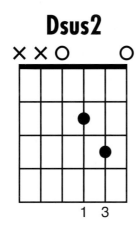

Above: Dsus2 shares the same sound properties as Asus2. In other words, it's built from root and 5th notes with a suspended 2nd replacing the more conventional 3rd.

D9

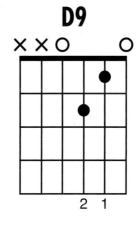

Above: Four different types of D chord are played at or around this particular position, including D9. An open top E provides the jazzy 9th harmony.

G7

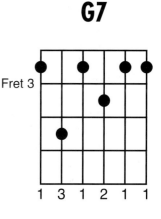

Above: The session's first full barre chord is a useful shape to know. Later, a sus4 note is added to G7 by placing finger 4 at fret 5 on the G string.

A⁷sus⁴

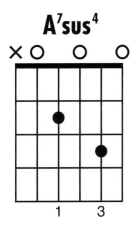
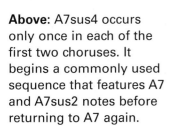

Above: A7sus4 occurs only once in each of the first two choruses. It begins a commonly used sequence that features A7 and A7sus2 notes before returning to A7 again.

H⁷

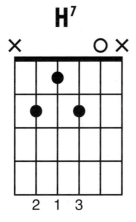

Above: You played this form of B7 in *Folsom Prison Blues*. Just as on that occasion, the fret 2 note on the top string associated with this shape is omitted.

Am

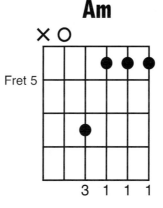

Above: A new variation on the frequently used A minor chord. It's played in 5th position with a half barred 1st finger and an open 5th string.

Dsus⁴

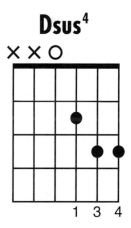

Above: Dsus4 begins a sequence similar to that of the A7 chords. The lower string notes stay static while the top string changes alter the chords from Dsus4 to D, Dsus2 and back to D again.

CHORD CHART - 35

Chord shapes feature heavily in this session's practice pieces. The famous Police riff from *Message In A Bottle* is based around add9 chords, while other parts of the song provide a chance to revise two-string power chords and some barre chord shapes. It's also worth recapping on four of the most used guitar chords – A minor, F, C and G.

C#madd⁹

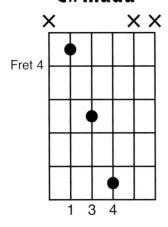

Above: C#madd9 is a chord with a mouthful of a name and an exacting finger stretch. The five-fret reach from finger 1 at fret 4 up to finger 4 at fret 8 is unforgiving but crucial to the Police riff.

Aadd⁹

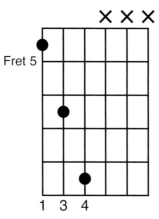

Above: Aadd9 shares the same finger pattern as C#madd9, but is played on the bottom three strings in 5th position. Badd9 and F#madd9 also use this shape in 7th and 2nd position, respectively.

A⁵

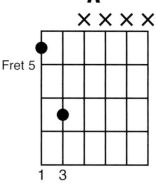

Above: In a session that is dominated by challenging chords, this A5 pattern comes as something of a relief. The same two-finger shape is used to play D5 and E5 on the A and D strings.

C#m

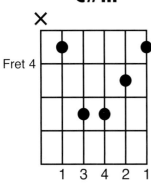

Above: C#m is the key chord for *Message In A Bottle*. This 4th position barred shape is the most common form of the chord, which contains the notes C#, E and G#.

A

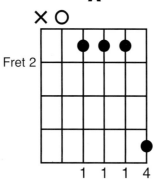

Above: This 2nd position form of A is rarely used because of the awkward 4th finger stretch. The top-string note smooths out the sound of the chord change from C#m.

F#m

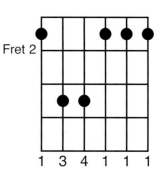

Above: F# minor is used sparingly in the exercises, but the hanging quality of its long, sustained strums has a dramatic impact. Aim for a straight finger barre right across the 2nd fret.

CHORD CHART - 36

Joni Mitchell uses dropped D tuning in a totally different way from any examples covered in *The Guitar Book* so far. The main difference is that she also drops the tuning of the top string, allowing greater potential for uncommon chord shapes in the accompaniment to *Free Man In Paris*. These tend to be full chords that imaginatively combine fretted and open strings to great effect. Remember to adapt your standard tuning before trying out any of these shapes.

① = D   ② = H   ③ = G   ④ = D   ⑤ = A   ⑥ = D

C⁽¹⁾

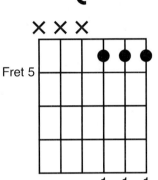

Above: Thanks to the dropped D tuning, a half-barre at fret 5 takes care of all three notes of C major. The same shape moved up to 7th position is used to form D major.

F

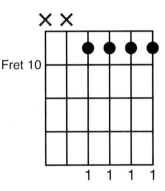

Above: This is an extended version of the C shape. Technically, it should be referred to as F/C, but most of the time it features only the major chord notes on the top three strings.

Aadd⁹

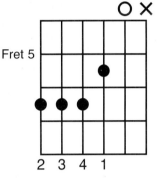

Above: Aadd9 is the song's key chord. The dropped D bass string necessitates a new finger pattern for the major chord notes on the bottom four strings.

C⁽²⁾

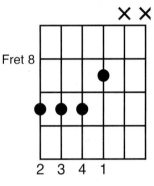

Above: The Aadd9 chord shape moved up to frets 9 and 10 makes another type of C major chord. The open B string is omitted on this occasion.

G

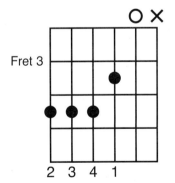

Above: This is yet another way to play a G chord. Notice the return of the open B string, which doubles the major 3rd of the chord when played in this position.

D/A

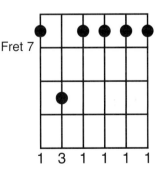

Above: The shape of this fully barred D chord with an A in the bass is used frequently in *Free Man In Paris*. It also features in 5th position as C/G and in 10th position as F/C.

Fadd²/C

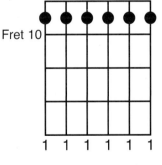

Above: The removal of finger 3 from the A string produces the add2 note for this six-string Fadd2/C chord, which is played solely with a finger barre in 10th position.

Em¹¹/A

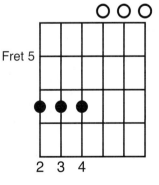

Above: Em11/A combines three fret 7 notes on the lower strings with the top three open strings. The chord's full sound will lift any instrumental break in the song.

CHORD CHART - 37

The dropped D tuning in *Place Your Hands* by Reef produces a set of less common chord shapes. The song's riff is built from D and G/D chords, although for most of the song you need to play the bass string before the other notes of the chords. The de-tuned 6th string means that the power chords played on the 5th and 6th strings can be barred across the same fret. The G and E chords based on the A barre chord shape are unaffected by the change of tuning.

⑥ = **D** (for all six chords)

D

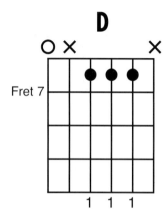

Fret 7

Above: D major is the key chord of the song – its sound is dominated by the de-tuned open 6th string. Mute the 5th string with the tip of the 7th fret finger barre.

G/D

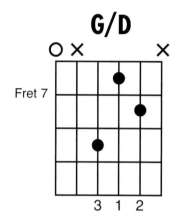

Fret 7

Above: G/D is always paired with the D chord in the riff and uses the same finger barre at fret 7. Be careful not to strum through the unwanted top string.

G⁽¹⁾

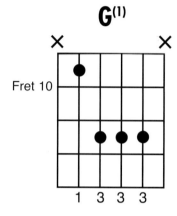

Fret 10

Above: You should be familiar with this A barre chord shape. Played in 10th position, it produces a G chord. Use the 3rd finger to barre the B, G and D strings.

B⁵

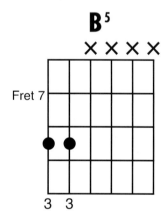

Fret 7

Above: Dropped D tuning results in power chords with both notes played at the same fret. In the context of the song, it's best to use finger 3 to form the necessary barre.

G⁽²⁾

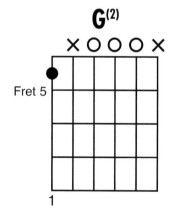

Fret 5

Above: This is an unusual form of G major, consisting mostly of open strings. Use the underside of the 1st finger to damp out the 5th string. The top string is, once again, unused.

E

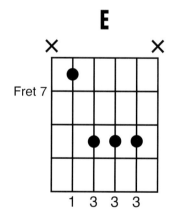

Fret 7

Above: E major is the second A barre chord shape in this session. Place your hand in 7th position. The 3rd finger barre can be substituted with fingers 2, 3 and 4.

CHORD CHART - 38

Shortened chord shapes form the backbone of the principal riffs featured in this session's song. However, these shapes change fret position so often that it would be pointless to label each and every one. Instead, the overall harmony of each passage is marked, such as the Em7 label that applies to the whole of the 1st bar of *There's No Other Way*. Listed below are some of the fuller chords that are played either in the chorus or the outro sections. All these chords are played in standard tuning.

E

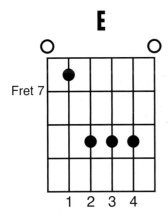

Above: E major is the key chord of the song's chorus. Although closely related to the A barre chord shape, the open top and bottom strings remove the need for a 1st finger barre.

Dadd⁹

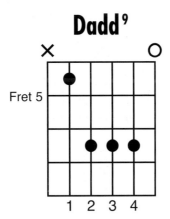

Above: Dadd9 shares exactly the same finger pattern as the 7th position E chord. It is played two frets lower, however, with the open top E string lending the add9 note.

G⁽¹⁾

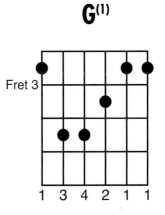

Above: G major is formed by shifting the six-string E barre chord shape to 3rd position. This chord features both with and without the top string note.

A

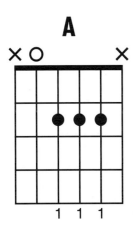

Above: This is a less common form of A major. In the context of the Blur song, it requires a barred 1st finger for the fretted notes. The top string should be avoided.

G⁽²⁾

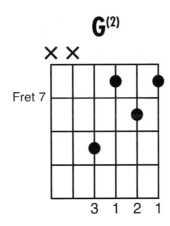

Above: Although the lowest note of this chord shape is B, a strong G major harmony is suggested. A two-fret shift up the neck gives another version of A major, as used in the chorus.

D

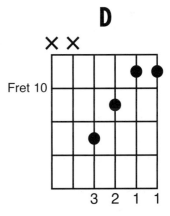

Above: In the song, this D major chord has finger 1 barring the top four strings. The same shape is used in 12th and 7th positions for E and B major respectively.

CHORD CHART - 39

Many of the chord shapes you use on a regular basis are present in this session. Queen's *Crazy Little Thing Called Love* is firmly rooted in the key of D major, so the frequent appearance of D and Dsus4 shapes should come as no surprise.

The other primary chords of G (chord IV) and A (chord V) are also involved. The appearance of an E, A and F major sequence within a Fifties-style rock'n'roll tune in the key of D is evidence of an imaginative band writing at the peak of its powers.

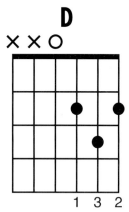
D
× × ○

1 3 2

Above: D major uses its distinctive triangular finger shape. For a tidier effect when strumming, try to mute the bottom E string with the tip of the left thumb.

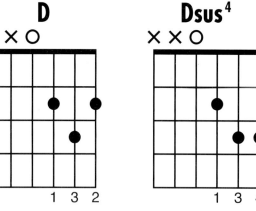
Dsus⁴
× × ○

1 3 4

Above: The D chords are interspersed with single Dsus4 chords. Although not labelled in the box, keep finger 2 on the top string at fret 2 for smooth exchanges with D major.

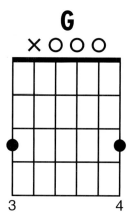
G
× ○ ○ ○

3   4

Above: This uncommon form of G has a muted A string. The use of fingers 3 and 4 for the fretted notes is likely to cause the 3rd finger to automatically mute the 5th string.

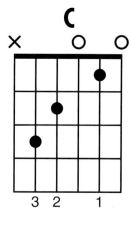
C
×   ○   ○

3 2   1

Above: The best-known form of C major, with fingers 1, 2 and 3 set up diagonally across the strings. Try muting the 6th string with your thumb.

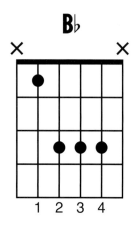
B♭
×   ×

1 2 3 4

Above: This B♭ major shape is best barred with finger 1 across the top five strings at fret 1. Rest finger 4 against the top E string to mute any accidental contact.

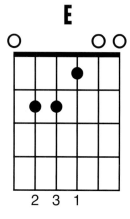
E
○   ○ ○

2 3 1

Above: This form of E major is the template for the six-string major barre chord. Make sure the bottom string is allowed to ring.

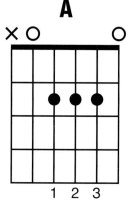
A
× ○   ○

1 2 3

Above: Our old favourite, A major, appears only fleetingly. This finger pattern forms the basis of the five-string major barre chord shape.

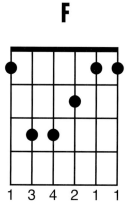
F

1 3 4 2 1 1

Above: Although you play F major only once in the practice pieces, it's a chord you are bound to come across time and again as you learn more songs to play on your guitar.

INDEX

MUSIC CREDITS

All Along The Watchtower
Words and Music by Bob Dylan. © 1968 Dwarf Music, USA. B Feldman and Co Ltd, London WC2H 0QY. Reproduced by permission of International Music Publications Ltd. All Rights Reserved.

All Day And All Of The Night
Written and composed by Ray Davies. © 1964 by Edward Kassner Music Co. Ltd. Copyright © 1964 Jayboy Music Corp. Copyright Renewed. All Rights Administered by Sony/ATV Music Publishing, 8 Music Square West, Nashville, TN 37203. International Copyright Secured. All Rights Reserved.

Black Night
Words and Music by Jon Lord, Ritchie Blackmore, Ian Gillan, Roger Glover and Ian Paice. © 1970 B Feldman and Co Ltd trading as Hec Music, London WC2H 0QY. Reproduced by permission of International Music Publications Ltd. All Rights for the United States and Canada Controlled and Administered by Glenwood Music Corp. For Australia and New Zealand: EMI Music Publishing Australia Pty Limited (ABN 83 000 040 951) PO Box 481, Spit Junction, NSW 2088, Australia. International copyright secured. All Rights Reserved. Used by Permission.

Bohemian Rhapsody
Words and Music by Freddie Mercury. © 1975 (Renewed 2003) B Feldman and Co Ltd trading as Trident Music Ltd, London WC2H 0QY. All Rights Controlled and Administered by Glenwood Music Corp. Reproduced by permission of International Music Publications Ltd. All Rights Reserved.

Brown Sugar
Written by Mick Jagger, Keith Richards. Published by ABKCO Music, Inc.

Cross Road Blues (Crossroads)
Words and Music by Robert Johnson. Copyright © (1978), 1990, 1991 Lehsem II, LLC and Claud L. Johnson. Administered by Music and Media International, Inc. International Copyright Secured. All Rights Reserved.

Dark Star
Words and Music by Jerry Garcia and Robert Hunter. © 1968 Ice Nine Publishing Co Inc, USA. Warner/Chappell North America Ltd, London W6 8BS. Reproduced by permission of International Music Publications Ltd. All Rights Reserved.

Get It On
Words and music by Marc Bolan. © 1971 Westminster Music Limited of Suite 1.07, Plaza 535 Kings Road, London SW10 0SZ. International Copyright Secured. All Rights Reserved. Used by Permission.

Heartbreak Hotel
Words and Music by Mae Boren Axton, Tommy Durden and Elvis Presley. Copyright © 1956 Sony/ATV Songs LLC. Copyright Renewed. All Rights Administered by Sony/ATV Music Publishing, 8 Music Square West, Nashville, TN 37203. International Copyright Secured. All Rights Reserved.

Heartbreaker
Words and music by Jimmy Page, Robert Plant, John Paul Jones and John Bonham. © 1969 (renewed) Flames Of Albion Music Inc, USA. Warner/Chappell Music Ltd, London W6 8BS. Reproduced by permission of International Music Publications Ltd. All Rights Reserved.

Hey Joe
Words and Music by Billy Roberts. © 1962 Third Story Music Inc, USA. Carlin Music Corp, London NW1 8BD for PRS Territories only. Reproduced by permission of International Music Publications Ltd. All Rights Reserved.

I Ain't Superstitious
Words and Music by Willie Dixon. © Copyright 1963 Arc Music Corporation, USA. Tristan Music Limited. Used by permission of Music Sales Limited. All Rights Reserved. International Copyright Secured.

(I Can't Get No) Satisfaction
Written by Mick Jagger, Keith Richards. Published by ABKCO Music, Inc.

I've Found A New Baby
Words by Spencer Williams. Music by Jack Palmer. © 1926 Clarence Williams Music Publishing Co Inc and Pickwick Music Corp, USA (50%) B. Feldman and Co Ltd, London WC2H 0QY (50%). Redwood Music Ltd, London NW1 8BD for the Commonwealth of Nations, Germany, Austria, Switzerland, South Africa and Spain. Reproduced by permission of International Music Publications Ltd. All Rights Reserved.

Iron Man
Words and Music by Terence Butler, John Osbourne, Tony Iommi and William Ward. © 1969 Westminster Music Limited of Suite 2.07, Plaza 535 Kings Road, London SW10 0SZ.

Jessica
Words and Music by Forrest Richard Betts. © 1973 (renewed) Unichappell Music Inc and Forrest Richard Betts Music, USA. Warner/Chappell North America Ltd, London W6 8BS. Reproduced by permission of International Music Publications Ltd. All Rights Reserved.

Jumpin' Jack Flash
Written by Mick Jagger, Keith Richards. Published by ABKCO Music, Inc.

Kashmir
Words and music by Jimmy Page, Robert Plant and John Bonham. © 1975 Flames Of Albion Music Inc, USA. Warner/Chappell Music Ltd, London W6 8BS. Reproduced by permission of International Music Publications Ltd. All Rights Reserved.

Layla
Words and Music by Eric Clapton and Jim Gordon. © Copyright 1970, 1998 and 2005 Eric Clapton and Throat Music Ltd. Used by permission of Music Sales Limited and International Music Publications Ltd. All Rights Reserved. International Copyright Secured.

Le Freak
Words and Music by Bernard Edwards and Nile Rodgers. © Copyright 1979 Bernard's Other Music/Sony/ATV Songs LLC, USA. Warner/Chappell Music Limited (50%)/Sony/ATV Music Publishing (UK) Limited (50%). All Rights on behalf of Sony/ATV Songs LLC Administered by Sony/ATV Music Publishing, 8 Music Square West, Nashville, TN 37203. Used by permission of Music Sales Limited and International Music Publications Ltd. All Rights Reserved. International Copyright Secured.

Live And Let Die
Words and Music by Paul McCartney and Linda McCartney. © Copyright 1973 MPL Communications Limited (75%)/EMI United Partnership Limited, worldwide print rights controlled by Alfred Publishing/IMP Limited (25%). Used by permission of Music Sales Limited and International Music Publications Ltd. All Rights Reserved. International Copyright Secured.

Me And The Devil Blues
Words and Music by Robert Johnson. Copyright © (1978), 1990, 1991 Lehsem II, LLC and Claud L. Johnson. Administered by Music and Media International, Inc. International Copyright Secured. All Rights Reserved.

Money
Words and Music by George Roger Waters. © 1973 Roger Waters Music Overseas Ltd. Warner/Chappell Artemis Music Ltd, London W6 8BS. Reproduced by permission of International Music Publications Ltd. All Rights Reserved.

Mr Bojangles
Words and Music by Jerry Jeff Walker. © 1968 (renewed) Cotillion Music Inc and Mijac Music, USA. Warner/Chappell North America Ltd, London W6 8BS. Reproduced by permission of International Music Publications Ltd. All Rights Reserved.

Mystery Train
Words and Music by Sam C Phillips and Herman Parker Jr. © 1955 (renewed) Hi-Lo Music and Mijac Music, USA. Carlin Music Corp, London, NW1 8BD for the Commonwealth of Nations (excluding Canada/Australasia) Eire and Israel. Warner/Chappell North America Ltd, London W6 8BS for the Rest Of The World. Reproduced by permission of International Music Publications Ltd. All Rights Reserved.

Nuages
Music by Django Reinhardt and Jacques Larue. © 1980 Peter Maurice Music Ltd. All Rights for the U.S. and Canada Controlled and Administered by Colgems-EMI Music Inc. All Rights Reserved. International Copyright Secured. Used by Permission.

Paranoid
Words and Music by Terence Butler, John Osbourne, Tony Iommi and William Ward. © 1969 Westminster Music Limited of Suite 2.07, Plaza 535 Kings Road, London SW10 0SZ.

Phase Dance
Music by Pat Metheny and Lyle Mays. © Copyright 1978 Pat Meth Music Corporation and Lyle Mays Music, USA. BMG Music Publishing Limited. Used by permission of Music Sales Limited. All Rights Reserved. International Copyright Secured.

Pinball Wizard
Words and Music by Pete Townshend. Copyright © 1969 by Towser Tunes, Inc., ABKCO Music and Fabulous Music Ltd. Copyright Renewed. All Rights for Towser Tunes, Inc. administered by BMG Music Publishing International. All Rights for BMG Music Publishing International in the U.S. Administered by Careers-BMG Music Publishing, a division of BMG Music Publishing NA, Inc. International Copyright Secured. All Rights Reserved.

Pride And Joy
Written by Stevie Ray Vaughan. © 1985 Ray Vaughan Music (ASCAP)/Administered by Bug Music. All Rights Reserved. Used by Permission

Purple Rain
Words and Music by Prince. © Copyright 1984 Controversy Music, USA. All Rights Controlled and Administered by Universal/MCA Music Limited. Used by permission of Music Sales Limited. All Rights Reserved. International Copyright Secured.

Rebel Rebel
Words and Music by David Bowie. © Copyright 1974 Jones Music America/RZO Music Limited (37.5%)/ Moth Music, Bewlay Brothers Music and EMI Music Publishing Ltd (37.5%)/Chrysalis Music Limited (25%). Used by permission of Music Sales Limited and International Music Publications Ltd. © 1974 Mainman Saag Ltd for Australia and New Zealand: EMI Music Publishing Australia Pty Limited (ABN 83 000 040 951) PO Box 481, Spit Junction, NSW 2088, Australia. All Rights for EMI Music Publishing Ltd controlled and administered by Colgems-EMI Music Inc. All Rights for Jones Music America administered by Arzo Publishing. All Rights for Moth Music administered by Chrysalis Songs. International copyright secured. All rights reserved. Used by permission.

Ride A White Swan
Words and Music by Marc Bolan. © 1970 Westminster Music Limited of Suite 1.07, Plaza 535 Kings Road, London SW10 0SZ. International Copyright Secured. All Rights Reserved. Used by Permission.

River Man
Written by Nick Drake. © 1969 Warlock Music Ltd.

Scuttle Buttin'
Written by Stevie Ray Vaughan. © 1984 Ray Vaughan Music (ASCAP)/Administered by Bug Music. All Rights Reserved. Used by Permission.

Seven Nation Army
Words and Music by Jack White. © 2002 Peppermint Stripe Music (BMI), USA. EMI Music Publishing Ltd, London WC2H 0QY. Reproduced by permission of International Music Publications Ltd. All Rights Reserved. Used by Permission.

She's Not There
Words and Music by Rod Argent. © 1964 Marquis Music Co Ltd, 1 Wyndham Yard, London W1H 2QF. Used by Permission.

Since You've Been Gone
Words and Music by Russ Ballard (Complete Music Ltd). © 1978 Complete Music Ltd. Printed by kind permission of Complete Music Ltd.

Smells Like Teen Spirit
Words and Music by Kurt Cobain, Krist Novoselic and Dave Grohl. © 1991 EMI Virgin Songs, Inc., The End of Music, M.J. Twelve Music and Murky Slough Music. All Rights Controlled and Administered by EMI Virgin Songs, Inc. All Rights Reserved. International Copyright Secured. Used by Permission.

Smoke On The Water
Words and Music by Jon Lord, Ritchie Blackmore, Ian Gillan, Roger Glover and Ian Paice. © 1972 B Feldman and Co Ltd trading as Hec Music, London WC2H 0QY. All Rights for the United States and Canada Controlled and Administered by Glenwood Music Corp. For Australia and New Zealand: EMI Music Publishing Australia Pty Limited (ABN 83 000 040 951) PO Box 481, Spit Junction, NSW 2088, Australia. International Copyright Secured. All Rights Reserved. Used by Permission.

Smooth
Words and Music by Itaal Shur and Robert Thomas. © 1999 Itaal Shur Music and Bidnis Inc, USA (60%) Warner/Chappell Music Ltd, London W6 8BS (40%) EMI Music Publishing Ltd, London WC2H 0QY. © 1999 EMI Blackwood Music, Inc., Bidnis, Inc. and Itaal Shur Music. All Rights for Bidnis, Inc. controlled and administered by EMI Blackwood Music, Inc. Reproduced by permission of International Music Publications Ltd. All Rights Reserved. International Copyright Secured. Used by Permission.

St Stephen
Words and Music by Robert Hunter, Jerry Garcia and Phil Lesh. © 1968 Ice Nine Publishing Co Inc, USA. Warner/Chappell North America Ltd, London W6 8BS. Reproduced by permission of International Music Publications Ltd. All Rights Reserved.

Stairway To Heaven
Words and Music by Jimmy Page and Robert Plant. © 1972 Superhype Music Ltd, London W6 8BS. Reproduced by permission of International Music Publications Ltd. All Rights Reserved.

Start Me Up
Words and Music by Mick Jagger and Keith Richards. © 1978 Promopub BV, Netherlands. EMI Music Publishing Ltd, London WC2H 0QY. Reproduced by permission of International Music Publications Ltd. All Rights Reserved.

Stormy Monday Blues
Words and Music by Aaron 'T-Bone' Walker. Copyright © 1947; Renewed 1975 Gregmark Music, Inc. (BMI). Worldwide Rights excluding the British Reversionary Territories but including Canada for Gregmark Music, Inc. Administered by Cherry River Music Co. International Copyright Secured. All Rights Reserved.

Sunshine Of Your Love
Words and Music by Jack Bruce, Pete Brown and Eric Clapton. © Copyright 1967 and 1996 Eric Clapton (33.33%)/Warner/Chappell Music Limited (66.67%). Copyright © 1968, 1973 by Dratleaf Ltd. Copyright Renewed. All Rights Administered by Unichappell Music Inc. Used by permission of Music Sales Limited and International Music Publications Ltd. All Rights Reserved. International Copyright Secured.

Sweet Baby James
Words and Music by James Taylor. © 1970 (Renewed 1998) EMI Blackwood Music Inc. and Country Road Music Inc. All Rights Controlled and Administered by EMI Blackwood Music Inc. All Rights Reserved. International Copyright Secured. Used by Permission

Sweet Little Angel
Words and Music by B.B. King and Jules Bihari. Copyright © 1956 by Careers-BMG Music Publishing, a division of BMG Music Publishing NA, Inc. Copyright Renewed. International Copyright Secured. All Rights Reserved.

Sweet Sixteen
Words and Music by B.B. King and Joe Bihari. Copyright © 1967 by Careers-BMG Music Publishing, a division of BMG Music Publishing NA, Inc. Copyright Renewed. International Copyright Secured. All Rights Reserved.

Three O'Clock Blues
Words and Music by B.B. King and Jules Bihari. Copyright © 1952 by Careers-BMG Music Publishing, a division of BMG Music Publishing NA, Inc. Copyright Renewed. International Copyright Secured. All Rights Reserved.

Tie Your Mother Down
Words and Music by Brian May. © 1976 Queen Music Ltd, London WC2H 0QY./ All Rights for the U.S. and Canada controlled and administered by Beechwood Music Corp. All Rights for the World excluding the U.S. and Canada controlled and administered by EMI Music Publishing Ltd. Reproduced by permission of International Music Publications Ltd. All Rights Reserved.

Time
Words and Music by George Roger Waters, David Gilmour, Nicholas Mason and Richard Wright. © 1973 Roger Waters Music Overseas Ltd and Pink Floyd Music Publishers Ltd (25%) Warner/Chappell Artemis Music Ltd, London W6 8BS. Reproduced by permission of International Music Publications Ltd. All Rights Reserved.

Tired Of Waiting For You
Written and composed by Ray Davies. © 1964 by Edward Kassner Music Co. Ltd. Copyright © 1964 Jayboy Music Corp. Copyright Renewed. All Rights Administered by Sony/ATV Music Publishing, 8 Music Square West, Nashville, TN 37203. International Copyright Secured. All Rights Reserved.

Travels
Words and Music by Pat Metheny and Lyle Mays. © Copyright BMG Music Publishing Limited. Used by permission of Music Sales Limited. All Rights Reserved. International Copyright Secured.

We Will Rock You
Words and Music by Brian May. © 1977 Queen Music Ltd, London WC2H 0QY. All Rights for the U.S. and Canada controlled and administered by Beechwood Music Corp. All Rights for the World excluding the U.S. and Canada controlled and administered by EMI Music Publishing Ltd. Reproduced by permission of International Music Publications Ltd. All Rights Reserved.

Where Were You?
Words and Music by Jeff Beck, Terry Bozzio and Tony Hymas. © 1989 BHB Music Ltd, USA. Warner/Chappell North America Ltd, London W6 8BS. Reproduced by permission of International Music Publications Ltd. All Rights Reserved.

Who Do You Love
Words and Music by Ellas McDaniel. © Copyright 1956 (renewed), 1991 MCA Music Limited (BMI). Tristan Music Limited. Used by permission of Music Sales Limited. All Rights Reserved. International Copyright Secured.

Whole Lotta Love
Words and Music by Jimmy Page, Robert Plant, John Bonham, John Paul Jones and Willie Dixon. © 1970 Flames Of Albion Music Inc, USA. Warner/Chappell Music Ltd, London W6 8BS. Reproduced by permission of International Music Publications Ltd. All Rights Reserved.

Wildwood Flower
Words and Music by A.P. Carter. © Copyright 1935 Peer International Corporation, USA. Peermusic (UK) Limited. Copyright Renewed. Used by permission of Music Sales Limited. All Rights Reserved. International Copyright Secured.

Wish You Were Here
Words and Music by George Roger Waters and David Gilmour. © 1975 Roger Waters Music Overseas Ltd and Pink Floyd Music Publishers Ltd. (50%) Warner/Chappell Artemis Music Ltd, London W6 8BS. Reproduced by permission of International Music Publications Ltd. All Rights Reserved.

The Yellow Princess
Words and Music by John Fahey. © 1966 Terrapin Music. Carlin Music Corp, London, NW1 8BD for the Commonwealth of Nations (excluding Canada/Australasia) and Eire.

You Really Got Me
Written and composed by Ray Davies. © 1964 by Edward Kassner Music Co. Ltd. Copyright © 1964 Jayboy Music Corp. Copyright Renewed. All Rights Administered by Sony/ATV Music Publishing, 8 Music Square West, Nashville, TN 37203. International Copyright Secured. All Rights Reserved.

You've Got A Friend
Words and Music by Carole King. © 1971 (Renewed 1999) Colgems-EMI Music Inc. All Rights Reserved. International Copyright Secured. Used by Permission.

Ziggy Stardust
Words and Music by David Bowie. © Copyright 1972 Tintoretto Music/RZO Music Ltd (37.5%)/ Moth Music, EMI Music Publishing Ltd (37.5%)/Chrysalis Music Ltd, (25%). Used by permission of Music Sales Limited and International Music Publications Ltd. All Rights Reserved. International Copyright Secured. © 1972 Mainman Saag Ltd for Australia and New Zealand: EMI Music Publishing Australia Pty Limited (ABN 83 000 040 951) PO Box 481, Spit Junction, NSW 2088, Australia. All Rights for EMI Music Publishing Ltd. Controlled and administered by Screen Gems-EMI Music Inc. All Rights for Tintoretto Music administered by RZO Music. All Rights for Moth Music administered by Chrysalis Songs. International Copyright Secured. All Rights Reserved. Used by Permission.

PHOTOGRAPHY CREDITS

All studio photography © Amber Books Ltd

Dorling Kindersley: 256 (top – Dave King)

Fender Europe: 217 (left)

Getty Images: 223 (Frank Micelotta, 334 (Keystone Features / Hulton Archive), 342 (Frank Micelotta), 358 (Sebastian Artz), 374 (Sebastian Artz), 390 (Miguel Rojo / AFP), 401 (Frank Driggs), 409 (Frank Driggs), 439 (Eric Schaal / Time & Life Pictures)

Guitar Traders: 280 (courtesy Mr. Naoki Washida)
Keith Morris: 443, 449, 450

Redferns: 218 (David Redfern), 219 (Michael Ochs), 220 (Ian Dickson), 221 (Richard E. Aaron), 222 (Richard Ecclestone), 225–226 (Michael Ochs), 229 (Don Paulsen), 230 (Bernd Muller), 232 (David Redfern), 234 (Bob King), 236 (Paul Bergen), 242 (Ebet Roberts), 244 (David Redfern), 247 (David Redfern), 248 (K & K Ulf Kruger), 250 (Robert Knight), 253 (Richard E. Aaron), 254 (Ian Dickson), 256(bottom – Grant Davis), 258 (Richard E. Aaron), 263 (GEMS), 264 (Michael Ochs), 267 (Mick Hutson), 268 (David Redfern), 271 (Ebet Roberts), 272 (Michael Ochs), 277 (David Redfern), 278 (Mick Hutson), 283 (Ron Howard), 289 (Fotex Agentur), 290 (Robert Knight), 292 (Jim McCary), 295 (David Redfern), 296 (Paul Reed Smith), 298 (bottom – David Redfern), 301 (Ebet Roberts), 302 (Fin Costello), 304 (Andrew Lepley), 309 (Richard E. Aaron), 310 (Fin Costello), 312 (Ebet Roberts), 315 (Harry Goodwin), 316 (Ian Dickson), 318 (Colin Fuller), 321 (Alain Dister), 322 (Richard Ecclestone), 324 (Richard Ecclestone), 326 (Ebet Roberts), 329 (Phil Dent), 330 (Geoff Dann), 332 (Bob King), 337–338 (Ebet Roberts), 341 (Richard E. Aaron), 345–346 (Mick Hutson), 349 (Peter Pakvis), 350 (Ebet Roberts), 353 (Tabatha Fireman), 354 (Paul Reed Smith), 356 (Michael Ochs), 357 (Deltahaze Corporation), 359–360 (David Redfern), 361 (Chuck Stewart), 363–364 (Deltahaze Corporation), 366 (Leon Morris), 369 (Jan Persson), 370(Michael Ochs), 373 (Mick Hutson), 376 (Michael Ochs), 378 (David Redfern), 381–383 (David Redfern), 385 (Ebet Roberts), 386 (Richard E. Aaron), 393 (Ebet Roberts), 394 (Robert Knight), 396 (David Redfern), 398 (Michael Ochs), 402 (Bob Willoughby), 405 (Michael Ochs), 406 (Paul Reed Smith), 410 (William Gottlieb), 413 (Mick Hutson), 414 (Bob Willoughby), 416 (Robert Knight), 418–421 (Michael Ochs), 422 (Geoff Dann), 425 (Geoff Dann), 426 (Geoff Dann), 429 (Michael Ochs), 430 (Paul Reed Smith), 433–434 (Michael Ochs), 436 (Michael Ochs), 440 (Michael Ochs), 445 (Ebet Roberts), 446 (Michael Ochs)

Rex Features: 239 (Andre Csillag), 240 (Alan Messer), 274 (Andre Csillag), 284 (Alan Messer), 286 (London Weekend Television), 306 (Andre Csillag)

496